MĪMĀṂSĀ AND VEDĀNTA

PAPERS OF THE 12TH WORLD SANSKRIT CONFERENCE
Vol. 10.3

Mīmāṃsā and Vedānta

Interaction and Continuity

Edited by
JOHANNES BRONKHORST

MOTILAL BANARSIDASS PUBLISHERS
PRIVATE LIMITED • DELHI

PAPERS OF THE 12TH WORLD SANSKRIT CONFERENCE
HELD IN HELSINKI, FINLAND, 13-18 JULY 2003
VOL. 10.3

General Editors
PETTERI KOSKIKALLIO & ASKO PARPOLA

First Edition: Delhi, 2007

ISBN: 81-208-3174-8

MOTILAL BANARSIDASS
41 U.A. Bungalow Road, Jawahar Nagar, Delhi 110 007
8 Mahalaxmi Chamber, 22 Bhulabhai Desai Road, Mumbai 400 026
203 Royapettah High Road, Mylapore, Chennai 600 004
236, 9th Main III Block, Jayanagar, Bangalore 560 011
Sanas Plaza, 1302 Baji Rao Road, Pune 411 002
8 Camac Street, Kolkata 700 017
Ashok Rajpath, Patna 800 004
Chowk, Varanasi 221 001

Printed in India
BY JAINENDRA PRAKASH JAIN AT SHRI JAINENDRA PRESS,
A-45 NARAINA, PHASE-I, NEW DELHI 110 028
AND PUBLISHED BY NARENDRA PRAKASH JAIN FOR
MOTILAL BANARSIDASS PUBLISHERS PRIVATE LIMITED,
BUNGALOW ROAD, DELHI 110 007

PREFACE

The second half of the first millennium witnessed various important developments in Indian thought. Among these, the increasingly active participation in philosophical debates of those who maintained that everything worth knowing is found in the Veda is particularly striking. Vedānta established itself as an independent school of thought during this period, ready to defend its positions against other schools, whether Brahmanical or non-Brahmanical. More or less simultaneously, Mīmāṃsā underwent important modifications which brought it closer to certain Vedānta positions.

Interestingly, both the most important representatives of Vedānta (Śaṅkara and others) and the Mīmāṃsakas with "Vedāntic" inclinations (Kumārila Bhaṭṭa is a prominent example) claimed that they faithfully applied the rules of interpretation that were characteristic of Mīmāṃsā. They were all Mīmāṃsakas in a certain way. They did not however agree with each other. They differed on fundamental points, such as the role of, and need for ritual activity to reach the ultimate goal, liberation.

A panel of the 12th World Sanskrit Conference in Helsinki was dedicated to the transitions just described. This volume is the outcome of this panel. Its participants concentrated, inevitably, on a limited number of key figures from that period, with particular emphasis on Kumārila Bhaṭṭa. The contributions by John Taber and Kiyotaka Yoshimizu contribute valuable new insights to the understanding of this voluminous and sometimes difficult author. Other thinkers of the period are not neglected, however. Marcus Schmücker, J. M. Verpoorten and Johannes Bronkhorst deal with early Vedānta thinkers in their relationship with ritual Mīmāṃsā. Walter Slaje, finally, analyses the role which the Vedic seer Yājña-valkya may have played in developing Mīmāṃsā and Vedānta thought.

A word of thanks to the organisers of the 12th World Sanskrit Conference may here be added. They have created a unique opportunity to compare notes to a number of scholars who had not so far collaborated, and seen to it that the results be published. Thanks are also due to the Finnish Cultural Foundation for having supported the conference.

The sequence of the articles in this volume follows the alphabetical order of the names of their authors.

JOHANNES BRONKHORST

CONTENTS

Preface v

Abbreviations ix

Contributors xi

JOHANNES BRONKHORST
Vedānta as Mīmāṃsā 1

MARCUS SCHMÜCKER
Debates about the Object of Perception in the Traditions of Advaita and Viśiṣṭādvaita Vedānta 93

WALTER SLAJE
Yājñavalkya-*brāhmaṇa*s and the Early Mīmāṃsā 115

JOHN TABER
Kumārila the Vedāntin? 159

J. M. VERPOORTEN
Mīmāṃsā- and Vedānta-sentences in Padmapāda's *Pañcapādikā* (Chapter 2) 185

KIYOTAKA YOSHIMIZU
Kumārila's Reevaluation of the Sacrifice and the Veda from a Vedānta Perspective 201

Index 255

ABBREVIATIONS

(More specific lists of abbreviations are given in the bibliographies)

ABORI	Annals of the Bhandarkar Oriental Research Institute, Poona
ĀSS	Ānandāśrama Sanskrit Series, Poona
BORI	Bhandarkar Oriental Research Institute, Poona
GOS	Gaekwad's Oriental Series, Baroda
HOS	Harvard Oriental Series
JIP	Journal of Indian Philosophy
Kl. Schr.	Kleine Schriften
SB ÖAW	Sitzungsberichte der Akademie der Wissenschaften in Wien, Philologisch-historische Klasse, Wien
VKSKS[O]	Veröffentlichungen der Kommission für Sprachen und Kulturen Süd[- und Ost]asiens,
WZKS[O]	Wiener Zeitschrift für die Kunde Süd[- und Ost]asiens
ZDMG	Zeitschrift der Deutschen Morgenländischen Gesellschaft

CONTRIBUTORS

JOHANNES BRONKHORST
Section de langues et civilisations orientales
Université de Lausanne
BFSH 2, CH-1015 Lausanne
SWITZERLAND
e-mail: johannes.bronkhorst@unil.ch

MARCUS SCHMÜCKER
Institute for the Cultural and Intellectual History of Asia
Strohgasse 45/2/4, 1030 Vienna
AUSTRIA
e-mail: marcus.schmuecker@oeaw.ac.at

WALTER SLAJE
Institute for Indology
Martin Luther-University Halle-Wittenberg
H.-u. Th. Mann-Strasse 22, D-06108 Halle
GERMANY
e-mail: walter.slaje@indologie.uni-halle.de

JOHN TABER
Department of Philosophy
MSC03 2140, 1 University of New Mexico
Albuquerque NM 87131-0001
U.S.A.
e-mail: jataber@unm.edu

JEAN-MARIE VERPOORTEN
Rue des Coteaux 17, 4800 Verviers
BELGIUM
e-mail: jverpoorten2003@yahoo.fr

KIYOTAKA YOSHIMIZU
Faculty of Letters, Hokkaido University
Kita 10 Nishi 7, Kita-Ku, Sapporo 060-0810
JAPAN
e-mail: tantris@let.hokudai.ac.jp

Vedānta as Mīmāṃsā

JOHANNES BRONKHORST

0. INTRODUCTION

The *Śābarabhāṣya* is the oldest surviving commentary on the *Pūrvamīmāṃsāsūtra*. Śabara's Bhāṣya is remarkable for various reasons. Śabara here expresses ideas which differ from those of most of his contemporaries. Most remarkable is the absence of any reference whatsoever to the ideas of rebirth and liberation. Śabara's Bhāṣya deals with Vedic ritual, which as a rule leads to heaven.

The absence of ideas which yet pervade much of Indian thought from the days of the early Upaniṣads onward could be explained by the conservative nature of Pūrvamīmāṃsā. As a matter of fact, most of Vedic literature is not concerned with rebirth and liberation either, and the Upaniṣads themselves reveal that this doctrine was an innovation. It may not necessarily have been accepted by all sacrificing Brahmins, and indeed, later texts such as the *Mahābhārata* show very little awareness of rebirth and liberation in their narrative parts, even though there can be no doubt that these texts are more recent than the early Upaniṣads. One might therefore think that the new ideas of rebirth and liberation took a long time to find general acceptance, and that conservative Brahmins at the time of Śabara – i.e., in the 5th or 6th century CE – still did not accept them. Indeed, Śabara's commentator Prabhākara still has no place for liberation in the 7th century CE, whereas his other commentator Kumārila opens up to this idea at around the same time.

All this fits in with the general picture according to which the belief in rebirth and liberation did not originate within Vedic Brahmanism. This belief originally belonged to others, and found its way into the Vedic Upaniṣads from outside, as is indeed confirmed by some Upaniṣadic passages. Vedic Brahmanism, far from being the source of these ideas, resisted them for some thousand years after their first appearance in the Upaniṣads. Seen in this way, the positions of Śabara and Prabhākara constitute additional evidence for the originally non-Vedic character of the belief in rebirth and liberation.

This simple and elegant way of understanding the spread in time of the belief in rebirth and liberation in India is jeopardised by certain ideas about the early history of the Vedānta philosophy. It is well known that the Vedānta philosophy – which is to be distinguished from the Upaniṣads upon which it claims to be based – played no role in the philosophical debates of the early centuries of the common era. For centuries debates took place, and were recorded, between Sāṃkhyas, Naiyāyikas, Vaiśeṣikas and various schools of Buddhism, without any reference to the Vedānta philosophy. The first mention of this school of thought by others may well occur in the *Madhyamakahṛdaya*, a text belonging to the 6th century whose author was a Buddhist called Bhavya. This absence of evidence for Vedānta as a school of philosophy might be interpreted as evidence for its relatively late appearance.[1]

In spite of this, a number of scholars are of the opinion that Vedānta as a system of philosophy was there right from the beginning, that is to say, right from the period immediately following the early Upaniṣads. The Vedānta philosophy, for which the name

---

[1] Frauwallner (1992: 173) represents a different point of view, which however is not very plausible: "In den folgenden Jahrhunderten [i.e., in the centuries following the composition of the Brahmasūtras, presumably already before the Common Era, JB] beschäftigte man sich damit, das System Bādarāyaṇas weiter auszugestalten und auszudeuten. Aber alles da liess sich mit den Leistungen der gleichzeitigen grossen philosophischen Schulen nicht vergleichen. Daher blieb das Vedānta-System zunächst unbeachtet und wurde auch in der Polemik dieser Schulen kaum einer Erwähnung wert gefunden."

Uttaramīmāṃsā is sometimes used, was, according to these scholars, part of original Mīmāṃsā, which covered both Pūrva- and Uttara-Mīmāṃsā. Together they constituted at the beginning one single school of thought. Some extend this idea, and maintain that this single school of thought originally had one basic text, the *Mīmāṃsāsūtra*. This original text had two parts: the former or first part of the *Mīmāṃsāsūtra*, and the latter or second part of the *Mīmāṃsāsūtra*; in Sanskrit: Pūrva-Mīmāṃsāsūtra and Uttara-Mīmāṃsāsūtra. The later expressions Pūrvamīmāṃsā and Uttaramīmāṃsā can then be explained as having (erroneously) evolved from these book-titles.

It is easy to see that the view according to which the Vedānta philosophy was in the beginning inseparably linked to Pūrvamīmāṃsā contradicts the idea that Pūrvamīmāṃsā for a long time was not interested in liberation and related concepts. The Vedānta philosophy, we must assume, has always been interested in liberation, through knowledge of Brahman. If the two schools of thought were originally one, we are virtually forced to conclude that the earliest ritualistic Mīmāṃsakas were also convinced Vedāntins. The abandonment by Pūrvamīmāṃsā of the ideal of liberation would then be a later development within the school, a development which soon, with Kumārila, yielded again to the lure of liberation.

It will be clear that the idea of an original unity of Pūrvamīmāṃsā and Uttaramīmāṃsā raises serious questions. It is therefore justified to ask what evidence it is based on. Several arguments have been presented in the secondary literature. The present article will deal with them.

1. WERE THE PŪRVA- AND UTTARA-MĪMĀṂSĀ ORIGINALLY ONE SYSTEM?

Hermann Jacobi remarked in 1911 that

> at Śabarasvāmin's time the Pūrva and Uttara Mīmāṃsā still formed *one* philosophical system, while after Kumārila and Śaṅkara they were practically two mutually exclusive philosophies.[2]

This remark, if true, has rather troubling consequences. It raises the general question what this single philosophical system at the time of, and before, Śabara may have looked like. More in particular, it raises the specific question why Śabara shows no awareness of the notion of liberation in his commentary on the ritual *Mīmāṃsāsūtra*, as observed by several scholars (Biardeau 1964: 90, n. 1; Halbfass 1980: 273 f; 1991: 300 f; Bronkhorst 2000: 99 f).[3] Uttaramīmāṃsā has, presumably from its beginning, always been about liberation through knowledge of Brahma. Is Śabara's silence in this regard to be explained by the presumed fact that he left this issue to the part of the single philosophical system that he adhered to but which he

---

[2] Jacobi 1911: 18 (576).

[3] Cf. Halbfass 1991: 301: "the Mīmāṃsā carries the heritage of the 'pre-karmic' past of the Indian tradition into an epoch for which karma and saṃsāra have become basic premises. As well as their counterpart, mokṣa, the concepts of karma and saṃsāra do not play any role in the Mīmāṃsāsūtra and remain negligible in its oldest extant commentary, Śabara's Bhāṣya." Biardeau 1968: 109: "[La Mīmāṃsā] n'accepte, au moins à date ancienne, ni l'idée des renaissances ni celle d'une délivrance."

Mesquita (1994) argues that both Jaimini and Śabara were concerned with liberation. For Jaimini he bases this opinion on the mention of the name Jaimini in the *Brahmasūtra* and in Śaṅkara's commentary thereon; this issue will be dealt with in section 6, below. Śabara's interest in liberation is presumably shown by his use of the expression *niḥśreyasa* in the *Tarkapāda* of his Bhāṣya (Frauwallner 1968: 16, l. 12). This expression by itself refers to "something that has no better", i.e. to the best there is, without specifying whether in Śabara's opinion heaven or liberation is the best there is. Elsewhere Śabara explains that heaven (*svarga*) is happiness (*prīti*) and that man makes efforts to attain happiness (see Bronkhorst 2000: 104; Heesterman 2003: 290 ff); liberation is never mentioned. The conclusion is inevitable that for Śabara heaven is the best there is, and therefore that *niḥśreyasa* is *svarga*.

had no occasion to comment upon? Or does it simply show that he did not accept the notion of liberation, or even that he was not, or barely, aware of it?

Jacobi's remark is cited with approval by Asko Parpola (1981: 155) in an article which tries to establish that not only were Pūrva- and Uttara-Mīmāṃsā originally one system, but that the fundamental texts of the two (the Pūrva-mīmāṃsāsūtra and the Uttara-mīmāṃsāsūtra respectively) were originally the initial and final parts of one single text, the original *Mīmāṃsāsūtra*. He supports this claim with the testimony of classical authors, to which he adds an argument based on the teacher quotations in the two texts.

Reacting to Jacobi's remark, A. B. Keith already observed: "This, of course, would give the Pūrvamīmāṃsā a very different aspect, as merely a part of a philosophy, not the whole." Keith himself considered Jacobi's remark dubious, and believed that syncretism of the systems would rather be due to the commentators.[4] It is indeed difficult to believe that the earliest Mīmāṃsakas, far from being the pure Vedic ritualistic thinkers that the texts present us with, were in their heart of hearts early Vedāntins, and that non-Vedāntic, "pure" Mīmāṃsakas did not exist until later. At first sight this would appear to turn the historical development on its head.[5] The improbability of such a development does not, of course, in

---

[4] Keith 1920: 473.

[5] It would not, of course, disagree with certain Indian traditionalists, who see the history of Indian thought as one of ongoing decline. Yudhiṣṭhira Mīmāṃsaka (1987, Introduction, p. 15-16), for example, speaks of the period of the teachers (*ācārya-yuga*) during which certain teachers, under the influence of Buddhists, Jainas and Cārvākas, started neglecting the earlier writings of Ṛṣis and Munis in order to press their own views. Y. Mīmāṃsaka mentions in particular Bhartṛhari, Śabarasvāmin and Śaṅkara in this connection, Śabarasvāmin's innovation being to deny the existence of Brahma. (*etasminn eva kāle Bhartṛhariṇā Vākyapadīya-prabhṛtayo granthā viracayya śabdādvaitavādaḥ pravartitaḥ, Śabara-svāminā ca brahmaṇaḥ sattām apalapya Pūrvamīmāṃsāyā bhāṣyaṃ viracitam, Bhaṭṭa-kumārilena ca Śābarabhāṣye Vārtikagranthā vilikhitāḥ | Śaṅkarācāryeṇa Bhartṛhareḥ śabdādvaitavādaṃ bauddhadārśanikamatāni cānurudhya tato vā preraṇāṃ labdhvā brahma satyaṃ jagan mithyā jīvo brahmaiva nāparaḥ iti matasya siddhyai vedāntadarśanasya bhāṣyaṃ viracitam*). See also Subrahmanya Sastri 1961, Bhūmikā, p. 13 f.

itself constitute proof that it may not have taken place. It does however justify us to review the evidence with great care.

Jacobi bases his opinion to the extent that "at Śabarasvāmin's time the Pūrva and Uttara Mīmāṃsā still formed *one* philosophical system" on the fact that Śabara is mentioned in an important passage in Śaṅkara's *Brahmasūtrabhāṣya* on sūtra 3.3.53. The passage needs to be studied in its context. This context is primarily provided by the sūtra 3.3.53 (*eka ātmanaḥ śarīre bhāvāt*) which, in Śaṅkara's interpretation, establishes the existence of the self. In this context Śaṅkara states:

> *nanu śāstrapramukha eva prathame pāde śāstraphalopabhogayogyasya dehavyatiriktasyātmano 'stitvam uktam* | *satyam uktaṃ bhāṣyakṛtā* | *na tu tatrātmāstitve sūtram asti* | *iha tu svayam eva sūtrakṛtā tadastitvam ākṣepapuraḥsaraṃ pratiṣṭhāpitam* | *ita eva cākṛṣyācāryeṇa śabarasvāminā pramāṇalakṣaṇe varṇitam* | *ata eva ca bhagavatopavarṣeṇa prathame tantre ātmāstitvābhidhānaprasaktau śārīrake vakṣyāma ity uddhāraḥ kṛtaḥ* |[6]

> [Objection:] Has the existence of a self that is different from the body and capable of enjoying the fruit of the Śāstra not [already] been stated at the very beginning of the Śāstra, in the first Pāda?
>
> [Answer:] That is true; it has been stated by the author of the Bhāṣya. But there (i.e., at the beginning of the Śāstra) there is no sūtra about the existence of a self. Here (i.e., in BraSū 3.3.53), on the other hand, the existence of the [self] has been established, after an initial objection, by the author of the Sūtra himself. And having taken it from here itself, Ācārya Śabarasvāmin has described [the existence of the self] in [the section] dealing with the means of valid cognition. Therefore also the revered Upavarṣa in the first Tantra, when he had to discuss the existence of the self, contented himself with saying: "We shall explain this in the Śārīraka".

The passage contains a number of puzzling expressions. It is particularly important to find out whether the expression 'at the very beginning of the Śāstra, in the first Pāda' (*śāstrapramukha eva prathame pāde*) is to be taken as referring to the same thing as 'in the first Tantra' (*prathame tantre*), or not. Since "the first Tantra"

---

[6] BSūBhā on sūtra 3.3.53 (ed. J. L. Shastri, p. 764, l. 9 – p. 765, l. 1); cf. Parpola 1981: 153.

is explicitly contrasted with and therefore differentiated from "the Śārīraka" – the Śārīraka being no doubt Upavarṣa's planned (or executed) commentary on the *Brahmasūtra* –, it seems safe to conclude that "the first Tantra" is the *Mīmāṃsāsūtra* (or Upavarṣa's commentary on it).[7] Many interpreters (e.g. Deussen 1887: 624; Thibaut 1890-96: II: 268; Gambhirananda 1972: 740; Hiriyanna 1925: 231; Kane 1960: 120; 1977: 1160; Parpola 1981: 153; Ramachandrudu 1989: 234-235; Bouy 2000: 23, n. 92; Govindānanda and Ānandagiri on BraSū 3.3.53) identify "the very beginning of the Śāstra" with MīmSū 1.1.5. But is this correct? Why should our short passage refer to one and the same discussion in three different ways: (i) "at the very beginning of the Śāstra, in the first Pāda", (ii) "in [the section] dealing with the means of valid cognition" and (iii) "in the first Tantra"?

We have to find out what Śaṅkara meant by "the beginning of the Śāstra". Related to this is the question whether Śaṅkara looked upon *Mīmāṃsāsūtra* and *Brahmasūtra* as together constituting one Śāstra, or as two different Śāstras. Jacobi and Parpola, as we have seen, invoke the passage under discussion to prove that the two together were originally one Śāstra, but their proof may be, at least in part, circular: The two disciplines were originally one because Śaṅkara refers to the *Mīmāṃsāsūtra* as "the beginning of the Śāstra", and "the beginning of the Śāstra" must refer to the *Mīmāṃsāsūtra* because the two disciplines were originally one. How do we get out of this circular argument?

There is another passage in Śaṅkara's *Brahmasūtrabhāṣya* which may throw light on his understanding of his own Śāstra. It occurs under sūtra 1.1.4 and reads:

---

[7] Cf. Kane 1977: 1160: "Śaṅkarācārya refers to the extant Pūrvamīmāṃsā as Dvādaśalakṣaṇī in his bhāṣya on *Vedāntasūtra* 3.3.26, as 'Prathamatantra' in bhāṣya on V.S. III.3.25, III.3.53 and III.4.27, as Prathama-kāṇḍa in bhāṣya on V.S. III.3.1, III.3.33, III.3.44, III.3.50, as Pramāṇalakṣaṇa in bhāṣya on V.S. [2.1.1 and] III.4.42." Similarly Kane 1960: 120.

evaṃ ca sati "athāto brahmajijñāsā" iti tadviṣayaḥ pṛthakśāstrārambha upapadyate | pratipattividhiparatve hi "athāto dharmajijñāsā" ity evārabdhatvān na pṛthakśāstram ārabhyeta | ārabhyamāṇaṃ caivam ārabhyate: "athātaḥ pariśiṣṭadharmajijñāsā" iti, "athātaḥ kratvarthapuruṣārthayor jijñāsā" itivat | brahmātmaikyāvagatis tv apratijñāteti tadartho yuktaḥ śāstrārambhaḥ "athāto brahmajijñāsā" iti |[8]

Such being the case, it is proper to begin a separate Śāstra with the words "Then therefore the enquiry into Brahma" (BraSū 1.1.1) because it deals with that. For in case [this Śāstra] were to deal with injunctions that one has to know [Brahma], no separate Śāstra could be begun, because [the Śāstra of injunctions (viz. the *Mīmāṃsāsūtra*)] has already begun with the words "Then therefore the enquiry into Dharma" (MīmSū 1.1.1). Something that has already begun would begin like this "Then therefore the enquiry into the remaining Dharma", just like "Then therefore the enquiry into the purpose of the sacrifice and into the purpose of man" (which is a sūtra (4.1.1) that introduces a chapter of the *Mīmāṃsāsūtra*). But because knowledge of the identity of Brahma and *ātman* has not been stated (in the Mīmāṃsā), the beginning of a [new] Śāstra in the form "Then therefore the enquiry into Brahma" in order to convey that [knowledge] is appropriate.

As the translation shows, this passage lends itself easily to an interpretation in which the *Brahmasūtra* belongs to a separate Śāstra (*pṛthakśāstra*), different from ritual Mīmāṃsā.

There is more. According to Śaṅkara in his comments on BraSū 3.3.53 which we studied above,

> the existence of a self that is different from the body and capable of enjoying the fruit of the Śāstra has [already] been stated at the very beginning of the Śāstra, in the first Pāda.

The very first Pāda of Śabara's Bhāṣya on the *Mīmāṃsāsūtra* does indeed contain a long passage dealing with the existence of the self (edited in Frauwallner 1968: p. 50, l. 5 – p. 60, l. 23; translated pp. 51-61). This self is, as a matter of fact, stated to be different from the body, but the passage says nothing about its being "capable of enjoying the fruit of the Śāstra". The first Pāda of Śaṅkara's *Brahmasūtrabhāṣya*, on the other hand, repeatedly deals with these

---

[8] BSūBhā on sūtra 1.1.4 (ed. J. L. Shastri, p. 98, ll. 3-7).

issues. As a short example we can take the following statement from Śaṅkara's comments on BraSū 1.1.4:

> *"aśarīraṃ vāva santaṃ na priyāpriye spṛśataḥ" iti priyāpriyasparśana-pratiṣedhāc codanālakṣaṇadharmakāryatvaṃ mokṣākhyasyāśarīratvasya pratiṣidhyata iti gamyate*[9]
>
> From the denial of being affected by joy and sorrow expressed in the statement "Joy and sorrow do not affect the one without body" (ChānUp 8.12.1) we understand that the state of being without body, called liberation, is denied to be the effect of Dharma characterised as injunction.

The "one without body" is the self. The present passage tells us that this self, which is without body, is capable of enjoying the fruit of the Śāstra, viz. liberation.

As an example of a short passage dealing with the existence of the self we can quote from Śaṅkara's comments on BraSū 1.1.1:

> *sarvo hy ātmāstitvaṃ pratyeti, na nāham asmīti* | *yadi hi nātmāstitva-prasiddhiḥ syāt sarvo loko nāham asmīti pratīyāt* |[10]
>
> For everyone is conscious of the existence of (his) self, and never thinks "I am not". If the existence of the self were not known, every one would think "I am not" (transl. Thibaut 1890-96: I: 14).

There are therefore good reasons to interpret the passage from Śaṅkara's *Brahmasūtrabhāṣya* on sūtra 3.3.53 cited above in the following manner:

> [Objection:] Has the existence of a self that is different from the body and capable of enjoying the fruits of the Śāstra not [already] been stated at the very beginning of the [present] Śāstra, in the first Pāda [of the *Brahmasūtra* and its Bhāṣya]?
>
> [Answer:] That is true; it has been stated by the author of the [*Brahma-sūtra-*]Bhāṣya (i.e., by Śaṅkara himself).[11] But there (i.e., at the beginning of

---

[9] BSūBhā on sūtra 1.1.4 (ed. J. L. Shastri, p. 72, ll. 1-3).

[10] BSūBhā on sūtra 1.1.1 (ed. J. L. Shastri, p. 43, ll. 1-2).

[11] The use of the third person to refer to one's own work finds a parallel, e.g., in Maṇḍana Miśra's *Brahmasiddhi* (e.g., p. 75, l. 4: *vakṣyati*; p. 23, l. 17: *āha*), and is particularly common where an author has himself composed a commentary

the *Brahmasūtra*) there is no sūtra about the existence of a self. Here (i.e., in BraSū 3.3.53), on the other hand, the existence of the [self] has been established, after an initial objection, by the author of the Sūtra himself. And having taken it from here itself, Ācārya Śabarasvāmin has described [the existence of the self] in [the section of the *Mīmāṃsābhāṣya*] dealing with the means of valid cognition. Therefore also the revered Upavarṣa in the first Tantra (i.e. in his commentary on the *Mīmāṃsāsūtra*), when he had to discuss the existence of the self, contented himself with saying: "We shall explain this in the Śārīraka".

This way of understanding Śaṅkara's reference to the first Pāda agrees with the way in which he refers to the first, second and third Adhyāyas. Wherever in his *Brahmasūtrabhāṣya* he refers to Adhyāyas, they are Adhyāyas of his *Brahmasūtrabhāṣya* (or of the *Brahmasūtra*), numbered according to the position they have in his own work. Śaṅkara refers to the "first Adhyāya" at the very beginning of the second Adhyāya of his *Brahmasūtrabhāṣya*; here there can be no doubt that it concerns the first Adhyāya of the *Brahmasūtra* (Bhāṣya), not of ritual Mīmāṃsā. Similarly, the "second Adhyāya" referred to at the very beginning of the third Adhyāya and under BraSū 2.1.1 clearly refers to Śaṅkara's own second chapter (or to that chapter of the *Brahmasūtra*). The same applies to the "third Adhyāya" referred to at the beginning of chapter four and under BraSū 3.1.1.[12]

Let us now turn to Śabara. The above passage shows that, in Śaṅkara's opinion, Śabara took a topic, or a passage, which be-

---

on his own work. Compare in this context Medhātithi's remark under Manu 1.4 (I, p. 7, ll. 28-29): *prāyeṇa granthakārāḥ svamataṃ parāpadeśena bruvate: "atrāha" "atra pariharanti" iti* "it is a well known fact that in most cases the authors of Treatises state their own views as if emanating from other persons, making use of such expression as 'in this connection *he says*' or '*they* meet this argument thus', and so forth" (transl. Jha, III, p. 20, modified). Nowhere else in his *Brahmasūtrabhāṣya* does Śaṅkara mention an 'author of the Bhāṣya' (*bhāṣyakṛt*; see Mahadevan 1971-73, II: 723).

[12] The fact that Bhāskara on sūtra 1.1.1 (ed. Dvivedin, p. 6, ll. 19-20) uses "in the first Pāda" where Śaṅkara says "in the first Tantra" (*ata evopavarṣācāryeṇoktaṃ prathamapāde ātmavādaṃ tu śārīrake vakṣyāma iti*) suggests that he already misinterpreted Śaṅkara.

longed under BraSū 3.3.53 and placed it in his *Mīmāṃsābhāṣya*. The passage does not say what exactly he took, nor does it state that he took it from his own commentary on the *Brahmasūtra*.

Śaṅkara testimony loses most of its value in the light of Erich Frauwallner's (1968) analysis of Śabara's Bhāṣya on MīmSū 1.1.1-5. It is this portion of Śabara's Bhāṣya that contains a discussion of the self in a section dealing with the means of valid cognition, as noted by Śaṅkara. However, both the discussion of the self and the section on means of valid cognition in which it finds itself belong to the so-called Vṛttikāra-grantha. That is to say, they belong to a portion which Śabara's explicitly cites from another author, whom he calls the Vṛttikāra. No one, not even Śaṅkara, claims that the Vṛttikāra-grantha as a whole was taken from a commentary on BraSū 3.3.53; the fact that the Vṛttikāra-grantha comments several Mīmāṃsāsūtras excludes this as a possibility. Within the Vṛttikāra-grantha the section on the existence of the self is an insertion (Frauwallner 1968: 109-110). This implies that if someone has taken this section from a commentary on BraSū 3.3.53, it was not Śabara, but the Vṛttikāra. It is therefore excluded that Śaṅkara still knew a commentary by Śabara on the *Brahmasūtra* which presumably contained the passage which is now part of the Vṛttikāra-grantha. Stated differently, it is open to question whether Śaṅkara knew more about Śabara than we do.

This may not be all that surprising. Even Kumārila, who commented upon Śabara's Bhāṣya itself and is commonly regarded as having lived before Śaṅkara (Pande 1994: 46-47), did no longer know the extent of the Vṛttikāra-grantha (Jacobi 1911: 15 [573] f).[13] Śaṅkara's incorrect attribution of the discussion of the self to Śabara is therefore understandable. His claim to know where this passage came from, on the other hand, is no more reliable than this incorrect attribution.

---

[13] Yoshimizu's contribution to this volume shows that Kumārila subsequently changed his mind about the extent of the Vṛttikāra-grantha.

Since Frauwallner's analysis may not be generally known, I cite here the most relevant passage:

> Der ganze Vṛttikāragranthaḥ ist, im grossen gesehen, folgendermassen aufgebaut. Nach der Besprechung der Erkenntnismittel ergreift ein Gegner das Wort und bringt eine Reihe von Gründen gegen die Glaubwürdigkeit des Veda vor. Die späteren Kommentatoren nennen diesen Abschnitt Citrākṣepavādaḥ, weil der Gegner von der vedischen Vorschrift *"citrayā yajeta paśukāmaḥ"* ausgeht. Die Antwort lautet zunächst im Anschluss an das Sūtram 5, dass der Veda glaubwürdig ist wegen der Naturgegebenheit der Verknüpfung von Wort und Gegenstand. Das wird weit ausholend besprochen: Wesen des Wortes, Gegenstand des Wortes, Wesen der Verknüpfung und ihre Naturgegebenheit. Dann wird nochmal auf die Angriffe des Gegners im Citrākṣepaḥ zurückgegriffen und sie werden der Reihe nach widerlegt. Damit ist die ganze Auseinandersetzung abgeschlossen.
>
> In die abschliessende Zurückweisung des Citrākṣepaḥ ist nun eine lange Erörterung über das Vorhandensein einer Seele eingefügt. Dass es sich dabei um einen sekundären Einschub handelt, zeigt schon das grobe Missverhältnis im Umfang dieses Einschubs gegenüber dem ganzen Abschnitt. Die ganze übrige Widerlegung des Citrākṣepaḥ umfasst nur 16 Zeilen, der Einschub 133 Zeilen. Ebenso krass ist die Äusserlichkeit der Einfügung. Auf diese lange Abschweifung folgt plötzlich ganz unvermittelt noch eine kurze Erwiderung auf einen der Einwände im Citrākṣepaḥ, so dass der Leser zunächst erstaunt fragt, wovon denn eigentlich die Rede ist. (Frauwallner 1968: 109-110.)

This analysis clearly shows that the portion on the soul is an insertion into the Vṛttikāra-grantha, and not into Śabara's commentary. Śaṅkara obviously had it wrong.[14]

There is less reason to be sceptical with regard to Śaṅkara's statement about Upavarṣa. There is no reason to doubt that Śaṅkara knew a commentary by Upavarṣa on the *Mīmāṃsāsūtra* in which its author stated: "We shall explain [the existence of the self] in the Śārīraka". What does this prove?

[14] Regarding Śaṅkara's date, see Slaje's contribution to this volume, fn. 1 (just before 700 CE). Slaje (fn. 61) also gives a survey of opinions as to Śabara's date, which does not however take into consideration that Śabara was not yet known to Bhartṛhari (Bronkhorst 1989), so that it is highly unlikely that Śabara lived before the 5th century CE.

It seems plausible to conclude from this that Upavarṣa commented, or intended to comment, on both the *Mīmāṃsāsūtra* and the *Brahmasūtra*. Does this mean that he "seems to have treated the two sets of aphorisms as one connected work" (Nakamura 1983: 398, n. 4, referring to Belvalkar)? This is far from certain. We know that another author, Maṇḍana Miśra, wrote treatises both on Mīmāṃsā and on Vedānta around the time of Śaṅkara, and yet it cannot be maintained that he treated the two sets of aphorisms as one connected work. Not much later Vācaspati Miśra commented upon works belonging to a variety of schools of thought. The fact, therefore, that Upavarṣa commented (or wanted to comment) upon the classical texts of two schools of thought does not, in and by itself, prove that he looked upon these as fundamentally the same, or upon their classical texts as really being parts of one single text. Indeed, the very circumstance that he speaks in this connection of "the Śārīraka" suggests that he did not look upon that work as simply a later part of the same commentary. And the fact that Śaṅkara speaks about Upavarṣa's "first Tantra" without further specification while referring to his commentary on the *Mīmāṃsāsūtra* may simply suggest that Śaṅkara did not know Upavarṣa's commentary on the *Brahmaṣūtra*.

The analysis of Śaṅkara's statements does not, therefore, provide us with reliable evidence that would allow to conclude that until Śaṅkara, and more particularly at the time of Upavarṣa and Śabara, the *Mīmāṃsāsūtra* and the *Brahmasūtra* were looked upon as parts of one single work. Even less do these statements prove that the two systems of thought that find expression in those texts were believed to be in reality just one system of thought.

Only one classical Sanskrit author appears to have made a statement suggesting that the two Sūtra texts were originally part of one undivided text. This author is Sureśvara.

Sureśvara is an early commentator, and apparently also a direct disciple, of Śaṅkara (EIP III, p. 420 ff;. Hacker 1951: 1918-19 [= (12)-(13)]; Ungemach 1996) His *Naiṣkarmyasiddhi* contains a critique of MīmSū 1.2.1 *āmnāyasya kriyārthatvād ānarthakyam atadarthānāṃ* ... "Since the Veda is for [ritual] activity, [passages] that are not for that are without purpose ...". Sureśvara states:

> *yad api jaiminīyaṃ vacanam udghāṭayasi, tad api tadvivakṣāparijñānād evodbhāvyate | kiṃ kāraṇam | yato na jaiminer ayam abhiprāya āmnāyaḥ sarva eva kriyārtha iti | yadi hy ayam abhiprāyo 'bhaviṣyat "athāto brahmajijñāsā | janmādy asya yataḥ" ity evamādi brahmavastusvarūpamātra-yāthātmyaprakāśanaparaṃ gambhīranyāyasaṃdṛbdhaṃ sarvavedāntārtha-mīmāṃsanaṃ śrīmacchārīrakaṃ nāsūtrayiṣyat | asūtrayac ca | tasmāj jaiminer evāyam abhiprāyo yathaiva vidhivākyānāṃ svārthamātre prāmāṇyam evam aikātmyavākyānām apy anadhigatavastuparicchedasāmyād iti |*[15]

> Also the words of Jaimini which you present, they too are based on an incorrect understanding of his intention. For Jaimini did not intend to say that the whole Veda is for [ritual] activity. Indeed, **had this been his intention, he would not have composed the sūtras of the venerable Śārīraka, viz. *athāto brahmajijñāsā, janmādy asya yataḥ*** (BraSū 1.1.1-2) etc., whose aim is to elucidate the real nature of the essence of Brahma and nothing else, and which is an investigation into the meaning of the Upaniṣads as a whole accompanied by profound reasoning. **But he has composed those sūtras.** Therefore Jaimini's intention is as follows: just as injunctive sentences are authoritative in their semantic space, in the same way too the sentences proclaiming the identity [of the self with Brahma], this because [both types of sentences] are equally limited to matters not known [from other sources].

It appears from this passage that Sureśvara believed that Jaimini the author of the *Mīmāṃsāsūtra* had also composed the *Brahmasūtra*.[16] It is of course a small step from there to the position that both Sūtra texts had once been one single text. Sureśvara maintained this common authorship even in the face of MīmSū 1.2.1, which he proposed to reinterpret in the light of Jaimini's "real" intentions.

---

[15] Sureśvara, p. 52, introducing verse 1.91; cf. Alston 1959: 65-66; Maximilien 1975: 43-44.

[16] Kane (1960: 135 f; 1977: 1174 f) concludes that Jaimini had composed a *Śārīrakasūtra* different from the present *Brahmasūtra*; similarly already Belvalkar 1927.

No independent scholar could possibly accept Sureśvara's argument as it is presented in this passage.[17] MīmSū 1.2.1 constitutes, as a matter of fact, a major argument against the original unity of Pūrva- and Uttara-Mīmāṃsā. It is true that this sūtra – at any rate in Śabara's interpretation – presents a *pūrvapakṣa*, i.e., an opinion that will subsequently be discarded. But what is going to be discarded (from sūtra 1.2.7 onward) is not the position that the whole Veda is for ritual activity, but the conclusion that therefore passages that are not for ritual activity are for that reason without purpose. Sureśvara on the other hand claims that Jaimini did not intend to say that the whole Veda is for ritual activity, which is a position which seems difficult to defend, even though he was not the only Vedāntin to hold it. Sureśvara's reinterpretation of this sūtra – or more precisely: his rejection of the straightforward interpretation of this sūtra without offering something credible in its place[18] – may therefore be understood to indicate that he attempted to impose a vision on the two Mīmāṃsās which does not easily fit the texts.

It goes without saying that MīmSū 1.2.1 constituted a challenge for many Vedāntins. Śaṅkara's *Brahmasūtrabhāṣya*, for example, cites MīmSū 1.2.1 in its introduction to BraSū 1.1.4, and subsequently enters in great detail to show that the Upaniṣadic statements about Brahma do not prescribe activity, and are not to be construed with other statements that do. In the end Śaṅkara does not reject MīmSū 1.2.1, but he limits its range to such an extent that it cannot do much harm any longer:

> *tasmāt puruṣārthānupayogyupākhyānādibhūtārthavādaviṣayam ānarthakyābhidhānaṃ draṣṭavyam*[19]

---

[17] Parpola draws attention to Keith's (1920: xx f) scepticism as to the value of this attestation. Hiriyanna (1925: 230) observed, similarly: "It would not ... be right to conclude on the strength of this passage alone ... that Sureśvara regarded Jaimini as the author of the Vedānta-sūtras."

[18] Sureśvara repeats his position again in the immediately following sentence: "It is only the Vedic texts related to commands that bear on action" (*adhicodanaṃ ya āmnāyas tasyaiva syāt kriyārthatā*; transl. Alston 1959: 67).

> That is why the mention of purposelessness (in MīmSū 1.2.1) is to be understood as concerning *arthavāda*s in the form of stories and the like that do not serve a human purpose (*puruṣārtha*)

Padmapāda – like Sureśvara probably a pupil of Śaṅkara (Hacker 1951: 1929-30 [= (23)-(24)]; Ungemach 1996) and therefore a contemporary of the former – disagrees with Sureśvara where the authorship of the *Brahmasūtra* is concerned.[20] He does so in the following passage:

> *sa ca svarūpāvagamaḥ kasmin kathaṃ veti dharmamātravicāraṃ pratijñāya tatraiva prayatamānena bhagavatā jaimininā na mīmāṃsitam upayogābhāvāt, bhagavāṃs tu punar bādarāyaṇaḥ pṛthakvicāraṃ pratijñāya vyacīcarat samanvayalakṣaṇena.*[21]

Venkataramiah (1948: 116) translates this as follows:

> And as to where or how the Vedic texts relating to the cognition of the existent entity (serve as a *pramāṇa*) is not explained by the revered Jaimini since in accordance with this resolve he set about investigating into the nature of Dharma only and since such knowledge (i.e., of *ātman* as distinguished from the body) is not to the purpose. But the revered Bādarāyaṇa on the other hand having resolved to inquire into a different topic altogether, has expounded (the subject of the separate existence of *ātman*) in the "*samanvayādhikaraṇa*" – [BraSū] I.1.1-4.

Padmapāda's disagreement with Sureśvara in this respect does not change the fact that he, too, has to limit the range of applicability of MīmSū 1.2.1. He does so in the following passage:

> *nanu "dṛṣṭo hi tasyārthaḥ karmāvabodhanam", "tadbhūtānāṃ kriyārthena samāmnāyaḥ", "āmnāyasya kriyārthatvād" iti ca sarvasya kāryārthatvaṃ*

---

[19] BSūBhā on sūtra 1.1.4 (ed. J. L. Shastri, p. 94, ll. 1-2); see further section 3.1 below.

[20] This was pointed out by van Buitenen (1956: 21, n. 57), who refers in this context to "Pañcapādika 40, 153-54" without indication what this means or what edition he has used; I presume that the passage cited here corresponds to the one intended by him.

[21] *Pañcapādikā* of Padmapāda, ed. S. Śrīrāma Śāstrī and S. R. Krishnamurthi Śāstrī, p. 149-150.

> *darśitam? satyam; tatprakramabalāt tanniṣṭho vedabhāga iti gamyate, na sarvatra* |[22]
>
> [Objection:] It has been shown in [Śabara on MīmSū 1.1.1 (Frauwallner 1968: 12, ll. 12-13):] *dṛṣṭo hi tasyārthaḥ karmāvabodhanam*, [and in MīmSū 1.1.15:] *tadbhūtānāṃ kriyārthena samāmnāyaḥ* ... [and 1.2.1] *āmnāyasya kriyārthatvād* ... that all [Vedic statements] have actions that are to be performed as purpose.
>
> [Reply:] True; because it begins with those [sūtras] (viz. *athāto dharmajijñāsā* MīmSū 1.1.1, and *codanālakṣaṇo 'rtho dharmaḥ* MīmSū 1.1.2), the portion of the Veda that is related to those [notions] (i.e., *dharma* and *codanā*) is understood. [These notions] do not pertain to the whole [of the Veda].

Sureśvara himself, in his Sambandhavārttika on Śaṅkara's *Bṛhadāraṇyakopaniṣadbhāṣya*,[23] points out that "in the *Mīmāṃsāsūtra* passage (1.2.1) 'since scripture (*āmnāya*) has action as its subject' the word 'scripture' refers only to the *karmakāṇḍa*, not to the Upaniṣads" (EIP III, p. 428).

Returning now to Sureśvara's remark about the authorship of the *Brahmasūtra*, the fact that his passage stands alone, is not confirmed by others and is indeed contradicted by statements from other authors (among them Padmapāda), does not add to its credibility. It is therefore all the more surprising that Parpola (1981: 150) cites this passage – without translation and without discussion – as supporting evidence for the hypothesis that

> the founder of the Mīmāṃsā [is to] be credited with the authorship of a treatise upon the Vedānta, which the [present *Brahmasūtra*] would have replaced, not without thereby utilizing some of its elements.

Note that Parpola's conclusion goes well beyond Sureśvara's evidence. Sureśvara's remark, if correct, would show that Jaimini was the author of the *Brahmasūtra*, not – *pace* Kane, Belvalkar (see

---

[22] Padmapāda's *Pañcapādikā*, ed. S. Subrahmanyaśāstri, p. 344.

[23] §§ 268-288. See especially §§ 272-273: *kriyāprakaraṇasthānāṃ vidhiśeṣātmanāṃ satām | vacasām akriyārthānām ānarthakyāya tad vacaḥ || na tūpaniṣadāṃ nyāyyaṃ pārthagarthyasya saṃbhavāt | pūrvoktenaiva nyāyena nātas tadvidhiśeṣatā ||*

note 16) and Parpola – "of a treatise upon the Vedānta, which the [present *Brahmasūtra*] would have replaced, not without thereby utilizing some of its elements". This artificial interpretation of Sureśvara's words by these modern scholars, including the postulated existence of an early Vedāntic work by Jaimini, finds its explanation in the fact that the extant *Brahmasūtra* is obviously a far more recent work than the ritual *Mīmāṃsāsūtra* and dates from a time many centuries after the late-Vedic period; its references to other systems of thought which did not yet exist in the late-Vedic period leave little doubt in this regard (see Jacobi 1911: 13 [571] f). However, it seems a lot more reasonable to take Sureśvara's remark at its face value and conclude that it is mistaken, rather than take it as a justification to postulate the existence of an earlier composition for which no independent evidence exists.

Let us now consider some further passages that have a bearing on the relationship between ritual Mīmāṃsā and Vedānta. Rāmānuja introduces his *Śrībhāṣya* on the *Brahmasūtra* in the following manner:

> *bhagavadbodhāyanakṛtāṃ vistīrṇāṃ brahmasūtravṛttiṃ pūrvācāryāḥ sañcikṣipuḥ, tanmatānusāreṇa sūtrākṣarāṇi vyākhyāsyante* | (*Śrībhāṣya* I, p. 2).
>
> Earlier Ācāryas have condensed the extensive *Brahmasūtravṛtti* composed by the venerable Bodhāyana. The sounds of the sūtras will be explained in accordance with their/his opinions.

It is not clear from this statement whether Rāmānuja still knew the long commentary of Bodhāyana or only the condensed versions prepared by the Ācāryas he mentions.[24] Mesquita (1984: 179-180)

---

[24] Rāmānuja's *Vedārthasaṃgraha* (§ 93; van Buitenen 1956: 128; Matsumoto 2003: 39) refers to "old commentaries on [Veda and] Vedānta, accepted by recognised scholars, [and composed] by Bodhāyana, Ṭaṅka, Dramiḍa, Guhadeva, Kapardi(n), Bhāruci etc." (*bodhāyanaṭaṅkadramiḍaguhadevakapardibhārucìprabhṛtyavigītaśiṣṭaparigṛhītapurātanavedavedāntavyākhyāna-*; some manuscripts omit °*veda*°). Rāmānuja's predecessor Yāmuna mentions as commentators on the *Brahmasūtra* Dramiḍa (some editions merely say *bhāṣyakṛt*) and Śrīvatsāṅkamiśra, and enumerates furthermore the following thinkers: Ṭaṅka, Bhartṛprapañca, Bhartṛmitra, Bhartṛhari, Brahmadatta, Śaṅkara, Śrīvatsāṅka and

surmises that he knew Bodhāyana's commentary in fragmentary form; this would explain that there are only seven quotations from this Vṛtti, all from the first Adhyāya, in the *Śrībhāṣya*. When, therefore, Rāmānuja cites a few pages later an unspecified Vṛtti-kāra, it is not fully clear whether the author cited is Bodhāyana (which seems probable), or someone else. The unspecified Vṛtti-kāra is cited in the following passage:

> *tad āha vṛttikāraḥ* । *"vṛttāt karmādhigamād anantaraṃ brahmavividiṣā" iti* । *vakṣyati ca karmabrahmamīmāṃsayor aikaśāstryaṃ: "saṃhitam etat śārīrakaṃ jaiminīyena ṣoḍaśalakṣaṇena iti śāstraikatvasiddhiḥ"* । (*Śrībhāṣya* I, p. 4)[25]
>
> The Vṛttikāra states this [in the following words]: "After the knowledge of karma which has been acquired, there is desire to know Brahma." And he will state that Karmamīmāṃsā and Brahmamīmāṃsā are one Śāstra, in the words: "This Śārīraka has been joined with the sixteen-fold [composition] of Jaimini,[26] and that proves that the two Śāstras are one."

Unlike Sureśvara, the Vṛttikāra cited by Rāmānuja does not appear to look upon the *Brahmasūtra* as a composition of Jaimini. His words rather create the impression that, according to him, the unity

---

Bhāskara (*Ātmasiddhi*, p. 9-10; cf. Neevel 1977: 66 ff, 100; Mesquita 1979: 165-166). A 17th-century work in the tradition of Viśiṣṭādvaita, Śrīnivāsa's *Yatipatimatadīpikā* (= *Yatīndramatadīpikā*; p. 1), enumerates Vyāsa, Bodhāyana, Guhadeva, Bhāṇaruci, Brahmānandi(n), Draviḍācārya, Śrīparāṃkuśa, Nātha, Yāmunamuni, Yatīśvara etc. as the names of earlier teachers. For the twenty-one earlier commentators of the *Brahmasūtra* enumerated by Madhva, see Sharma 1981: 98.

[25] Quoted in Kane 1960: 120, n. 2; 1977: 1159, n. 1886; Parpola 1981: 147, n. 7a.

[26] The sixteenfold composition of Jaimini is no doubt the combination of the twelve chapters commented upon by Śabara with the four chapters known as Saṃkarṣakāṇḍa or Devatākāṇḍa; along with the four chapters of the *Brahmasūtra* this adds up to twenty chapters in total. It is noteworthy that the four chapters of the Devatākāṇḍa – which in the opinion of Rāmānuja's Vṛttikāra are part of the sixteenfold Karmamīmāṃsā – are united with the four chapters commented upon by Śaṅkara (i.e. with the *Brahmasūtra*) to account for an Uttaramīmāṃsā in eight chapters in the *Sarva(darśana)siddhāntasaṃgraha* ascribed to (another) Śaṅkara, as noted in Hacker 1947: 55. According to the *Tattvaratnākara* the author of the Devatākāṇḍa is Kāśakṛtsna; see Subrahmanya Sastri 1961, Preface, p. iii; Bhūmikā, pp. 5-6.

of the two Śāstras came about later, after the composition of their classical texts. Note further that these passages from Rāmānuja's *Śrībhāṣya* (unlike the *Prapañcahṛdaya*, to be considered below) do not state that either Bodhāyana or the Vṛttikāra (who may well have been one and the same person) commented upon both the *Mīmāṃsāsūtra* **and** the *Brahmasūtra*.

Also the *Prapañcahṛdaya*, an anonymous work of unknown date,[27] creates the impression that the two Śāstras were combined at some moment of time after the composition of their classical texts:

> *tatra sāṅgopāṅgasya vedasya pūrvottarakāṇḍasaṃbhinnasyāśeṣavākyārthavicāraparāyaṇaṃ mīmāṃsāśāstram | tad idaṃ viṃśatyadhyāyanibaddham | tatra ṣoḍaśādhyāyanibaddhaṃ pūrvamīmāṃsāśāstraṃ pūrvakāṇḍasya dharmavicāraparāyaṇaṃ jaiminikṛtam | tadanyad adhyāyacatuṣkam uttaramīmāṃsāśāstram uttarakāṇḍasya brahmavicāraparāyaṇaṃ vyāsakṛtam |*[28]

> The Mīmāṃsāśāstra reflects on the meanings of all sentences belonging to the Veda, Pūrvakāṇḍa and Uttarakāṇḍa combined, along with its Aṅgas and Upāṅgas. It has been composed in twenty chapters. Among these, the Pūrvamīmāṃsāśāstra composed in sixteen chapters,[29] by Jaimini, reflects upon the Dharma connected with the Pūrvakāṇḍa. Different from that is the Uttaramīmāṃsāśāstra, four chapters composed by Vyāsa,[30] which reflects upon Brahma of the Uttarakāṇḍa.

---

[27] Witzel (1982: 212) characterizes the *Prapañcahṛdaya* as a "im frühen Mittelalter, vielleicht noch vor Śaṅkara entstandene Enzyklopädie". He gives no evidence for this claim: a note merely states that this text is already acquainted with the medical author Vāhaṭa, so that it must date from after ca. 600 CE. Witzel repeats this claim in a more recent publication (Witzel 1985: 40: "wohl in die 2. Hälfte des 1. Jts. n. Chr. zu setzen"), adds however in a note (p. 66, n. 19): "Parpola, (cf. WZKS, 25, p. 153 ff.), datiert den Text ins 11. Jht." See further fn. 98, below.

[28] *Prapañcahṛdaya*, p. 26-27 (38-39), chapter 4; cited in Parpola 1981: 146, n. 4; Kane 1977: 1159, n. 1886.

[29] See fn. 26, above.

[30] Note that also Govindānanda's *Bhāṣyaratnaprabhā* on BrSBh 1.1.4 (p. 98) ascribes the *Brahmasūtra* to Vyāsa: *uktarītyā brahmaṇaḥ svātantrye saty eva bhagavato* ***vyāsasya*** *pṛthak śāstrakṛtir yuktā* ...; similarly Sāyaṇa in the introduction to his *Ṛgvedabhāṣya* (e.g., p. 10, l. 12), Vācaspati in the fifth introductory verse of his *Bhāmatī*, Kullūka Bhaṭṭa on Manu 1.8 and 21. Kauṇḍa Bhaṭṭa in his *Vaiyākaraṇabhūṣaṇa* on verses 23 and 24 ascribes both the

This same text adds that Bodhāyana and Upavarsa commented upon the combined work:

> *tasya viṃśatyadhyāyanibaddhasya mīmāṃsāśāstrasya kṛtakoṭināmadheyaṃ bhāṣyaṃ bodhāyanena kṛtam* | *tad granthabāhulyabhayād upekṣya kiṃcit saṃkṣiptam upavarṣeṇa kṛtam* | *tad api mandamatīn prati duṣpratipādaṃ vistīrṇatvād ity upekṣya ṣoḍaśalakṣaṇapūrvamīmāṃsāśāstrasya devasvāminātisaṃkṣiptaṃ kṛtam* | *bhavadāsenāpi kṛtaṃ jaiminīyabhāṣyam* | *punar dvikāṇḍe dharmamīmāṃsāśāstre pūrvasya tantrakāṇḍasyācāryaśabarasvāminātisaṃkṣepeṇa saṃkarṣakāṇḍaṃ dvitīyam upekṣya kṛtaṃ bhāṣyam* |[31]

> Bodhāyana wrote a commentary, called *Kṛtakoṭi*, on the [entire] Mīmāṃsāśāstra composed in twenty chapters. Because the great bulk of [that] work was frightening, Upavarṣa abridged it by omitting some things. Considering even that to be difficult to understand for the dull-witted on account of its extent, Devasvāmin wrote a much abridged [commentary] pertaining only to the Pūrvamīmāṃsāśāstra defined by the [first] 16 [chapters]. Bhavadāsa, too, wrote a commentary upon [this] work of Jaimini's. Again, Ācārya Śabarasvāmin wrote, with much abbreviation, a commentary upon the first of the two kāṇḍas of the Dharmamīmāṃsāśāstra, Tantrakāṇḍa, omitting the second Saṅkarṣakāṇḍa. (transl. Parpola 1981: 153-154; modified)

It is hard to determine with certainty the extent to which the accounts of the *Prapañcahṛdaya* are trustworthy. Yudhiṣṭhira Mī-

---

Brahmasūtra and the *Yogabhāṣya* to Vyāsa. Cf. further Kane 1960: 129 ff; 1977: 1166. Vyāsa is also mentioned at *Upadeśasāhasrī*, Padyabandha 16.67, but the editor and translator of this passage believes that "[i]n Śaṅkara's works Vyāsa indicates the author of the Smṛtis and not Bādarāyaṇa, the author of the B[rahma] S[ūtra]" (Mayeda 1979: 159, n. 41; cf. 1965: 187; 1973: 40-41). Yāmuna bases an argument on the presumed identity of Vyāsa the author of the *Mahābhārata* and Vyāsa the author of the *Brahmasūtra*; see Neevel 1977: 56. Madhusūdana Sarasvatī's *Vedāntakalpalatikā* sometimes mentions Vyāsa (p. 2 verse 4), sometimes Bādarāyaṇa (p. 12), apparently referring to one and the same person. The fact that the *Prapañcahṛdaya* elsewhere (p. 46 [67]) identifies Bādarāyaṇa and Vyāsa has not received sufficient attention in the secondary literature.

[31] *Prapañcahṛdaya*, p. 27 (39); cited in Kane 1977: 1159, n. 1886; Parpola 1981: 154, n. 37; Mīmāṃsaka 1987, Introduction, p. 27. The passage continues (cited in Mīmāṃsaka 1987, Introduction, p. 27): *tathā ca devatākāṇḍasya saṃkarṣeṇa* | *brahmakāṇḍasya bhagavatpādabrahmadattabhāskarādibhir matabhedenāpi kṛtam* | *tathā śābarabhāṣyaṃ vākyārthabhedam abhyupagamya bhaṭṭaprabhākarābhyāṃ dvidhā vyākhyātam: tatra bhāvanāparatvena bhaṭṭakumāreṇa, niyogaparatayā prabhākareṇa.*

māṃsaka (1987, Introduction, pp. 29-30) has pointed out that according to various early testimonies Kṛtakoti, far from being the name of a commentary, is another name for Upavarṣa. He further draws attention to the fact that the *Prapañcahṛdaya*, while mentioning Brahmadatta and Bhāskara as commentators on the *Brahmasūtra*,[32] does not mention Śaṅkara.[33] Christian Bouy (2000: 24, n. 96), moreover, reminds us that according to Vedāntadeśika, Bodhāyana and Upavarṣa appear to be one and the same person.[34]

However that may be, the *Prapañcahṛdaya* does not tell us that Pūrva- and Uttara-Mīmāṃsā were originally one system. It rather suggests that at some point in time efforts were made to combine the two fundamental texts – the *Mīmāṃsāsūtra* and the *Brahmasūtra* – in order to create one single system. Bodhāyana and Upavarṣa (whether one or two persons) may have played a role in this attempt. Judging by later developments, this attempt did not meet with lasting success. Devasvāmin and other commentators returned to a separate treatment of the *Mīmāṃsāsūtra*, the commentators mentioned by Rāmānuja and others apparently confined themselves to the *Brahmasūtra*.

We must conclude from the evidence so far considered that the testimony from later authors does not support the hypothesis that the Pūrva- and the Uttara-Mīmāṃsā originally were one system,

---

[32] See the preceding footnote.

[33] This is surprising in view of the fact that the author of the *Prapañcahṛdaya* may have been an Advaitin, as might follow from the following statement (p. 17 [23]): *nirupādhikas tanubhuvanaprapañcapratibhāsarahito nityaśuddhabuddhamuktaparamānandādvaitabrahmabhāvo mokṣaḥ*; see also his characterisation of the fourth chapter of the *Brahmasūtra* (p. 29 [42]): *caturthe sakalasaṃsāraduḥkhānāṃ nivṛttilakṣaṇam ātmādvaitabrahmamātramokṣaphalam*. It is on the other hand surprising that the last two chapters of the *Prapañcahṛdaya* (*prakaraṇas* 7 and 8) extensively deal with Sāṃkhya and Yoga.

It is here to be noted (i) that Śaṅkara *may* have thought that Śabara had also composed a commentary on the *Brahmasūtra*, as we have seen above, and (ii) that Śabara refers twice (on PMS 10.4.32; 12.2.11) to the Saṅkarṣakāṇḍa in his *Mīmāṃsābhāṣya*, without clear indication to the effect that he himself had composed a commentary on it.

[34] Cf. Mesquita 1984: 181-182, n. 9.

even less that the Pūrva- and Uttara-Mīmāmsāsūtra were originally part of one single work. The following sections will bring to light that all the available evidence agrees as well – in fact, better – with an altogether different hypothesis, the hypothesis namely that at least some Vedāntins at some point of the history of this current of thought made a effort to turn themselves into, or become recognised as, some kind of Mīmāṃsakas, different from the ritual Mīmāṃsakas, but Mīmāṃsakas none the less, this because these Vedāntins, too, followed the same strict rules of Vedic interpretation as the ritual Mīmāṃsakas.

2. VEDĀNTINS WHO ARE NOT MĪMĀṂSAKAS

The question we have to address at this point is the following: why should a philosophy that draws its inspiration from the Upaniṣads consider itself a form of Mīmāṃsā? This would at first sight only make sense if Mīmāṃsā were some kind of philosophy. The fact is that it isn't. Ritual Mīmāṃsā, at any rate, never was a philosophy until later thinkers of the school – primarily Kumārila Bhaṭṭa and Prabhākara – adopted philosophical positions in their confrontations with thinkers of other schools. Until that time ritual Mīmāṃsā was a school of Vedic hermeneutics. The whole of Śabara's Bhāṣya contains very little that one might be tempted to call "philosophy" and all the more that is Vedic interpretation. In other words, a philosophy that shares features with the teachings of the Upaniṣads and which draws its inspiration from these texts is not automatically a form of Mīmāṃsā.

Let us not forget that ritual Mīmāṃsā is not a school of ritual practice that invokes the Veda in order to justify its practices. The texts present the situation the other way round. Mīmāṃsā describes the manner in which an open-minded student reacts to the teachings of the Veda. That is to say, a properly qualified student learns the Veda by heart and also comes to understand its meaning. He is in this way confronted with injunctions, which tell him that he must carry out certain ritual acts. Realising that these injunctions cannot but be correct, he now knows that he has to sacrifice and does so. Combining these injunctions with other injunctions and with different Vedic statements, our student finds out how exactly to perform these sacrifices. If in this way he is going to perform the same sacrifices which his elders had performed before him, this is not, strictly speaking, because he imitates his elders, but because he, individually, has been confronted with the same Vedic injunctions as had his elders before him.

If we apply this way of thinking to Vedānta as Mīmāṃsā – for which the passages cited in section 1 above use various names: Śārīraka-, Vedāntārtha-, Brahma- and Uttara-Mīmāṃsā –, we find that this cannot be merely a philosophy which justifies its tenets by invoking the Veda. In order to be a form of Mīmāṃsā, the situation has to be reversed here too. Any qualified person is free to invoke passages from the Veda to support this or that position, and later thinkers maintain that all the Smṛtis are in fact based on the Veda. This does not however turn these Smṛtis into Mīmāṃsā. In order to be a form of Mīmāṃsā, Vedānta thought must claim to directly derive from the Veda. In fact, the expression "Vedānta thought" or "Vedānta philosophy" is dubious in this connection; it is no doubt more correct to speak of the "Vedāntic transformation" that is claimed to affect the qualified student who correctly studies the Veda.

At this point it is important to recall that Vedāntic Mīmāṃsā, in order to be a form of Mīmāṃsā, has to describe the reaction of the learner to the whole of the Veda, not exclusively the Upaniṣads. Since no Vedāntic Mīmāṃsaka, to my knowledge, has ever rejected ritual Mīmāṃsā for being totally mistaken, Vedāntic Mīmāṃsā presents itself as a superstructure on top of ritual Mīmāṃsā. This does not necessarily entail that every Mīmāṃsaka must also be, or have been, a ritualist (even though many Vedāntic Mīmāṃsakas adopted this position). It means that they fully recognise that many Vedic statements require those who study them to perform sacrifices; the knowledge obtained from Upaniṣadic statements may annul these injunctions for certain adepts (this is the opinion of several Vedāntic Mīmāṃsakas, among them Śaṅkara), but this does not change the fact that those Vedic injunctions in and by themselves require such behaviour. In other words, Vedāntic Mīmāṃsā in a certain way recognises ritual Mīmāṃsā.

However, to come back to the point of departure, one may very well adhere to Vedāntic ideas without having a Mīmāṃsā-like conception as to how a student of the Veda supposedly will undergo the effects of the relevant Upaniṣadic statements. This is a very important point: there is no reason whatsoever to believe that all Vedāntins were Mīmāṃsakas, even Vedāntic Mīmāṃsakas. There is no theoretical reason to think so, and there are practical indications that there were indeed Vedāntins who recognised no link with Mīmāṃsā. In the present section we will briefly consider testimony that shows that there apparently were, during the centuries preceding Śaṅkara, Vedāntins who did not consider themselves Mīmāṃsakas. These early Vedāntins held on to a position in which knowledge of Brahma was the precondition for liberation, they apparently believed that this position was the one also taught in the Upaniṣads (sometimes only their name would betray this), but they did not waste a word on what exact role the Veda played in obtaining this liberating knowledge. In other words, these Vedāntins were not, or at any rate did not present themselves as Mīmāṃsakas.

The first text here to be considered is the so-called *Gauḍapādīyakārikā* or *Āgamaśāstra* ascribed to Gauḍapāda, in whom later tradition sees the teacher of the teacher of Śaṅkara.[35] It must here briefly be recalled that this ascription of the *Āgamaśāstra* to a single author is highly problematic. This text really consists of four treatises (*prakaraṇa*), already in the opinion of the Śaṅkara who commented upon all four of them, and about whose identity there is difference of opinion.[36] The second of these four treatises (known

[35] Mahadevan 1952: 2; but Hacker 1951: 1922 (16).

[36] See Mayeda 1968a; Vetter 1969b; 1978a; Bronkhorst 1991a; King 1995; Stephan 2002: 29 ff; Hanneder 2003.

by the name Vaitathyaprakaraṇa) refers at two occasions to the Upaniṣads (GK 2.12: *vedāntaviniścaya*; GK 2.31: *vedānteṣu vicakṣaṇa*) but contains no hint how, or indeed that, its doctrine is derived from the Upaniṣads. Its central message, that the objects of our waking consciousness are no more real than the objects seen in a dream, is presented as 'handed down by tradition' (*smṛta*) in verse 2.4, rather than as 'known from the Veda' (*śruta*), which would metrically have been possible. The third treatise (*Advaitaprakaraṇa*) frequently mentions Brahma, but its point is not that Brahma can only be known through the Veda. The emphasis is on mental states without thought, sometimes called *samādhi* (3.37), sometimes *asparśayoga* 'contactless Yoga': "This is what is called 'contactless Yoga', very difficult to be looked at by all yogins; for the yogins shrink from it seeing fear where [in fact] there is no fear."[37] A further message of this treatise is that nothing can come into existence. This position is argued for in a series of verses (GK 3.20-28) with the help of both Upaniṣadic references and logic (cf. Bronkhorst 1999: 53 f). The third treatise does also elsewhere refer to Upaniṣadic passages (e.g. GK 3.11: *taittirīyake*; 3.12: *madhujñāne*; etc.) but, like the second treatise, it does not suggest that the knowledge it communicates, or the aim it preaches, can only be obtained from the Upaniṣads by applying the principles of Mīmāṃsā. Some of the themes of the third treatise (*asparśayoga*; and the idea that nothing can come into existence) recur in the fourth one (Alātaśāntiprakaraṇa), with this difference that the fourth treatise heavily uses Buddhist ideas and terminology, so much so that the position can be, and has been, defended that this treatise was composed by a Buddhist. It is therefore open to question whether it was conceived as an expression of Vedāntic thought, and no trace of concern with the text of the Upaniṣads can, of course, be found in it. The first treatise, finally, is often considered as commenting

[37] GK 3.39: *asparśayogo nāmaiṣa* (Bouy 2000: 73, 181 reads *vai nāma*) *durdarśaḥ sarvayogibhiḥ* | *yogino bibhyati hy asmād abhaye bhayadarśinaḥ* || Transl. Bhattacharya, modified. Cf. Divanji 1940; King 1992; Slaje 1994b.

upon an Upaniṣad, the *Māṇḍūkya-Upaniṣad*. However, the commentator Śaṅkara does not look upon this text as an Upaniṣad, as *śruti*, and nor does the famous Śaṅkara who composed the *Brahmasūtrabhāṣya* ever cite this Upaniṣad (Mayeda 1968a: 81; Vetter 1979: 34-35).[38] The first treatise itself contains no indication that its teaching is based on an Upaniṣad, nor on several Upaniṣads or on the Veda for that matter. Its emphasis is on the syllable OM, which is identical with Brahma, and knowledge of which leads to the highest goal: "He and no other person is a sage (*muni*) who knows OM which has no measure and yet has an unlimited measure, and which is the cessation of duality, and which is bliss."[39]

Another early Vedānta treatise – the *Paramārthasāra* of Ādiśeṣa, which appears to be younger than the *Āgamaśāstra* and older than the *Yuktidīpikā*[40] (Danielson 1980: 1-2) – is an even clearer example of Vedāntic thought in which the link with the Veda receives no attention whatsoever. Indeed, the word Vedānta itself occurs only in its concluding verse, in the compound *vedāntaśāstra*. Nothing else in the eighty-seven verses that make up this small treatise as much as suggests that the message it communicates has anything whatsoever to do with the Upaniṣads. On the other hand, Brahma is frequently mentioned, and it is made clear that knowledge of Brahma leads to liberation.

---

[38] With regard to Śaṅkara, Mayeda (1968a: 82) observes: "It is strange but true that the commentator of the Gauḍapādīyakārikā keeps totally silent about the Māṇḍūkyopaniṣad, even while commenting on its twelve prose sentences. Of course he has to cite to interpret it, but he does so as if it were a part of the Gauḍapādīyakārikā." It is to be noted that a number of later authors refer to both the Māṇḍūkya and the Gauḍapādīyakārikā as *śruti*, and therefore as part of the Veda (Mayeda 1968a: 81 f; Bouy 2000: 33). Note further that "Śaṃkara cite ..., dans son com[mentaire] sur les Brahmasūtra, [*Gauḍapādīyakārikā*] III.15 et I.16, en les attribuant respectivement au *saṃpradāyavid* et au 'maître' (*ācārya*) *vedāntārthasaṃpradāyavid* ([*Brahmasūtrabhāṣya*] I.4,14; II.1,9)" (Bouy 2000: 33, n. 154).

[39] GK 1.29: *amātro 'nantamātraś ca dvaitasyopaśamaḥ śivaḥ* | *oṅkāro vidito yena sa munir netaro janaḥ* || Transl. Bhattacharya.

[40] Nothing stands in the way of dating the *Yuktidīpikā* in the second half of the 6th century CE; see Bronkhorst 2003.

The Buddhist author Bhavya provides us with further early testimony regarding what he calls the Vedāntavādins.[41] His testimony creates the impression that the school of philosophy that he describes was not much concerned with the details of Vedic interpretation that is characteristic of Mīmāṃsā. Theirs was a school of philosophy, whose link with the Upaniṣads receives no attention whatsoever in Bhavya's exposition. What is more, we learn from Qvarnström's (1989: 102 f) study of the material that Bhavya believed that the Vedāntavādins had adopted or stolen their ideas from the Buddhists. Bhavya claims:[42] "Being convinced that this infallible system of the Tathāgata is a good one, here [in the Vedānta system] the heterodox sectarians, being desirous of [that doctrine], have therefore [even] made it their own." This accusation, too, suggests that Bhavya was confronted with people or texts whose prime concern was not to derive their philosophy from Vedic texts.

Also the Jaina tradition has preserved a small text – dating perhaps from the 6th century and attributed to Siddhasena Divākara – which presents a Vedāntic position. This text draws upon Upaniṣadic and other Vedic sources, without however subjecting them to anything like a Mīmāṃsā-like analysis.[43]

As a further example of Vedānta-like philosophising without excessive concern for Vedic hermeneutics the 5th-century thinker Bhartṛhari may be mentioned. His Vākyapadīya appears to refer to Vedāntins once (*trayyantavedinaḥ*; Vkp 3.3.72), but there is no reason to think that Bhartṛhari counted himself amongst them (cf. Houben 1995: 293 f; Bronkhorst, forthcoming (a)). And yet Bhartṛhari's thought resembles classical Vedāntic philosophy in many

---

[41] Earlier authors maintained that Bhavya quotes a verse from Gauḍapāda in his work and is therefore posterior to him, but this seems less certain now; cf. Bouy 2000: 20 f.

[42] *Madhyamakahṛdayakārikā* 8.86: *tāthāgatīm avitathāṃ matvā nītim imāṃ śubhām | tasmāj jātaspṛhais tīrthyaiḥ kṛtaṃ tatra mamāpi tat* || Text and translation as in Qvarnström 1989: 44, 91.

[43] Qvarnström 2003.

respects. Brahma is mentioned in the very first verse of the Vākyapadīya, and a few more times later on. Brahma is Bhartṛhari's absolute, which is one, the totality of all there is.[44] This totality is divided into unreal entities under the influence of the powers of Brahma. This is not, to be sure, identical in all details with the philosophy of Śaṅkara, or Gauḍapāda. Indeed, a major difference is that Bhartṛhari never identifies the self with Brahma. Yet Bhartṛhari's respect for the Veda is beyond doubt, and the resemblance of some of his notions with the ideas normally associated with Vedāntic thought is clear. But Bhartṛhari does not present his views as the mere result of correct Vedic interpretation.

One more text must be mentioned here. The recent researches of Walter Slaje (especially 1994a) have made it probable that the *Yogavāsiṣṭha* was originally an independent work called *Mokṣopāya*, a work whose author and precise date remain unknown.[45] The attitude toward authority of the author of the original *Mokṣopāya* finds expression in the following words:

> Even when it has been composed by a human being, a treatise must be accepted if it teaches on the basis of arguments (*yukti*). [Everything] else, on the other hand, should be abandoned, even if it derives from seers (*ṛṣi*). One should exclusively adhere to rules of logic (*nyāya*). Statements supported by arguments (*yukti*) must be accepted even from a child. [Everything] else should be abandoned like [useless] grass, even if it has been uttered by [the god] Brahmā.[46]

And again:

---

[44] Cf. Bronkhorst 1991b; 1998. The parallelism with the early Sāṃkhya notion of *pradhāna* is striking; see Bronkhorst, forthcoming (b).

[45] Regarding the date of the original *Mokṣopāya* Slaje makes the following observation (1994a: 56): "Mit seinem erkenntnistheoretischen Illusionismus und seiner Lehre vom nicht wirklich Entstandensein der Erscheinungswelt (*ajātatva*) könnte das Werk – historisch betrachtet – eine Nebenlinie zu Gauḍapāda (um 500), dem Laṅkāvatārasūtra, und Maṇḍana (um 700) bilden."

[46] YogV 2.18.2-3: *api pauruṣam, ādeyam śāstraṃ ced yuktibodhakam* I *anyat tv, ārṣam api, tyājyam; bhāvyaṃ nyāyaikasevinā* II *yuktiyuktam upādeyaṃ vacanaṃ bālakād api* I *anyat tṛṇam iva tyājyam, apy uktaṃ padmajanmanā* II Cf. Slaje 1994a: 167.

> Never and in no case should one be satisfied with the author of a treatise; one should be satisfied with the contents of the treatise, [on condition that] it provides experience supported by arguments (*yukti*).[47]

These and many other passages allow us to conclude that the author of the *Mokṣopāya* was of the opinion that his philosophical position was not based on traditional authority, but supported by arguments presented in his text. This does not necessarily mean that he claimed to have created an altogether new philosophy, but he certainly was of the opinion that someone who was sufficiently informed about the world and who seriously considered the arguments concerned, would arrive at the same philosophy as he, quite independently of the tradition he might belong to. Which is this philosophical position? The author of the *Mokṣopāya* teaches a subjective illusionism, which denies the existence of a real, objectively existing world.[48] The world is nothing beyond imagination; even the creator-god Brahmā is no more real than the model in the mind of a painter.[49] All that exists is consciousness.

This is not the place to deal with the arguments which the *Mokṣopāya* presents to prove its view of the world (see Bronkhorst 2001: 207 ff). It is however important to note that its philosophy is in various respects close to Vedānta.[50] Yet this text explicitly denies dependence on anything but logical reasoning.

The texts considered so far can be looked upon as being more or less closely associated with one or more Vedāntic traditions that remained unconnected with Mīmāṃsā. There are of course nume-

---

[47] YogV 7.103.45: *śāstrakartari rantavyaṃ na kadācana kutracit* | *śāstrārtha eva rantavyaṃ yuktiyuktānubhūtide* | The reading is the one adopted by Slaje (1994a: 165) on the basis of supplementary manuscript evidence. Where possible, I use the readings accepted by Slaje in his book *Vom Mokṣopāya-Śāstra zum Yogavāsiṣṭha-Mahārāmāyaṇa* (1994), or in his editions of Bhāskarakaṇṭha's *Mokṣopāyaṭīkā* (1993, 1995, 1996). I also follow Slaje in referring to the Uttarārdha of book 6 as book 7.

[48] E.g. YogV 6.95.16 (Slaje 1994a: 260, n. 230): *jagadādi na vidyate.*

[49] YogV 3.2.55: *yathā citrakṛdantaḥsthā nirdehā bhāti putrikā* | *tathaiva bhāsate brahmā cidākāśāccharañjanam* || (Slaje 1994a: 198)

[50] Cf. Chenet 1998-99.

rous other texts which preach Vedānta-like ideas without being in any way linked to Mīmāṃsā.[51] It serves no purpose in the present context to try to be exhaustive. However, mention must be made of the relatively late Upaniṣads that were composed during the period that interests us. These texts propound Vedāntic ideas (such as "I am Brahma") without basing themselves on the old Upaniṣads; they do not need to, because they present themselves as Upaniṣads. And yet these texts are younger than the early Upaniṣads, many much younger, some younger than Śaṅkara himself. It may here suffice to mention the so-called Saṃnyāsa Upaniṣads, which have been studied in detail by scholars such as Sprockhoff (1976) and Olivelle (1992). The dates of these texts range from the last centuries preceding the common era to the 15th century CE, according to Sprockhoff (1976). It is not impossible that some of these Upaniṣads have at a late date been "vedanticised" (Sprockhoff 1976: 263), but this can hardly be true of all the Upaniṣads that have been composed during this period. Obviously the Vedāntic ideas of these and other Upaniṣads cannot be looked upon as some kind of Mīmāṃsā, because these texts claim to be parts of the Veda themselves. Perhaps this claim was never meant to be taken too seriously – after all, these Upaniṣads were not part of the repertoire of traditional Veda reciters – but this would show all the more clearly that the Vedānta philosophy, in the opinion of many, could very well survive and thrive without a close link to the Veda of the traditional reciters.

Relatively early evidence for Vedānta-like ideas is also found elsewhere. Aśvaghoṣa's *Buddhacarita*, for example, contains the following verse, put in the mouth of the future Buddha's teacher

---

[51] Cf. Gonda 1985: 82: "D'une manière générale, à travers toute l'histoire de l'hindouisme, on peut distinguer les penseurs plutôt philosophes et les fidèles sentimentaux. Les premiers ont tendance à croire à l'existence du seul Brahman et à son identité avec les âmes empiriques et la matière; ils estiment que la rédemption consiste en ceci que, par une vision directe, on fait l'expérience de l'unité éternelle du brahman et de l'âme ... Quant aux croyants plus ou moins bhaktiques, ils insistent, avec la Bhagavadgītā, sur le fait que le Brahman est l'Ātman et le maître des êtres vivants, ..." Cf. Sheridan 1986.

Arāḍa Kālāma (12.42): "For this purpose the Brahmans in the world, who follow the doctrine of the supreme Absolute (*paramabrahma*), practise here the brahman-course and instruct the Brahmans in it." (*ityarthaṃ brāhmaṇā loke paramabrahmavādinaḥ* | *brahmacaryaṃ carantīha brāhmaṇān vāsayanti ca* ||).[52]

[The question of the relation of certain Vedāntic traditions with Mīmāṃsā presents itself emphatically in connection with the school of Rāmānuja. Gerhard Oberhammer (1997: 97) makes the following pertinent remarks:

> In der Darstellung der Geschichte der Rāmānuja-Schule werden ihre Anfänge üblicherweise durch die Namen Nāthamuni, Yāmunamuni und Rāmānuja charakterisiert, auch wenn einige verlorene Autoren dem Namen nach bekannt sind und erwähnt werden. Dadurch ergibt sich ein im Grunde eindimensionales Bild der Anfänge dieser Schule, das letztlich auch ihre historische Verflechtung in das philosophisch-theologische Geschehen der Zeit im Dunkeln lässt. Woher stammt die philosophische Tradition dieser Denker, von denen jedenfalls Yāmunamuni ein Pāñcarātrin gewesen sein dürfte, und wie war ihre Beziehung zur Vedānta-Tradition? Denn selbst bei der üblichen Darstellung der Geschichte der Schule fällt auf, dass im Grunde Rāmānuja der erste Autor ist, der einen Kommentar zu den Brahmasūtren schreibt. Weder Nāthamuni noch Yāmunamuni haben einen solchen verfasst. Yāmunamuni kennt zwar die Brahmasūtren und zitiert sie. Er kennt sogar eine grosse Zahl von Kommentatoren der Brahmasūtren, man tut sich aber schwer *vor* Rāmānuja von einer echten Vedānta-Tradition der Schule im engeren Sinne zu sprechen. Es fällt selbst schwer, genau zu bestimmen, woher Rāmānujas eigene Vedānta-Tradition kommt. Es ist bezeichnend, dass Rāmānuja, wenigstens der Legende nach, Schüler eines Vedānta-Lehrers gewesen ist, nämlich Yādavaprakāśas, der mit seiner Lehre nicht dem Typus des Viśiṣṭādvaita angehört hat, wie er etwa bei Yāmunamuni fassbar ist. Die Anfänge der Vedānta-Tradition Rāmānujas bleiben im Dunkel und können beim heutigen Stand der Forschung auch nicht geklärt werden.

In view of the questions raised in this article, one may wonder to what extent Rāmānuja's predecessors can be looked upon as Vedāntic Mīmāṃsakas.[53] Roque Mesquita's researches (1990: 19),

---

[52] Johnston 1936: 133 (text), 174 (translation). Cf. Nakamura 1955: 83 f; 1983: 146 f.

[53] Cf. Oberhammer 1971: 6.

for example, have led to the conclusion that Nāthamuni was of the opinion that God's existence had to be proved, not only on the basis of the Veda, but also with the help of inference. Yāmunamuni defended initially (e.g., in his *Ātmasiddhi* and *Īśvarasiddhi*) the same position, but abandoned the idea of a logical proof of the existence of God in his later works (*Puruṣanirṇaya*, *Āgama-prāmāṇya*; see Mesquita 1971; 1973: 187 f; 1974: 188 f; 1980: 203 f). Vedānta as Mīmāṃsā – as has been pointed out above and will further be shown below – allows no other means of obtaining liberating knowledge of Brahma, or of God, than the Veda. Vedāntic Mīmāṃsā has no place for logical proofs of God, for it would no longer be a form of Mīmāṃsā.]

3. VEDĀNTINS WHO ARE MĪMĀṂSAKAS

Beside those Vedāntins who do not show much concern with the details of Vedic hermeneutics, there are others who do. We will see that a number of Vedāntins did not just use the principles of Mīmāṃsā in order to arrive at a correct interpretation of the Upaniṣads which they could then use to prove their philosophies right. They went further by presenting their philosophies as being themselves Mīmāṃsā at heart. A correct use of the principles of Mīmāṃsā, they argued, leads the qualified student to liberation through the knowledge of Brahma. These philosophers do not therefore present themselves, strictly speaking, as philosophers, a fact that has often been overlooked in modern research.[54] Modern research has therefore frequently dealt with questions such as that of the relationship between human reason and Vedic revelation in these thinkers.[55] To the extent that these thinkers present them-

[54] See however Mayeda 1968b: 221: "Early Vedānta philosophers did not pay much attention to the epistemological and logical problems which were important, even essential, topics among other schools of Indian philosophy."

[55] This question is explicitly thematised in works such as Murty 1959; Brückner 1979; Halbfass 1991, chapter 5 ("Human reason and Vedic revelation in Advaita Vedānta"; an earlier version of this chapter in Halbfass 1983, chapter 2).

selves as Mīmāṃsakas (and we will see that they do not always stick to this position in all their writings), there can be no doubt that knowledge derived from the Veda must have priority over any form of reasoning. Being self-proclaimed Mīmāṃsakas they maintain, and have to maintain, that the Veda provides knowledge that cannot be obtained by any other means. Vedānta conceived of as Mīmāṃsā is **not** a form of philosophy which uses various means of knowledge to establish its positions; quite on the contrary, it **is** Vedic interpretation which starts from the assumption that knowledge correctly derived from the Veda cannot but be correct itself.[56] Let me hasten to add that the knowledge about Brahma that can be obtained from the Veda and from nowhere else is not just any kind of knowledge; for the student who is ripe for it, it is knowledge which liberates him from this world.

We have seen that by far not all Vedāntins have presented themselves as Mīmāṃsakas, and it seems a priori likely that Vedānta as Mīmāṃsā was an innovation that was at some time made in certain Vedāntic circles. We may assume that the author or authors of the *Brahmasūtra* as well as the various commentators of this text only whose names have reached us belonged to those who welcomed this way of presenting Vedānta.[57] In the following pages

---

Krishna (2001: 94) protests, no doubt rightly, against the use of the term "revelation" in this context.

[56] One is tempted to conclude from Vātsyāyana's laconic characterisation in the *Nyāyabhāṣya* of the Upaniṣads as being "mere knowledge of the self" (*adhyātmavidyāmātra*) and distinct from "investigative science" (*ānvīkṣikī*) that he was acquainted with some form of early Vedāntic Mīmāṃsā; see NBh, p. 35, ll. 3-4 (on sūtra 1.1.1).

[57] It is not clear to what extent all Vedāntins in the tradition of *Brahmasūtra* commentators considered themselves Mīmāṃsakas. Sureśvara's use, in his *Naiṣkarmyasiddhi* 2.24, of the simple term *mīmāṃsaka* to designate a follower of Kumārila Bhaṭṭa is suggestive in this respect; cf. Hacker 1951: 1954 (48). There is however no doubt in the case of the most important ones: Śaṅkara calls his own work *Vedāntavākyamīmāṃsā* under BSū 1.1.1 (and *Śārīrakamīmāṃsābhāṣya* in the colophons); Bhāskara's commentary is called *Śārīrakamīmāṃsābhāṣya* in a number of colophons; attention has been drawn in section 1 to Rāmānuja's use of the expression Brahmamīmāṃsā.

we will consider some of the thinkers of this kind whose works have survived. The earliest commentator on the *Brahmasūtra* whose work has been preserved is Śaṅkara. Let us examine his position in some detail.

3.1. Śaṅkara

In the beginning of his *Brahmasūtrabhāṣya*, Śaṅkara presents a justification of the way he interprets the Upaniṣads. Since this way would at first sight seem to be in contradiction with the Mīmāṃsā methods of Vedic interpretation, he first presents the latter's point of view as a *pūrvapakṣa*:

> *kathaṃ punar brahmaṇaḥ śāstrapramāṇakatvam ucyate, yāvatā "āmnāyasya kriyārthatvād ānarthakyam atadarthānām" iti kriyāparatvaṃ śāstrasya pradarśitam | ato vedāntānām ānarthakyaṃ, akriyārthatvāt | kartṛdevatādiprakāśanārthatvena vā kriyāvidhiśeṣatvaṃ, upāsanādikriyāntaravidhānārthatvaṃ vā | na hi pariniṣṭhitavastupratipādanaṃ saṃbhavati, pratyakṣādiviṣayatvāt pariniṣṭhitavastunaḥ, tatpratipādane ca heyopādeyarahite puruṣārthābhāvāt | ata eva 'so 'rodīt' ity evamādīnām ānarthakyaṃ mā bhūd iti "vidhinā tv ekavākyatvāt stutyarthena vidhīnāṃ syuḥ" iti stāvakatvenārthavattvam uktam | mantrāṇāṃ ca "iṣe tvā" ityādīnāṃ kriyātatsādhanābhidhāyakatvena karmasamavāyitvam uktam | ato na kvacid api vedavākyānāṃ vidhisaṃsparśam antareṇārthavattā dṛṣṭopapannā vā | na ca pariniṣṭhite vastusvarūpe vidhiḥ saṃbhavati, kriyāviṣayatvād vidheḥ | tasmāt karmāpekṣitakartṛdevatādisvarūpaprakāśanena kriyāvidhiśeṣatvaṃ vedāntānām | atha prakaraṇāntarabhayān naitad abhyupagamyate, tathāpi svavākyagatopāsanādikarmaparatvam | tasmān na brahmaṇaḥ śāstrayonitvam*[58]
>
> How [can] it be stated that the Veda (*śāstra*) is the means of knowing Brahma, in view of the fact that it has been shown – (in MīmSū 1.2.1 which reads:) "Since the Veda is for [ritual] activity, [passages] that are not for that are without purpose" – that the Veda concerns [ritual] activity? The Upaniṣads are therefore without purpose, since they are not for [ritual] activity. Alternatively, they are adjuncts to injunctions [that prescribe ritual] activities in order to make known their agent, deity, etc.; or they are meant to enjoin other activities such as adoration. For it is not possible that they provide information about an existing thing, because an existing thing is the object of

[58] BSūBhā introducing sūtra 1.1.4 (ed. J. L. Shastri, p. 58, l. 6 – p. 61, l. 4).

> [other means of knowledge] such as perception, and because no human purpose (*puruṣārtha*) is served in providing information about [an existing thing], by which nothing is to be gained or lost. It is for this reason that, in order to avoid that [Vedic statements] like "He wept" be without purpose, [such statements] are stated to serve a purpose in that they eulogise [an injunction], in (MīmSū 1.2.7:) "Because they form one sentence with an injunction, they [serve a purpose] by eulogising injunctions." *Mantra*s such as *iṣe tvā* (TaitS 1.1.1) have been stated to be connected with ritual acts as being expressive of [ritual] activity and the means thereto. For this reason Vedic sentences are nowhere seen to have purpose except in connection with injunctions, nor would this be possible. Nor is an injunction possible that pertains to the existing aspect of a thing, because an injunction concerns an activity. It follows that the Upaniṣads are adjuncts of injunctions [that prescribe ritual] activities by making known the own forms of the agent, deity etc. required by the ritual act. And if this is not accepted out of concern for the different contexts [of Upaniṣads and Vedic injunctions], they [must be accepted as] concerning adoration and other things mentioned in their own sentences. It follows that Brahma is not known from the Veda.

This passage admirably presents, and in few words, what we know is the position of classical Mīmāṃsā. In this position there is no place for information in the Veda about existing things. The Veda, not having been composed by fallible beings, cannot possibly contain incorrect information, and therefore no information that could be in conflict with other means of knowledge such as perception. For this reason it cannot contain information about what the world is like. However, it can and does contain information about what human beings must do, for this information cannot be obtained in any other way. The result is that injunctions have to be taken literally, whereas all other Vedic pronouncements may have to be understood metaphorically.

Śaṅkara does not agree with this. He claims that the principles of Mīmāṃsā do not exclude that information about Brahma can be obtained from the Vedic texts. His logic is simple. He agrees with Mīmāṃsā that the Veda can on no account be in conflict with other means of knowledge and that, therefore, the Veda can only provide information about things that we cannot gain information about in any other way. For Mīmāṃsā the only things that fulfill this requirement are the injunctions. Śaṅkara argues that Brahma, too, falls in the same category: the only way to obtain knowledge about Brahma is through the Veda.

It is to be emphasised that Śaṅkara does not express disagreement with the basic principles of Mīmāṃsā. On the contrary, he agrees with all of them.[59] He only maintains that in applying these principles the traditional Mīmāṃsakas overlook something. They are, to be sure, right in thinking that the Veda should never be in conflict with other means of knowledge. They are also correct in maintaining that the injunctions, by their very nature, cannot be in conflict with any other means of knowledge and must therefore be taken literally. He only adds that the same reasoning applies to the passages that provide information about Brahma, for Brahma, too, cannot be known by any other means of knowledge.[60]

Śaṅkara sets out his arguments in a long passage, of which the following parts are most important in the present context:

> *na ca pariniṣṭhitavastusvarūpatve 'pi pratyakṣādiviṣayatvaṃ brahmaṇaḥ, "tat tvam asi" iti brahmātmabhāvasya śāstram antareṇānavagamyamānatvāt* | ... | *yady apy anyatra vedavākyānāṃ vidhisaṃsparśam antareṇa pramāṇatvaṃ na dṛṣṭaṃ, tathāpy ātmavijñānasya phalaparyantatvān na tadviṣayasya śāstrasya prāmāṇyaṃ śakyaṃ pratyākhyātum* |[61]

---

[59] This idea is still present in the much more recent Śaṅkara legends. According to these, Maṇḍana Miśra was a Mīmāṃsaka who lost a debate with Śaṅkara. However, "[i]n ihm regte sich Zweifel, denn etwas konnte er nicht verstehen: Wie konnte der grosse Weise Jaimini, der selbst ein Schüler Vyāsas war, eine Lehrmeinung vertreten, die offensichtlich falsch und nicht im Einklang mit den heiligen Schriften war? Auch Śaṅkaras grossartige Erklärungen konnten Maṇḍanamiśras Zweifel nicht ausräumen. Um letzte Gewissheit zu erlangen, richtete Maṇḍanamiśra seine Gedanken auf Jaimini, der daraufhin erschien und ihn davon überzeugte, dass Śaṅkaras Advaita-Lehre nicht die Gültigkeit der ritualistischen Mīmāṃsā-Lehre ausschliesse, sondern diese in sich begreife." (Ungemach 1996: 301.)

[60] The central role of the *śruti* constitutes what Michael Comans calls the "method of early Advaita Vedānta" (2000, especially p. 467 ff).

[61] BSūBhā on sūtra 1.1.4 (ed. J. L. Shastri, p. 63, l. 4 – p. 65, l. 2). See further Rambachan 1997.

> And Brahma, even though by its nature an existing thing, is not the object of perception etc., because the identity of Brahma and the self known from "That's who you are" (ChānUp 6.8.7) [can] not be known without the Veda. ... Although elsewhere Vedic sentences are not seen to be authoritative without being connected with injunctions, the authority of Vedic texts that concern [knowledge of the self] cannot be rejected, because knowledge of the self leads to a result.

Put differently, traditional Mīmāṃsā is completely correct but for the fact that its very principles should oblige it to include among the statements that will have to be taken literally, beside injunctions, also Upaniṣadic sentences pertaining to Brahma. Śaṅkara, far from being a critic of Mīmāṃsā, presents himself here as an even more conscientious applier of Mīmāṃsā principles than the traditional Mīmāṃsakas themselves.

Elsewhere in his *Brahmasūtrabhāṣya* Śaṅkara emphasises again that Brahma cannot be known by any other means than only the Veda:

> *yat tūktaṃ pariniṣpannatvād brahmaṇi pramāṇāntarāṇi saṃbhaveyur iti tad api manorathamātram* | *rūpādyabhāvād dhi nāyam arthaḥ pratyakṣasya gocaraḥ* | *liṅgādyabhāvāc ca nānumānādīnām* | *āgamamātrasamadhigamya eva tv ayam artho dharmavat* |[62]

> As to what has been claimed, namely that other means of knowledge may be possible with respect to Brahma because the latter is a completed thing, [the answer is:] That, too, is wishful thinking. For this object (viz., Brahma), not possessing colour etc., [can] not be the object of perception; nor of inference and so on, because there is no inferential mark. This object can rather only be known through the Veda (*āgama*), just like Dharma (which can only be known through Vedic injunctions).

Śaṅkara's acceptance of Mīmāṃsā principles does not mean that he always reaches the same conclusions as the ritual Mīmāṃsakas. Statements about Brahma have to be accepted for reasons which the traditional Mīmāṃsaka should find convincing. But Śaṅkara goes further. Information contained in *arthavāda*s (i.e., statements like "He wept", cited by Śaṅkara's Mīmāṃsā opponent) and in *mantra*s,

[62] BSūBhā on sūtra 2.1.6 (ed. J. L. Shastri, p. 360, ll. 6-8).

if it is not in conflict with other sources of knowledge, will have to be accepted, too. In this way we learn that the gods have bodies etc., a position that had been rejected by Śabara Śaṅkara explains this in his commentary on BraSū 1.3.33:

yad apy uktaṃ mantrārthavādayor anyārthatvān na devatāvigrahādiprakāśanasāmarthyam iti | atra brūmaḥ: pratyayāpratyayau hi sadbhāvāsadbhāvayoḥ kāraṇam, nānyārthatvam ananyārthatvaṃ vā | tathā hy anyārtham api prasthitaḥ pathi patitaṃ tṛṇaparṇādy astīty eva pratipad-yate | atrāha: viṣama upanyāsaḥ | tatra hi tṛṇaparṇādiviṣayaṃ pratyakṣaṃ pravṛttam asti yena tadastitvaṃ pratipadyate | atra punar vidhyuddeśaikavākyabhāvena stutyarthe 'rthavāde na pārthagarthyena vṛttāntaviṣayā pravṛttiḥ śakyādhyavasātum | na hi mahāvākye 'rthapratyāyake 'vāntaravākyasya pṛthak pratyāyakatvam asti | yathā "na surāṃ pibet" iti nañvati vākye padatrayasaṃbandhāt surāpānapratiṣedha evaiko 'rtho 'vagamyate | na punaḥ surāṃ pibed iti padadvayasaṃbandhāt surāpānavidhir apīti | atrocyate: viṣama upanyāsaḥ | yuktaṃ yat surāpānapratiṣedhe padānvayasyaikatvād avāntaravākyārthasyāgrahaṇam | vidhyuddeśārthavādayos tv arthavādasthāni padāni pṛthag anvayaṃ vṛttāntaviṣayaṃ pratipadyānantaraṃ kaimarthyavaśena kāmaṃ vidheḥ stāvakatvaṃ pratipadyante | ... | tad yatra so 'vāntaravākyārthaḥ pramāṇāntaragocaro bhavati tatra tadanuvādenārthavādaḥ pravartate | yatra pramāṇāntaraviruddhas tatra guṇavādena | yatra tu tad ubhayaṃ nāsti tatra kiṃ pramāṇāntarābhāvād guṇavādaḥ syād āhosvit pramāṇāntarāvirodhād vidyamānavāda iti pratītiśaraṇair vidyamānavāda āśrayaṇīyaḥ na guṇavādaḥ | etena mantro vyākhyātaḥ |[63]

With regard to what has been said – viz., that neither a *mantra* nor an *arthavāda* is capable of revealing the body and other [features] of divinities, this because [*mantra* and *arthavāda*] have another purpose – we answer: Cognition and absence of cognition, not the fact of having or not having another purpose, are the cause for [accepting] the existence and non-existence [respectively of something]. For example, a man, though traveling for another purpose, knows that the grass, leaves and other things that have fallen on his path are there.

At this point [the opponent] objects: The comparison is not appropriate. For in that [comparison] perception with grass, leaves and other things as objects has taken place, with the help of which [the traveler] knows that these [objects] are there. In the present case, on the other hand, since the *arthavāda* has praise [of some sacrificial injunction] as purpose by being united into one sentence with that injunction, it is not possible to determine

[63] BSūBhā on sūtra 1.3.33 (ed. J. L. Shastri, p. 269, l. 12 – p. 272, l. 2).

> that it has, by having a different purpose [as well], an event as object. For a sentence that is included in a larger sentence that expresses a meaning, does not separately express [another meaning]. For example, in the negative sentence "One should not drink alcoholic beverages" (*na surāṃ pibet*), because of the connection between the three constituent words, only one meaning, viz. the prohibition of drinking alcoholic beverages, is understood; but not also the injunction to drink alcoholic beverages on account of the connection between the two words *surāṃ pibet* "One should drink alcoholic beverages".
>
> Here the following reply is given: The comparison is not appropriate. It is correct that in the prohibition of alcoholic beverages the meaning of the included sentence (*surāṃ pibet*) is not understood because there is only one syntactical connection between the words. However, in the case of an injunction and its accompanying *arthavāda*, the words of the *arthavāda*, having [first and] separately reached syntactic agreement with an event as object, they subsequently, under the influence of the question "what for?", do indeed praise the injunction. ... Therefore, where the meaning of an included sentence belongs to the realm of another means of valid cognition (and is corroborated by it), there the *arthavāda* plays its role in accordance with that [other means of valid cognition]. Where [the meaning of the included sentence] is contradicted by another means of valid cognition, [there the *arthavāda* plays its role] through secondary communication. But where neither of the two is the case, there those who rely upon cognition must accept that [the *arthavāda*] communicates something existing, on the basis of the following reflection: "Should it be secondary communication on account of the fact that there is no other means of valid cognition (with regard to its contents), or a communication of something existing because it is not in contradiction with another means of valid cognition?". In this same way the *mantra* has been explained.

It is striking that here, once again, Śaṅkara turns the methods of Mīmāṃsā against itself. He does not deny that *arthavāda*s are to be understood with injunctions. He merely adds, on the basis of a semantic analysis, that this does not do away with their literal contents, which have to be accepted if no other means of valid cognition militates against this.

Śaṅkara applies essentially the same method to distinguish between statements about Brahma that are literally true and such that are not. He clearly distinguishes between these two in his commentary on BraSū 4.3.14:

jagadutpattisthitipralayahetutvaśruter anekaśaktitvaṃ brahmaṇa iti cet । *na* । *viśeṣanirākaraṇaśrutīnām ananyārthatvāt* । *utpattyādiśrutīnām api samānam ananyārthatvam*[64] *iti cet* । *na* । *tāsām ekatvapratipādanaparatvāt* । *mṛdādidṛṣṭāntair hi sato brahmaṇa ekasya satyatvaṃ vikārasya cānṛtatvaṃ pratipādayac chāstraṃ notpattyādiparaṃ bhavitum arhati* । *kasmāt punar utpattyādiśrutīnāṃ viśeṣanirākaraṇaśrutiśeṣatvaṃ na punar itaraśeṣatvam itarāsām iti* । *ucyata: viśeṣanirākaraṇaśrutīnāṃ nirākāṅkṣārthatvāt* । *na hy ātmana ekatvanityatvaśuddhatvādyavagatau satyāṃ bhūyaḥ kācid ākāṅkṣopajāyate puruṣārthasamāptibuddhyupapatteḥ* ... । ... *na viśeṣa-nirākaraṇaśrutīnām anyaśeṣatvam avagantuṃ śakyate* । *naivam utpatty-ādiśrutīnāṃ nirākāṅkṣārthapratipādanasāmarthyam asti* । *pratyakṣaṃ tu tāsām anyārthatvaṃ samanugamyate* । ... *evam utpattyādiśrutīnām aikātmyāvagamaparatvān nānekaśaktiyogo brahmaṇaḥ* ।[65]

Opponent: Brahma can have different powers since the Upaniṣads show It to be the cause of the origin, continuance, and dissolution of the universe.
Vedāntin: Not so, since the Upaniṣadic texts denying distinctive attributes cannot be interpreted in any other way.
Opponent: In the same way the texts about origin etc. cannot be interpreted otherwise.
Vedāntin: Not so, for their purpose is to establish unity. The text that propounds the reality of Brahma, existing alone without a second, and that proves the unreality of all modifications with the help of illustrations like clay, cannot be meant for establishing the truth of origin etc.
Opponent: Why again should the texts about origin etc. be subservient to the texts denying distinction and not the other way round?
Vedāntin: The answer is that this is so because the texts denying distinction lead to a knowledge which is complete by itself (and leaves behind no more curiosity to be satisfied). For when one has realized that the Self is one, eternal, pure, and so on, one cannot have any more curiosity to be satisfied as a result of the rise in him of the conviction that the highest human goal has been reached ... [T]he texts denying distinctions cannot be understood to be subservient to others. But the texts about origin etc. cannot give rise to any such self-contained knowledge (that allays further curiosity). As a matter of fact, they are seen to aim at something else. ... Thus since the texts about creation etc. are meant for imparting the knowledge of oneness, Brahma cannot be possessed of many powers.

---

[64] J. L. Shastri's edition has incorrect *anyārthatvam*.

[65] BSūBhā on sūtra 4.3.14 (ed. J. L. Shastri, p. 884, l. 5 – p. 885, l. 5). Transl. Gambhirananda 1972: 885-886, modified; cf. Comans 2000: 223.

[There is one important domain in which Śaṅkara does not always follow the example of classical Mīmāṃsā as we find it in Śabara's Bhāṣya. The latter's exegetical efforts follow the fundamental principle that an interpretation that is "nearer", i.e. presents itself more directly, is to be preferred to one that is more "remote".[66] Śaṅkara, following the *Brahmasūtra*, sometimes deviates from this principle. Under BraSū 1.1.22 he admits that in connection with the word *ākāśa* the meaning *bhūtākāśa* 'the element ether' presents itself immediately to the mind (*śīghraṃ buddhim ārohati*); yet he rejects this sense in favour of another one: Brahma. The principle of "proximity" as a yard-stick for comparing interpretations is yet behind the important *Mīmāṃsāsūtra* (3.3.14), known to Śaṅkara,[67] which enumerates a number of criteria of interpretation in order of decreasing importance (and justifies this with the word *arthaviprakarṣāt* "because the meaning obtained with their help is more remote").[68]]

If then Śaṅkara makes an effort to present the Vedāntic way to liberation as a form of Mīmāṃsā, does this have any effect on the precise nature of this path? Here it is to be remembered that Mīmāṃsā – i.e., first of all ritual Mīmāṃsā – takes as point of departure the hypothetical situation of a man with an open mind and without prior expectations who is being confronted with the contents of the Veda, presumably during the process of learning it by heart. Coming across an injunction this man will know that he must execute this or that activity, he will interpret other Vedic sentences along with injunctions, etc. etc. The whole of Mīmāṃsā in its sometimes confusing complexity is presented as resulting naturally from this confrontation, in which the learner must however preserve his unbiased openness to the text. In the end this learner will carry out rituals and do all the other things that are required, not

---

[66] See Bronkhorst 1997.

[67] Renou 1957: 125 / 473 / 411 sq.

[68] MīmSū 3.3.14: *śruti-liṅga-vākya-prakaraṇa-sthāna-samākhyānāṃ samavāye pradaulbalyam arthaviprakarṣāt.*

(according to the theory) because someone told or taught him to do so, but simply because this is the natural reaction to a confrontation with the texts he has learnt.

This same hypothetical situation applies to Brahma-Mīmāṃsā. Imagine the same man as before now learning the Upaniṣads by heart. He will come across, and by hypothesis understand, sentences that teach him e.g. that his self is identical with Brahma. Śaṅkara makes a point of arguing that these sentences are no injunctions, so that there is no prescription to meditate on Brahma or the like. That is to say, these sentences do nothing beyond passing some information. But important information it is! It is the kind of information that informs a person that the snake which had given him a fright is really a rope. Such information does not prescribe anything, yet totally changes the situation of those who receive it. Our Vedic student will all of a sudden know that his self is Brahma and therefore be liberated. By hypothesis he does not have to do anything to attain this state; indeed, there is nothing he *can* do. Liberation in this way is the result of an unbiased confrontation with the relevant parts of the Veda, and of nothing else.

It is important to realise that Śaṅkara's determination to present Vedānta as Mīmāṃsā inevitably leads him to the position that liberation is the result of the mere confrontation with the relevant Upaniṣadic statements.[69] He does indeed emphasise in various places that only knowledge is required to attain that goal, which may be attained either from the mere hearing of Upaniṣadic sentences or from contemplation on them. However, John A. Taber (1983: 13 ff) has plausibly argued, citing a variety of passages, that Śaṅkara's position must have been somewhat more complex. On several occasions Śaṅkara states quite clearly that works can purify

[69] This is not the same as stating that Śaṅkara felt obliged to present it in this way "by the conventions of the literary genre he has chosen", as Taber (1983: 7) maintains. Also other Vedāntins, most notably Śaṅkara's disciple Sureśvara, attribute the same importance to the Upaniṣadic statements; see Hacker 1951: 2001 (95) f.

a person so that he can then know the self. A clear example is Śaṅkara's Bhāṣya on *Bṛhadāraṇyaka-Upaniṣad* 4.4.22:

> *kathaṃ punar nityasvādhyāyādibhiḥ karmabhir ātmānaṃ vividiṣanti? naiva hi tāny ātmānaṃ prakāśayanti yathopaniṣadaḥ | naiṣa doṣaḥ | karmaṇāṃ viśuddhihetutvāt | karmabhiḥ saṃskṛtā hi viśuddhātmānaḥ śaknuvanty ātmānam upaniṣatprakāśitam apratibandhena veditum |*[70]
>
> But how do [Brahmins] desire to know the self by means of works such as the obligatory recitation of the Veda? For those [works] do not illuminate the self, as do the Upaniṣads. Nothing wrong here, because [these] works are the cause of purification. For those who have been purified by works, whose selves are pure, are able to know the self revealed by the Upaniṣads without obstruction.

The Bhāṣya on *Taittirīya-Upaniṣad* 1.11 is equally clear:

> *virodhād eva ca vidyā mokṣaṃ prati na karmāṇy apekṣate | svātmalābhe tu pūrvopacitaduritapratibandhāpanayadvāreṇa vidyāhetutvaṃ pratipadyante karmāṇi nityānīti | ... | evaṃ cāvirodhaḥ karmavidhiśrutīnām | ataḥ kevalāyā eva vidyāyāḥ paraṃ śreya iti siddham |*[71]
>
> It is precisely because of this conflict [between karma and knowledge] that knowledge does not depend on karma as far as *mokṣa* is concerned. With respect to its own attainment, however, we have said that obligatory karma becomes the *cause* of knowledge insofar as it removes previously accumulated hindrances. ... Thus there is no contradiction of those scriptural passages that enjoin karma. Hence, that the highest good is a consequence of knowledge alone is proved.

Taber concludes (1983: 23) that there is "little doubt that Śaṅkara conceives of religious practice as an important aid in achieving *mokṣa*, even if it is not, strictly speaking, its cause".

The beginning of the *Upadeśasāhasrī* (prose) confirms that liberating knowledge will not be the share of those who do not fulfil a number of demanding preconditions:

---

[70] Śaṅkara: *Bṛhadāraṇyakopaniṣadbhāṣya*, p. 300. Cf. Taber 1983: 17.

[71] Śaṅkara: *Taittirīyopaniṣadbhāṣya*, p. 352-353. Transl. Taber 1983: 20; cf. Hulin 2001: 162 ff.

tad idaṃ mokṣasādhanaṃ jñānaṃ sādhanasādhyād anityāt sarvasmād viraktāya tyaktaputravittalokaiṣaṇāya pratipannaparamahaṃsapārivrājyāya śamadamadayādiyuktāya śāstraprasiddhaśiṣyaguṇasampannāya śucaye brāhmaṇāya vidhivad upasannāya śiṣyāya jātikarmavṛttavidyābhijanaiḥ parīkṣitāya brūyāt punaḥ punar yāvad grahaṇaṃ dṛḍhībhavati.[72]

The [direct] means to liberation, that is, knowledge, should be imparted again and again until it is firmly grasped – to a Brahmin disciple who is pure, indifferent to everything that is transitory and achievable through worldly means, who has given up the desire for a son, for wealth, and for this world and the next, who has adopted the life of a wandering monk and is endowed with control over his mind and senses as well as with the other qualities of a disciple well known in the scriptures, and who has approached the teacher in the prescribed manner and has been examined with respect to his caste, profession, conduct, learning, and parentage.

Śaṅkara's *Brahmasūtrabhāṣya* enumerates, under the very first sūtra, the following preconditions for an aspiring student: (1) an ability to distinguish between the temporal and the eternal; (2) dispassion for the enjoyment of the fruits of one's actions both here and hereafter; (3) attainment of the means of tranquillity, self restraint and the like; (4) the desire for liberation.[73]

It should be clear from these and similar passages that not just anyone who is confronted with the Upaniṣads will attain liberation. Some will, others won't. The difference lies in the degree of preparedness of the students. The preliminary requirements are far from negligible; they exclude all those who have not studied the Veda in the prescribed manner (and therefore presumably Śūdras and women), and further reduce the numbers of those who have properly carried out their Vedic studies to those who have practised the intellectual and ascetic virtues indicated.[74]

Regarding Śaṅkara's "improved Mīmāṃsā", Tilmann Vetter (1979: 125) makes the following observation:

---

[72] Śaṅkara: *Upadeśasāhasrī*, Gadyabandha 1.2 (Mayeda 1973: 191); transl. Taber 1983: 24.

[73] BSūBhā on sūtra 1.1.1 (ed. J. L. Shastri, p. 36, l. 3 – p. 37, l. 1): *nityānityavastuvivekaḥ, ihāmutrārthabhogavirāgaḥ, śamadamādisādhanasampat, mumukṣutvaṃ ca.* Cf. Bader 1990: 59.

[74] See further Sawai 1986.

> [*Brahmasūtrabhāṣya*] Einleitung und I 1 1-4 haben ... vor allem die Aufgabe die Vedānta-Schule (als Untersuchung des Brahman) deutlich von der Mīmāṃsā-Schule (als der Untersuchung des rituellen Werks) abzusetzen. Die prinzipielle Kompromisslosigkeit, mit der dies geschieht und eigentlich erst eine von der alten Schule der Veda-Interpretation unabhängige Schule der Upaniṣad-Interpretation geschaffen wird, mit der zumindest alle Versuche zurückgewiesen werden, die immer selbständiger werdende Upaniṣad-Interpretation doch noch als eine Abteilung der Karma-Mīmāṃsā zu deuten, darf man wohl als eine der bedeutendsten Leistungen Ś[aṅkara]s ansehen, bei der er wenig von Vorgängern übernommen haben dürfte.

Vetter may well be right in thinking that Śaṅkara may have been the first to think out the principles of interpretation to be used for the Upaniṣads. But this is not so much a demarcation from traditional Mīmāṃsā, but rather an extension of Mīmāṃsā so as to include Upaniṣadic interpretation, too. Strictly speaking, and following Śaṅkara's logic, the traditional Mīmāṃsakas had done a good job, but had overlooked the crucial fact that, beside the injunctions, the Veda contains other sentences that provide information about things that cannot be contradicted by experience or by any other means of knowledge. These other sentences are the famous *mahāvākyas* of the Upaniṣads.

If it is true that Śaṅkara fundamentally approved of traditional Mīmāṃsā and its methods, what did he think of the ritual activity which that school of interpretation had found to be the main, or even the only, message to be drawn from the Veda? Did he consider this conclusion mistaken? By no means. For those who aspire to the aims that can be obtained by sacrificing, sacrificing is the appropriate way. For those, however, who aspire for liberation, ritual activity plays no role. The question whether rites can play an introductory or purifying role seems to be answered differently in different works of Śaṅkara. With regard to the first prose portion of the *Upadeśasāhasrī* (Gadyabandha 1), Vetter (1979: 139) makes the following observation:

> Nirgends wird etwas davon gesagt, dass rituelle Werke, die man vor dem Stadium des strengen Entsagens tut eine vorbereitende (das Innere reinigende) Funktion haben können.

We read for example in Gadyabandha 1.30:

> ... *pratiṣiddhatvād bhedadarśanasya, bhedaviṣayatvāc ca karmopādānasya, karmasādhanatvāc ca yajñopavītādeḥ karmasādhanopādānasya paramātmābhedapratipattyā pratiṣedhaḥ kṛto veditavyaḥ* I *karmaṇāṃ tatsādhanānāṃ ca yajñopavītādīnāṃ paramātmābhedapratipattiviruddhatvāt* I *saṃsāriṇo hi karmāṇi vidhīyante tatsādhanāni ca yajñopavītādīni, na paramātmano 'bhedadarśinaḥ* I *bhedadarśanamātreṇa ca tato 'nyatvam* I[75]

> ... it is prohibited [by the Śrutis] to hold the view that [Ātman] is different [from Brahma]; use of the rituals is [made] in the sphere of [the view] that [Ātman] is different [from Brahma]; and the sacred thread and the like are requisites for the rituals. Therefore, it should be known that the use of rituals and their requisites is prohibited, if the identity [of Ātman] with the highest Ātman is realized, since [the use of] rituals and their requisites such as the sacred thread is contradictory to the realization of the identity [of Ātman] with the highest Ātman. [The use of] rituals and their requisites such as the sacred thread is indeed enjoined upon a transmigrator [but] not upon one who holds the view of the identity [of Ātman] with the highest Ātman; and the difference [of Ātman] from It is merely due to the view that [Ātman] is different [from Brahma].

And Padyabandha 1.15 has:

> *viruddhatvād ataḥ śakyaṃ karma kartuṃ na vidyayā* I
> *sahaivaṃ viduṣā tasmāt karma heyaṃ mumukṣuṇā* II[76]

> Because of the incompatibility [of knowledge with action], therefore, one who knows so, being possessed of this knowledge, cannot perform action. For this reason action should be renounced by a seeker after final release.

The *Upadeśasāhasrī* also contains some passages which seem to indicate that ritual activity should be carried out, perhaps even until the moment at which cessation of nescience is attained. Mayeda

---

[75] Mayeda 1973: 197; transl. Mayeda 1979: 85, 220, modified. Mayeda (1979: 85 ff) gives further citations confirming this position.

[76] Mayeda 1973: 73; transl. Mayeda 1979: 87, 104.

(1979: 88 ff) discusses these passages and suggests that Śaṅkara's drastic denial of action was intended to shock his pupils into an insight into the true nature of the Self.

Given that Vedāntic Mīmāṃsā presents itself as the correct interpretation of the Veda, and of its final parts in particular, it goes without saying that a precondition for the useful study of the *Brahmasūtra* – or more precisely, for the enquiry into Brahma – should be the study of the Veda. Depending on the inclination of the student, the study of ritual Mīmāṃsā – i.e. of the enquiry into Dharma – can at that point be skipped, allowing the student to concentrate on the insight to be obtained from the Upaniṣads, altogether leaving aside all ritual activity. This is what Śaṅkara says in his *Brahmasūtrabhāṣya*. In his explanation of BraSū 1.1.1 (*athāto brahmajijñāsā* "Then therefore the enquiry into Brahma") he raises the issue that *atha* 'then' indicates that enquiry into Brahma has to follow something else and asks what that could be. The answer is found in the following passages:

> *sati cānantaryārthatve yathā dharmajijñāsā pūrvavṛttaṃ vedādhyayanaṃ niyamenāpekṣate, evaṃ brahmajijñāsāpi yat pūrvavṛttaṃ niyamenāpekṣate tad vaktavyam* | *svādhyāyānantaryaṃ tu samānam* | *nanv iha karmāvabodhānantaryaṃ viśeṣaḥ* | *na, dharmajijñāsāyāḥ prāg apy adhītavedāntasya brahmajijñāsopapatteḥ* |[77]
>
> Given that the meaning "immediate succession" is [expressed by the word *atha*], it should be stated what it is that enquiry into Brahma requires as necessarily preceding it, just as enquiry into Dharma requires study of the Veda as necessarily preceding it. The fact of being preceded by Vedic study is however common [both to the enquiry into Brahma and to the enquiry into Dharma]. [Question:] Isn't the difference in this case [of enquiry into Brahma] that it is [to be] preceded by understanding ritual activity (i.e., Pūrvamīmāṃsā)? [Answer:] No, for enquiry into Brahma is possible for one who has studied the Veda, even before enquiry into Dharma.

What further preconditions are there, then, for someone to enter upon "enquiry into Brahma"? The answer is to be found in the following sequel to the preceding passage:

[77] BSūBhā on sūtra 1.1.1 (ed. J. L. Shastri, p. 29, l. 1 – p. 33, l. 1).

> *tasmāt kim api vaktavyaṃ yadanantaraṃ brahmajijñāsopadiśyata iti* I *ucyate: nityānityavastuvivekaḥ, ihāmutrārthabhogavirāgaḥ, śamadamādisādhanasampat, mumukṣutvaṃ ca* I *teṣu hi satsu prāg api dharmajijñāsāyā ūrdhvaṃ ca śakyate jijñāsituṃ jñātuṃ ca, na viparyaye* I[78]
>
> Something must therefore be stated after which enquiry into Brahma is taught.
>
> The answer is: [The requirements for entering upon enquiry into Brahma are] discernment between eternal and non-eternal things; renunciation with regard to enjoyment in this and the next world; excellence in means such as peace, restraint, etc.; and desire to become liberated. For when these [elements] are present, one can desire to know, and know, even before enquiry into Dharma, as well as after it, not [however] in the opposite case.

These and other passages show that Śaṅkara's "improved" Mīmāṃsā disposes, for all intents and purposes, of ritual Mīmāṃsā, leaving place only for Brahma-Mīmāṃsā. Śaṅkara does not say this in so many words, but his admission that one does not miss out if one does not study ritual Mīmāṃsā and does not perform sacrificial rites says it all. Śaṅkara's is a "palace revolution" inside Mīmāṃsā, leaving an altogether different ideology in charge.

If the preceding pages have shown that Śaṅkara presents himself more often as a Mīmāṃsaka than as a philosopher, some features of his writing that have puzzled earlier commentators become understandable. Paul Hacker (1968: 120 [214] ff) has expressed surprise about the fact that Śaṅkara offers few if any rational arguments in defence of monism, which is yet a central part of his philosophy. Hacker looks for a solution in a hypothesis concerning the biography of Śaṅkara (first Yogin, then Advaitin). However, Śaṅkara the Mīmāṃsaka had no need for proofs of monism. What is more, knowledge derived from the Veda should be unobtainable by other means. This includes knowledge of monism.

The realisation that Śaṅkara presents himself as a Mīmāṃsaka and that for this reason he has no need to argue for positions which, he claims, can only be learnt from the Veda, gives rise to difficulties in some isolated cases. Hacker already drew attention to the

---

[78] BSūBhā on sūtra 1.1.1 (ed. J. L. Shastri, p. 36, l. 2 – p. 37, l. 2).

second prose portion of the *Upadeśasāhasrī*, and Vetter has dedicated a chapter of his book *Studien zur Lehre und Entwicklung Śaṅkaras* (1979: 75 ff) to it. This portion presents an argument for monism, if only a short one (Gadyabandha 2.109: ... *ātmajyotiṣaḥ ... advaitabhāvaś ca sarvapratyayabhedeṣv avyabhicārāt* "Dass das Licht des Selbst ... zweitlos ist, folgt daraus, dass es in keiner der verschiedenen Vorstellungen fehlt" transl. Hacker). This same second prose portion distinguishes itself further by the fact that it does not cite a single Upaniṣadic passage, and yet ends with the statement of the teacher who declares to his pupil: "Henceforth ... you are liberated from the suffering of transmigratory existence" (Gadyabandha 2.109: *[a]taḥ paraṃ ... saṃsāraduḥkhān mukto 'sīti*).

A passage like this is problematic in the light of what we now know about Śaṇkara as a Mīmāṃsaka. Vetter has cogently argued (1979: 75 f) that this portion of the *Upadeśasāhasrī* is an independent text,[79] so that one is entitled to wonder whether it was composed before Śaṅkara had come to think as a Mīmāṃsaka. (This comes close to Vetter own position.)[80] Alternatively, one may wonder whether this particular portion was really composed by Śaṅkara himself. It is true that Mayeda (1965; 1973: 22-64) gives a long list of arguments in order to show that Śaṅkara is the author of the *Upadeśasāhasrī*. These arguments start however from the assumption that all the texts brought together in the *Upadeśasāhasrī* have one and the same author. If we confine our attention to the second prose portion (which covers 13 pages in Mayeda's edition and has therefore a decent size) the situation changes drastically. Most of Mayeda's arguments cannot be applied to this portion. Where various early author have cited from the *Upadeśasāhasrī* (though with-

---

[79] Vetter argues in particular against the reasons adduced by Hacker (1949: 7-9) and Mayeda (1973: 66-67) to demonstrate that the three prose portions belong together and form a unity. He shows most notably that the notion according to which they respectively deal with hearing (*śravaṇa*), thinking (*manana*) and meditation (*nididhyāsana*) is in conflict with the precise wording of the text.

[80] See also Vetter 1978b: 52.

out using this name), none of them appear to have cited from its prose parts. Of the terms which are used in a fashion which is typical for Śaṅkara, only one occurs in the second prose portion. In other words, of all the arguments presented by Mayeda, only one applies to the second prose portion of the *Upadeśasāhasrī*, viz., the fact that here *avidyā* is used much in the way it is used in Śaṅkara's *Brahmasūtrabhāṣya*. There is, finally, a third way to make sense of the peculiarities of the second prose portion of the *Upadeśasāhasrī*. They may indicate that the line between mīmāṃsic and non-mīmāṃsic Vedānta, even in the case of this important thinker, was not always as clearly drawn as we might expect. This does not change the fact that there where Śaṅkara speaks as a (Brahma-) Mīmāṃsaka, Upaniṣadic statements are not merely cited to support his thought; they are an essential part of it. They are not cited to support views that are also supported otherwise. Quite on the contrary, they are the source of knowledge which cannot be obtained otherwise.

3.2. Other early commentators on the *Brahmasūtra*

Having discussed in some detail the way in which Śaṅkara presents his thought as an improved form of Mīmāṃsā, we can be brief with regard to the other early commentators of the *Brahmasūtra* whose works have survived. Chronologically next to Śaṅkara comes Bhāskara.[81] Like Śaṅkara, Bhāskara establishes under BraSū 1.1.4 that the proper application of the principles of Mīmāṃsā support his claim that Upaniṣadic statements can provide knowledge about an established thing, viz. Brahma. Bhāskara states here:

> *vaidikānām apauruṣeyatvād anapekṣatvaṃ pramāṇāntarānadhigatatvāc ca mūlakāraṇasya nāpariniṣṭhitatvaṃ kāryatvaṃ vā prāmāṇye kāraṇaṃ kiṃ tv anadhigatārthagantṛtvam* (Bhāskara, *Brahmasūtrabhāṣya*, p. 13, ll. 14-16):

---

[81] Ingalls 1952; 1954: 293, n. 4; van Buitenen 1961; Raghavan 1967; Rüping 1977: 12 ff.

> Since Vedic [statements] are without author, they do not depend upon [other means of knowledge]. Since moreover the root cause [of the world] (i.e., Brahma) is not known through any other means of knowledge, it is not its not being established or its having to be carried out that is the cause of the authoritativeness [of the relevant Vedic statements]. On the contrary, it is the fact that [those Vedic statements] make known an object that is [otherwise] unknown [which is the cause for those statements being authoritative].

Bhāskara's formulation is a bit complex, but his intentions are clear. The ritual Mīmāṃsakas may maintain that only things that are not established and that have to be carried out, i.e., activities, can be made known through the appropriate Vedic statements, i.e., the injunctions, Bhāskara formulates the criterion differently. Vedic statements must make known what is not known by other means. This includes activities that are to be carried out, to be sure, but not only those. It also includes the root cause of the world, for this cannot be known by other means either.

Rāmānuja introduces his discussion of BraSū 1.1.4 as follows in his *Śrībhāṣya*:

> *yady api pramāṇāntarāgocaraṃ brahma, tathāpi pravṛttinivṛttiparatvābhāvena siddharūpaṃ brahma na śāstraṃ pratipādayati, ity āśaṅkyāha: ...* (*Śrībhāṣya*, p. 306)

> If one has the doubt that, even though Brahma is not covered by any other means of knowledge [but the Veda], yet the Veda (*śāstra*) does not teach Brahma because, being an established thing, it has nothing to do with activity and abstention from activity, the answer is given in what follows.

These two short passages should suffice to show that Bhāskara and Rāmānuja share with Śaṅkara one fundamental tenet: Brahma can only be known through the Veda. That is to say, like Śaṅkara they treat Vedānta as a form of Mīmāṃsā.

3.3. Maṇḍana Miśra

We can compare Śaṅkara's position with that of his possible contemporary[82] Maṇḍana Miśra. Maṇḍana is familiar with various views regarding the Upaniṣads, as he points out at the very beginning of his *Brahmasiddhi*:

> *vedānteṣu vipratipadyante vipaścitaḥ: kecid aprāmāṇyaṃ manyante, ātmanaḥ pramāṇāntarasiddhatve teṣām anuvādakatvāt, asiddhatve saṃbandhāgrahaṇāt apadārthatve vākyasyāviṣayatvāt, pravṛttinivṛttyanupadeśe cāpuruṣārthatvāt* | *anye tu pratipattikartavyatāprāmāṇyavyājenāprāmāṇyam evāhuḥ* | *anye tu karmavidhivirodhāt pratyakṣādivirodhāc ca śrutārthaparigrahe upacaritārthān manyante* | (*Brahmasiddhi*, p. 1, ll. 7-11).

> The learned disagree with respect to the Upaniṣads.
> – Some think that they are not a means of valid cognition, (i) because, if the self is known through another means of knowledge, the [Upaniṣads do nothing but] repeat [what is already known]; (ii) if [on the other hand, the self] is not [already] known, it cannot be the object of a sentence, given that it is not the object of a word because the link [between word and object] cannot [in that case] be grasped; (iii) since they do not give instruction into what to do and what not to do, they serve no human purpose.
> – Others state that they are not really a means of valid cognition, using the excuse that they are a means providing the cognition that knowledge [of the self] must be accomplished.
> – Others again think that the Upaniṣads express figurative meanings, this because they are in conflict with the ritual injunctions and with perception etc.

Maṇḍana's own rejection of these positions finds expression in the immediately following sentence: *tannirāsāyedam ārabhyate* "To reject these [positions] this [work] is begun."

Like Śaṅkara, Maṇḍana, too, maintains in his *Brahmasiddhi* that Brahma can and must be known from the Veda. However, he believes that Brahma can be known through perception as well. The chapter called Tarkakāṇḍa shows elaborately that perception presents non-difference (*abheda*), whereas the distinctions (or particulars) which we believe to perceive are due to mental construction (*vikalpa*): "Perception is first, without mental construction, and

---

[82] For a recent discussion, see Thrasher 1993: 112 ff; further 1979.

has for its object the bare thing. The constructive cognitions which follow it plunge into particulars." (p. 71, ll. 1-2: *vastumātraviṣayaṃ prathamam avikalpakaṃ pratyakṣam; tatpūrvās tu vikalpabuddhayo viśeṣān avagāhant[e]*; transl. Thrasher 1993: 80). Maṇḍana does not say explicitly that non-difference (*abheda*) or the bare thing (*vastumātra*) are identical with Brahma, but Tilmann Vetter (1969a: 98, n. 165) and much more elaborately Allen Wright Thrasher (1993: 77-87) argue convincingly that such is the case. In fact, the characteristics of the "bare thing" of the Tarkakāṇḍa coincide largely with the features by which Brahma is described in the Brahmakāṇḍa. We must therefore assume that the following passage in the final chapter (Siddhikāṇḍa) of the *Brahmasiddhi* presents Maṇḍana's own position:

> *athavā na loke 'tyantam aprasiddhaṃ brahma, sarvapratyayavedyatvāt, brahmaṇo vyatirekeṇa pratyetavyasyābhāvāt, viśeṣapratyayānāṃ ca sāmānyarūpānugamāt* ... (*Brahmasiddhi*, p. 157, ll. 14-15; cf. Thrasher 1993: 86).
>
> Or rather, Brahma is not totally unknown in ordinary experience, because it is knowable in every cognition, because no object of cognition except Brahma exists, and cognitions of particulars are always accompanied by the form of the universal, ...[83]

Maṇḍana, then, maintains that Brahma is the object of perception. In the chapter called Brahmakāṇḍa he also suggests that a certain kind of reasoning leads to knowledge of Brahma; this reasoning runs as follows:[84]

> *viśeṣanivṛttyaiva tat śabdena buddhau nidhīyate, suvarṇatattvavat; na hi suvarṇatattvaṃ piṇḍarucakādisaṃsthānabhedopaplavarahitaṃ dṛśyate; na ca ta eva suvarṇatattvam, tatparityāge 'pi bhāvāt saṃsthānāntare; atha cādṛṣṭasaṃsthānabhedopaplavavivekam api buddhyā bhedāpohadvāreṇa svayaṃ pratīyate, parasmai ca pratipādyate.* (*Brahmasiddhi*, p. 26, ll. 16-20.)

---

[83] Nicholson (2003: 585) speaks of "the intellectually jarring situation of identifying the *vastu-mātra* ... with the universal (*sāmānya*)" into which Maṇḍana forces himself.

[84] Cf. Vetter 1969a: 99, and 98, n. 165.

> Only by removing distinctions one obtains, with the help of the word, knowledge of it (i.e. of Brahma), as of the essence of gold. For the essence of gold, free from distractions in the form of specific shapes like that of a clump, neck ornament, etc., is not observed. Nor do those [specific shapes] themselves constitute the essence of gold, because [the essence] is still there, in the form of another shape, even when those particular shapes are abandoned. And yet [the essence of gold] itself, even though its distinction from distractions in the form of specific shapes [can] not be seen, is known by means of the removal of the specificities with the help of thought, and it can be communicated to someone else.

However, because perception is always sullied by ignorance, Maṇḍana holds on to the position that knowledge of Brahma is based on the Veda alone:

> *āmnāyaikanibandhanatvaṃ tu tasyocyate, pratyakṣādīnam avidyāsaṃbhinnatvāt; pratyastamitanikhilabhedena rūpeṇāviṣayīkaraṇād bhedapratyastamayasyāmnāyāvagamyatvād iti* I (*Brahmasiddhi*, p. 157, ll. 19-21; cf. Thrasher 1993: 86)
>
> But this [Brahma as the non-existence of phenomenal diversity] is said to be based on the Veda (*āmnāya*) alone, because perception etc. are associated with *avidyā*. For, because they do not take [Brahma] as their object under the form where all difference has disappeared, the disappearance of difference is knowable from the Veda [alone].

Verse 2 of the Brahmakāṇḍa is no doubt to be understood in the same way:

> *āmnāyataḥ prasiddhiṃ ca kavayo 'sya pracakṣate* I
> *bhedaprapañcavilayadvāreṇa ca nirūpaṇām* II
> (*Brahmasiddhi*, p. 23, l. 18-19)
>
> The wise proclaim knowledge of this (i.e., Brahma) on the basis of the Veda, and its determination through the dissolution of the manifoldness of divisions.

Verses 3 and 4 of the Siddhikāṇḍa leave perhaps least occasion for ambiguity:

> *sarvapratyayavedye vā brahmarūpe vyavasthite* |
> *prapañcasya pravilayaḥ śabdena pratipādyate* ||
> *pravilīnaprapañcena tadrūpeṇa na gocaraḥ* |
> *mānāntarasyeti matam āmnāyaikanibandhanam* ||
> (*Brahmasiddhi*, p. 157, ll. 10-13)
>
> Or rather (*vā*), though the form of Brahma is established as being known in each cognition, the resorption of manifoldness is conveyed by the word [only].
> Since [Brahma] in that form, in which manifoldness has been resorbed, is not the object of any other means of cognition, it is considered to exclusively depend on the Veda.

Thrasher (1993: 81 f) draws attention to the fact that Maṇḍana was not the first to hold the view that perception gives access to Brahma. Kumārila Bhaṭṭa is acquainted with (and criticizes) the view that perception has the highest universal as object, and that constructive cognitions add the distinctions.[85] Kumārila's commentators Umbeka and Pārthasārathi Miśra, moreover, attribute this view to Vedāntins. Kumārila's brief remarks do not however permit us to find out whether those other Vedāntins yet maintained, like Maṇḍana, that knowledge of Brahma is based on the Veda only. It is therefore possible that Maṇḍana, while continuing an earlier tradition to the extent that perception has Brahma as object, gives a mīmāṃsic twist to this tradition by emphasizing that perception gives imperfect access to Brahma, which must therefore be completed through the Veda, so much so that in the end knowledge of Brahma is based on the Veda alone. If this understanding of Maṇḍana's role in the history of Vedāntic thought is correct, we must conclude that this thinker made a determined effort to join the two kinds of Vedānta that existed in his time: Vedānta as speculative philosophy and Vedānta as Mīmāṃsā. His *Brahmasiddhi* shows that in the end he opted for Vedānta as Mīmāṃsā, without

---

[85] *Ślokavārttika*, Pratyakṣa, 114-116: *mahāsāmānyam anyais tu dravyaṃ sad iti cocyate* | *sāmānyaviṣayatvaṃ ca pratyakṣasyaivam āśritam* || *viśeṣās tu pratīyante savikalpakabuddhibhiḥ* | *te ca kecit pratidravyaṃ kecid bahuṣu saṃśritāḥ* || *tān akalpayad utpannaṃ vyāvṛttānugatātmanā* | *gavy aśve copajātaṃ tu pratyakṣaṃ na viśiṣyate* ||

however doing away with all the ideas that more philosophically oriented Vedāntins before him had developed.

4. VEDĀNTA AND LIBERATION AS PART OF KARMA-MĪMĀṂSĀ

The preceding sections have shown that we may have to distinguish two forms of Vedāntic philosophy, one which is quite independent of the details of Vedic interpretation, and one which presents itself as an improved form of Mīmāṃsā, the most sophisticated manner of Vedic interpretation. The former is primarily a religico-philosophical movement, which claims allegiance, to be sure, to the Upaniṣads, but develops its way to liberation more or less independently, without claiming that this way is the outcome of the correct study of the Veda. The latter form of Vedāntic philosophy does precisely that, presenting itself as a school of Vedic hermeneutics.

It may not be possible to determine with certainty why and how the link between Vedāntic philosophy and Mīmāṃsā has come about. It seems however clear that a certain tension between the two must have existed from an early date onward. If and to the extent that the Vedāntists wanted "their" Upaniṣads to be included among those part of the Veda that had to be taken literally, a confrontation with Mīmāṃsā could hardly be avoided. Those Mīmāṃsakas, on the other hand, who felt attracted to the new ideas about liberation, rebirth etc. that were gaining ground all around them, were challenged to find a way to extend their hermeneutical rules so as to include the views expressed in the Upaniṣads. We do not know for sure who took the initiative. However, there are various indications which suggest that efforts were made within Mīmāṃsā to extend its scope.

About the attempts to include Vedāntic thought into the Karma-Mīmāṃsā, Vetter says the following:

> Die Mīmāṃsā versuchte zu jener Zeit einen Erlösungsweg in ihr System aufzunehmen und dadurch vor allem die konkurrierende vedische Schule des Vedānta zu absorbieren. Wie wir aus der Polemik bei Śankara und Maṇḍana erfahren, lautete dabei die wichtigste Behauptung der Mīmāṃsā, die Erkenntnis des Selbst sei als für die Erlösung 'vorgeschrieben' zu betrachten. Formal lässt sich das durch gewisse Upaniṣadsätze stützen, z.B. 'das Selbst soll man schauen' usw. ([BĀrUp] II, 4, 5). Damit wäre der Vedānta keine von der Mīmāṃsā getrennte Disziplin mehr; denn dann wird vom Veda zum Ziel der Erlösung ein Mittel bereitgestellt, das man auszuführen hat. (Vetter 1969a: 18-19.)

Unfortunately no early texts belonging to these kinds of Mīmāṃsakas are known to have survived. However, as pointed out by Vetter, Śaṅkara and Maṇḍana criticise this position. Maṇḍana does so, for example, at the very beginning of his *Brahmasiddhi*, in the passage cited in section 3.3 above. A passage where Śaṅkara does the same occurs in the first chapter of the verse section of his *Upadeśasāhasrī*:

> *nanu karma tathā nityaṃ kartavyaṃ jīvane sati* |
> *vidyāyāḥ sahakāritvaṃ mokṣaṃ prati hi tad vrajet* ||
> *yathā vidyā tathā karma coditatvāviśeṣataḥ* |
> *pratyavāyaśmṛteś caiva kāryaṃ karma mumukṣibhiḥ* ||
> *nanu dhruvaphalā vidyā nānyat kiṃcid apekṣate* |
> *nāgniṣṭomo yathaivānyad dhruvakāryo 'py apekṣate* ||
> *tathā dhruvaphalā vidyā karma nityam apekṣate* |
> *ity evaṃ kecid icchanti na karma pratikūlataḥ* ||[86]

> [Objection:] "Should not [certain] action too always be performed while life lasts? For this [action], being concomitant with knowledge [of Brahma], leads to final release.[87]
>
> "**Action, like knowledge [of Brahma, should be adhered to], since [both of them] are equally enjoined [by the Śrutis]**. As the Smṛti also [lays it down that] transgression [results from the neglect of action, so] action should be performed by seekers after final release.

---

[86] *Upadeśasāhasrī*, Padyabandha 1.8-11; text Mayeda 1973: 72; transl. Mayeda 1979: 103-104. For other passages from Śaṅkara's works, see Alston 1989a; 1989b.

[87] I am not sure that this translation does full justice to the original. A more literal translation might be: "For that concomitance of knowledge [with action] leads to final release".

> "[If you say that] as knowledge [of Brahma] has permanent fruit, and so does not depend upon anything else, [we reply:] Not so! Just as the Agniṣṭoma sacrifice, though it has permanent fruit, depends upon things other than itself,
>
> "so, though knowledge [of Brahma] has permanent fruit, it always depends upon action. Thus some people think." [Reply:] Not so, because action is incompatible [with knowledge].

There were other Mīmāṃsakas, who decided to include the notion of liberation into their own system without introducing knowledge of Brahma as a condition. It has already been pointed out above that Śabara shows no awareness of the notion of liberation. Attention has also been drawn to MīmSū 1.2.1 (*āmnāyasya kriyārthatvād ānarthakyam atadarthānāṃ* ... "Since the Veda is for [ritual] activity, [passages] that are not for that are without purpose ..."), which constitutes an argument against the original unity of Pūrva- and Uttara-Mīmāṃsā, and for the absence of the notion of liberation – or stronger: for the rejection of that notion – in ritual Mīmāṃsā. Attention can furthermore be drawn to MīmSū 4.3.14: *sa svargaḥ syāt sarvān praty aviśiṣṭatvāt* "The [result of the Viśvajit-sacrifice] must be heaven, because [desire for heaven] is present, without distinction, in all [people]"; this sūtra can hardly have been composed by someone who "really" aimed for liberation. Prabhākara – who commented upon the *Śābarabhāṣya* and appears to have lived and worked in the first half of the 7th century CE (Yoshimizu 1997: 37-49) – still maintains that heaven is the one thing which all humans without exception desire to attain (Yoshimizu 1997: 179-180, with n. 81). However, other ritualists did become interested in the notion of liberation. Yoshimizu contrasts the position of Kumārila in this regard with that of Prabhākara, probably his contemporary:[88]

> Kumārila hingegen schliesst sich nicht an die traditionnelle Ansicht der Mīmāṃsā-Schule an, dass der Himmel das endgültige Ziel des Menschen ist und das Nitya-Opfer das Mittel zum Erlangen des Himmels ist. Um die Veranstaltung des Nitya-Opfers in den Übungsweg zur Erlösung einzu-

[88] See also Taber's and Yoshimizu's contributions to this volume.

schliessen, behauptet Kumārila vielmehr in allen seinen Werken, dass das Nitya-Opfer in der Tat nur zur Beseitigung der von ihm begangenen Sünde beiträgt; vgl. [*Ślokavārttika*] Sambandhākṣepaparihāra k. 110: "Wer sich Erlösung wünscht, soll sich unter den (im Veda vorgeschriebenen Handlungen) nicht mit dem fakultativen Opfer und der verbotenen (Handlung) beschäftigen, soll aber das periodische Opfer und das gelegentliche Opfer verrichten, indem er sich die Beseitigung der Sünde wünscht" (*mokṣārthī na pravarteta tatra kāmyaniṣiddhayoḥ* I *nityanaimittike kuryāt pratyavāya-jihāsayā* II); [*Tantravārttika*] ii, 228, 16-17 ... : "Die je nach der Lebensstufe und der Sozialklasse festgelegten periodischen und gelegentlichen Opfer soll man verrichten, um [durch die gelegentlichen Opfer] die früher begangene Sünde zu vernichten und [durch die periodischen Opfer] der wegen des Versäumnisses zu verursachenden künftigen Sünde vorzubeugen" (*pratyāśramavarṇaniyatāni nityanaimittikakarmāṇy api pūrvakṛtaduritakṣayārtham akaraṇanimittānāgatapratyavāyaparihārārthaṃ ca kartavyāni*); [*Ṭupṭīkā*] v, 246, 4-6: "Es gibt fürwahr keinen Menschen, der bei [der Ausführung] des unbedingt zu tuenden (Opfers) kein Ergebnis begehren würde. Wenn [der Gegner meint]: 'Wer sich Erlösung wünscht, [begehrt kein Ergebnis]', stimmt das nicht. Auch der (Erlösung begehrende Mensch) kann die Vernichtung der Sünde [als Ergebnis des Opfers] begehren, weil die Erlösung unmöglich ist, wenn die (Sünde) vorhanden ist." (*na hīdṛśaḥ puruṣo 'sti yo 'vaśyakartavye phalaṃ na kāmayate. mokṣārthī cet. tan na. tenāpy avaśyaṃ pāpakṣaya eṣitavyaḥ. tasmin sati mokṣābhāvāt*). (Yoshimizu 1997: 179-180, n. 80.)

In the hands of Kumārila, therefore, the performance of Vedic ritual becomes a means to attain liberation.[89]

The Buddhist Bhavya criticises Mīmāṃsā in chapter 9 of his *Madhyamakahṛdaya*. Surprisingly, he attributes to the Mīmāṃsakas only one aim, liberation (*apavarga*, *mokṣa*), and does not even mention heaven. This suggests one of two things: Either Bhavya was not well informed about the real concerns of the Mīmāṃsakas of his time, or he was acquainted with Mīmāṃsakas who maintained that ritual action leads to liberation. The very first verses of the chapter concerned, the *Mīmāṃsātattvanirṇayāvatāra*, states Bhavya's understanding of Mīmāṃsā quite explicitly:

eke 'pavargasanmārgadhyānajñānāpavādinaḥ I
kriyāmātreṇa tatprāptiṃ pratipādyānapatrapāḥ II

[89] For details see Mesquita 1994; Bronkhorst, forthcoming (c).

śāstroktavrīhipaśvājyapatnīsaṃbandhakarmaṇaḥ |
nānyo mārgo 'pavargāya yukta ity āhur āgamāt ||[90]

Without any sense of shame some (i.e., Mīmāṃsakas) deny that meditation and insight [constitute] the true way to deliverance (*apavarga*). They insist that it can only be achieved by rituals.

They say that according to tradition (*āgama*) there is no other correct way to deliverance (*apavarga*) than the rituals prescribed in the sacred texts, i.e. [rituals that involve] rice, cattle, butter and participation of one's wife.

This might be taken to mean that the idea of liberation came to be grafted upon Vedic sacrifice already at the time of Bhavya, at least in the opinion of some Mīmāṃsakas. Alternatively, we may have to accept that Bhavya's information about Mīmāṃsā was incomplete.

It will be useful here to draw attention to the fact that certain Vedāntins, among them Bhāskara and Rāmānuja, represent the view that a combination of ritual activity and insight into the true nature of the self lead to liberation (see below, section 5). They were not the first to do so. The following passage from the *Manusmṛti* expresses essentially the same point of view:

sukhābhyudayikaṃ caiva naiḥśreyasikam eva ca |
pravṛttaṃ ca nivṛttaṃ ca dvividhaṃ karma vaidikam ||
iha cāmutra vā kāmyaṃ pravṛttaṃ karma kīrtyate |
niṣkāmaṃ jñānapūrvaṃ tu nivṛttam upadiśyate ||
pravṛttaṃ karma saṃsevya devānām eti sāmyatām |
nivṛttaṃ sevamānas tu bhūtāny atyeti pañca vai || (Manu 12.88-90)

Vedic ritual acts are of two kinds: engaging in activity (*pravṛtta*) and abstaining from activity (*nivṛtta*). [The former] leads to the rise of happiness, [the latter] to liberation.

In this world and in the next, optional ritual acts are known as "engaging in activity", whereas obligatory ritual acts accompanied by knowledge are taught to be "abstaining from activity".

Having been dedicated to ritual acts that are "engaging in activity" one becomes equal to the gods; being dedicated to [ritual acts that are] "abstaining from activity", on the other hand, one passes beyond the five elements.[91]

---

[90] Lindtner 1999: 253 (text and translation); 2001: 92 (text).

These few passages illustrate well enough that inside the ritual tradition forces were at work to incorporate the notion of liberation, either by including knowledge of Brahma among the things enjoined in the Veda, or by adding it as a precondition for carrying out ritual, or finally by simply claiming that the correct execution of the ritual by itself was an essential step on the way to liberation.

5. PŪRVA-MĪMĀṂSĀSŪTRA, UTTARA-MĪMĀṂSĀ-SŪTRA AND THE TEACHER QUOTATIONS

Asko Parpola, in some articles that have already been referred to above, makes the suggestion that the terms Pūrvamīmāṃsā and Uttaramīmāṃsā "seem to have come to being as a result of an erroneous analysis as PM-S and UM-S respectively of the names *Pūrvamīmāṃsāsūtra* (abbreviated PMS) and *Uttaramīmāṃsāsūtra* (UMS)." (Parpola 1981: 147-148). He continues:

> I suspect that originally the terms PM and UM did not occur at all outside the book titles or rather headings PMS and UMS, but have evolved from these, and that the correct analysis of the latter is P-MS and U-MS. In other words, I suggest that the references of the words *pūrva* and *uttara* is not the two branches of Mīmāṃsā as a philosophical system, **but the two portions of one single work called Mīmāṃsāsūtra**. PMS would thus have originally meant 'the former or first part of the Mīmāṃsāsūtra', and UMS correspondingly 'the latter or second part of the Mīmāṃsāsūtra', not 'the Sūtra of Pūrva-Mīmāṃsā/Uttara-Mīmāṃsā'.[92]

[91] Two verses later, interestingly, the *Manusmṛti* states the opposite, viz., that a Brahmin should abandon ritual activity: "A priest should give up even the activities described above and devote himself diligently to the knowledge of the self, to tranquillity, and to the recitation of the Veda" (Manu 12.92: *yathoktāny api karmāṇi parihāya dvijottamaḥ* | *ātmajñāne śame ca syād vedābhyāse ca yatnavān* || transl. Doniger & Smith 1991: 287). The translators point out in a footnote: "A similar passage in favour of renunciation, even in preference to the Vedic ritual that is otherwise Manu's first concern, appears at 6.86 and 6.96."

[92] Parpola's (1994: 293, n. 2) statement to the effect that "This hypothesis is endorsed by Clooney 1990: 25ff." seems premature. Clooney (1990: 27) says: "But without proposing that [Parpola's] efforts to relate the two Mīmāṃsās are entirely premature, I suggest that we must study in depth and detail the twelve Adhyāya's of Jaimini and four Adhyāyas of Bādarāyaṇa in order to understand

Parpola provides a number of arguments in defence of his thesis, some of which have already been dealt with above. He does not however address the question to what extent the textual evidence supports the priority of the expressions *Pūrvamīmāṃsāsūtra* and *Uttaramīmāṃsāsūtra* to Pūrvamīmāṃsā and Uttaramīmāṃsā respectively. And yet, this is an issue that cannot be ignored.

The *Mīmāṃsākoṣa* has no entries for (or beginning with) Pūrvamīmāṃsā and Uttaramīmāṃsā. This raises the question whether the two terms can be found in surviving Pūrvamīmāṃsā works. No such occurrences are known to me.[93]

The colophons to Śaṅkara's commentary on the *Brahmasūtra* call his commentary *Śārīrakamīmāṃsābhāṣya*. This text never uses the terms Uttaramīmāṃsā or *Uttaramīmāṃsāsūtra* according to the Word Index brought out under the general editorship of T. M. P. Mahadevan (1971-73).[94] They do not occur in Śaṅkara's *Upadeśasāhasrī*, according to the Index of Words in Mayeda's (1973) edition, nor in his *Gītābhāṣya*, according to D'Sa's Word-Index (1985). I have not found these terms in Padmapāda's *Pañcapādikā*. Sureśvara, too, in the passage considered above, speaks of the Śārīraka which, in view of the context, must stand for *Śārīrakasūtra*. Bhāskara, a commentator on the *Brahmasūtra* who must be slightly younger than Śaṅkara, does not appear to use the terms Pūrvamīmāṃsā and Uttaramīmāṃsā. The fact that he uses the term Mīmāṃsā to refer to ritual Mīmāṃsā (e.g. p. 6, ll. 12-13: *na ca brahmaviṣayo vicāro mīmāṃsāyāṃ kvacid adhikaraṇe vartate* ...; p. 15, ll. 20-21: *na ca niyogasya vākyārthatve mīmāṃsāyāṃ bhāṣ-*

---

what is actually being said and in what manner in the Pūrva and Uttara Mīmāṃsās. Working 'from within' will shed a great deal of light on the question of the unity of the two systems and do so in a more fruitful fashion than by considering the 'Mīmīṃsā' titles (which in any case did not belong to the texts in the very beginning)."

[93] They do not, for example, occur in Megumu Honda's *Index to the Ślokavārttika* (1993).

[94] Cf. e.g. Padmapāda's *Pañcapādikā* (ed. S. Subrahmanyaśāstri) pp. 69, 298, 300, 511: *vedāntamīmāṃsā*; p. 510: *vedāntavākyamīmāṃsā*.

yākṣaraṃ śārīrake vā sūtrākṣaraṃ sūcakam asti[95]) would seem to confirm this, in spite of the fact that his commentary calls itself in the colophons *Śārīrakamīmāṃsābhāṣya*.

An early attestation of Pūrva- and Uttara-Mīmāṃsā occurs in Yāmuna's *Ātmasiddhi*,[96] where it is stated:

> *prapañcitaś ca pūrvottaramīmāṃsābhāgayor nirālambanatvapratiṣedhaḥ; yathārthakhyātisamarthanena ca śāstra iti na vyāvarṇyate.* (*Ātmasiddhi*, p. 25, ll. 12-13)[97]

Mesquita translates:

> Und die Widerlegung der [von den Buddhisten gelehrten] Objektlosigkeit [der Erkenntnis] wurde [in den Werken] der beiden Teile[, nämlich der] Pūrva- und der Uttaramīmāṃsā, ausführlich vorgetragen, und [zuletzt auch] in [Nāthamunis] Lehrbuch [Nyāyatattva] zusammen mit der Rechtfertigung der [Irrtumslehre] Yathārthakhyāti. Deshalb wird [sie hier] nicht dargelegt. (Mesquita 1988: 62, n. 77)

Rāmānuja's *Śrībhāṣya* speaks of Pūrva- and Uttara-Mīmāṃsā in a passage which points out the difference between the two (p. 4, ll. 9-10: ... *pūrvottaramīmāṃsayoḥ bhedaḥ*). The *Prapañcahṛdaya*, as we have seen, speaks of the Pūrvamīmāṃsāśāstra which it considers to reflect upon the Dharma connected with the Pūrvakāṇḍa, and of the Uttaramīmāṃsāśāstra which reflects upon Brahma of the Uttarakāṇḍa.[98]

---

[95] Bhāskara's subsequent remarks cite a sentence from the Bhāṣya (*ye prāhuḥ kim api bhāvayed iti te svargakāmapadasambandhāt svargaṃ bhāvayed iti brūyuḥ*) which is Śabara on MīmSū 2.1.1, p. 340; and a sūtra (*kṛtaprayatnāpekṣas tu* ...) which is BraSū 2.3.42.

[96] The *Ātmasiddhi* is traditionally considered part of Yāmuna's *Siddhitraya*, but was originally an independent work; see Mesquita 1973: 184.

[97] Cited in Mesquita 1988: 62.

[98] This might be taken as an indication that the *Prapañcahṛdaya* is a relatively recent text, dating roughly from the time of Yāmuna and Rāmānuja. See fn. 27, above.

Among more recent texts that mention Pūrva- and Uttara-Mīmāṃsā Sāyaṇa's commentary on the *Ṛgveda* (e.g. vol. I, p. 10, ll. 4 and 6) may be mentioned. See further Śrīnivāsa's *Yatipatimatadīpikā* (= *Yatīndramatadīpikā*) p. 12: *sa*

It will be clear that, as long as no earlier occurrences of the expressions Pūrva- and Uttara-Mīmāṃsā will have been identified, Parpola's proposal as to the original use of these expressions will not be based on any direct evidence.

However, a more plausible interpretation of these terms is possible. Consider first the four hypotheses presented and rejected as *pūrvapakṣas* by Parpola (1981: 145-146):

1) "the Pūrva-mīmāṃsā has come into being as a philosophical system earlier than the Uttara-mīmāṃsā";

2) "Pūrva-mīmāṃsā is so called because it deals with that part of the Vedic literature which was composed earlier, ... while the Uttara-mīmāṃsā is concerned with the later part of the Śruti";

3) "Pūrva- and Uttara-mīmāṃsā [are] 'the discussion of the first and second (part of the Veda)' respectively";

4) "Pūrva-mīmāṃsā [is] 'the preliminary investigation', ... establishing beyond doubt the authority and reliability of the Veda and elaborating methods of interpreting it. It thus provides the requirements needed for the Uttara-mīmāṃsā or 'the final investigation'."

Parpola is probably right in rejecting all these four hypotheses, but his reason for doing so, viz. that all these interpretations erroneously take the existence of the terms Pūrvamīmāṃsā and Uttaramīmāṃsā for granted, does not appear to be valid, as we have seen. The fourth hypothesis may however be closest to the truth. This can be seen as follows.

For Śaṅkara, as we have seen, Vedāntic thought (which he calls Śārīraka- or Brahma-Mīmāṃsā) can be studied instead of ritual Mīmāṃsā (which he does not call Pūrva-Mīmāṃsā). The two are not therefore ordered in time for him. The situation is however altogether different for other commentators of the *Brahmasūtra*.

---

ca vedaḥ karmabrahmapratipādakapūrvottarabhāgābhyāṃ dvidhā bhinnaḥ | *ārādhanakarmapratipādakaṃ pūrvakāṇḍam* | *ārādhyapratipādakam uttarakāṇḍam* | *ubhayor mīmāṃsayor aikaśāstryam* |

Bhāskara states that reflection on Dharma has to precede reflection on Brahma (p. 2, ll. 25-26: *pūrvaṃ tu dharmajijñāsā kartavyā*; p. 3, l. 25-26: *tasmāt pūrvavṛttād dharmajñānād anantaraṃ brahmajijñāseti yuktam*). Reflection on Dharma is the business of ritual Mīmāṃsā, whose first sūtra begins with the words: *athāto dharmajijñāsā*. Rāmānuja states the same in different words (*Śrībhāṣya*, p. 4, ll. 3-4: *pūrvavṛttāt karmajñānād anantaraṃ ... brahma jñātavyam*).[99] That is to say, for these thinkers Pūrva-Mīmāṃsā has to precede Uttara-Mīmāṃsā in the life of a man (even if Bhāskara does not appear to use these precise terms). The fact that we find these terms first in the writings of Rāmānuja and his predecessor Yāmuna suggests that the terms have to be interpreted quite simply as earlier and later Mīmāṃsā in the sense that the study of these two "sciences" were meant to occupy the attention of the thinkers concerned "earlier" respectively "later" in their lives.[100] It appears that only later these terms came to be used by Advaitins, as in the passage from the *Prapañcahṛdaya* cited in section 1 above.

We have already seen that the new argument which Parpola adduces to show that originally the *Pūrvamīmāṃsāsūtra* and the *Brahmasūtra*[101] were part of one single text is the fact that both quote the same teachers; teacher quotations figure, as a matter of fact, in the subtitle of his articles.[102] After our preceding considera-

---

[99] See further Sawai 1993.

[100] Renou (1942: 117 [442, 323]) is no doubt right in thinking that "[la prévalence de l'ultériorité] est constante au fond de la notion d'*uttara-mīmāṃsā* appliquée au Vedānta en tant que spéculation postérieure et supérieure à la fois à la Mīmāṃsā première", but the claimed link with the grammatical sūtra *vipratiṣedhe paraṃ kāryam* (P. 1.4.2) is far from evident.

[101] We have already seen (in section 1) that Parpola, following others, prefers to speak "of a treatise upon the Vedānta, which the [present *Brahmasūtra*] would have replaced, not without thereby utilizing some of its elements". About the difference in style between *Mīmāṃsāsūtra* and *Brahmasūtra*, see Renou 1962; on the references in the *Brahmasūtra* to relatively late developments in Indian philosophy, see Jacobi 1911: 13 (571) f.

[102] Cf. further Parpola 1981: 165: "The teacher quotations of the PMS and the UMS are important as a proof of the original unity of these two texts ..."

tions, it will be clear that this argument, if it is one, is the only one remaining. Let us therefore look at these quotations more closely.

Parpola (1981: 155-157) provides an "exhaustive tabulation" which shows "that both texts cite what is in practice an identical selection of named authorities". The exceptions, Parpola continues, concern a few rarely occurring names only. It can easily be seen from this tabulation that the *Brahmasūtra* never cites the name of a teacher that is not also cited in the *Pūrvamīmāṃsāsūtra* (along with the Saṅkarṣakāṇḍa). There is only one exception: the name of Kāśakṛtsna, which only occurs in the *Brahmasūtra* (1.4.22), but not in the ritual *Mīmāṃsāsūtra*.

It must be admitted that this state of affairs is quite extraordinary. It becomes even more extraordinary if we take into consideration Renou's (1962: 197 [623]) observation to the extent that these cited teachers never express a dissident view in the *Brahmasūtra*. If taken at its face value, all this implies that the authorities responsible for the development of "Vedāntic" thought were the same as those who developed ritual thought. Parpola (1981: 158) concludes from this that

> it is quite clear that both Jaimini and Bādarāyaṇa, as well as the other authorities quoted, were well acquainted with both branches of the Mīmāṃsā, just like the earliest commentators of the unified Mīmāṃsāsūtra.

This conclusion seems reasonable enough, but raises the question which we formulated at the beginning of this article, but this time in a more extreme form: Must we really believe that all those early ritualists – this time not only Jaimini and his early commentators, but also the authorities he quotes – were in their heart of hearts Vedāntins? Moreover, how is it possible that only recognised ritual teachers contributed to Vedāntic thought?

What do we know about the early development of Vedāntic thought? Parpola paints the following picture. Having pointed out that there was a "twofold mīmāṃsā" connected with Vedic ritual from the very beginning (1981: 158 ff), he states with regard to its late-Vedic history:

> I have no doubt that this twofold mīmāṃsā continued to be practised by the Vedic ritualists even after the Upaniṣadic period right down to the days of the *Mīmāṃsāsūtra*, although the ceremonial and speculative (or practical and theoretical) sides of this early scholarly activity were henceforth recorded separately, in the Kalpasūtras and in the (later) Upaniṣads (Parpola 1981: 162).

This picture gives rise to several questions.

First of all, whatever may have been the case in early days, at the time of and following the Vedic Upaniṣads Vedāntic thought is not just the theoretical side of ritual activity. This is particularly clear from passages in the Upaniṣads that express themselves critically with regard to the Vedic ritual tradition.[103] There is also the tendency, which manifests itself in late-Vedic texts, to "interiorize" ritual practice, to "deritualize" it.[104] Then there are passages which distinguish those who reach the world of Brahma by reason of a special insight from those who sacrifice and are as a result reborn in this world.[105] Criticism of Vedic ritualism perhaps finds its culmination in the late-Vedic *Muṇḍaka-Upaniṣad* (still commented upon by Śaṅkara); the following passage illustrates this:

> *avidyāyāṃ bahudhā vartamānā, vayaṃ kṛtārthā ity abhimanyanti bālāḥ* |
> *yat karmiṇo na pravedayanti rāgāt, tenāturāḥ kṣīṇalokāś cyavante* ||
> *iṣṭāpūrtaṃ manyamānā variṣṭaṃ nānyac chreyo vedayante pramūḍhāḥ* |
> *nākasya pṛṣṭhe te sukṛte 'nubhūtvemaṃ lokaṃ hīnataraṃ vā viśanti* ||
> *tapaḥśraddhe ye hy upavasanty araṇye, śāntā vidvāṃso bhaikṣacaryāṃ carantaḥ* |
> *sūryadvāreṇa te virajāḥ prayānti, yatrāmṛtaḥ sa puruṣo hy avyayātmā* ||[106]

> Wallowing in ignorance time and again, the fools imagine, "We have reached our aim!" Because of their passion, they do not understand, these people

[103] Cf. Sarup 1921, Introduction, pp. 71-80 ("Early anti-Vedic scepticism").
[104] Cf. Bodewitz 1973: 211-338 ("Agnihotra and Prāṇāgnihotra").
[105] ChānUp 5.10; BĀrUp 6.2.15-16.
[106] MuṇUp 1.2.9-11; text and transl. Olivelle 1998: 440-441.

> who are given to rites. Therefore, they fall, wretched and forlorn, when their heavenly stay comes to a close.
>
> Deeming sacrifices and gifts as the best, the imbeciles know nothing better. When they have enjoyed their good work, atop the firmament, they return again to this abject world.
>
> But those in the wilderness, calm and wise, who live a life of penance and faith, as they beg their food; through the sun's door they go, spotless, to where that immortal Person is, that immutable self.

Scepticism with regard to the Vedic sacrifice does not stop with the late-Vedic Upaniṣads. The *Bhagavadgītā* – in which the supreme Brahma plays an important role, and which refers to its chapters in the colophons as Upaniṣad (Schreiner 1991: 234) – is a particularly prominent example of such continued criticism, as scholars have repeatedly observed (e.g. Sarup 1921: 75; Lamotte 1929: 105; references to Bhag 2.42-46; 9.20-21; 11.48, 53).[107] Critical gāthās and ślokas have been preserved, which have been studied by Paul Horsch (1966, especially p. 468 ff). All this shows that it is far from evident that the Upaniṣadic tradition is simply the theoretical part of the practical tradition which led from Vedic ritual to post-Vedic ritual thought (Mīmāṃsā).

Texts such as the *Mahābhārata* – which in its present form is certainly more recent than the early Upaniṣads – demonstrate that the Vedic ritualistic tradition did continue in post-Upaniṣadic times while remaining largely unaffected by ideas about rebirth and liberation. It is true that these issues play an important role in the philosophical parts of this text; in the narrative parts, on the other hand, they are far less common. Indeed, Brockington (1998: 232) refers to the significance of Vedic sacrifice within the *Mahābhārata*, and observes: "this is clearly a feature which tends to align it more with the Brāhmaṇas than with classical Hinduism". The concepts of *karma* and *saṃsāra* do occasionally appear in the narrative

107 Peter Schreiner (1991: 142) observes: "Die Tatsache, dass der Text (= Bhagavadgītā) Zitate aus einer Upaniṣad enthält (2.19-20, vgl. Kaṭha-Upaniṣad 2.20 und 2.19 [i.e., 2.19 and 2.18 in Olivelle's edition]) unterstreicht, dass der Text in einer Tradition steht und, so darf man annehmen, sich dieser Tradition bewusst zuordnet."

books, beside various other determinants of human destiny (Brockington 1998: 244 f), but they do not play the important role which they should be expected to play if we assume that the Vedic tradition had accepted these concepts from the days of the early Upaniṣads onward. Hopkins, citing a passage from the Śāntiparvan, paraphrases (1901: 186): "The priest, orthodox, is recognized as still striving for heaven and likely to go to hell, in the old way."[108] There can be no doubt that the Brahmins made fun of in this passage are not Vedāntins in their heart of hearts.

Second, if it is true that the speculative (or theoretical) sides of the early scholarly activity which led to Uttaramīmāṃsā was recorded in the (later) Upaniṣads, one might expect to find the names of the authorities cited in the *Brahmasūtra* in those Upaniṣads. However, none of these cited names occur in the surviving Upaniṣads, as we can learn from Vishva Bandhu's *Vedic Word-Concordance*. Most of them do occur in the Kalpasūtras (as shown by Parpola). Do we have to assume that these names occurred in later Upaniṣads that are now lost? or in other pre-Brahmasūtra "Vedāntic" texts that are now lost? The uncomfortable fact is that we have plenty of independent evidence pertaining to the ritualistic activity of the authorities cited in the ritual *Mīmāṃsāsūtra*, but none whatsoever with regard to their Vedāntic interests. To be more precise, we know from independent sources that the authorities cited in the *Brahmasūtra* were interested in ritual, but we have not one bit of independent evidence that they were interested in Vedāntic thought and concerns.

The above reflections call for another way of looking at the teacher quotations in the *Brahmasūtra*. We have seen that one branch of later Vedāntic thinkers (Śaṅkara, Maṇḍana Miśra and others) took great pain to show that their discipline is really a form – the best form – of Mīmāṃsā, that they applied the methods and techniques of Mīmāṃsā with even more rigour than the ritualist

---

[108] Cf. Mhbh 12.192.14-15: *nirayaṃ naiva yātāsi yatra yātā dvijarṣabhāḥ* | *yāsyasi brahmaṇaḥ sthānam animittam aninditam* |

Mīmāṃsakas. The *Brahmasūtra* belongs to this branch of Vedāntic thought. As such, the *Brahmasūtra* had to justify its teachings by invoking the same authorities as the ritual *Mīmāṃsāsūtra.*[109] That is to say, it did not wish to proclaim a different discipline based on the teachings of different authorities, because this would suggest, or even imply, that the *Brahmasūtra* belonged to a different tradition, just as the teachings of Kapila (Sāṃkhya) and of Gautama (Nyāya) constitute different traditions. By basing itself on the same authorities as the ritual *Mīmāṃsāsūtra* and using the same exegetical principles, the *Brahmasūtra* presents itself as teaching the same Mīmāṃsā, only better. Teaching Mīmāṃsā better means, of course, that in the *Brahmasūtra* due attention is given to the statements about Brahma in the Upaniṣads. This in its turn, the Vedāntic Mīmāṃsakas claim, is a necessary consequence of the correct application of the rules of Mīmāṃsā.

This does not necessarily imply that all the references to authorities in the *Brahmasūtra* are bogus. It is certainly conceivable that early "Uttaramīmāṃsakas" made major efforts to extend the views of ritual authorities so as to make them applicable to Vedāntic thought and procedures, to draw new conclusions out of their old positions. The unfortunate truth is that we have practically no evidence to come to anything approaching certainty in this regard. The well-nigh impossible style of the *Brahmasūtra*[110] itself

---

[109] Already Renou (1962: 197 [623]) wondered: "Dans quelle mesure ces attributions sont-elles réelles, dans quelle mesure s'agit-il de fictions destinées à rendre un exposé plus vivant?"

[110] Renou (1962: 202 [628]) characterizes it as follows: "Cette économie aboutit souvent à l'ellipse. Si chez Pāṇini rien d'essentiel n'est omis qui ne puisse se reconstituer par les [sūtra] précédents ou en faisant appel aux *adhikāra*, ici dans les [*Brahmasūtra*] il arrive que des mots importants manquent, ceux-là même dont la définition est en cause. Ainsi le mot *brahman* est omis partout ... '; and again (1961: 197 [553]): "Les [sūtra] du Vedānta ... ont une teneur elliptique qui, le plus souvent, défie la compréhension directe." Already Thibaut (1890-96: I: xiii-xiv) complained: "The two Mīmāṃsā-sūtras occupy, however, an altogether exceptional position in point of style. All Sūtras aim at conciseness .... At the same time the manifest intention of the Sūtra writers is to express themselves

– which, as Rüping (1977: 2) points out, may well have been cultivated on purpose[111] – prevents us in most cases from being sure that this text itself ascribes Vedāntic positions to these ritual authorities.

And yet, a closer look at the positions ascribed to Jaimini in the *Brahmasūtra*[112] shows that these ascribed views are often very close to positions known to be held by the ritual Mīmāṃsakas. This may indicate that the *Brahmasūtra* occasionally mentions the name of Jaimini in order to present a ritual Mīmāṃsā view which it then rejects. The conclusion that Jaimini must have been a Vedāntin of sorts may in that case have to be abandoned.

Consider first BraSū 1.3.31 which mentions the name of Jaimini. The sūtra reads: *madhvādiṣv asaṃbhavād anadhikāraṃ jaiminiḥ*; it stands out, in comparison with many other sūtras in the same text, by the relative clarity of its formulation. It is yet difficult to determine, on the basis of these words alone, what this sūtra means. If we assume that Śaṅkara was aware of the intention of the

with as much clearness as the conciseness affected by them admits of. ... Altogether different is the case of the two Mīmāṃsā-sūtras. There scarcely one single Sūtra is intelligible without a commentary. The most essential words are habitually dispensed with; nothing is, for instance, more common than the simple omission of the subject or predicate of a sentence."

[111] Similarly Renou 1961: 206 (562): "On est donc conduit à penser que l'auteur des [*Brahmasūtra*] a cherché à restreindre l'intelligibilité, au-delà même de ce que se permet d'habitude le style en *sūtra*"; and Renou 1942: 122 (444, 328): "[Les sūtra des deux Mīmāṃsā sont] elliptiques ... et apparemment dédaigneux de faciliter au lecteur l'intelligence du texte. La concision dans les deux Mīmāṃsā, qui conduit à supprimer des éléments essentiels et amoindrit en fait l'intelligibilité ... est aux antipodes de la concision pāṇinéenne, où tout ce qui importe est formulé." Cf. already Deussen 1923: 28: "Dieser Thatbestand der Brahma-sûtra's lässt sich weder aus dem Streben nach Kürze, noch aus einer Vorliebe für charakteristische Ausdrucksweise hinlänglich erklären. Vielmehr müssen wir annehmen, dass der oder die Verfasser absichtlich das Dunkle suchten, um ihr die Geheimlehre des Veda behandelndes Werk allen denen unzugänglich zu machen, welchen es nicht durch die Erklärungen eines Lehrers erschlossen wurde."

[112] Cf. Kane 1960: 126 f; 1977: 1162 f; and Taber's contribution to this volume.

sūtra, and that we are therefore entitled to invoke his help, we may then translate:

> On account of the impossibility [on the part of the gods to be qualified to knowledge] with regard to honey etc., Jaimini [thinks that the gods] are not qualified [to knowledge of Brahma].

According to the editions of Śaṅkara's commentary, sūtra 1.3.31 is part of the Devatādhikaraṇa, which covers sūtras 1.3.26-33. None of these sūtras, to be sure, contains any indication that this section is concerned with gods or with the qualification to knowledge of Brahma, so it is probably impossible to confirm that Śaṅkara's understanding of sūtra 1.3.31 is correct.[113] Assuming nonetheless that it is, some interesting observations can be made. We know from Śabara's Bhāṣya on MīmSū 6.1.5 that gods are not qualified to perform Vedic rites. The statement from Śabara concerned, *na devānāṃ devatāntarābhāvāt*, is even cited by Śaṅkara in the beginning of the Devatādhikaraṇa (on BraSū 1.3.26). MīmSū 6.1.5 itself, though rather obscure, can be understood to express the same position.[114] The position presumably attributed to Jaimini in BraSū 1.3.31 may therefore very well be an extension of the view held by the "real" Jaimini, i.e., by the author of MīmSū 6.1.5. It certainly is an extension of what Śabara – and perhaps others before him – believed was Jaimini's view.

It is less obvious that the reason given in BraSū 1.3.31 corresponds to anything Jaimini may have ever thought of. According to Śaṅkara, the words *madhvādiṣv asaṃbhavād* "On account of the

[113] The sūtras read: *tadupary api bādarayaṇaḥ saṃbhavāt* (26); *virodhaḥ karmaṇīti cen nānekapratipatter darśanāt* (27); *śabda iti cen nātaḥ prabhavāt pratyakṣānumānābhyām* (28); *ata eva ca nityatvam* (29); *samānanāmarūpatvāc cāvṛttāv apy avirodho darśanāt smṛteś ca* (30); *madhvādiṣv asaṃbhavād anadhikāraṃ jaiminiḥ* (31); *jyotiṣi bhāvāc ca* (32); *bhāvaṃ tu bādarāyaṇo 'sti hi* (33).

[114] *Pūrvamīmāṃsāsūtra* 6.1.5 reads: *kartur vā śrutisaṃyogād vidhiḥ kārtsnyena gamyate*, which Jha (1933, II: 973) translates, or rather paraphrases: "In reality, the injunction of an act should be taken to apply to only such an agent as may be able to carry out the entire details of the act; because such is the sense of the Vedic texts."

impossibility [on the part of the gods to be qualified to knowledge] with regard to honey etc." refer to ChānUp 3.1.1 *asau vā ādityo devamadhu* "The honey of the gods, clearly, is the sun up there" (transl. Olivelle 1998: 201). The interpretation which, according to Śaṅkara, Jaimini gives of this statement is that human beings should worship the sun by superimposing the idea of honey on it (*manuṣyā ādityaṃ madhvadhyāsenopāsīran*). No such interpretation is found in Śaṅkara's commentary on the *Chāndogya-Upaniṣad.* And it is very surprising to find such an interpretation attributed to Jaimini. From the point of view of ritual Mīmāṃsā this is a simple *arthavāda.* And Śaṅkara himself, under the immediately following sūtra 1.3.32, presents Jaimini's ideas about *arthavāda*s as follows:

> *arthavādā api vidhinaikavākyatvāt stutyarthāḥ santo na pārthagarthyena devādīnāṃ vigrahādisadbhāve kāraṇabhāvaṃ pratipadyante*
>
> *Arthavāda*s, too, having as purpose to praise [an activity] on account of the fact that they are to be understood in connection with an injunction, are no independent (*pārthagarthyena*) grounds for [accepting] that the gods etc. have bodies and so on.

This is indeed the position of ritual Mīmāṃsā, and this same reasoning might be used to refuse drawing conclusions from the statement from the *Chāndogya-Upaniṣad* on which Jaimini is yet supposed to base his conclusion that the gods are not qualified to knowledge.

Jaimini is again mentioned in BraSū 3.2.40: *dharmaṃ jaiminir ata eva.*[115] Śaṅkara interprets this to mean that in Jaimini's opinion not God (*īśvara*) but Dharma, or Apūrva, links the sacrificial activity with its result. This agrees with what we know from Śabara's Bhāṣya, and sūtra 3.2.40 may therefore correctly represent Jaimini's opinion without obliging us to conclude that Jaimini was (also) a Vedāntin.

---

[115] Modi (1943?: 77) translates: "Jaimini [says that the fruit is] Dharma (religious merit), because of this very reason (viz., the support of the Śruti)."

Jaimini's mention in BraSū 4.4.11 (*bhāvaṃ jaiminir vikalpāmananāt*)[116] is at first sight more problematic, for it concerns – at least in Śaṅkara's interpretation – the question whether a liberated soul still has a body and organs; according to Jaimini, it does. Far from concluding from this sūtra that Jaimini had ideas about the state of liberation, it seems much more prudent to read no more in it than an extension of the ritual Mīmāṃsā idea that sacrificers will remain in possession of body and organs in the state which they strive to attain above all, viz. heaven.

Jaimini defends the subordinate nature of knowledge of the self in BraSū 3.4.2[117] (in Śaṅkara's interpretation) and the non-injunction of other stages of life (*āśrama*) in sūtra 3.4.18[118] (again according to Śaṅkara), both times in opposition to Bādarāyaṇa, and both times in agreement with ritual Mīmāṃsā doctrine.

Let it here once more be repeated that the obscure formulation of the *Brahmasūtra* makes any study of its contents extremely difficult. Few would be more qualified than Parpola to study the extent to which the opinions attributed to the various teachers in this text can be looked upon as extensions of what we know about them from elsewhere, but unfortunately his articles almost completely abandon the *Brahmasūtra* after the challenging initial remarks. The observations about Jaimini presented above are however suggestive. They suggest indeed that Jaimini in the *Brahmasūtra*, far from being the name of an individual who had outspoken ideas about Vedānta, stands there for a collection of views which

---

[116] Modi (1943?: 441) translates: "Jaimini holds that there is existence of a body in his case, because of the mention in the Śruti of an option regarding the number of bodies of a liberated soul."

[117] BraSū 3.4.2: *śeṣatvāt puruṣārthavādo yathānyeṣv iti jaiminiḥ*. Transl. Modi 1943?: 242: "'The name of *the aim of human life* is applied [to the goal of the Lore of the Upaniṣads] because that knowledge is subsidiary [to the sacrifice] as is the case with other knowledges or other puruṣārthas', so says Jaimini."

[118] BraSū 3.4.18: *parāmarśaṃ jaiminir acodanā cāpavadati hi.* Modi (1943?: 252) translates: "Jaimini holds the knowledge of Brahman to be a thought; and [he says] 'It is not of the form of an Injunction, because the Scripture denies all actions [as a help to the realization of Brahman].'"

agree more or less well with the ritual Mīmāṃsā position. Something similar may be true for the remaining teachers whose names are cited in the *Brahmasūtra*. Unfortunately this will have to remain a hypothesis as long as the *Brahmasūtra* remains almost completely unintelligible.

The view that the *Brahmasūtra* made an effort to show itself to be a Mīmāṃsā text that does not in any essential aspect deviate from classical Mīmāṃsā can explain various other features as well. The *Brahmasūtra* refers on some occasions to Mīmāṃsā rules, which it obviously accepts. Mīmāṃsaka (1987, Introduction, p. 7) illustrates this with a number of examples,[119] but points out that no borrowing of rules has taken place in the opposite direction, from *Brahmasūtra* to ritual *Mīmāṃsāsūtra*. He concludes from this that the names Pūrvamīmāṃsā and Uttaramīmāṃsā are appropriate, no doubt in the meanings of earlier and later Mīmāṃsā respectively. Whatever one thinks of this interpretation (which differs widely from the one proposed by Parpola), it is clear that Uttaramīmāṃsā was influenced by and followed the example of Pūrvamīmāṃsā, but not vice-versa. This of course agrees with our suggestion that the thinkers of Uttaramīmāṃsā went out of their way to show their teaching to be an improved version of ritual Mīmāṃsā. The extensive use made by Śaṅkara of Mīmāṃsā principles (Devasthali 1952; Moghe 1984) points in the same direction.

Seen in the way here suggested the *Brahmasūtra* and its early commentaries are the embodiment of the attempt to lend the respectability of serious Vedic interpretation to the speculations about Brahma which had continued without interruption since Upaniṣadic times. Such respectability so far only belonged to the (Pūrva-)Mīmāṃsā. By basing all their doctrines on properly interpreted Upaniṣadic statements, the speculations about Brahma became a form of Mīmāṃsā, even a better form of Mīmāṃsā than the ritualistic one. Some traces of non-mīmāṃsic Vedāntic thought

---

[119] See further Subrahmanya Sastri 1961, Bhūmikā, p. 2 f; Renou 1962: 195 (621), n. 2.

have however survived, allowing us to see that post-Vedic Vedāntic philosophy had not always been a form of Mīmāṃsā (e.g., Uttaramīmāṃsā, Śārīraka-Mīmāṃsā, etc.).

6. CONCLUSIONS

It will be clear from the preceding reflections that Uttaramīmāṃsā, far from being part of original Mīmāṃsā, attached itself at some time to it in order to provide speculations about Brahma with the solid underpinning of serious Vedic interpretation. Speculations about Brahma, more or less continuing the ideas found in the Vedic Upaniṣads, had been around probably without interruption since Upaniṣadic times. They had not always profited from the sophisticated instruments of Vedic interpretation that had been developed in Mīmāṃsā for the sake of Vedic ritual. Using these instruments to solidly anchor Vedāntic ideas into the eternal Veda was an aim that gave rise to a new – or perhaps better: supplementary – school of Vedic interpretation: the Uttaramīmāṃsā.

This way of looking at the historical origins of Uttaramīmāṃsā does away with the need to believe that the early ritual Mīmāṃsakas – Śabara, but also Jaimini, and even the authorities cited in the Sūtra – were really convinced Vedāntins, who believed in liberation from this world as a possibility beside and above the rewards offered for Vedic ritual practice. It is no longer necessary to think that Śabara, in spite of showing no awareness whatsoever of the notion of liberation in his massive commentary on the *Mīmāṃsāsūtra*, yet was familiar with it and may therefore himself have hoped to attain liberation one day. We can now stick to the far simpler and far more plausible position that Śabara – and Jaimini, and all those they cite – never mention liberation because they did not believe in it. They did not believe in it because there was no place for liberation in their vision of the world which was in this respect still rather close to, and continued, the Vedic ritualistic world view. This in its turn constitutes evidence that Vedic Brahmins had not, from the time of the Upaniṣads onward, embraced the new ideas of karmic retribution and liberation. Far from it, the most conservative among them continued to resist these ideas for at least one thousand years, from the time of the early Upaniṣads until that of Śabara and Prabhākara. We can now also understand how later ritual Mīmāṃsakas – prominent among them Kumārila Bhaṭṭa – could no longer resist the lure of the notion of liberation and yielded to it without becoming Vedāntins. From the point of view of ritual Mīmāṃsā the two Mīmāṃsās were not fundamentally one, and had never been one. Vedānta had attached itself to the older school of Vedic interpretation, claiming that it had always been part of it; that ritual Mīmāṃsā had never been complete without it. The ritual Mīmāṃsakas knew better, and historically speaking they were right.[120]

REFERENCES

Texts and abbreviations

Ādiśeṣa: *Paramārthasāra*. See under Danielson 1980.

Ānandagiri: *Nyāyanirṇaya*. See under Śaṅkara: *Brahmasūtrabhāṣya*.

Bhāskara: *Brahmasūtrabhāṣya*. In: *Brahmasūtrabhāṣyam Bhāskarācārya viracitam*. Brahmasūtra with a commentary by Bhâskarâchârya. Ed. by Vindhyeshavari Prasâda Dvivedin. (Chowkhamba Sanskrit Series, 70, 185, 209.) Benares 1915. (Reprint: Chowkhamba Sanskrit Series, 20. Varanasi: Chowkhamba Sanskrit Series Office, 1991.)

Govindānanda: *Bhāṣyaratnaprabhā*. See under Śaṅkara: *Brahmasūtrabhāṣya*.

Kullūka Bhaṭṭa: *Manvartha-Muktāvalī*. For the edition see *Manusmṛti*.

Madhusūdana Sarasvatī: *Vedāntakalpalatikā*. Edited, with an introduction, English translation and appendices, by R. D. Karmarkar. Poona: BORI, 1962.

Maṇḍana Miśra: *Brahmasiddhi*. Ed. by S. Kuppuswami Sastri. Madras 1937. (Second edition: Delhi: Sri Satguru, 1984.)

Manusmṛti, with the Sanskrit commentary Manvartha-Muktāvalī of Kullūka Bhaṭṭa. Ed. J. L. Shastri. Delhi: Motilal Banarsidass, 1983.

Medhātithi: *Manubhāṣya*. For the edition see Jha 1920-39.

---

[120] I thank Roque Mesquita for help and advise.

Padmapāda: *Pañcapādika.* 1) In: *Śrī Padmapādācārya's Pañcapādikā*, with the commentaries Vivaraṇa by Śrī Prakāśātmamuni, Tattvadīpana by Śrī Akhaṇḍānanda Muni and Ṛjuvivaraṇa by Śrī Viṣṇubhaṭṭopādhyāya. Ed. by Paṇḍitrājā Śāstraratnākara S. Subrahmanyaśāstri. (Advaita Grantha Ratna Manjusha, 33.) Mount Abu and Varanasi: Mahesh Research Institute, 1992. 2) In: *Pañcapādikā of Śrī Padmapādācārya*, with Prabodhapariśodhinī of Ātmasvarūpa and Tātparyārthadyotinī of Vijñānātman and Pañcapādikāvivaraṇa of Śrī Prakāśātman with Tātparyadīpikā of Citsukhācārya and Bhāvaprakāśikā of Nṛsiṃhāśrama. Ed. by S. Śrīrāma Śāstrī & S. R. Krishnamurthi Śāstrī. Madras: Government Oriental Manuscripts Library, 1958. For and English translation see Venkataramiah 1948.

Prapañcahṛdaya. In: *Prapañca-hṛdayam tathā Prasthāna-bhedaḥ.* Ed. by Yudhiṣṭhira Mīmāṃsaka. Bahālagaḍha: Rāmalāla Kapūra Trust, 1987. [Page numbers in brackets refer to the first edition of this text by T. Ganapati Sastri 1915 (Trivandrum Sanskrit Series, 45).]

Rāmānuja: *Śrībhāṣya*, I. Ed. by N. S. Ramabhadracharya Melkote: The Academy of Sanskrit Research, 1985.

Rāmānuja: *Vedāntadīpa.* In: *Vedāntadeepa. A Gloss on Brahmasūtras by Rāmānujāchārya.* Ed. by Bhattanāthaswāmi. (Benares Sanskrit Series, 69, 70 and 80.) Benares 1904.

Rāmānuja: *Vedārthasaṃgraha.* See under van Buitenen 1956.

Śaṅkara: *Brahmasūtrabhāṣya.* Editions used: 1) *Brahmasūtra-Śāṅkarabhāṣyam.* Edited, with the commentaries Bhāṣyaratnaprabhā of Govindānanda, Bhāmatī of Vācaspati, Nyāyanirṇaya of Ānandagiri, by J. L. Shastri. (Reprint: Delhi: Motilal Banarsidass, 1996.) 2) *Brahmasūtra with Śāṅkarabhāṣya.* (Works of Śaṅkarācārya in original Sanskrit, 3.) Delhi: Motilal Banarsidass, 1964.

Śaṅkara: *Bṛhadāraṇyakopaniṣad-bhāṣya, Chāndogyopaniṣad-bhāṣya, Taittirīyopaniṣad-bhāṣya.* In: *Ten Principal Upanishads with Śāṅkarabhāṣya.* (Works of Śaṅkarācārya in original Sanskrit, 1.) Delhi: Motilal Banarsidass, 1964.

Sāyaṇa: *Ṛgvedabhāṣya.* In: *Ṛgveda-Saṃhitā with the commentary of Sāyaṇācārya*, I. Ed. by V. K. Rājawade et al. Second edition. Poona: Tilaka Mahārāṣṭra Vidyāpīṭha – Vaidika Saṃśodhana Maṇḍala, 1972.

Śrīnivāsadāsa: *Yatīndramatadīpikā.* In: *Śrī Bhāshya Vārtika, a Treatise on Viśishtādvaita Philosophy*; also Yatīndra Mat Dīpikā by Nivāsā Chārya son of Govindā Chārya, and Sakalāchāryamat Saṅgrah. Ed. by Ratna Gopāl Bhaṭṭa. Benares: Vidyā Vilās Press, 1907.

Sureśvara: *Sambandhavārttika* on Śaṅkara's *Bṛhadāraṇyakopaniṣad-bhāṣya.* Edition used: *Shri Sureshvaracharya's Brihadaranyakopanishad-Sambandhabhashyavartikam*, with the commentary of Shri Aanandagiri

Aacharya. ... Edited with introduction notes, etc. by ... S. Subrahmanya Shastri. (Advaita Grantha Ratna Manjusha, 22.) Mount Abu, Varanasi: Mahesh Research Institute, 1980.

Sureśvara: *Naiṣkarmyasiddhi*. Edition used: *The Naiṣkarmya-siddhi of Sureśvarācārya*, with the Candrikā of Jñānottama. Edited with notes and index by the late Colonel G. A. Jacob. Revised edition, with introduction and explanatory notes by M. Hiriyanna. (Bombay Sanskrit and Prakrit Series, 38.) 1925. (Reprint: Poona: BORI, 1980.)

Vācaspati Miśra: *Bhāmatī*. See under Śaṅkara, *Brahmasūtrabhāṣya*.

Yāmuna: *Ātmasiddhi*. In: *Sri Yamunacharya's Siddhi Traya*, with a Sanskrit commentary ... by ... Uttamur T. Viraraghavacharya ... and translation in English by R. Ramanujachari & ... K. Srinivasacharya. Madras: Ubhaya Vedanta Granthamala Book Trust, 1972. (The edition was first published in Tirupatti 1942.)

BĀrUp *Bṛhadāraṇyaka-Upaniṣad*

Bhag *Bhagavadgītā*

BraSū *Brahmasūtra*

BSūBhā *Brahmasūtrabhāṣya* of Śaṅkara

ChānUp *Chāndogya-Upaniṣad*

EIP *The Encyclopedia of Indian Philosophies*. Ed. by Karl H. Potter. Delhi, 1970-.

GK *The Āgamaśāstra of Gauḍapāda*. Ed. by Vidhushekhara Bhattacharya. 1943. (Reprint: Delhi: Motilal Banarsidass, 1989.)

Mhbh *The Mahābhārata*. For the first time critically edited, I-XIX. Ed. by V. S. Sukthankar and others. Poona: BORI, 1933-66.

MīmSū *Mīmāṃsāsūtra*

MuṇUp *Muṇḍaka-Upaniṣad*

NBh *Nyāyabhāṣya* of Pakṣilasvāmin Vātsyāyana. Nyāyadarśanam with Vātsyāyana's Bhāṣya, Uddyotakara's Vārttika, Vācaspati Miśra's Tātparyaṭīkā & Viśvanātha's Vṛtti. Chapter I, section I critically edited with notes by Taranatha Nyaya-Tarkatirtha and chapters I-ii–V by Amarendramohan Tarkatirtha, with an introduction by Narendra Chandra Vedantatirtha. Calcutta: Metropolitan Printing & Publishing House, 1936.

TaitS *Taittirīyasaṃhitā*

TanVār *Tantravārttika* of Kumārilabhaṭṭa. (ĀSS, 97.)

Vkp *Vākyapadīya* of Bhartṛhari. Ed. by W. Rau. Wiesbaden 1977.

YogV *Yogavāsiṣṭha*. For the edition see Pansikar 1918. [YogV 6 refers to the Pūrvārdha and YogV 7 to the Uttarārdha of Prakaraṇa 6.]

Other sources

ALSTON, A. J. (transl.) 1959. *The Realization of the Absolute. The "Naiṣkarmya Siddhi" of Śrī Sureśvara*. Second edition: Shanti Sadan, London, 1971.

—— 1989a. *Śaṃkara on Ritual Views*. (A Śaṃkara Source-Book, 4.) London: Shanti Sadan.

—— 1989b. *Śaṃkara on Discipleship*. (A Śaṃkara Source-Book, 5.) London: Shanti Sadan.

BADER, Jonathan 1990. *Meditation in Śaṅkara's Vedānta*. New Delhi: Aditya Prakashan.

BELVALKAR, Shripad Krishna 1927. Jaimini's Śārīraka-sūtra. In: *Aus Indiens Kultur. Festgabe Richard von Garbe*: 163-170. Erlangen: Verlag vom Palm & Enke.

BHADKAMKAR, H. M. & R. G. BHADKAMKAR (eds.) 1918. *The Nirukta of Yāska (with Nighaṇṭu). Edited with Durga's Commentary*, I. (Bombay Sanskrit and Prakrit Series, 73.) Bombay: Government Central Press. (Reprint: Poona: BORI, 1985.)

BIARDEAU, Madeleine 1964. *Théorie de la connaissance et philosophie de la parole dans le brahmanisme classique*. (Le Monde d'Outre-mer Passé et Présent, première série, études, 23.) Paris: Mouton.

—— 1968. L'ātman dans le commentaire de Śabarasvāmin. In: *Mélanges d'Indianisme à la Mémoire de Louis Renou*: 109-125. Paris: E. de Boccard.

BODEWITZ, H. W. 1973. *Jaiminīya Brāhmaṇa I, 1-65. Translation and Commentary, with a Study Agnohotra and Prāṇāgnihotra*. Leiden: E.J. Brill.

BOUY, Christian 2000. *Gauḍapāda, l'Āgamaśāstra. Un traité vedāntique en quatre chapitres*. Texte, traduction et notes. (Collège de France, Publications de l'Institut de Civilisation Indienne, Série in-8°, 69.) Paris: Édition-Diffusion de Boccard.

BROCKINGTON, John 1998. *The Sanskrit Epics*. (Handbuch der Orientalistik, Abteilung Indien, 12.) Leiden: E.J. Brill.

BRONKHORST, Johannes 1989. Studies on Bhartṛhari, 2: Bhartṛhari and Mīmāṃsā. *Studien zur Indologie und Iranistik* 15: 101-117. (Reprint in: R. C. Dwivedi (ed.), *Studies in Mīmāṃsā. Dr. Mandan Mishra Felicitation Volume*: 371-388. Delhi: Motilal Banarsidass, 1994.)

—— 1991a. Review of Wood 1990. *Asiatische Studien / Études Asiatiques* 45.2: 324-333.

—— 1991b. Studies on Bhartṛhari, 3: Bhartṛhari on sphoṭa and universals. *Asiatische Studien / Études Asiatiques* 45.1: 5-18.

—— 1997. Philosophy and Vedic exegesis in the Mīmāṃsā. In: Eli Franco & Karin Preisendanz (eds.), *Beyond Orientalism. The Work of Wilhelm*

Halbfass and its Impact on Indian and Cross-Cultural Studies. (Poznan Studies in the Philosophy of the Sciences and the Humanities, 59.): 359-371. Amsterdam: Rodopi.

—— 1998. Bhartṛhari (c. 5th century). In: Edward Craig (ed.), *Routledge Encyclopedia of Philosophy*, I: 764-766. London: Routledge

—— 1999. *Langage et réalité: sur un épisode de la pensée indienne*. (Bibliothèque de l'École des Hautes Études, Sciences Religieuses, 105.) Turnhout: Brepols.

—— 2000. *Karma and Teleology. A problem and its Solutions in Indian Philosophy*. (Studia Philologica, Monograph Series, 15.) Tokyo: International Institute for Buddhist Studies.

—— 2001. Pour comprendre la philosophie indienne. In: Johannes Bronkhorst (ed.), *La rationalité en Asie* I *Rationality in Asia* (Études de Lettres, 2001.3): 195-221. Lausanne: Université de Lausanne: Faculté des lettres.

—— 2003. Review of *Yuktidīpikā. The Most Significant Commentary on the Sāṃkhyakārikā*, I. Critically edited by Albrecht Wezler & Shujun Motegi. *ZDMG* 153.1: 242-247.

——, forthcoming (a). Bhartṛhari and his Vedic tradition. Paper read at the International Seminar on Language, Thought and Reality in Bhartṛhari on the occasion of the Centennial Year of MLBD. New Delhi, 12-14 December 2003.

——, forthcoming (b). On the nature of *pradhāna*. In: Karin Preisendanz & Eli Franco (eds.), *Commemoration Volume Wilhelm Halbfass*.

——, forthcoming (c). Echoes of Ājīvikism in medieval Indian philosophy.

BRÜCKNER, Heidrun 1979. *Zum Beweisverfahren Śaṃkaras. Eine Untersuchung der Form und Funktion von dṛṣṭāntas im Bṛhadāraṇyakopaniṣadbhāṣya und im Chāndogyopaniṣadbhāṣya des Śaṃkara Bhagavatpāda*. (Marburger Studien zur Afrika- und Asienkunde, Serie B: Asien, 5.) Berlin: Dietrich Reimer.

CHENET, François 1998-99. *Psychogenèse et cosmogonie selon le Yoga-Vāsiṣṭha: «Le monde est dans l'âme»*, I-II. (Collège de France, Publications de l'Institut de Civilisation Indienne, Série in-8°, 67.) Paris: Édition-Diffusion de Boccard.

CLOONEY, Francis X. 1990. *Thinking Ritually. Rediscovering the Pūrva Mīmāṃsā of Jaimini*. (Publications of the De Nobili Research Library, 17.) Vienna: Institute for Indology, Vienna University.

COMANS, Michael 2000. *The Method of Early Advaita Vedānta. A Study of Gauḍapāda, Śaṅkara, Sureśvara, and Padmapāda*. Delhi: Motilal Banarsidass.

DANIELSON, Henry 1980. *Ādiśeṣa, the Essence of Supreme Truth (Paramārthasāra).* Sanskrit text with translation and notes. (Religious texts translation series NISABA, 10.) Leiden: E.J. Brill.

DEUSSEN, Paul 1923. *Das System des Vedānta.* Vierte Auflage. Leipzig: F. A. Brockhaus. [First edition: 1883.]

—— 1887. *Die Sûtra's des Vedânta oder die Çârîraka-Mîmâṅsâ des Bâdarâyaṇa nebst dem vollständigen Commentare des Çaṅkara aus dem Sanskrit übersetzt.* Leipzig: F.A. Brockhaus. (Reprint: Hildesheim: Georg Olms Verlag.)

DEVASTHALI, G. V. 1952. Śaṅkarācārya's indebtedness to Mīmāṃsā. *Journal of the Oriental Institute (Baroda)* 1: 23-30.

DIVANJI, P. C. 1940. Gauḍapāda's asparśayoga and Śaṃkara's jñānavāda. *Poona Orientalist* 4.4: 149-158.

DONIGER, Wendy & Brian K. SMITH (transl.) 1991. *The Laws of Manu.* Harmondsworth: Penguin.

D'SA, Francis X. 1985. *Word-Index to Śaṅkara's Gītābhāṣya.* (Linguistic Aids for the Study of Indian Religious Texts, 1.) Pune: Institute for the Study of Religion.

FRAUWALLNER, Erich 1968. *Materialien zur ältesten Erkenntnislehre der Karmamīmāṃsā.* (SB ÖAW, 259.2; VKSKSO, 6.) Wien: Österreichische Akademie der Wissenschaften.

—— 1992. *Nachgelassene Werke II: Philosophische Texte des Hinduismus.* Hrsg. Gerhard Oberhammer und Chlodwig H. Werba. (SB ÖAW, 588; VKSKS, 26.) Wien: Verlag der Österreichischen Akademie der Wissenschaften.

GAMBHIRANANDA, Swami (transl.) 1972. *Brahma-Sūtra-Bhāṣya of Śrī Śaṅkarācārya.* Second edition. Calcutta: Advaita Ashrama.

GONDA, Jan 1985. *Les religions de l'Inde,* II: *L'hindouisme récent.* Traduit de l'allemand par L. Jospin. Paris: Payot. (French translation of *Die Religionen Indiens,* II: *Der jüngere Hinduismus.* Stuttgart: W. Kohlhammer, 1963.)

HACKER, Paul 1947. Śaṅkarācārya and Śaṅkarabhagavatpāda. Preliminary remarks concerning the authorship problem. *New Indian Antiquary* 9: 175-186. Corrected version in: Lambert Schmithausen (ed.), *Kleine Schriften*: 41-58. Wiesbaden: Franz Steiner, 1978. (Reprinted: Halbfass 1995: 41-56). [References are to the corrected version in *Kl. Schr.*]

—— 1949. *Upadeśasāhasrī, Unterweisung in der All-Einheits-Lehre der Inder von Meister Shankara, Ĝadyaprabandha oder das Buch in Prosa,* aus dem Sanskrit übersetzt und erläutert. Bonn: Ludwig Röhrscheid.

—— 1951. *Untersuchungen über Texte des frühen Advaitavāda. I. Die Schüler Śaṅkaras.* (Abhandlungen der Akademie der Wissenschaften und der Literatur, Mainz, Geistes- und Sozialwissenschaftliche Klasse, 1950.26.) Mainz: Akademie der Wissenschaften und der Literatur; in Kommission bei Franz Steiner, Wiesbaden.

—— 1968. Śaṅkara der Yogin und Śaṅkara der Advaitin: einige Beobachtungen. In: *Beiträge zur Geistesgeschichte Indiens, Festschrift für Erich Frauwallner* (WZKSO, 12-13 [1968-69]): 119-148. (Reprint: Lambert Schmithausen (ed.), *Kleine Schriften*: 213-242. Wiesbaden: Franz Steiner, 1978.) (English translation: Halbfass 1995: 101-134.)

HALBFASS, Wilhelm 1980. Karma, *apūrva*, and 'natural' causes: observations on the growths and limits of the theory of *saṃsāra*. In: Wendy Doniger O'Flaherty (ed.), *Karma and Rebirth in Classical Indian Traditions*: 268-302. Berkeley: University of California Press.

—— 1983. *Studies in Kumārila and Śaṅkara*. (Studien zur Indologie und Iranistik, Monographie 9.) Reinbek: Inge Wezler.

—— 1991. *Tradition and Reflection. Explorations in Indian Thought*. Albany: State University of New York Press.

—— 1995. *Philology and Confrontation. Paul Hacker on Traditional and Modern Vedānta*. Albany: State University of New York Press.

HANNEDER, J. 2003. Review of Bouy 2000. *Indo-Iranian Journal* 46.2, 161-165.

HEESTERMAN, J. C. 2003. Opfer, Transzendenz und Dharma in der Sicht der Mīmāṃsā. In: Gerhard Oberhammer & Marcus Schmücker (Hrsg.), *Mythisierung der Transzendenz als Entwurf ihrer Erfahrung*. (SB ÖAW, 706; Beiträge zur Kultur- und Geistesgeschichte Asiens, 41): 281-298. Wien: Verlag der Österreichischen Akademie der Wissenschaften.

HIRIYANNA, J. 1925. See under Sureśvara: *Naiṣkarmyasiddhi*.

HOHENBERGER, A. (transl.) 1964. *Rāmānuja's Vedāntadīpa. Seine Kurzauslegung der Brahmasūtren des Bādarāyaṇa*. (Bonner Orientalistische Studien, N.S. 14.) Bonn: Selbstverlag des Orientalischen Seminars der Universität.

HONDA, Megumu 1993. Index to the Ślokavārttika. *Dōhō Daigaku Kiyō* 7: 148-33 (= (1)-(116)).

HOPKINS, E. Washburn 1901. *The Great Epic of India. Its Character and Origin*. New York: Schribner. (Reprint: Calcutta: Punthi Pustak, 1978.)

HORSCH, Paul 1966. *Die vedische Gāthā- und Śloka-Literatur*. Bern: Francke.

HOUBEN, Jan E. M. 1995. *The Saṃbandha-Samuddeśa (Chapter on Relation) and Bhartṛhari's Philosophy of Language*. (Gonda Indological Studies, 2.) Groningen: Egbert Forsten.

HULIN, Michel 2001. *Śaṅkara et la non-dualité*. Paris: Bayard.

INGALLS, Daniel H. H. 1952. The study of Śaṃkarācārya. *ABORI* 33: 1-14.

INGALLS, Daniel H. H. 1954. Śaṃkara's arguments against the Buddhists. *Philosophy East and West* 3: 291-306.

JACOBI, Hermann 1911. The dates of the philosophical Sūtras of the Brahmans. *Journal of the American Oriental Society* 31: 1-29 (Reprint: *Kl. Schr.* [1970], II: 559-587).

JHA, Ganganath (ed. & transl.) 1920-39. *Manusmṛti, with the 'Manubhāṣya' of Medhātithi*, I-X. Second edition. Delhi: Motilal Banarsidass, 1999.

—— (transl.) 1933. *Śābara-Bhāṣya*, I-III. (GOS, 66, 70, 73.) Baroda: Oriental Institute. (Reprint: 1973-74.)

JOHNSTON, E. H. 1936. *Aśvaghoṣa's Buddhacarita or Acts of the Buddha.* Sanskrit text of Cantos I-XIV with English translation of Cantos I-XXVIII. Calcutta: Baptist Mission Press. (New enlarged edition: Delhi Motilal Banarsidass, 1984.)

KANE, Pandurang Vaman 1960. Pūrvamīmāṃsāsūtra, Brahmasūtra, Jaimini, Vyāsa and Bādarāyaṇa. *Bulletin of the Deccan College Research Institute* 20.1-4: 119-139.

—— 1977. *History of Dharmaśāstra*, V.2. (Government Oriental Series B, 6.) Second edition. Poona: BORI. [First edition: 1962.]

KEITH, A. Berriedale 1920 [?; the preface is signed 1928]. *A History of Sanskrit Literature.* Oxford: Oxford University Press.

KING, Richard 1992. Asparśa-yoga: meditation and epistemology in the Gauḍapādīya-kārikā. *JIP* 20: 89-131.

—— 1995. Early Advaita Vedānta: the date and authorship of the Gauḍapādīyakārikā. *Indo-Iranian Journal* 38: 317-355.

KRISHNA, Daya 2001. *New Perspectives in Indian Philosophy*. Jaipu: Rawat Publications.

LAMOTTE, Étienne 1929. *Notes sur la Bhagavadgītā*. Paris: Paul Geuthner.

LINDTNER, Christian 1999. Bhavya on Mīmāṃsā, Mīmāṃsātattvanirṇayāvatāraḥ, with English translation. *Adyar Library Bulletin* 1999: 245-302.

—— (ed.) 2001. *Madhyamakahṛdayam of Bhavya*. Adyar: The Adyar Library and Research Centre, The Theosophical Society.

MAHADEVAN, T. M. P. 1952. *Gauḍapāda: A Study in Early Advaita*. Madras: University of Madras.

—— (ed.) 1971-73. *Word Index to the Brahma-Sūtra-Bhāṣya of Śaṅkara*, I-II. (Madras University Philosophical Series, 17.) Madras: Centre of Advanced Study in Philosophy, University of Madras.

MATSUMOTO, Shokei 2003. *A Study of Rāmānuja's Vedārthasaṃgrahaḥ*, I: *Sanskrit text*; II: *Japanese translation*; III: *Studies*. (Acta Indologica, 8.) Chiba-ken: Naritasan Shinshoji.

MAXIMILIEN, Guy 1975. *Sureśvara, La démonstration du non-agir (Naiṣkarmyasiddhi).* Introduction et traduction. (Publications de l'Institut de Civilisation Indienne, série in-8°, 37.) Paris: Institut de civilisation indienne / E. de Boccard.

MAYEDA, Sengaku 1965. The authenticity of the Upadeśasāhasrī ascribed to Śaṅkara. *Journal of the American Oriental Society* 85: 178-196.

—— 1968a. On the author of the Māṇḍūkyopaniṣad- and the Gauḍapādīya-bhāṣya. In: *V. Raghavan Felicitation Volume* (Adyar Library Bulletin 31-32 [1967-68]): 73-94.

—— 1968b. The advaita theory of perception. In: *Beiträge zur Geistesgeschichte Indiens, Festschrift für Erich Frauwallner* (WZKSO, 12-13 [1968-69]): 221-239.

—— (ed.) 1973. *Śaṅkara's Upadeśasāhasrī.* Critically edited with introduction and indices. Tokyo: Hokuseido Press.

—— 1979. *A Thousand Teachings. The Upadeśasāhasrī of Śaṅkara.* Tokyo: Tokyo University Press. (Reprint: Albany: State University of New York Press, 1992.)

MESQUITA, Roque 1971. *Das Problem der Gotteserkenntnis bei Yāmunamuni.* Dissertation zur Erlangung des Doktorgrades an der philosophischen Fakultät der Universität Wien. Wien.

—— 1973. Yāmunamuni: Leben, Datierung und Werke. *WZKS* 17: 177-193.

—— 1974. Recent research on Yāmuna. *WZKS* 18: 183-208.

—— 1979. Zur Vedānta- und Pāñcarātra-Tradition Nāthamunis. *WZKS* 23: 163-193.

—— 1980. Yāmuna's Vedānta and Pāñcarātra: a review. *WZKS* 24: 199-224.

—— 1984. Rāmānujas Quellen im Mahāpūrvapakṣa und Mahāsiddhānta des Śrībhāṣya. *WZKS* 28: 179-222.

—— 1988. *Yāmunācāryas Saṃvitsiddhi: Kritische Edition, Übersetzung und Anmerkungen.* Mit einem Rekonstruktionsversuch der verlorenen Abschnitte. (SB ÖAW, 504; VKSKS, 21.) Wien: Verlag der Österreichischen Akademie der Wissenschaften.

—— 1990. *Yāmunācāryas Philosophie der Erkenntnis: Eine Studie zu seiner Saṃvitsiddhi.* (SB ÖAW, 563; VKSKS, 24.) Wien: Verlag der Österreichischen Akademie der Wissenschaften.

—— 1994. Die Idee der Erlösung bei Kumārilabhaṭṭa. In: R. Mesquita & C. H. Verba (Hrsg.), *Orbis indicus – Festschrift für Gerhard Oberhammer zum 65 Geburtsdag* (WZKS 38): 451-484.

MĪMĀṂSAKA, Yudhiṣṭhira 1987. *Mīmāṃsā-Śābara-Bhāṣya [prathamo bhāgaḥ], śāstrāvatāra-vedaśrutyāmnāyasaṃjñāmīmāṃsā-śrautayajña-mīmāṃsā''khyais tribhir nibandhair yuktaḥ, vividhaprakārakaiṣ ṭippa-*

ṇībhir vividhapariśiṣṭaiś ca samalaṃkṛtaḥ. Bahālagadha: Ramlal Kapur Trust.

Mīmāṃsākoṣa, I-VII. Ed. by Kevalānandasaraswatī. Wai: Prajna Pathashala Mandal, 1952-66.

MODI, P. M. 1943?. *A Critique of the Brahmasūtra (III.2.11–IV). With Special Reference to Śaṅkarācārya's Commentary*, I: *Interpretation of the Sūtras (III.2.11–IV)*. Bhavnagar, n.d.

MOGHE, S. G. 1984. Śaṅkarācārya and Pūrva-Mīmāṃsā. In: *Studies in the Pūrva Mīmāṃsā*: 1-13. Delhi: Ajanta Publications.

MURTY, K. Satchidananda 1959. *Revelation and Reason in Advaita Vedānta*. London: Asia Publishing House – Waltair: Andhra University – New York: Columbia University Press. (Reprint: 1961.)

NAKAMURA, Hajime 1955. Upaniṣadic tradition and the early school of Vedānta as noticed in Buddhist scripture. *Harvard Journal of Asiatic Studies* 18: 74-104.

—— 1983. *A History of Early Vedānta Philosophy*, I. Translated into English by Trevor Leggett et al. (Religions of Asia Series, 1.) Delhi: Motilal Banarsidass.

NEEVEL, Walter G. 1977. *Yāmuna's Vedānta and Pāñcarātra. Integrating the Classical and the Popular*. (Harvard Theological Review, Harvard Dissertations in Religion, 10.) Missoula, Montana: Scholars Press.

NICHOLSON, Hugh 2003. Apologetics and philosophy in Maṇḍana Miśra's Brahmasiddhi. *JIP* 30 (2002): 575-596.

OBERHAMMER, Gerhard 1971. *Yāmunamunis Interpretation von Brahmasūtram 2, 2, 42-45. Eine Untersuchung zur Pāñcarātra-Tradition der Rāmānuja-Schule*. (SB ÖAW, 274.4; VKSKS, 10.) Wien: Hermann Böhlaus.

—— 1997. *Materialien zur Geschichte der Rāmānuja-Schule*, III: *Yādavaprakāśa, der vergessene Lehrer Rāmānujas*. (SB ÖAW, 646; VKSKS, 29.) Wien: Verlag der Österreichischen Akademie der Wissenschaften.

OLIVELLE, Patrick 1992. *Saṃnyāsa Upaniṣads. Hindu Scriptures on Asceticism and Renunciation*. New York: Oxford University Press.

—— 1998. *The Early Upaniṣads*. Annotated text and translation. New York: Oxford University Press.

PANDE, Govind Chandra 1994. *Life and Thought of Śaṅkarācārya*. Delhi: Motilal Banarsidass.

PANSIKAR, Vasudeva Laxmana Sharma (ed.) 1918. *The Yogavāsiṣṭha of Valmīki, with the Commentary Vāsiṣṭhamahārāmāyaṇatātparyaprakāśa*, I-II. (Reprint of the Third Edition: Delhi: Motilal Banarsidass, 1984.)

PARPOLA, Asko 1981. On the formation of the Mīmāṃsā and the problems concerning Jaimini, with particular reference to the teacher quotations and the Vedic schools. *WZKS* 25: 145-177.

—— 1994. On the formation of the Mīmāṃsā and the problems concerning Jaimini, with particular reference to the teacher quotations and the Vedic schools (Part II). *WZKS* 38: 293-308.

QVARNSTRÖM, Olle 1989. *Hindu Philosophy in Buddhist Perspective. The Vedāntatattvaviniścaya Chapter of Bhavya's Madhyamakahṛdayakārikā.* (Lund Studies in African and Asian Religions, 4.) Lund: Plus Ultra.

—— 2003. Early Vedānta philosophy preserved by the Jain tradition: The Vedavādadvātriṃśikā of Siddhasena Divākara. In: Olle Qvarnström (ed.), *Jainism and Early Buddhism: Essays in Honor of Padmanabh S. Jaini*: 575-593. Fremont, California: Asian Humanities Press.

RAGHAVAN, V. 1967. The Upadeśasāhasrī of Śaṃkarācārya and the mutual chronology of Śaṃkarācārya and Bhāskara. *WZKSO* 11: 137-140.

RĀJAVĀḌE, Vaijanātha Kāśīnātha (ed.) 1921. *Durgācāryakṛtavṛttisametam Niruktam. Pūrvaṣaṭkātmakaḥ prathamo bhāgaḥ.* (ĀSS, 88.) Poona: Ānandāśrama.

RAMACHANDRUDU, P. 1989. Śaṅkara and Pūrvamīmāṃsā. In: R. Balasubramanian & Sibajiban Bhattacharyya (eds.), *Perspectives of Śaṅkara. Rashtriya Śaṅkara Jayanti Mahotsava Commemoration Volume*: 233-240. Government of India: Department of Culture, Ministry of Human Resource Development.

RAMBACHAN, Anantanand 1997. Where words can set free. The liberating potency of Vedic words in the hermeneutics of Śaṅkara. In: Jeffrey R. Timm (ed.), *Texts in Context. Traditional Hermeneutics in South Asia*: 33-46. Delhi: Sri Satguru Publications.

RENOU, Louis 1942. Les connexions entre le rituel et la grammaire en sanskrit. *Journal Asiatique* 233 (1941-42): 105-165. (Reprints: Staal 1972: 435-469; Renou 1997, I: 311-371.)

—— 1957. Grammaire et Vedānta. *Journal Asiatique* 245: 121-133. (= Staal 1972: 470-478; Renou 1997, I: 407-419.)

—— 1961. Sur la forme de quelques textes sanskrits. *Journal Asiatique* 249: 163-211. (= Renou 1997, II: 519-567.)

—— 1962. Sur la forme des Brahmasūtra. In: Ernest Bender (ed.), *Indological Studies in Honor of W. Norman Brown* (American Oriental Series, 47): 195-203. New Haven, Connecticut: American Oriental Society. (= Renou 1997, II: 621-629.)

—— 1997. *Choix d'études indiennes*, I-II. Réunies par Nalini Balbir et Georges-Jean Pinault. (Réimpressions, n° 9.) Paris: Presses de l'Ecole française d'Extrême-Orient.

RÜPING, Klaus 1977. *Studien zur Frühgeschichte der Vedānta-Philosophie*, I: *Philologische Untersuchungen zu den Brahmasūtra-Kommentaren des Śaṅkara und des Bhāskara*. (Alt- und Neu-Indische Studien, 17.) Stuttgart: Franz Steiner.

SARUP, Lakshman 1921. *The Nighaṇṭu and the Nirukta*. Introduction, English translation and notes. Delhi: Motilal Banarsidass. 1966.

SAWAI, Yoshitsugu 1986. Śaṅkara's theory of saṃnyāsa. *JIP* 14: 371-387.

—— 1993. Rāmānuja's theory of karman. *JIP* 21: 11-29.

SCHREINER, Peter 1991. *Bhagavad-Gita: Wege und Weisungen*. Übersetzt und eingeleitet. Zürich: Benziger.

SHARMA, B. N. K. 1981. *History of the Dvaita School of Vedānta and its Literature*. Second revised edition. Delhi: Motilal Banarsidass.

SHERIDAN, Daniel P. 1986. *The Advaitic Theism of the Bhāgavata Purāṇa*. Delhi: Motilal Banarsidass.

SLAJE, Walter (ed.) 1993. *Bhāskarakaṇṭhas Mokṣopāya-Ṭīkā. Ein Kommentar in der Tradition der kaschmirischen Yogavāsiṣṭha-Überlieferung. 2. Prakaraṇa (Mumukṣuvyavahāra)*. (Materialien für eine kritische Ausgabe des Mokṣopāya, 1.) Graz: Leykam.

—— 1994a. *Vom Mokṣopāya-Śāstra zum Yogavāsiṣṭha-Mahārāmāyaṇa. Philologische Untersuchungen zur Entwicklungs- und Überlieferungsgeschichte eines indischen Lehrwerks mit Anspruch auf Heilsrelevanz*. (SB ÖAW, 609.) Wien: Österreichische Akademie der Wissenschaften.

—— 1994b. Die Angst der Yogis vor der Versenkung. *WZKS* 38: 273-291.

—— 1995. *Bhāskarakaṇṭhas Mokṣopāya-Ṭīkā. Ein Kommentar in der Tradition der kaschmirischen Yogavāsiṣṭha-Überlieferung. Die Fragmente des 3. (Utpatti-) Prakaraṇa*. (Materialien für eine kritische Ausgabe des Mokṣopāya, 2.) Graz: EWS-Fachverlag.

—— 1996. *Bhāskarakaṇṭhas Mokṣopāya-Ṭīkā. Ein Kommentar in der Tradition der kaschmirischen Yogavāsiṣṭha-Überlieferung. 1. (Vairāgya-) Prakaraṇa*. (Materialien für eine kritische Ausgabe des Mokṣopāya, 3.) Unter Mitarbeit von Jutta Valent ausgegeben. Graz: EWS-Fachverlag.

——, this volume. Yājñavalkya-brāhmaṇas and the early Mīmāṃsā.

SPROCKHOFF, Joachim Friedrich 1976. *Saṃnyāsa. Quellenstudien zur Askese im Hinduismus*, I: *Untersuchungen über die Saṃnyāsa-Upaniṣads*. (Abhandlungen für die Kunde des Morgenlandes, 42.1.) Wiesbaden: Franz Steiner.

STAAL, J. F. (ed.) 1972. *A Reader on the Sanskrit Grammarians*. Cambridge, Mass.: MIT Press. (Reprint: Delhi: Motilal Banarsidass, 1985.)

STEPHAN, Peter 2002. *Erlösung im Spannungsfeld von aktivem Leben und Entsagung. Eine Studie zu Śaṅkaras Exegese der Bhagavadgītā*. (Geisteskultur Indiens, Texte und Studien, 3; Indologica Halensis.) Aachen: Shaker Verlag.

SUBRAHMANYA Sastri, A. (ed.) 1961. *Prakaraṇa Pañcikā of Sri Śālikanātha Miśra with Nyāya-Siddhi.* Edited with introduction and notes. (Banaras Hindu University Darśana Series, 4.) Banaras Hindu University.

TABER, John 1983. *Transformative Philosophy. A study of Śaṅkara, Fichte, and Heidegger.* Honolulu: University of Hawaii Press.

——, this volume. Kumārila and Śaṅkara on liberation.

THIBAUT, George (transl.) 1890-96. *Vedânta-Sûtras with the Commentary by Śaṅkarācārya,* I-II. (The Sacred Books of the East, 34 & 38.) Oxford: Clarendon Press. (Reprint: Delhi: Motilal Banarsidass, 1973.)

THRASHER, Allen Wright 1979. The dates of Maṇḍana Miśra and Śaṃkara. *WZKS* 23: 117-139.

—— 1993. *The Advaita-Vedānta of Brahma-siddhi.* Delhi: Motilal Banarsidass.

UNGEMACH, Anton 1996. Die vier Hauptschüler Śaṅkaras in den Śaṅkara-Legenden. In: Dieter B. Kapp (Hrsg.), *Nānāvidhaikatā. Festschrift für Hermann Berger* (Beiträge zur Kenntnis südasiatischer Sprachen und Literaturen, 4): 292-310. Wiesbaden: Harrassowitz.

VAN BUITENEN, J. A. B. 1956. *Rāmānuja's Vedārthasaṃgraha.* Introduction, critical edition and annotated translation. Poona: Deccan College. (Deccan College Monograph Series, 16.)

—— 1961. The relative dates of Śaṃkara and Bhāskara. *Adyar Library Bulletin* 25: 268-273. (Reprint: van Buitenen 1988: 187-190.)

—— 1988. *Studies in Indian Literature and Philosophy: Collected Articles.* Edited by Ludo Rocher. Delhi: Motilal Banarsidass.

VENKATARAMIAH, D. (transl.) 1948. *The Pañcapādikā of Padmapāda (Translated into English).* (GOS, 107.) Baroda: Oriental Institute.

VETTER, Tilmann 1969a. *Maṇḍanamiśra's Brahmasiddhiḥ, Brahmakāṇḍa.* Übersetzung, Einleitung und Anmerkungen. (SB ÖAW 262.2.) Wien: Österreichische Akademie der Wissenschaften.

—— 1969b. Zur Bedeutung des Illusionismus bei Śaṅkara. In: *Beiträge zur Geistesgeschichte Indiens, Festschrift für Erich Frauwallner* (WZKSO, 12-13 [1968-69]): 407-423.

—— 1978a. Die Gauḍapādīya-Kārikās: zur Entstehung und zur Bedeutung von (A)dvaita. *WZKS* 22: 95-131.

—— 1978b. Erfahrung des Unerfahrbaren bei Śaṅkara. In: Gerhard Oberhammer (Hrsg.), *Transzendenzerfahrung, Vollzugshorizont des Heils. Das Problem in indischer und christlicher Tradition.* (Publications of the De Nobili Research Library, 5): 45-59. Vienna: Institute for Indology, Vienna University.

VETTER, Tilmann 1979. *Studien zur Lehre und Entwicklung Śaṅkaras*. (Publications of the De Nobili Research Library, 6.) Vienna: Institute for Indology, Vienna University.

VISHVA BANDHU (ed.), 1955-65. *A Vedic Word Concordance*, I-V. Hoshiarpur: V.V.R. Institute.

WITZEL, Michael 1982. Materialien zu den vedischen Schulen, 1: Über die Caraka-Śākhā. *Studien zur Indologie und Iranistik* 8/9: 171-240.

—— 1985. Regionale und überregionale Faktoren in der Entwicklung vedischer Brahmanengruppen im Mittelalter (Materialien zu den vedischen Schulen, 5). In: Hermann Kulke & Dietmar Rothermund (Hrsg.), *Regionale Tradition in Südasien*: 37-76 (Beiträge zur Südasienforschung, Südasien-Institut, Universität Heidelberg, 104.) Wiesbaden: Franz Steiner.

WOOD, Thomas E. 1990. *The Māṇḍūkya Upaniṣad and the Āgama Śāstra. An Investigation into the Meaning of the Vedānta.* (Society for Asian and Comparative Philosophy, Monograph no. 8.) Honolulu: University of Hawaii Press.

YOSHIMIZU, Kiyotaka 1997. *Der ,Organismus' des urheberlosen Veda*. (Publications of the De Nobili Research Library, 25.) Vienna: Institute for South Asian, Tibetan and Buddhist Studies, Vienna University.

——, this volume. Kumārila's reevaluation of the sacrifice and the Veda from a Vedānta perspective

Debates about the Object of Perception in the Traditions of Advaita and Viśiṣṭādvaita Vedānta

MARCUS SCHMÜCKER

I

In the tradition of Advaita and Viśiṣṭādvaita Vedānta disparate views on the highest Being were long disputed. The divergence of their views is reflected, among others, in the contrasting teachings about perception (*pratyakṣa*). In this article a part of their controversy and its historical development will be given as follows: I shall begin with Maṇḍana Miśra's (7th century) attempt to avoid the contradiction between two means of valid cognition, i.e. perception and the meaning of Brahman in the 'great utterances' (*mahāvākya*) of the Upaniṣads. In the Tarkakāṇḍa of the *Brahmasiddhi*, he develops his position mainly in confrontation with an opponent who identifies an existing entity (*vastu*), i.e. the object of perception, with the particular (*viśeṣa*). In contrast Maṇḍana identifies an existing entity (*vastu*) with a universal (*sāmānya*) 'beingness' or as he expresses it, with 'mere being' (*sanmātra*). One can pursue these thoughts of Maṇḍana by looking at some of the earliest criticism thereof, beginning with that of Śālikanātha (9th century). He refers to Maṇḍana's as well as to Maṇḍana's opponents views about the object of perception and rejects both: neither the particular (*viśeṣa*) nor the universal (*sāmānya*) <u>alone</u> are verifiable by perception. In Śālikanātha's view, universal and particular are connected to each other (*parasparasaṃbaddha*) and therefore two entities (*dve vastunī*) are perceived in every perception. The first Advaitic response to Śālikanātha's criticism came from Ānandabodha (11th century) in his *Nyāyamakaranda*, who defended Maṇḍana's thoughts against Śālikanātha's attack. The debate between Advaita Vedānta and Pūrva Mīmāṃsā is repeated along these general lines by an exponent of the Viśiṣṭādvaitic tradition of the Rāmānuja School, Meghanādārisūri (13th century), in a chapter called the Vākyārthapradīpa in his *Nayadyumaṇi*. Meghanādārisūri reproduces the position of Maṇḍana at some length and repeats Śālikanātha's criticism to refute Maṇḍana's view. Finally he presents his own theory about the object of perception. For him, an entity (*vastu*) is only perceptible if it is qualified (*viśiṣṭa*) by a universal and a particular. I will conclude this paper by presenting Meghanādārisūri's reason for this position. His different concept of perception seems to be an alternative to the positions outlined before and is based on a different understanding of the absolute Being. He defines Brahman as qualified (*viśiṣṭa*) by the universe, i.e. by every mental/conscious (*cit/cetana*) and inanimate (*acit/acetana*) entity.

II

What are Maṇḍana's reasons for arguing that perception can only perceive 'mere being' (*sanmātra*)? The context in which he develops his argument is the following: The Advaitic understanding of the authoritative scriptures restricts the meaning of the Veda as pointing only to Brahman as the One without a second. Maṇḍana now argues that our valid means of cognition do not contradict the non-duality of Brahman as declared in the great utterances (*mahāvākya*) of the Veda, because perception has 'mere being' as its object. He demonstrates this fact by bringing forward logical arguments (see BS 39.1 ff) stating that even in our habitual and ordinary use of perception we do not initially perceive the diversity of objects, but rather 'mere being' (*sanmātra*). This 'mere being' is also called *vastumātra* (BS 49.24) or *arthamātra* (BS 58.23). However, in the second act of knowledge, called mental construction (*vikalpabuddhi*) (see BS 71.1-2) by Maṇḍana, a difference (*bheda*) is recognized, caused by a delimitation (*vyavaccheda*) and brought about by beginningless nescience (*anādyavidyā*) (see BS 48.14): Due to this influence of nescience on perception there may be a contradiction between perception and the Veda. While perception seems to know difference by Avidyā the Veda declares non-difference (*abheda*) for Brahman. To avoid any conflict Maṇḍana argues that difference (*bheda*) cannot be an object of perception, but only 'mere being' (*sanmātra*). An important passage in the Tarkakāṇḍa of his *Brahmasiddhi*, in which Maṇḍana unfolds[1] his central thesis, refers to the doctrine of his main opponent.[2] The opponent teaches the opposite of Maṇḍana's concept of the object of perception: only particulars (*viśeṣa*) are the object of perception and every universal (*sāmānya*) is known by a second knowledge and is therefore unreal. For this opponent – to whom he gives the name *ātyantikabhedavādin* – only particulars are called the real object of perception. All knowledge of universals lies in the realm of the conceptual construction (*kalpanājñānagocara*). Because the sentence structure of Maṇḍana's and his opponent's view is parallel, one can compare them to each other and see which important words are changed by Maṇḍana.

---

[1] In BS 60.10-18 Maṇḍana presents four views. He attributes the first view to the *saṃsargavādins*: *jñānabhedāt sāmānyavyaktibhāgena vastudvayam* (Biardeau 1969: 221, n. 1 comments on this view: "Cependent, il est difficile de reconnaître les Vaiśeṣika dans ces *saṃsargavādin* qui opposent *sāmānya* et *vyakti*, alors que les Vaiśeṣika opposent *sāmānya* et *viśeṣa* comme déterminants de la substance – *dravya* – et n'accordent *sattā* qu'à *dravya* parmi ces trois éléments. Mais l'inexactitude vient sans doute de l'angle particulier et inhabituel sous lequel est envisagé ici le système de Kaṇāda. D'ailleurs, comme la suite du texte le montre, Maṇḍana ne semble pas faire de distinction entre *viśeṣa* et *vyakti*"). Maṇḍana attributes the second view to the Jainas (*anekāntavādin*) and says: *ekaṃ vā sāmānyaviśeṣātmakaṃ vastu*. The third and fourth views are given here.

[2] Various secondary sources have identified this opponent as Dharmakīrti. See Vetter 1964: 96-98; Schmithausen 1963: 245-246; Thrasher 1993: 54-56.

Opponent (BS 60.12-15):	Maṇḍana (BS 60.15-17):
viśeṣā eva vā vastūni. *teṣām ātyantikabhedaniścayāsāmar-thyāt tadupādānas tadviṣaya evābhedaḥ kalpanājñānagocaraḥ.* *dṛṣṭā hi bhinneṣv abhedakalpanā vanam iti yathāhur ātyantikabheda-vādinaḥ.*	*abhedo vā paramārthaḥ.* *tasyānavacchinnasyānantasya tathā niścetum aśakter anāditvāc cāvidyāyās tadupādānās tadviṣayās bhedaparikalpanāḥ.* *dṛṣṭā hi taraṅgabhedād abhinne candramasi bhedakalpanā.*
Or [an alternative explanation to the views given is:] entities are only particulars. Because it is not possible to determine the absolute difference of these (particulars), the non-difference, which has these as support, whose object are these (particulars) lies in the realm of conceptual construction. For, in respect to different things we do observe the conceptual construction of non-difference [namely] in the use of the word 'forest' [in respect to different trees]. So say those who teach an absolute particular.	Or [an alternative explanation to the opponent's view is:] Non-difference is the highest reality. Because this [non-difference], which is unseparated and without limitation, cannot be determined as such and because nescience is beginningless, the conceptual constructions of difference, have this (*abheda*) as their support, and this (*abheda*) as their object. For we observe the conceptual construction of difference in respect to something that is undifferentiated, [namely] the moon [when it appears as differentiated] because of differences in the waves.

Countering the view of his opponent and demonstrating his own opinion, Maṇḍana transposes the terms referring to the objects of perception and the subsequent knowledge. In the above-quoted passage we can observe how Maṇḍana substitutes 'mere being' (*sanmātra*), called here non-difference (*abheda*), for the particulars (*viśeṣa*) that are the first (and only) object of perception for the *ātyantikabhedavādin*. For the latter, perception cognizes no particular in the first moment of its function. Like his opponent, Maṇḍana maintains the distinction between non-conceptual perception and conceptual knowledge, but he switches exactly that upon which the perception aligns itself in the first moment of its function (*vyāpāra*). Thus, we can compare Maṇḍana's substitutions of his opponent's terms word by word:

Opponent (BS 60.12-15):	Maṇḍana (BS 60.15-17):
viśeṣāḥ	*abhedaḥ*
vastūni	*paramārthaḥ*
teṣām (viśeṣāṇām)	*tasya (abhedasya)*
ātyantikabheda-	*(tasya) anavacchinnasya anantasya*
tad(bheda)upādānaḥ	*tad(abheda)upādānāḥ*
tad(bheda)viṣayaḥ	*tad(abheda)viṣayā*
abhedaḥ kalpanājñānagocaraḥ	*bhedaparikalpanāḥ*
abhedakalpanā	*bhedakalpanā*

Just as only particulars were known in the first moment of perception for Maṇḍana's opponent, in Maṇḍana's own view no particularity is knowable, because for him ignorance causes the unreal construction of particulars. Therefore, Maṇḍana says that by virtue of nescience we see something as different that in reality is not different, but rather one (*eka*) and undivided, as for example the moon that is one, but seems to be manifold if it is reflected in the waves.[3] Thus, it is logically proven for Maṇḍana that it is not possible to perceive a particular object in the first moment, i.e. to have knowledge of difference and subsequently knowledge of non-difference. From this fact he concludes that only beingness of something perceived can be perception's first and only object. For him, beingness or 'mere being' is an entity in itself, and different from the individual existence of each particular.[4] It is on this

[3] For further explanations of the example of the moon in contrast to the unreal perception of the particulars, see BS 72.17.

[4] It also differs therefore from the Vaiśeṣika's concept of "being", see Halbfass 1975: 197, n. 71: "How the 'facticity' and 'positivity' implied in the perception of the actual thing (*dravya*) qua *viśeṣya* has to be related to the apprehension of *sattā* qua *viśeṣaṇa* is a question which does not really become thematic in Vaiśeṣika; and there is nothing like the Vedānta attempt to equate what is given to indeterminate perception with 'pure being'." In another article Halbfass (1976: 159, n. 61) even mentions Maṇḍana's concept of *sanmātra* and, contrasting it to Praśastapāda's concept of "being" he says: "In der Tat wäre es in Praśastapādas System ganz unzulässig, eine Erkenntnis dadurch als unbestimmt zu kennzeichnen, daß man ihr die 'Substanz allein', d.h. den bloßen Bestimmungsträger, als Inhalt zuweist."

account that Maṇḍana characterizes perception's function as an affirmation (*vidhi*) and not as a delimitation (*vyavaccheda*) in which every other possibility for the perception is eliminated. In BS 44.10-18 he states three alternatives, of which only the first contains no presupposition of difference (*bheda*):

> **(1)** *vastusvarūpavidhiḥ,* **(2)** *vastvantarasya vyavacchedaḥ,* **(3)** *ubhayaṃ veti. ubhayasminn api traividhyam.* **(3a)** *yaugapadyam,* **(3b)** *vyavacchedapūrvako vidhiḥ,* **(3c)** *vidhipūrvako vyavaccheda iti. tatra vastvantaravyavacchede ubhayasmin vā bhedaḥ pratyakṣagocara iti bhavati virodhaḥ. svarūpavidhimātre tu kasya cid vyavacchedena śūnye na bhedaḥ pramāṇārthaḥ, na hi vyavacchedād ṛte bhedasiddhiḥ vidhimātravyāpāraṃ ca pratyakṣam.*

> [perception functions as] **(1)** the affirmation of the proper form of an entity, **(2)** as the delimitation from another thing, or **(3)** as both [at the same time]. The last case results in three alternatives: **(3a)** simultaneity, **(3b)** the affirmation preceded by the delimitation, **(3c)** the delimitation preceded by the affirmation. Among these [alternatives], in the case of delimitation from another object or in the case of both the difference lies in the realm of perception. Thus, a contradiction arises [with your own position]. In the case of a mere affirmation of the proper form without delimitation from something the difference is not an object of a means of valid cognition. For, without delimitation no difference is established and perception consists in the function of mere affirmation.

III

The concept of perception as an affirmation (*vidhi*) of 'mere being' (*sanmātra/vastumātra*) without any relation to any concrete particular entity was provoking and therefore criticised, first of all by Śālikanātha. He objects to the idea that perception cognise 'mere being' (*sanmātra*) as a universal (*sāmānya*), and in his reply argues that beingness (*sattā*) cannot be known independently of word-referents (*padārtha*). He unfolds his concept of the object of perception in opposition to the two positions mentioned above. First he counters the assumption of mere beingness as Maṇḍana claimed it. Śālikanātha interprets this to be the great universal (*mahāsāmānya*).

It exists without any relation to a real particular (*viśeṣa*). Secondly he unfolds his concept in opposition to the thesis that the particular (*viśeṣa*) exists without the universal, as was the case for the *ātyantikabhedavādin*. That upon which the perception aligns itself in its first moment is also substituted by Śālikanātha. Rethinking both extremes – Maṇḍana's and the *ātyantikabhedavādin*'s object of perception – he says in his *Pramāṇaparāyaṇa* (PrP 162.1-2):

> *tasya (svarūpamātragrahaṇasya) na svalakṣaṇamātraṃ viṣayaḥ, jātyādy-ākārāvabhāsasya spaṣṭatvāt. nāpi sāmānyamātraṃ viṣayaḥ, bhedagraha-ṇasya pratītisiddhatvāt.*
>
> For this [apprehending of the mere proper form] neither the bare particular is the object, because one can clearly perceive that [something] appears in form of a universal etc., nor is the mere universal the object [of perception], because the knowledge of difference is a fact cognized by apprehension.

For Śālikanātha, beingness (*sattā*), now as a universal, cannot be supposed to exist without a relation to a particular and is only possible as beingness of a proper form (*svarūpa*) of word-referents (*padārtha*). If the non-duality of Brahman could be verified empirically, Maṇḍana's view would be justifiable – says Śālikanātha. But if one could verify it, precisely the Advaitic proposition of Brahman's being without a second (*advaita*) would be contradicted.[5] Therefore, Śālikanātha denies that 'beingness' (*sattā*) can be a mere universal (*sāmānyamātra*) knowable independently of that which exists as a particular. For him, both the particular and the universal exist identifiably in spatio-temporal reality. Beingness is only cognizable if it is ascertainable by valid means of cognition, otherwise it could not be detected. Referring to Maṇḍana's view in the *Jātinirṇaya* (PrP 99.2-7) he says:

---

[5] Śālikanātha refutes Maṇḍana's thesis as contradiction in terms. In order to verify "mere being" by perception, either the highest Being, the Brahman, must be an object or the perception must be a never changing and constantly on-going knowledge (*dhārāvāhinī buddhi*). The first supposition contradicts Brahman's absoluteness in its being without a second. The second supposition does not allow the perception of an empirical entity. We will see that Meghanādārisūri gives in his reply to his Advaitic opponent (NDy 54.12 ff) exactly the same arguments.

> ... *yo hi mahāsāmānyaṃ sattāṃ saṅgirate, so 'pi svarūpasattāṃ padārthānāṃ manyata eva. ... tena svarūpasattaiva pramāṇasaṃbandhayogyatā. yasya hi svarūpam asti, tat pramāṇena paricchidyate.*
>
> ... For even he, who namely glorifies the great universal as beingness, accepts it very well as beingness of the proper form of word-referents. ... Therefore the suitability[6] for the connection with the means of knowledge is only the beingness of the proper form. For that which has a proper form is delimited by a means of knowledge.[7]

Nevertheless, Śālikanātha accepts Maṇḍana's opinion that the first perception is only affirmative (*vidhāyaka*). However, contrary to Maṇḍana's view of perception, it affirms not only a universal, but also particulars such as properties. This means that particularity and universality were both perceived. Thus he explains in his *Tattvāloka* (PrP 336.9):

> *sāmānyaviśeṣau tu parasparasaṃbaddhe dve vastunī pratyakṣam avagāhate tathā ca kutaḥ sattādvaitasiddhiḥ.*
>
> The perception knows both entities that are mutually connected, i.e. the universal and the particular, and thus, whence comes the proof that beingness is without a second?[8]

---

[6] For this term see Halbfass 1992: 153: "The Prābhākara school of Mīmāṃsā does not accept a universal 'reality'. In its view, as articulated most clearly in the works of Śālikanātha, the ideas of *sattā* and *sattāsaṃbandha* can be reduced to the imposed property (*upādhi*) 'suitability for valid cognition'." Halbfass 1992: 156: "The Prābhākaras, in particular Śālikanātha Miśra, argue that the assumption of a universal *sattā* is unnecessary. In their view, there is no reality in addition to what is real; there is nothing over and above the fact that things are what they are; that is, their peculiarity and identity as things (*vastusvarūpa*). The alleged universal *sattā* can be reduced to the non-objective property (*upādhi*) 'suitability for valid cognition' (*pramāṇasaṃbandhayogyatā*)."

[7] For a direct reference to Maṇḍana in the *Jātinirṇaya* see on PrP 100.2-4: *tad evam apākṛte padārthasvarūpātirekiṇi mahāsāmānye sattākhye yat svamanīṣānirmitakutarkabalena* ***sanmātraviṣayaṃ pratyakṣam*** *iti sādhitaṃ, tad atidūrotsāritam.* "Having refuted in this manner the all-surrounding universal, which is called beingness and which is different from the proper form of a word-referent, it is far-fetched, if, by virtue of bad reflection caused by self-desire, it is proved that perception has mere being as an object."

Śālikanātha understands Maṇḍana's concept of perception as demonstrating that this valid means of cognition can prove the fact of Brahman's being without any second, i.e. to perceive without perceiving a difference (*bheda*). But for Śālikanātha this would mean that one knew only *one* object by unchanging perception, i.e. a perception that never alters and that is therefore not able to inform about the diversities of objects. If anything is to be known in the empirical world, it is inescapable that perception centers on more than a single object. At the beginning of an elaborated reply to Maṇḍana's concept of liberation he gives further reasons for his refuting of perception's function as affirming the 'mere being'. In his *Tattvāloka* (PrP 336.5-7) Śālikanātha rejects Maṇḍana's remarks with the following words:

> *na caitad ittham. na khalv advaitaṃ kasya cit pramāṇasya gocaraḥ. syān matam, pratyakṣam eva vidhimātropakṣīnavyāpāram aparispṛṣṭānyonya-bhedam advitīyam ekaṃ tattvaṃ sākṣāt karotīti. tad asat. satyaṃ, vidhāya-kam eva pratyakṣam tac ca vidadhad api rūpaṃ rūpatayā rasaṃ ca rasatayā vidadhāti, na punaḥ sarvam ekatayā. yathā rūpe dhārāvāhinī buddhiḥ, tathābhūtaiva yadi rase 'pi syāt, tadā bhaved eva pratyakṣeṇa sākṣātkṛtam advaitam.*
>
> And the case is not so. The fact of being without a second is by no means the object of any valid means of cognition. If one were to think, perception itself, whose function is limited to mere affirmation, would reveal the only reality, which is without a second and whose mutual difference [from something else] is untouched, then it is not right. It is true, perception is only affirmative and it also affirms colour as being colour and taste as being taste, but it does not affirm everything as being one. If a constantly flowing [i.e. unchanging] knowledge/cognition [occurs] in response to a colour and exactly that kind of cognition were to occur in response to a taste also, then the Being without a second would be revealed by perception.

In which manner the entity is characterised in relation to other things and whether it has the same properties as another object or not, can be realized afterwards by the subsequent conceptual per-

---

[8] See also the parallel formulation in his *Pramāṇaparāyaṇa* (PrP) 163.5-6: *tasmāt sāmānyaviśeṣau dve vastunī pratipadyamānaṃ pratyakṣaṃ prathamam upapadyate.*

ception (*savikalpikapratyakṣa*).[9] What one can come to know for perception in the first moment of its function are for Śālikanātha single objects. A second following perception, knowing their difference to other objects further specifies these objects. The second knowledge is as real as the first and not caused by ignorance in contrast to Maṇḍana's opinion.

Moreover in this context we must mention that Śālikanātha's view of perception fits into a larger understanding of the Veda, especially in the teaching of the *vākyārtha* as being the 'what ought to be done' (*kārya*) in contrast to the being without a second, i.e. Brahman, expressed by the *akhaṇḍavākyārtha* (i.e. Brahman as the indivisible content of a Vedic sentence) as the only meaning of the great utterances (*mahāvākya*). If perception only knows 'mere being' one can never know what must be performed in a ritual action (*kārya*). For Śālikanātha, the sacred Vedic language is prescriptive and essentially concerned with ritual action (*kriyā*). For him, the content of a Vedic sentence (*vākyārtha*) fulfills its purpose in its portrayal of how a human being should behave. This is expressed in the linguistic form of the injunction (*vidhi*) to sacrifice and in the potential or optative mood (*vidhi liṅ*). The Vedic language indicates how to behave and is not to be used as an authoritative source of knowledge for the existence and description of an unverifiable transcendent entity such as 'mere being' that can never cause the proper performance of the ritual act.

---

[9] For the different functions of both perceptions according Śālikanātha, see Schmithausen 1963: 109: "Die Verschiedenheit von Dingen wird aber nicht durch ihr bloßes Dasein bewußt, sondern es bedarf hierzu des Erfassens unterscheidender Bestimmungen oder eigentuemlicher Charakteristika (*dharmāntarāṇi*)" (55.12-14) ... "Durchgängigkeit und Abgesondertheit kann man nur erkennen, wenn man ein anderes (gleichartiges) Ding hinzuzieht (*vastvantarānusandhānam*), d.h. das wahrgenommene Ding zu ihm in Beziehung setzt und vergleicht, welche Bestandteile des ersten Dinges sich hier finden und welche nicht" (55.2, 26.9 f).

IV

The Advaitic view of perception's content was not refuted once and for all with Śālikānātha's criticism. In the tradition of late Advaita Vedānta, Maṇḍana's view of perception was preserved and continued to be defended still more. One of the most detailed discussions can be found in Ānandabodha's *Nyāyamakaranda*. Ānandabodha adopts Maṇḍana's remarks about the object of perception (see NyM 32.1 ff). In his NyM he often refers to Maṇḍana's Tarkakāṇḍa, and defends his teachings against the criticism of Śālikanātha (see NyM 177.5 ff). The following passage continues the above-given debate about the object of perception. After quoting Śālikanātha's objections against Maṇḍana at length and quite verbatim,[10] Ānandabodha refers firstly to Śālikanātha's critical statement (*Tattvāloka*, PrP 336.5-7) mentioned above. I will quote only a small section to show Ānandabodha's reference to Śālikanātha's passage as quoted and translated above, but it suffices to show that he renders the position of Maṇḍana precisely by saying that perception cannot prove *advaita* and is therefore not capable of knowing the Brahman itself.[11]

PrP 336.5-7:	NyM 297.3-8:
na caitad ittham. na khalv advaitaṃ kasya cit pramāṇasya gocaraḥ. syān matam, ***pratyakṣam eva vidhimātropakṣīṇavyāpāram*** *aparispṛṣṭānyonya****bhedam*** *advitīyam ekaṃ tattvaṃ sākṣāt karotīti. tad asat. satyaṃ, vidhāyakam eva pratyakṣam*	*yat tāvad advaitaviṣayatābhāve pratyakṣasyābhihitaṃ* ***vidhimātrā****vasitavyāpāram api* ***pratyakṣaṃ rūpaṃ rūpatayā rasaṃ ca rasatayā*** *parasparavyāvṛttasvabhāvam* ***eva vidhatte, na punar*** *ekākāram evāśeṣaṃ.* ***yathā*** *hi* ***rūpe dhārāvāhinī*** *dhīs* ***tathā yadi***

[10] Compare NyM 290.1–297.1 to *Tattvāloka* (PrP) 336.1–343.1. As far as I know only the editors of the PrP refer to Ānandabodha's close citation of Śālikanātha's rejection of Maṇḍana's teachings. Because Ānandabodha's remarks that come after his quotations of Śālikanātha's objections and by which he refutes Śālikanātha's polemical utterances (see NyM 297.2–308.8) are so elaborate I will deal in another place with this debate in more detail.

[11] Words that coincide in both quotations are marked bold.

tac ca ***vidadhad rūpaṃ rūpatayā rasañ ca rasatayā vidadhāti, na punar*** *sarvam ekatayā,* ***yathā rūpe dhārāvāhinī*** *buddhiḥ,* ***tathā****bhūtaiva* ***yadi rase 'pi syāt, tadā*** *bhaved eva* ***pratyakṣe****ṇa sākṣātkṛtam* ***advaitam****.*	***rase 'pi syāt, tadā pratyakṣād advaitam*** *iti, tad etad vidhāyakasyaiva pratyakṣasya vyavacchedakatvam apākurvadbhir asmābhir adhastād eva nirastam ... na ca vayaṃ vastutaḥ pratyakṣād advaitasiddhiṃ brūmaḥ.*

Ānandabodha's quotation (NyM 297.3-8) can be translated as follows:

> First of all, that which is stated, namely that non-duality is no object for perception [in the following words]: 'perception, though its function is determined as mere affirmation, affirms only colour as being colour and taste as being taste having mutually delimited natures, but does not have entirely only one form. If a constantly flowing [i.e. unchanging] knowledge/cognition [occurs] in the same manner in response to a colour as [it occurs] in response to a taste, then the non-duality would be proved from perception' – this has been rejected earlier by us (NyM 31 ff) by refuting that perception, which is only affirmative, is delimitative. And as a matter of fact we do not say that the [complete] proof of [the One] without a second (*advaitasiddhi*) is due to perception.

It is important to notice in the last lines of this quotation that Ānandabodha understands Maṇḍana's concept of perception not as a direct cognition of Brahman as an object, but rather interprets it as a means that can prove the fact, that Brahman is the only being (*sat*) as it is described in the relevant Śruti-passages (see NyM 299.3).

However, valid means of cognition, the relevant Śruti-passages included, belongs to the realm of beginningless nescience (*māyā/avidyā*) for Ānandabodha. Similarly to his teacher Vimuktātman, he interprets everything that is different from the highest Being as belonging to Māyā/Avidyā. He defines the Māyā/Avidyā just as Vimuktātman as non determinable as real nor as unreal (*sadasadbhyām anirvacanīya*), and therefore as being strictly different from Brahman itself.[12] Perception and its object as well is different from

[12] Compare for example NyM 302.6-9 to IS 32.6 ff.

Brahman and also consists of Māyā/Avidyā. Therefore for Ānandabodha it is not determinable as real (*sat*) like Brahman, nor as unreal (*asat*). Consisting in Māyā/Avidyā it is not possible for perception to prove the *advaita* of Brahman. The object of perception is like its material cause (*upādānakāraṇa*), the Māyā/Avidyā, neither absolutely real nor unreal, and exists only as long as the individual being (*jīva*) does not know that his Self is identical to Brahman. If we look forward and compare this point to Meghanādārisūri's own teaching, we see some similarity in structure. Although for Ānandabodha perception belongs to the realm of beginningless Māyā/Avidyā, it has an object separate from Brahman and not Brahman itself. In the same manner we will see that for Meghanādārisūri perception has an object that is in fact real but separate from Brahman. The difference between the two is that in the former view the Māyā/Avidyā has ceased in the status of *mokṣa*, although before this ceasing Brahman is its support (*āśraya*), whereas for the latter the valid means of cognition belongs eternally to the body (*śarīra*) of Brahman. But before I deal with Meghanādārisūri's view in detail, I have to present the manner in which he refers to the Advaitic position.

V

We can find the topics developed in the polemical discussion between Advaitins and Śālikanātha in Meghanādārisūri's discussion of Maṇḍana's views that are set forth and refuted in his *Nayadyumaṇi* in the chapter concerning the 'light on the meaning of a [Vedic] sentence' (*vākyārthapradīpa*). In certain sections, this chapter deals with the polemic against Maṇḍana Miśra's teaching of the object of perception in connection with the meaning of Vedic sentences. After stating Maṇḍana's arguments for the view that perception is not able to know differences (*bheda*) and only Brahman is the real referent (*artha*) of a Vedic sentence (*vākyārtha*),[13]

[13] See NDy 50.16–54.11.

he uses Śālikanātha's criticism to refute Maṇḍana's teaching, bringing forward the argument that it is not Brahman that is the indivisible content of a Vedic sentence (*akhaṇḍavākyārtha*), but rather that 'which ought to be done' (*kārya*), whereby he shows that the condition needed to carry out the ritual performance is not the perception of 'mere being'.[14] That Meghanādārisūri refers to Maṇḍana's view here is evidenced by the fact that in the statement of his opponent Meghanādārisūri has adopted Maṇḍana's argumentation that delimitation (*vyavaccheda*) of the entity cannot be the first known fact. The difference of a proper form (*svarūpa*) cannot be proven, even if one says that perception is delimitative, nor if one says that it can act in both ways, i.e. affirmatively and delimitatively. The opponent's final view is that on the basis of perception one cannot decide what is earlier. Again I contrast both statements, so that one can easily see that Meghanādārisūri reproduces Maṇḍana's concept of affirmative perception:

BS 44,10-18:	NDy 50.21–51.5:
(1) *vastusvarūpavidhiḥ,* **(2)** *vastvantarasya vyavacchedaḥ,* **(3)** *ubhayaṃ veti. ubhayasminn api traividhyam.* **(3a)** *yaugapadyam,* **(3b)** *vyavacchedapūrvako vidhiḥ,* **(3c)** *vidhipūrvako vyavaccheda iti. tatra vastvantaravyavacchede ubhayasmin vā bhedaḥ pratyakṣagocara iti bhavati virodhaḥ. svarūpavidhimātre tu kasya cid vyavacchedena śūnye na bhedaḥ pramāṇārthaḥ, na hi vyavacchedād ṛte bhedasiddhiḥ vidhimātravyāpāraṃ ca pratyakṣam.*	*pratyakṣaṃ hi kiṃ* **(1)** *vidhāyakam?* **(2)** *vyavacchedakaṃ vā* **(3)** *ubhayaṃ vā?* **(1)** *prathame vastusvarūpavidhimātropakṣayān na bhedasiddhiḥ.* **(2)** *dvitīye 'pi niṣedhyasāpekṣatvena prāptir pūrvakatvāt, prāpteś ca vidhyapekṣatvāt, vidheś ca vastumātropakṣayāt tadasiddhiḥ. tṛtīyas tu vikalpaḥ –* **(3c)** *kiṃ vidhipūrvako vyavacchedaḥ* **(3b)** *etadvyatyayo vā?* **(3a)** *yugapad vobhayam iti? ādye 'navacchinnasanmātravirodhād vyavacchedāsiddhau bhedāsiddhiḥ. dvitīye 'pi vyavacchedasya vidhipūrvatvād eva vyavacchedapūrvatvānupapattes tadasiddhiḥ. ata eva tṛtīyapakṣānupapattes tatsiddhir nirastā. na caikavidhāyakatvam evānyavyavacchedakatvam iti.*

[14] See NDy 54.12 ff.

Further, it is important to mention that the opponent states that the perception of the 'unseparated mere being' (*anavacchinnasanmātra*) has false knowledge as its imposed property (*ajñānopādhikam*), and difference is established by virtue of nescience (*avidyāto bhedasiddhiḥ*):

> *pratyakṣasya sanmātraviṣayatve 'py ajñānaviśiṣṭavastuviṣayatvān nājñānopamardakatvam iti na tattvaikaviṣayatvam.*
>
> Even though the object of perception is 'mere being', it does not destroy ignorance, because its object is an entity that is qualified by ignorance [and] thus its object is not only the [highest] reality.

As was shown by Maṇḍana in the same manner, Meghanādārisūri's opponent draws the conclusion here that the Veda is, contrary to perception, without any fault and has therefore the stronger (*balīyas*) weight in the case of contradiction between the two means of valid cognition (see NDy 53.1 ff).

VI

When, in this chapter of his *Nayadyumaṇi*, Meghanādārisūri responds to the discussion about perception and to the proper meaning of the Vedic sentences (*vākyārtha*), he criticises the perceptibility of 'mere being' (*sanmātra*) just as Śālikanātha had done. But Meghanādārisūri's metaphysical background neither supposes Brahman to be the only reality (*sat*) as non-differentiated (*nirviśeṣa*), as ineffable (*avācya*) or as the support (*āśraya*) of ignorance (*avidyā*), nor does he consider the Brahman to be the only entity to which the content of a sentence refers. However, he also does not take the atheistic position of that 'which ought to be done' (*kārya*) held by exponents of the Prābhākara-Mīmāṃsā. I will show that he only uses their criticism against the Advaitin's idealistic concept of perception and, in the broader sense, against their idealistic concept of the highest Being having no relation to the world and being thus without any empirical evidence.

It is of further importance to see that though he accepts Śālikanātha's view for refuting the opponent's objections and though he defends him against a new attack[15] he does not stop at or adopt Śālikanātha's realistic position as a final position, but rather uses this viewpoint to refute the Advaitic interpretation of a Vedic sentence. Before I come to Meghanādārisūri's own concept of Brahman and its relation to the world, I will quote his reply to his Advaitic opponent. In NDy 54.12–55.6 he introduces his answer with the following question:

> *pratyakṣacidacidviṣayatvena abhimataṃ sattvaṃ kiṃ brahmasattākhyam sāmānyaṃ vā?*
>
> Is beingness, which is thought to be the mental/conscious and inanimate object of perception, called beingness of Brahman or a universal?

However, neither of these possibilities is without a self-contradiction and in no case can perception apprehend 'beingness' (*sattva*): the Advaitic opponent can neither bring forward the argument that beingness (*sattva*) is identical with Brahman, nor can he say that it is a universal (*sāmānya*) independent of a particular. To say that beingness is identical with Brahman is not verifiable, because Brahman is never the object of perception. And were one to suppose it to be such object, no liberation could take place. In Meghanādārisūri's words (NDy 54.13-15):

> *nādyaḥ, brahmaṇaḥ 'na cakṣuṣā gṛhyate'* [MuṇḍU 3.1.8] *ityādinā pramāṇāntarāviṣayatvapratīter virodhād. dṛśyatvāṅgīkāraś ca tvaddarśanaviruddhaḥ, tadaṅgīkāre ca tava muktau dṛśyatvena mithyātvāpātaḥ.*
>
> The first [consideration] is not the case, because it contradicts the knowledge that Brahman is no object of further valid means of cognition due to the declaration [of MuṇḍU 3.1.8], which begins with the words: 'Not perceptible with the sense of vision'. And the assumption that [Brahman] is a directly perceptible object contradicts your own opinion; and even if this were

[15] For an elaborate contribution on the status of the Veda in Rāmānuja's teachings and his debate with the Prābhākara-Mīmāṃsā, see Lipner 1986: 11 ff, and especially 17 ff.

accepted by you, falsity/unreality (*mithyātva*) would result, because according to you [Brahman] is perceptible [only] in the case of release.

The second alternative is not possible either. Such an independent universal is not verifiable by perception, because perception is momentary, cognizes the diversity of objects, and is therefore not unchanging like the eternal universal. But if such a universal exists Brahman's being without a second as well would contradict it. Therefore, Meghanādārisūri denies the second possibility in the following words (NDy 54.15-20):

> *nāpi dvitīyaḥ, sarṣapamahīdharādiṣu anuvṛttaikapratīter durlabhatvāt tatsāmānyāsiddheḥ, tadaṅgīkāre 'pi tasya sāmānyatvena vyaktinivṛttāv agrahaṇāt. tasya ca vyaktiparyantatvāt sāmānyamātragrahaṇam anupapannam. tatsaṃbhave ca vyaktividhurapradeśe 'pi grahaṇāpattiḥ, sāmānyasya sarvagatatvanityatvayor aṅgīkārāt. tasyaiva grāhyatve 'pi na brahmādvaitasiddhiḥ, tayor bhinnatvāt.*
>
> Nor is the second alternative possible, because this universal is not proven/given, because it is difficult to know by virtue of one single continuous knowledge as in the case of a mustard-seed, the earth, etc. And even if one concedes this, [it is not known], because, if the particular vanishes, it is not apprehended due to its being a universal. And knowing a mere universal is impossible, because the [universal] is delimited by the particular; and if this [i.e. knowing a mere universal] were to be possible, one could apprehend the universal also at a place that is separated from the concrete particular, because one supposes the universal to be omnipresent and eternal. Even if this [omnipresent and eternal universal] were to be knowable, the Brahman as being without a second would not be proven, because both [i.e universal and Brahman] are different [from each other].

It is plausible to say that here Meghanādārisūri repeats the arguments Śālikanātha brought forward in saying that beingness is by perception neither verifiable if it is supposed to be identical with Brahman nor is it knowable if it is held to be an independent mere universal. As far as I can see, Meghanādārisūri, in the same manner as Śālikanātha, reaches here the conclusion that the universal can never be proven without contradictions as separate from the particular. He presents his own view in the following words (NDy 57.10-12):

na ca bhedasya vastusvarūpatvāt pratyakṣasya kṣaṇikatve 'pi vastugrahānupapattiḥ. jātyādeḥ kṣanikagrāhyatvāt taddhiyo 'paryavasānād eva vyakter api viṣayatvam.

And even if perception is momentary, the knowledge of the (real) thing is not impossible, because the difference [is identical with] the proper form of the thing. Because the universal, etc., are cognizable in one moment, in the same manner the concrete thing is also an object of perception due to the fact that knowledge is not determinative.

If one realizes an object, in the first moment of perception one knows both the universal (*sāmānya*) and the particular, even though the perception is momentary. For Meghanādārisūri on the one hand the perception of a mere universal (*sāmānyamātra*) is not possible as beingness (*sattva*) or as 'mere being' (*sanmātra*), and on the other hand the restriction to a bare particular (*viśeṣa*) is not well founded. After the object is realized as an object, its special difference is known in comparison with a second object with the help of a special counter-positive (*pratiyogiviśeṣa*) (see NDy 57.12).

VII

But how does this concept of perception and its real object agree with the acceptance of the highest Being, i.e. Brahman, that is accepted in the same manner as it was for the Advaitin's view? And how does Meghanādārisūri integrate the realistic view of perception's concept as influenced by Śālikanātha into his own teaching of the relation between Brahman and world? Why does not the same contradiction arise for him? How can the perceivable world exist together with the highest Being?

We can see that Meghanādārisūri also applies the concept of togetherness of universal and particular for the relation between Brahman and every entity that can be known as different from it. His metaphysical concept is parallel to that of an object's conception: Brahman alone would lead back to the Advaitin's idealistic system and the empirical world alone would lead back to a realistic position as is the view of the Prābhākara-Mīmāṃsā. Meghanādārisūri himself argues both that the highest Being is not without the world, and that the world does not exist without the highest Being. His concept that was developed in his own tradition of the Rāmānuja School, to which he was closely attached, is as follows: Everything different from Brahman belongs to the body (*śarīra*) of Brahman. But contrary to the body of Māyā/Avidyā that disappears in the final knowledge of identity between the Self and Brahman, this body belongs eternally to the Brahman itself. It consists of a plurality of substantial, uncaused conscious (*jīvātman*) selves and of inanimate entities[16] and depends eternally (*nitya*) on Brahman in an asymmetrical form.

If something is different from Brahman it does not have to be seen as completely separate from it as in the manner of the Advaitin's understanding of its being produced by beginningless nescience. Rather it can be understood as a qualification (*viśeṣaṇa*) of Brahman. In this sense he says that the body as the entirety of individual selves and of inanimate entities specify the Brahman that is therefore called as qualified (*viśiṣṭārtha*). By this interpretation Meghanādārisūri takes both traditions that he deals with into account in a new way: on the one hand he can uphold the monism, because everything different from Brahman can be understood as belonging to his body. On the other hand he does not deny the concept of ritual activity of the individual self, but he is able to integrate it.

By carrying out the *kārya*, the highest aim is not only the attainment of heaven, but also Brahman[17] as specified by different words (*padaviśeṣaviśiṣṭabrahma*). Otherwise (*anyadā*), Meghanādārisūri says (NDy 79.13-14):

---

[16] And not, as claimed by the School of Advaita Vedānta, of insentient (*jaḍa*) individual souls.

[17] It is now the only and the real *padārtha*.

> *svargāditattadvastuviśiṣṭam eva prāpyam. tatprāptāv apy acinmātrabhoga eva teṣāṃ tātparyam.*
>
> That 'which has to be obtained' would only be specified by the respective entity such as heaven, etc. Even in the case of its attainment the purport of these (entities) would only be the enjoyment of something insentient.

The impersonal and insentient (*acetana*) *apūrva*-principle of the Mīmāṃsā School would never be able to give the fruit (*phala*) of an individual's ritual activity. Only if it is qualified by the highest self, i.e. Brahman or God, ritual activity will have a result. The highest self alone can bestow fruits and neither insentient and sentient entities alone by itself. Every insentient entity like fire is possessed by a sentient entity, but both must be directed or controlled by the highest self. Thus Meghanādārisūri continues NDy 80.12:

> *apūrvādes tu phaladātṛtvam acetanatvād anupapannam. agnyādicetanānāṃ ca paramātmaviśiṣṭānām eva phaladātṛtvam. sarveṣāṃ tadantarātmakatvatanniyāmyatvaccheṣatvānām 'yaḥ pṛthivyāṃ tiṣṭhan' ityādau śravaṇāt. ataḥ sarvāntarātmabhūtaṃ brahmaiva tattadvastuviśiṣṭaṃ śabdārthaḥ.*
>
> But the *apūrva* etc. can not be the bestower of the fruit, because it is insentient. And sentient entities [having] fire etc. are the bestower of the fruits, only if they are specified by the highest self, because it is revealed in scripture, in such passages as [BĀU 3.7.7] 'who resides in the earth', that everything [sentient and insentient entities] has him [i.e. the highest self] as its inner Self, and is to be directed/guided by him, and is its remnant. Therefore, Brahman alone, as the inner Self of everything and specified by the respective entities, is the real meaning of the word.

The simple word that refers to an entity that consists of universal and particular is a part of Brahman's body and can be understood as not referring to a simple object, but to an object that is a mode (*prakāra*) of Brahman. If the word (*pada/śabda*) expresses or refers to the mode (*prakāra*) of that Brahman, no contradiction arises for the highest Being, because every mode belongs to Brahman (*prakārin*). All specifications (*viśeṣaṇa*) are expressible in words, of which the Brahman is the real object, because the objects, to which the words refer to, qualify only Brahman. Thus it is expressed in every word, i.e. in Vedic words as well as in words of everyday language. In the following sentence Meghanādārisūri summarizes his own concept of the relationship between Brahman and the world. This sentence is at the same time the *siddhānta* to the discussion presented above in NDy 76.10-13:

> *laukikavaidikavākyānām aviśeṣeṇa parabrahmaivārthaḥ, tásyaiva sarvapadavācyatvāt. padāny eva hi vākyam sarvapadavācyatā ca brahmavyatiriktakṛtsnacidacidvastūnāṃ taccharīratvena tatprakāratvāt, prakāravācakaśabdānāṃ ca prakāraviśiṣṭārthaparatvāt.*
>
> In mundane and Vedic sentences, the highest Brahman is exclusively without distinction the meaning [of a sentence], because only this is expressible in every word. For, the sentence [consists of] words alone, and that it [i.e. Brahman] is expressible in every word [is possible], because mental/conscious and inanimate entities that are completely separated from Brahman are its mode, inasmuch as it has them as its body, and because the words that express its modes rest on an object/goal [i.e. Brahman] which is specified by its mode.[18]

REFERENCES

Texts and abbreviations

BS [(Maṇḍanamiśra:) *Brahmasiddhi*] *Brahmasiddhi by Ācārya Maṇḍanamiśra with Commentary by Śaṅkhapāṇi*. Ed. by S. Kuppaswami Sastri. (Madras Government Oriental Manuscripts Series, 4.) Madras 1937.

IS [(Vimuktātman:) *Iṣṭasiddhi*] *Iṣṭasiddhi of Vimuktātman with Extracts from the Vivaraṇa of Jñānottama*. Critically edited with Introduction and Notes by M. Hiriyanna. (GOS, 65.) Baroda 1933.

NDy [(Meghanādārisūri:) *Nayadyumaṇi*] *Nayadyumaṇiḥ by Meghanādārisūri*. Critical edition with introduction and notes by V. Krishnamacharya and T. Viraraghavacharya. (Madras Government Oriental Series, 141.) Madras 1956.

---

[18] Thanks to Prof. Dr. Eli Franco for critical remarks and corrections of my translations and of the English version. Thanks to Dr. Alex Watson, who also corrected parts of my translations and improved the English. Finally I am grateful to Cynthia Peck-Kubaczek, who is always the first to help me bring out an English version. An earlier draft of this paper was published in: Srinivasa Rao & Godabarisha Mishra (eds.), *Paramparā. Essays in Honour of R. Balasubramanian*: 341-362. New Delhi: Indian Council of Philosophical Research, 2003.

NyM [(Ānandabodha:) *Nyāyamakaranda*] *Nyāyamakaranda by Shree Ānanda Bodha Bhaṭṭārakāchārya. With the Commentary by Citsukh Muni, Pramāṇamālā and Nyāyadīpāvalī*, I-IV. Ed. by Svāmī Bālarāma Udaseen Māndalika. (Chowkhambā Sanskrit Series, 38, 62, 87, 117.) Benares 1907.

PrP [(Śālikanātha:) *Prakaraṇapañcikā*] *Prakaraṇa Pañcikā of Śālikanātha with Nyāsiddhi of Jaipuri Nārāyaṇa Bhaṭṭ*. Ed. by A. Subrahmanya Sastri. (Hindu University Darśana Series, 4.) Benares 1961.

Studies

BIARDEAU, Madeleine 1969. *La philosophie de Maṇḍana Miśra. Vue à partir de la Brahmasiddhi*. (Publications de l'École Française d'Extrême-Orient, 76). Paris: École Française d'Extrême-Orient.

HALBFASS, Wilhelm 1975. Conceptualisations of 'being' in Classical Vaiśeṣika. *WZKS* 19: 183-198.

—— 1976. Substanz (*dravya*) im Vaiśeṣika. *WZKS* 20: 141-166.

—— 1992. *On Being and What There Is. Classical Vaiśeṣika and the History of Indian Ontology*. Albany: State University of New York Press.

LIPNER, Julius 1986. *The Face of Truth. A Study of Meaning and Metaphysics in the Vedāntic Theology of Rāmānuja*. Albany: State University of New York Press.

SCHMITHAUSEN, Lambert 1963. Vorstellungsfreie und vorstellende Wahrnehmung bei Śālikanātha. *WZKSO* 7: 104-115.

THRASHER, Allen Wright 1993. *The Advaita Vedānta of Brahma-Siddhi*. Delhi: Motilal Banarsidass.

VETTER, Tilmann 1964. *Erkenntnisprobleme bei Dharmakīrti*. (VKSKSO, 1.) Wien: Österreichische Akademie der Wissenschaften.

Yājñavalkya-*brāhmaṇa*s and the Early Mīmāṃsā

WALTER SLAJE

I

Comparative investigations into the Pūrva- and Uttara-Mīmāṃsā tend in most cases to focus predominantly on differences of mainly a doctrinal nature by sharply contrasting them. The present paper, however, will – in its introductory part – rather be concerned with some features that have received less attention. They belong to the sphere of social and ideological aspects and are in a sense more related to everyday life than to philosophical doctrines. After briefly outlining some of such features in their intra- and inter-systemic contexts they will form the background for the argument to be made in the subsequent part, dealing with the so-called Yājñavalkya-*brāhmaṇa*s and their relationship to the early development of the Pūrva-Mīmāṃsā. Although my observations are of a more general nature, it is hoped that they will contribute to a future conspectus of connecting and dissociating peculiarities, as the case may be, of both the Mīmāṃsās.

1. Introduction: The Vedic dharma in its bifurcation and the purposes of the Karma- and Jñānakāṇḍas

1.1. Śaṅkara

According to the *Bhagavadgītābhāṣya* of Śaṅkara (the second half of the 7th century?)[1] the Vedic *dharma*, characterised by (ritual) activity (*pravṛtti*) as well as by its opposite, ritual inactivity or renunciation (*nivṛtti*), also supports the world in exactly such a twofold way. Śaṅkara and some of his followers[2] provide a mythical account for this claim: Viṣṇu Nārāyaṇa created Marīci,[3] the first of the Prajāpatis, and Sanaka, for making the world continue. To Marīci and the other Prajāpatis he taught the Vedic *dharma* of (sacrificial and social) activity. Through procreation they became

---

[1] Vetter (1969: 15) opts for the second half of the 7th century. In like manner also Thrasher (1993: 127), who accords with Vetter and demonstrates in detail (pp. 112-121) that Śaṅkara must indeed have been referred to by Maṇḍana in his *Brahmasiddhi*. Maṇḍana's literary activity has been fixed by Thrasher (1993: 127) as between 660 and 720 by the following reasons: Maṇḍana knew Dharmakīrti (600-660) and the latter's older contemporaries Kumārila (Steinkellner 1997: 642) and Prabhākara. Prabhākara displays knowledge of the doctrine adhered to by Kumārila and should therefore be dated in the the first half of the 7th century (Yoshimizu 1997: 49). Śaṅkara, too, knew Dharmakīrti and Kumārila (Mesquita 1994: 458, n. 33). Maṇḍana, who refers to Śaṅkara (Vetter 1979: 11, n. 2), is quoted himself by Sureśvara, Śaṅkara's direct disciple. So he seems to have been a contemporary of Śaṅkara. Umbeka, who demonstrably was active between 760 and 790, wrote a commentary on Maṇḍana's *Bhāvanāviveka*, reporting already a number of variant readings which must be accorded some time (at least half a century) for their gradual development. Thrasher consequently arrives at ca. 720 for a later limit of Maṇḍana. This is in accordance with the fact that Maṇḍana is also quoted by Karṇakagomin (750-810) (Vetter 1979: 11 f). Therefore Śaṅkara, who, as trustworthy (Thrasher 1993: 113 f) traditional belief has it, died comparatively young, could indeed have ended his life around or before 700 AD. Sureśvara quotes Maṇḍana. So also does Bhāskara, active perhaps immediately after Śaṅkara (Rüping 1977: 18; cf. also Stephan 2002: 19 f), who was himself refuted by Vimuktātman, whom Schmücker (2001: 21 f, n. 4) assigns to approximately the first half of the 10th century. It is in the sense of merely a working hypothesis that I adapt the established relative chronology to an absolute dating as follows: Śaṅkara (670-700) ← Maṇḍana (660-720) ← Sureśvara (680-740) ← Bhāskara (between 720 and the 10th century) ← Vimuktātman (between 740 and the first half of the10th century).

[2] See, e.g., Ātmasukha, VC, p. 2, 7 ff.

[3] For mythological details of his domestic life cf. Mani 1975: 487.

the first householders. The *dharma* of inactivity or renunciation, characterised by knowledge and dispassion, was taught to Sanaka and his three brothers, who thereupon became the first celibates.[4] We may consider both of them true archetypes of the *lifelong* householder (*gṛhastha*) and the *lifelong* renouncer (*saṃnyāsin*) respectively. Marīci, who as a Prajāpati begot offspring and never became a renouncer, archetypically represents the sacrificing householder. The renouncer-type, on the other hand, as represented by Sanaka, is the *lifelong* celibate. He never became a householder and never procreated offspring.[5] It is clear that Śaṅkara's bifurcation of the Vedic *dharma* mirrors the Karma- and Jñānakāṇḍas. In his opinion, the *dharma* of the Karmakāṇḍa causes bondage[6] and can at best bring about *abhyudaya* (a divine position in heaven).[7] The Jñānakāṇḍa alone was capable of effecting final release from transmigration (*niḥśreyasa*).[8] Although the *karmamārga* of a householder is thus assigned limited importance in terms of final release, it nevertheless contributes to the purification of the organ (/capacity) of discrimination (*sattvaśuddhi*)[9] and by way of this

---

[4] See BhGBh (Introduction), p. 1, 7-10: ... *marīcyādīn agre sṛṣṭvā prajāpatīn, pravṛttilakṣaṇaṃ dharmaṃ grāhayām āsa vedoktam. tato 'nyāṃś ca sanakasanandanādīn utpādya, nivṛttilakṣaṇaṃ dharmaṃ jñānavairāgyalakṣaṇaṃ grāhayām āsa. dvividho hi vedokto dharmaḥ pravṛttilakṣaṇo nivṛttilakṣaṇaś ca jagataḥ sthitikāraṇam.*

[5] For details cf. Mani 1975: 682.

[6] Cf. BhGBh (p. 270, 2 f) *ad* BhG 18.30: *pravṛttiḥ ... bandhahetuḥ karmamārgaḥ śāstravihitaviṣayaḥ, ... nivṛttir mokṣahetuḥ saṃnyāsamārgaḥ.*

[7] BhGBh (Introduction), p. 2, 12 f: *abhyudayārtho 'pi yaḥ pravṛttilakṣaṇo dharmo ... sa devādisthānaprāptihetur ...*

[8] BhGBh (Introduction), p. 2, 4 ff: ... *paraṃ niḥśreyasaṃ sahetukasya saṃsārasyātyantoparamalakṣaṇam. tac ca sarvakarmasaṃnyāsapūrvakād ātmajñānaniṣṭhārūpād dharmād bhavati.* It is interesting to compare Pārthasārathi's similar opinion on the difference between *abhyudaya* and *niḥśreyasa*: *adṛṣṭaṃ ca phalaṃ ... dvividham abhyudayarūpaṃ niḥśreyasarūpaṃ ca, 'sarvān kāmān āpnoti'* (ChU 7.10.2) *'so 'śnute sarvān kāmān'* (TaittU 2.1.1) *ityādy abhyudayaphalam. 'na sa punar āvartate'* (~ ChU 8.15.1) *ityādi niḥśreyasaphalam iti vivekaḥ* (ŚD 131.15 ff). Cf. also Mesquita 1994: 452 (n. 7), 460 ff.

[9] BhGBh (Introduction), p. 2, 12 ff: ... *yaḥ pravṛttilakṣaṇo dharmo ... sa ... īśvarārpaṇabuddhyānuṣṭhīyamānaḥ sattvaśuddhaye bhavati ...*

prepares for eventually entering the state of a knowledge-based renouncer.[10] The celibate renouncer would thus take advantage of the primacy of liberation over the householder.

1.2. *Kumārila*

Kumārila (the first half of the 7th century), on his part – whose *Ślokavārttika* was referred to by Śaṅkara[11] – held a slightly different opinion on the respective purposes of the Karma- and the Jñānakāṇḍa, and on the way in which they would exercise a beneficial effect on final release (*mokṣa*).[12] To his mind as laid down in the *Ślokavārttika*, the study of the Upaniṣads (*vedānta*) would have rendered the natural certainty about the existence of a self, as tacitly presupposed by Vedic injunctions,[13] a firm conviction (*dṛḍha niścaya*) – but nothing more:[14] *dṛḍhatvam etadviṣayaḥ prabodhaḥ*[15] *prayāti vedāntaniṣevaṇena* (ŚV, ātmav. 148cd).

[10] BhGBh (Introduction), p. 2, 12-16: ... *yaḥ pravṛttilakṣaṇo dharmo ... sa ... sattvaśuddhaye bhavati ... | śuddhasattvasya ca jñānaniṣṭhāyogyatāprāpti-dvāreṇa jñānotpattihetutvena ca niḥśreyasahetutvam api pratipadyate*. Cf. also Stephan 2002: 54 ff, 94.

[11] Mesquita 1994: 458, n. 33.

[12] For details regarding the development of Kumārila's ideas about *mokṣa* and related topics, from a purely ritual path (*karmamārga*) as expounded in the *Ślokavārttika*, to the *karmajñānasamuccaya*-path in the *Tantravārttika* (pp. 459, 463) and the *Bṛhaṭṭīkā* (pp. 465 ff), cf. Mesquita 1994 and the articles of John Taber and Kiyotaka Yoshimizu in the present volume. On the chronological order of the *Ślokavārttika* and the *Bṛhaṭṭīkā* (in this sequence), see Kataoka 2003: 65.

[13] So already Śabara, cf. Mesquita 1994: 453, n. 13. Kumārila: "An injunction depends on a self, because otherwise [the use of the injunction would be] improper. This [dependence] being the case (loc. abs.), the existence [of a self] is made manifest. Therefore the [*brāhmaṇa*-quotations under consideration] here justify [what] is referred to by these [injunctions] as a subject matter." (ŚV, ātmav. 141: *anyathānupapatteś ca vidhinātmany apekṣite | astitvadyotanād etair arthākṣiptasamarthanam* ||). See also NR (p. 513, 4 f) on ŚV 141: *na kevalam upaniṣadvacanād evātmāstitvam, agnihotrādividhayo 'pi hi nityaṃ bhoktāram antareṇānupapadyamānās tam arthād dyotayanty eva.*

[14] Cf. Mesquita 1994: 453; NR (p. 515, 6 f) on ŚV 148: *dārḍhyārthibhis tu vedāntavihiteṣv eva śravaṇamanananididhyāsanādiṣu yatitavyam iti.* Cf. Pārthasārathi elsewhere: ... *dṛḍhavivekapratipādakānām upaniṣadvākyānām* ... (ŚD, p. 131, 7)

Therefore, in Kumārila and Śaṅkara we meet with opposite opinions clearly distinguishing between the two *kāṇḍa*s and claiming a different purpose for each of them. For Kumārila the Jñānakāṇḍa was auxiliary to the Karmakāṇḍa in that it reinforces the given certainty of the existence of one's own self. Śaṅkara, on the other hand, belittled the Karmakāṇḍa by assigning it a mere preparatory value for, and thus subordinating it to, the Jñānakāṇḍa. All this is, however, not really new and would in no way come as a surprise to an Indologist.

2. Social aspects

2.1. The two Mīmāṃsās in the context of gṛhastha- and saṃnyāsa-āśramas

It is perhaps worthwhile to dwell on the probable impact the respective *kāṇḍa*s must have exercised on the chosen order of life (*āśrama*) of their dedicated followers, since we may assume an intrinsic relationship between these two *kāṇḍa*s and two particular *āśrama*s. For one thing, there is indeed good reason to assign the Pūrva-Mīmāṃsakas to the householder's order (*gṛhastha-āśrama*), since as followers of the Karmakāṇḍa they were sacrificing (*karmin*s). The Uttara-Mīmāṃsakas in contrast belonged to the order of renouncers (*saṃnyāsa-āśrama*). As followers of the Jñānakāṇḍa their emphasis was on gnosis alone (*jñānin*s), and they rejected performing sacrifices. From such a background an aged[16] Mīmāṃsaka could hardly have felt compelled to eventually take to an entirely opposite, the renouncer's mode of life. It would have rendered all their arguments in favour of life-long extended sacrificial duties a relative value, and their *kāṇḍa* a preparatory position only, exactly as claimed by Śaṅkara. For in this case they all would have ended their lives in a Saṃnyāsin's state[17]. This, however, would hardly stand to reason. Why?

---

[15] °*viṣayaḥ prabodhaḥ* with ŚD (p. 131, 9) against °*viṣayaś ca bodhaḥ* of the edition.

[16] See Olivelle 1993: 131 ff.

2.2 *Pūrva- and Uttara-Mīmāṃsakas as life-long sacrificers or renouncers*

The mere prospect of turning away one day from the regular fulfilment of Karmakāṇḍa obligations they as *gṛhastha*s had previously been affiliated to would certainly have eased tensions and rather caused a decrease in the zeal with which Mīmāṃsakas continuously and explicitly defended their lifelong ritual obligations against the opposite claims as made by Vedāntins. Nevertheless, this has not happened, quite on the contrary. In a way, the increase to be observed is somehow in line with Śaṅkara's presentation of the mythic archetypes of *lifelong* householders and *lifelong* celibates. It is difficult not to think of Śaṅkara and of the majority of Saṃnyāsins following his path as of *lifelong* celibates either, and right from the outset of their religious career at that. This may reflect the bipartite *āśrama*-structure of the early Vedic period, which knew of two stages in life only, celibate studentship and procreating householder.[18] And the Mīmāṃsakas, who always emphatically contested the legitimacy of celibate life orders, held all the Saṃnyāsins up to ridicule for precisely this reason. P. Olivelle, after having demonstrated that Jaimini, Śabara and Kumārila clearly took such a stance, came to the conclusion that

> at least some Mīmāṃsists totally rejected the legitimacy of celibate *āśrama*s for ordinary people, reserving them for the blind, the lame, the impotent, and other ritually incompetent people.

To Olivelle the central aim of the Mīmāṃsakas was

> to deny Vedic authority to celibate modes of life. ... The injunctions dealing with celibate *āśrama*s, if they had any validity at all, are directed not at normal people who are capable of marrying but at the handicapped ... whom these texts provide with an alternative mode of life.[19]

---

[17] Cf. below *sub* 2.3 on the possibility of a ritually active life as a *pravrājaka*.

[18] The early Vedic period knew only of two stages in life (studentship and householder), a third stage after the householder developed only later on. See Witzel 2003: §2, p. 105, n. 9.

Śabara even went so far as to insinuate to long-time celibates that they "lived as Vedic students for forty-eight years in order to hide their impotence," on which Olivelle remarked that this must "surely have been intended as a jab below the belt at ascetic celibates of his time."[20]

Thus, the celibate renouncers became the scorn of many a staunch Mīmāṃsaka personality such as Jaimini, Śabara and Kumārila as also pointed out by Olivelle. However, Maṇḍana, for instance, too, remained a householder and also refused to become a renouncer.[21] Fulfilling the three obligations (*ṛṇa*) of studying the Vedas, procreating offspring and of sacrificing was, to him no less than to Śabara,[22] a lifelong duty, in particular with regard to offering. Suspending the same by a turn to a renouncer's life in the search for nothing but pure self-knowledge would in Maṇḍana's opinion have inhibited the attainment of such a goal through causing a considerable delay.[23] It is in terms of acceleration that he recommended a combined procedure of continuing one's obligations *and* of searching for self-knowledge without, however, taking to renunciation.

At any rate it should be recorded that Jaimini, Śabara, Kumārila and Maṇḍana explicitly defended the ideal of the practice of lifelong sacrificing.

---

[19] Olivelle 1993: 239, 242.

[20] Olivelle 1993: 238.

[21] BS (Introduction), pp. xxxv, xlix, li, lvii, lxxiv.

[22] Cf. ŚBh *ad* MSū 6.2.31.

[23] Cf. BS 36.9 ff, probably a direct reference to Śaṅkara (BSūBh 789.3 f on BSū 3.4.17): *pratipannagārhasthyasyātmavidyayaiva kṛtakṛtyatāṃ manvānasya, ṛṇāpakaraṇaṃ praty anādṛtasya, vihitākaraṇanimittasya pāpmano vidyodayapratibandhṛtvaṃ darśayati – ṛṇāni trīṇy apākṛtya* [ManuS 6.35a; cf. MSū 6.2.31] – *iti.* BS 36.21–37.1: *ūrdhvaretasāṃ cāśramiṇāṃ vināpi tair* [i.e. *yajñādibhiḥ*] *viśuddhavidyodaya iṣyate, kiṃ tu kālakṛto viśeṣaḥ. ... karmāṇy apekṣyante vidyāyām abhyāsalabhyāyām api ...* And this is what Śaṅkara has to say about the *ūrdhvaretas* (BSūBh 788.16 on BSū 3.4.17): *na hy agnihotrādīni vaidikāni karmāṇi teṣāṃ santi.*

2.3. Symbolic elements: Triple staff and appellations

There are some more features keeping a Pūrva-Mīmāṃsaka apart from an Uttara-Mīmāṃsaka. The significant character is in their case rather of an emblematic, symbolic nature. It was used as a criterion to clearly distinguish between their respective representatives. Features of such a kind were the carrying of the single or the triple staff (*tridaṇḍin*)[24] as well as the habit of adding some peculiar appellations to their names. Advaita-Vedāntins who followed Śaṅkara were bearers of the single staff (*ekadaṇḍin*), thus demonstrating their state of renouncer of the highest order (*paramahaṃsa*). The triple-staffed (*tridaṇḍin*) Brahmins, however, belonged to factions connected with *karmajñānasamuccaya* and related doctrines, as represented by, e.g., Bhāskara, the Viśiṣṭādvaitins or, most interestingly, by the Mīmāṃsakas. They were assigned a minor state of renunciation only, such as *kuṭīcaka* or *bahūdaka*[25]. Ānandānubhava's *Nyāyaratnadīpāvali* (13th century) can be taken as a testimony to this assessment. On account of one unambiguous passage,[26] it becomes clear that at the time certain additions to names were indeed sufficiently "telling" for his contemporaries to identify[27] the respective order of life (*gṛhastha* or *saṃnyāsin*) the author of a particular text was belonging to.

The following is the context of this remarkable passage: Ānandānubhava reproaches Bhāskara for having denied to the

[24] Similarly also Bhāskara and the Viśiṣṭādvaitins. The single-staff tradition (*ekadaṇḍin, ekaveṇupāṇi*) "entailed the total withdrawal from all ritual activities. The other" (i.e. the triple-staff tradition) "considered some form of ritual life, in keeping with the *dharma* of one's *āśrama*, an essential feature even of renunciation." See Olivelle 1986: 52 f. On ascetics and the *tridaṇḍa* cf. also von Hinüber 1992: 52 (n. 83), 59, 62 (n. 110), 65.

[25] Cf. Olivelle 1986: 52 ff; cf. also TRD 284, 2-15 *ad* ṢDS, Adhikaraṇa 6: Jaiminīyas.

[26] The passage under consideration (NRD 317.4/12) was only briefly treated by Kuppuswami Sastri in his introduction to BS (pp. li f) and later reedited and translated by Olivelle 1986: 92-117.

[27] Strikingly enough, the *Brahmavaivartapurāṇa* makes also a clear distinction between respectable layman Brahmins (*bhaṭṭa*) and religious mendicants: *bhaṭṭāṃś ca bhikṣukāṃś caiva* ... (BVP 4.105.70).

Kaṭhaśruti- and other Saṃnyāsa Upaniṣads their Vedic authenticity and authoritativeness, and of having insinuated they were composed by some charlatan (NRD 316.6 ff). In continuation of his argument with Bhāskara he states that one should not reject texts accepted by venerable and reliable persons (*āptabhāva*),[28] in particular when they belong to the foremost of learned men (*śiṣṭāgraṇī*). He enumerates them by their names of Viśvarūpa, Prabhākara-Guru, Maṇḍana-Miśra, Vācaspati-Miśra and Sucarita-Miśra. Interestingly, Viśvarūpa and Prabhākara-Guru are both assigned to the faction of Ānandānubhava himself, in that they were considered bearers of the single-staff (*ekadaṇḍin*). The three "Miśras"[29], on the other hand, were in no way suspected of having been *ekadaṇḍins*. Quite on the contrary, their relationship with the *gṛhastha-āśrama* was seen in accordance with their carrying a triple-staff (*tridaṇḍa*), and this is made explicit.[30] It is further substantiated by pointing out particular appellations that permit discerning between authors of the householder and the renouncer type. By means of this Ānandānubhava identifies Viśvarūpa as Sureśvara, taking Viśvarūpa as his earlier name before he became an *ekadaṇḍin* under the name of Sureśvara. That Viśvarūpa wrote his *Bālakrīḍā* commentary as a householder (*gṛhastha*) can be recognized, he asserts, by the honorific "Bhaṭṭa" prefixed to his name in the colophon. Had a Saṃnyāsin written it, he would have identified himself by putting Parivrājakācārya before his Saṃnyāsin-name of Sureśvara.[31] Unfortunately, no similarly revealing remarks are made with reference

[28] Preferring the variant °*bhāvaiḥ* (apparatus) to text: °*vākyaiḥ* (NRD 317.10).

[29] The *dvandva* compound °*maṇḍana-vācaspati-sucarita-miśraiḥ* should be taken as an *ekaśeṣa* with the final member referring to each of the three preceding ones.

[30] See Olivelle 1986: 52 f.

[31] NRD 318.2-6: *gṛhasthāvasthāyāṃ viracite ca viśvarūpagranthe ... na cāsau granthaḥ saṃnyāsinā viracitaḥ. tathā hi – parivrājakācārya-sureśvaraviracite – iti granthe nāma likhet. likhitaṃ tu bhaṭṭa-viśvarūpaviracite – iti.* According to BS (Introduction), p. li f, n. 152 and Olivelle 1986: 105, n. 5-58 it is Viśvarūpa's Bālakrīḍā commentary on the *Yājñavalkyadharmaśāstra* which Ānandānubhava has in mind here.

to Prabhākara. Ānandānubhava might therefore have agreed with the opponent who held that Prabhākara was indeed an *ekadaṇḍin*, as was perhaps inferred from the appellation *guru*.

Therefore, we may come to the conclusion that aged Mīmāṃsakas possibly might have left their home, but in doing so they continued sacrificing and carrying their symbolic triple-staff. This does not necessarily mean they thereby would actually have changed their *āśrama*. Their state may rather have resembled either the *vānaprastha* or the late Vedic *pravrājaka* type,[32] who, when of old age, had the choice to emigrate voluntarily from his village or urban environment, without abandoning his sacrificial duties. Although a precursor of what later developed into renunciation (*saṃnyāsa*, *pari-vrāja*) in the strict sense of an *āśrama*, the *pravrāja* mode of life nevertheless survived as a householder's (*gṛhastha*) alternative to becoming an extreme renouncer (*saṃnyāsin*). While the latter had to break away totally from tradition, a former householder roaming about in his old age continued sacrificing by keeping also his sacrificial cord, topknot and other emblems such as the triple staff.[33] Whatever this may have been, a case of *pravrājaka* or the *vānaprastha-āśrama*, it was certainly not the *parivrājaka* mode a Mīmāṃsaka aspired or eventually took to. This can be substantiated by a revealing passage in Bhāskara's *Brahmasūtrabhāṣya*, where it has been stated that performing the rituals would very well go together with carrying the *tridaṇḍa* and that the meaning of the word *pravrajita* has nothing in common with 're-nouncement' (*tyāga*).[34] No less revealing is Guṇaratna's characterisation of Pūrva-Mīmāṃsakas as typical householders: *tatra pūrvamīmāṃsāvādinaḥ kukarmavivarjino yajanādiṣaṭkarmakāriṇo brahmasūtriṇo gṛhasthāśramasthitāḥ śūdrānnādivarjakā bhavanti. te ca dvedhā bhāṭṭāḥ prābhākarāś ca ṣaṭpañcapramāṇapra-*

---

[32] See Sprockhoff 1981: 84-87.

[33] See Olivelle 1986: 26 ff.

[34] See Bhāskara (ŚMBh 208.24 f): *tridaṇḍapakṣe ... karmatyāgo nāsti. na hi pravrajitaśabdas tyāgārtho* ... Cf. also below, footnotes 43 and 58.

rūpiṇaḥ. ye tūttaramīmāṃsāvādinaḥ ... (TRD 283.7-10 *ad* ṢDS, Adhikaraṇa 6: Jaiminīyas).

Given such a background, it is worthy of note that in perfect accordance with Ānandānubhava's information and Bhāskara's remarks we do indeed find specific appellations appended to the proper name of almost *every* Pūrva-Mīmāṃsaka recorded in literature. These additions such as "Miśra", "Bhaṭṭa" or "Svāmin" point to learned, respectable Brahmins of the "laity", but never to renouncers:[35] Śabara-Svāmin, Kumārila-Bhaṭṭa or Kumāra-Svāmin,[36] Prabhākara-Miśra, Maṇḍana-Miśra, Bhaṭṭa-Umbeka, Sucarita-Miśra, Śālikanātha-Miśra, Pārthasārathi-Miśra, Paritoṣa-Miśra, Bhavanātha-Miśra, Murāri-Miśra, and so on. This cannot be merely accidental. No Advaita-Vedānta renouncer is known to bear a similar addition to his name. I am therefore quite convinced that at the time of the circles we are concerned with here the appellation *bhaṭṭa* (> *bhartṛ*) connoted the meaning of a married man, a private citizen or 'Mister', so to speak. Hence, in terms of state (*āśrama*), the Bhaṭṭas were married men (*gṛhastha*s).

3. Ideologies

3.1. Activity (karman) and knowledge (jñāna)

It may be recalled from chapter 2.2 above that Maṇḍana had favoured the ideal of a combination of ritual activity and knowledge, which is also known as *karma-jñāna-samuccaya*.[37] In his investigation of 1994, R. Mesquita has convincingly shown that already before Maṇḍana also Kumārila (in his *Tantravārttika* and

[35] For traditional names and titles such as "Miśra", "Bhaṭṭa" and "Svāmin" as characteristic of Brahmins cf. Witzel 1994: 265. Kṣemendra, in his *Lokaprakāśa* (LPr, p. 1, v. 8), relates the title of a Bhaṭṭa to ritually active Brahmins: *ṛtvijo yājñiko yajvā sāmanto bhaṭṭa ucyate | trisandhyopāsakaś caiva vipraś caiva purohitaḥ* ||. Vidyabhusana (1915: 88) fails to supply a reason supporting his statement that °*svāmin* was related to people hailing from the southern regions: "The title Svāmi appended to Pakṣila in the name Pakṣilasvāmi also points to his birth-place having been in Draviḍa."

[36] Mesquita 1994: 474, n. 106.

[37] BS (Introduction), pp. xlvi f; Thrasher 1993: 32.

Bṛhaṭṭīkā) had supported a combined mode of life (*samuccaya*) in like manner.[38] Yet, Kumārila was certainly not the first to think along such lines and probably also not the first to lead his life accordingly, as can be judged from the example of Bhartṛprapañca, the ancient commentator on the BĀU, who was criticised by Śaṅkara for his *bhedābheda* views.[39] Householders were naturally bound to carry out activities (*karman*), the precise nature of which depended largely on their respective (*sva-*)*dharma*, from ritual to the fulfilment of various social obligations. Thus they must have conceived of themselves as being fundamentally related to the 'path of activities' (*karmamārga*, *pravṛtti*), which, quite contrary to the path concentrating on seeking only knowledge (*jñānamārga*, *nivṛtti*), was basically open for an expansion into a combined *karma-* and *jñāna-mārga*. No wonder then that in exactly this regard Śaṅkara's Vedāntic adversary Bhāskara has much more in common with Maṇḍana than with Śaṅkara. Apart from an explicitly formulated *jīvanmukti* doctrine he shared with Maṇḍana,[40] Bhāskara, too, besides his *bhedābheda* orientation, also held a *karmajñānasamuccaya* position[41] and – quite befittingly – refused to ever become a renouncer.[42] On account of this, he naturally incurred the hatred of ascetic and purely knowledge-orientated Advaita-

[38] On *Tantravārttika* and *Bṛhaṭṭīkā*, see Mesquita 1994: 459 ff and 465-469, 479 f.

[39] For Bhartṛprapañca in the present context see Rüping 1977 and Mesquita 1994: 463, n. 59.

[40] See below. For Maṇḍana, see BS (Introduction), xxxvi ff, 132.6, 151.7. For Bhāskara, cf. ŚMBh *passim*, in particular 220.13, 224.20.

[41] ŚMBh 207.24 ff: *tasmād yathaiva śamādayo* [cf. BSū 3.4.27] *yāvajjīvam anuvartante viduṣām apavargaprāptaye, tathāśramakarmāṇīti nāntarāle parityāgaḥ*. On Bhāskara and his relationship with Śaṅkara see Rüping 1977: 65 ff.

[42] ŚMBh 210.1 f: *tasmād yāvad idaṃ me śarīram iti karmanibandhanāvṛttir anuvartate, tāvad āśramakarmānuvṛttir aśakyā nivārayitum* ... As another example for a close relationship between *jñānakarmasamuccaya* and *jīvanmukti* one may draw upon Śrīdhara, the author of the *Nyāyakandalī*. See Mesquita 1994: 466, n. 73 and 469, n. 89. Pārthasārathi is equally explicit with regard to lifelong offering combined with *ātmajñāna* as the means to neutralize accumulated *karman* (ŚD 130.26 ff).

Vedāntins. In this connection it should be recalled that Bhāskara explicitly rejected also opinions according to which the *śruti* would indeed prescribe to refrain from a householder's duties at a certain stage and to enter another state, namely that of a renouncer. Such an ideology is merely based on the *smṛti*, Bhāskara clarifies. From a presupposed authoritativeness of the *śruti* in favour of a turn to an ascetic order of life, it would necessarily follow that the mendicant life of Buddhists and Jainas, too, was in accordance with the *śruti* (*śrauta*).[43]

Briefly, Bhartṛprapañca, Kumārila, Maṇḍana and Bhāskara were some outstanding personalities to support a *karmajñānasamuccaya* doctrine.

3.2. *Karmajñānasamuccaya and the jīvanmukti*

From the Bṛhaṭṭīkā fragments preserved in Śrīdhara's *Nyāyakandalī* and analysed by R. Mesquita it appears that Kumārila seems to have accepted a particular liberation concept,[44] the notion and term (*jīvanmukti*) of which is elaborately discussed first in Maṇḍana's *Brahmasiddhi*.[45] Indeed, the *karmajñānasamuccaya* as well as the state of *jīvanmukti* connected with it share in a closer relationship than discernible from perhaps only a superficial point of view. As is well known,[46] views of such a kind tend to trace back the idea of *jīvanmukti* exclusively to the Advaita-Vedānta movement, in

---

[43] See ŚMBh 207.26–208.4 and Bhāskara's harsh criticism of *saṃnyāsa* on pp 208-211. Despite this, the Jābālaśruti, not infrequently quoted in such contexts, leaves it to the decision of the person concerned to directly 'renounce' – *if pra-√vraj* bore at all the very connotation of 'renunciation' in the sense as claimed by later traditions (see footnotes 34 and 58) – from whatever the actual order of his life may be. *Jābālopaniṣad* 4: ... *brahmacaryaṃ samāpya gṛhī bhavet, gṛhī bhūtvā vanī bhavet, vanī bhūtvā pravrajet* | *yadi vetarathā brahmacaryād eva pravrajet, gṛhād vā, vanād vā* | ... See also footnotes 34, 58.

[44] Mesquita 1994: 470 ff, 480. From Pārthasārathi' s presentation of the matter it would, however, appear, that *mokṣa* realises itself only after death: *asati śarīrārambhe pūrvaśarīranipāte cāśarīro 'vasthito mukto bhavati* (ŚD 130.28 f).

[45] See, e.g., BS (Introduction), xxxvi ff, 130.17–134.18 [132.6], 151.7 (= quotation of Yogasūtrabhāṣya *ad* Yogasūtra 4.30).

[46] Cf. Slaje 2000b: 325 f.

particular to Śaṅkara. But only scarcely did the latter touch on it, and very reluctantly at that.[47] The first systematic representation of an Advaita-Vedāntic *jīvanmukti* doctrine becomes visible as late as in the 13th century through Ānandānubhava who dedicated the fourth chapter of his *Nyāyaratnadīpāvali* to this concept.[48] This was about one hundred years before Vidyāraṇya firmly established the *jīvanmukti* idea in Advaita-Vedānta circles by writing his famous *Jīvanmuktiviveka* treatise. Earlier on only Vimuktātman (between the second half of the 8th and the first half of the 10th century) pronounced himself more prominently in favour of a *jīvanmukti* doctrine as this had become unavoidable for safeguarding his *ekajīva-vāda*.[49] Moreover, Ānandānubhava, who as a commentator on the *Iṣṭasiddhi* was well acquainted with Vimuktātman's ideas, took the latter as a point of reference for his own *jīvanmukti* exposition. On the other hand, idea and term of *jīvanmukti* were already there in Mīmāṃsā circles in the 7th century, implicitly perhaps in Kumārila (the first half of the 7th century), but explicitly in Maṇḍana (660-720), and so also in the Bhedābheda-Vedāntin Bhāskara, who must be assigned a time between Maṇḍana and Vimuktātman. Apart from the two Mīmāṃsās, the *jīvanmukti* can terminologically and doctrinally be traced back to the Bhāṣyas on the *Yoga-* and on the *Nyāyasūtras* respectively, and Uddyotakara, too, is very explicit with regard to that idea.[50] So contrary to the "Vedānticized" mainstream opinion maintained uncritically by too many Indologists, the historical truth turns out rather as follows: the Vedānta tradition initially felt compelled to react to an idea gradually gaining predominance over their own claim of a primacy of renunciation.[51] This idea did not regard liberation as being

---

[47] Cf. BSūBh, pp. 97,3, 850,3–851,4; BhGBh *ad* BhG 6.27. See also Mesquita 1994: 470, n. 25 and 480, n. 129; Slaje 2000b: 326, n. 5.

[48] Translation and analysis by Hoffmann (2005).

[49] For this problem in Vimuktātman's doctrine cf. Schmücker 2001: 158-171. Cf. also Mesquita 2000: 181 f, n. 375 and 520 ff, n. 688 for a summary of the idea of *jīvanmukti* in Vimuktātman and other Advaitins.

[50] See Slaje 2000b: 343, n. 78 for references.

necessarily inhibited by ritual or social activities – quite on the contrary. The earlier *jīvanmukti* notions appear as intrinsically related to a *karma-* or a *karma-* and *jñāna*-path. The development and the early history of the *jīvanmukti* idea was – on the basis of the *Bhagavadgītā*, the *Mahābhārata* and the *Mokṣopāya* – demonstrably closely related to the *gṛhastha* order of life, in particular to *gṛhastha*s and the *kṣātra dharma* of the ruling class (*kṣatriya*), with an emphasis on their active participation in society (*karmin*).[52] Let it be noted that famous exponents of the nobility figure always prominently in such contexts: Arjuna in the *Bhagavadgītā*, Rāma in the *Mokṣopāya*, King Janaka[53] in the *Mahābhārata*. The latter in particular, who remained socially active throughout his life,[54] has not only become the model of a *jīvanmukta* in later tradition, but was – as Śaṅkara has it – referred to even by Jaimini with a view "to demonstrate that *householders* engaged in *procreation* and *ritual activities* can indeed attain the knowledge revealed in the Vedas."[55] Tradition has it that under the influence of Yājñavalkya's thought, advice and example he remained a house-holding king and did *not* renounce although he had already become a *jñānin* – the archetypical *jīvanmukta* as it were.

In short, our distorted picture of the history of *jīvanmukti* is largely due to a preconceived notion according to which the term would necessarily bear an Advaita-Vedānta coinage, considered to be the same in all traditions. This is not the case. It is true that in the broader context of Advaita-Vedānta *renunciation* the *jīvanmukti*

---

[51] Slaje 2000b: 325 ff.

[52] See Slaje 2000a; 2000b; 2001. Cf. Bhāskara [BhGBh(Bh) 165.6 on BhG 6.47]: *gṛhasthasyārjunasya* ..., and also Śaṅkara (BSūBh p. 783, 8 ff *ad* BSū 3.4.3). In Kashmir, *gṛhastha* traditions had typically been predominant, and works concerning this matter were still composed under Mogul rule in the late 17th century, as can be seen from Ānandavardhana's *jñānakarmasamuccaya*-exegesis of the *Bhagavadgītā* (Slaje, forthcoming).

[53] On his identity cf. Witzel 2003: §2, pp. 106 ff, n. 13.

[54] Slaje 2000b: 338-342.

[55] Olivelle 1993: 241. For this view as ascribed to Jaimini cf. Śaṅkara's Bhāṣya on BSū 3.4.18 (Olivelle 1993: 239 f).

must be taken as an anticipation of final liberation in the sense of an *attainment of a positive experience* (bliss, etc.), so to speak. In contrast to this, the doctrines as preserved in the epic, in the *Mokṣopāya*, and also in the Yoga- and Nyāya-commentaries, conceived of the *jīvanmukti* as of *liberation from attachment* to the fruits of actions and *from passionate involvement* in worldly things and matters. This would result in a lasting dispassionate attitude, the basis for *non-intentional activities* and participation *in* the world, which alone would be neutral in terms of karmic retribution. There is also a *subhāṣita* on the *gṛhastha-āśrama* evidently taken from the *Yājñavalkyasmṛti* and tying it nicely with some of the features just pointed out: *nyāyārjitadhanas tattvajñānaniṣṭho 'tithi-priyaḥ* | *śāstravit satyavādī ca gṛhastho 'pi vimucyate* ||.[56]

Thus, if we take R. Mesquita's pioneering investigation into passages pointing to Mīmāṃsā *jīvanmukti* ideas into consideration, as they were related to a *continuation* of ritual *activities*,[57] we may not be wrong in assuming that a similar conception may have prevailed among the Mīmāṃsaka householders. As an interim result it may therefore be maintained that the bifurcation of the two Mīmāṃsās fairly extended also to social, symbolic, ideological and soteriological aspects.

[56] SRBh, p. 93, 8 f (= 2nd Prakaraṇa, Gṛhastāśramapraśaṃsā, v. 1). Cf. YS 3.205. The *Yājñavalkyasmṛti*, and in particular Aparārka's commentary on it, were extensively exploited by Ānandavardhana to demonstrate that the *smṛtis* (including the *Mahābhārata*) favoured a householder's balanced way of life in that such a one combined sacrificial activities (*karmin*) with knowledge (*jñānin*), following the *jñānakarmasamuccaya*. Ontologically, it is the *bhedābheda-vāda*, which he ascribes to those traditions. In fact, this would separate them in more then only one aspect from Śaṅkara's *advaita-vāda*, who accepted only knowledge as the means to final release. On Ānandavardhana, see above, fn. 25.

[57] This is also supported by the emphasis put on the neutralisation of *karman* through fully experiencing (*bhoga*) its effects already brought into action (*prārabdha*) [cf. Mesquita 1994: 458 f, 479; cf. also ŚD 129.20 ff and 130.26 ff] and by a particular view-point according to which *mokṣa* means *liberation from* any relationship with the (material) world: *so 'yaṃ prapañcasaṃbandho bandhas, tad-vimokṣaś ca mokṣaḥ* (ŚD 125.32 f); *niḥsaṃbandho nirānandaś ca mokṣaḥ* (ŚD 128.30).

II

Let us now turn to Yājñavalkya, Janaka's adviser, and inquire into a possible historical relationship with the two Mīmāṃsās. Yājña-valkya is represented in the ŚPB as officiating priest and house-holder, as a seeker for self-knowledge and, in one place, seemingly also as a *pra-vrājaka.*[58] Yājñavalkya's outstanding personality and idiosyncratical manner of speech cannot be explained by literary fiction alone.[59]

In the Ātmavāda section of the "Vṛttikāragrantha",[60] as handed down by Śabara (ca. 4th/5th century AD)[61] in his Bhāṣya on MSū

---

[58] BĀU 4.5.2 (M/K): *pravrajiṣyan* ... *aham* ... (Yājñavalkya's direct speech); 4.5.25 (M): *pravavrāja* (redactional conclusion) for which K (4.5.15) reads: *vijahāra*. Hanefeld (1976: 72, n. 3) reports the reading *udyāsyan* for the direct speech *pravrajiṣyan* in M (4.5.2). On some doctrinal implications of the (historically later) *pra-√vraj* usage in the BĀU cf. Sprockhoff 1979: 396 ff; 1981: 68-76, 84 ff. Note that according to Bhāskara *pra-√vraj* does *not* mean 'renouncement' (*tyāga*) [see above, footnotes 34 and 43]. Śaṅkara, however, was conspicuously quick in identifying *pra-√vraj* with *pari-√vraj* (*pravrajiṣyan* [=] *pārivrājyaṃ kariṣyan* (BĀUBh 661.2 *ad* BĀU 4.5.2); so also in the case of *udyāsyan*: *udyāsyan* [=] *ūrdhvaṃ yāsyan* [=] *pārivrājyākhyam āśramāntaram* [BĀUBh 299.8 f *ad* BĀU 2.4.1], as he also was in excluding socially active classes from the renouncer's mode of life: *na hi kṣatriyavaiśyayoḥ pārivrājya-pratipattir asti* (BĀUBh *ad* 4.5.15 [cf. Sawai 1992: 129, n. 44, 131]).

[59] Parpola 1981: 159 ff; see Fišer 1984 and, in particular, Witzel 2003. Whether it was Yājñavalkya himself or the character depicted as "Yājñavalkya" in the Upaniṣads that may have served as a model for some peculiar develop-ments in both the Pūrva- and the Uttara-Mīmāṃsā respectively, is of no rele-vance for the point to be made here.

[60] Cf. Frauwallner 1972. For attempts at an exact demarcation of the Vṛtti-kāragrantha from Śabara's own words, which has not yet really been settled beyond doubt, cf. Strauss 1932: 487 ff, 516, n. 3 [= *Kl. Schr.*, pp. 397 ff, 426, n. 3]; Zangenberg 1962: 61 ff (62 f on the structure); Frauwallner 1968: 108 ff. On pp. 109-111 Frauwallner assigns also the *ātma-vāda* section to the Vṛttikāra. In contrast with Strauss, according to whom the Vṛttikāragrantha would have covered the text from p. 24, 16 to p. 48, 14 (ŚBh[F]), Frauwallner extends the section from p. 24, 16 to p. 60, 25, marking at the same time the end of his edi-tion. Pārthasārathi treats the "Vṛttikāra section" in his *Śāstradīpikā* (ŚD) from p. 89, 2 to p. 132, 15.

[61] As to Śabara's dating cf. Verpoorten 1987: 8 ("between 350 and 400 A.D."). Clooney (1990: 53) assigns him a time "two or three centuries" after "the

1.1.5, a number of Upaniṣadic statements are quoted.[62] All of them are authored by Yājñavalkya and correspond with the received Mādhyandina recension of the *Bṛhadāraṇyaka*. Let it be noted right at the outset, however, that the BĀU had been redacted comparatively late (ca. 200-100 BC),[63] and that in the Vṛttikāragrantha as such no direct reference is made to the names of either Yājñavalkya or of the *Bṛhadāraṇyaka-Upaniṣad*. All the quotations there go by the denotation of '*brāhmaṇa*'.[64] Unless they refer to the smallest divisional units of the BĀU or of the *Śatapathabrāhmaṇa*, which

---

second century A.D." and to Jaimini's Sūtras a time for taking their shape "between the fourth and second centuries B.C., and a redactional process until about 200 B.C." According to Parpola (1994) Jaimini is earlier than Kātyāyana (p. 303), who can be dated between 248-180 BC (p. 300, n. 40). Yoshimizu (1997: 33, n. 1) cautiously refrains from any determination of Śabara's *floruit*. It was Zangenberg (1962: 66) who established the time of the Vṛttikāra as the first half of the 5th century as a "preliminary working hypothesis". Frauwallner's inclination to assign to him the second half of the 5th century was based on the assumption ("augenscheinlich") that the Vṛttikāra had probably been aware of Vasubandhu's *Vādavidhi* (Frauwallner 1968: 101). This, however, is anything but certain. Zangenberg (1962: 65, 67) had already emphasised the highly speculative nature of such an assumption by using "vielleicht" and "unverkennbare Ähnlichkeit". Verpoorten (1987: 8) placed the Vṛttikāra in the first half of the 4th century ("between 300 and 350 A.D."), although by an obviously erroneous reference (note 38) to Frauwallner 1968: 113.

[62] H. Jacobi (1914: 153 ff [= *Kl. Schr.*, pp. 750 ff]) was the first to point to the fact that the oldest extant exegeses of the BĀU are contained in a Mīmāṃsā work, the *Śābarabhāṣya*. For subsequent treatments of this passage cf. Strauss 1932: 521-524 [= *Kl. Schr.*, pp. 431-434]; Biardeau 1968: 113 f; Frauwallner 1968: 54 f.

[63] Witzel 2003: § 9, p. 135.

[64] As already noted by Strauss: "Upaniṣad*stellen*", [emphasis mine] "die bezeichnenderweise hier immer Brāhmaṇa heißen, ..." (Strauss 1932: 493 [= *Kl. Schr.*, p. 403]). A comparable usage has been brought to light by Thieme's investigation on *bráhman*: *brāhmaṇa* (n.) is frequently (e.g., AiB, TS, ŚPB) used in the sense of "Wahrheitsformulierung", "was Wahrheitsformulierung[en] enthält", etc. (Thieme 1952: 118 ff [= *Kl. Schr.*, pp. 127 ff]). Formulations of such a kind may consist of a single statement ("Ausspruch") only. See, however, already Eggeling: "Single discourses of this kind were called *brāhmaṇa* ... or because they were ... the authoritative utterances of such as were thoroughly versed in Vedic and sacrificial lore and competent ... In later times a collection or digest of such detached pieces came to be likewise called a Brāhmaṇa." (Eggeling 1882: xxii f).

are as well called '*brāhmaṇas*', the particular way the '*brāhmaṇa*' references under consideration are arranged and used by the Vṛttikāra and Mīmāṃsā authors rather point to the meaning of 'direct authoritative instruction' or, as implied by the title of the present paper, of an 'instructional formulation'. This observation can claim confirmative support from the matching usage of other Mīmāṃsakas such as Kumārila and Pārthasārathi, Prabhākara and Śālikanātha,[65] and also from what L. Renou had independently assumed already in 1948, namely that the reference to *brāhmaṇas* of Yājñavalkya by Kātyāyana,[66] a "key figure in the early history of Mīmāṃsā"[67] and who, as of the 3rd/2nd century BC lived slightly before the final redaction of the BĀU took place, was entirely unlikely to have referred to the *whole* Yājñavalkyakāṇḍa of the BĀU:

> Il est tout-à-fait improbable ... que cette expression vise le Yājñavalkyakāṇḍa de la BĀU: le sū. IV. 3, 105, auquel se réfère l'exception de Kātyāyana, concerne 'les traités de Brāhmaṇa et de Kalpa', non des chapitres d'Upaniṣad.[68]

In a recent study, J. Bronkhorst[69] arrived at the exact opposite opinion. According to Bronkhorst "BĀU 3-4 *must* be meant by Kātyāyana" (p. 114). He takes it for granted that by '*brāhmaṇa*'

---

[65] Cf., e.g., ŚV (ātmav.) 140 f, 143, 146 (as explained by the NK) and ŚD, p. 131, 19 – p. 132, 13; Bṛ 165.9 (ṚjV 165.26), 176.1, 179.7, 11; (ṚjV 179.21, 28); 186.7 f (ṚjV 186.26 f).

[66] Vārttika 1 on Pāṇ 4.3.105 (Mbh 2.316.12-15): *purāṇaprokteṣu brāhmaṇakalpeṣu yājñavalkyādibhyaḥ pratiṣedhas tu tulyakālatvāt*. Patañjali states more precisely: *yājñavalkāni brāhmaṇāni* (MBh 2.316.15).

[67] Parpola 1994: 298.

[68] Renou 1948: 75 [885]. "The weakness of Goldstücker's argument lies in his identification of the Yājñavalkāni Brāhmaṇāni with the Brāhmaṇa of the Vājasaneyins. ... The Yājñavalkāni Brāhmaṇāni ... seem to me to stand somewhat on a par with the 'Tittiriṇā proktāḥ ślokāḥ', which, in Patañjali's time, were excluded from the term 'Taittirīyāḥ' as uncanonical. ... Both kinds of tracts probably belong to the last floating materials of Ad[h]varyu tradition, which had not yet been incorporated with the canon. ..." (Eggeling 1882: xxxviii). Recently, Reinvang (2000) referred to the "*brāhmaṇas*" of Yājñavalkya as "pericopes".

[69] Bronkhorst 1993: 113 f.

Kātyāyana and Patañjali were referring to recently composed 'works', and translates Patañjali's *yājñavalkāni brāhmaṇāni* accordingly as: "the Brāhmaṇa *works* uttered by Yājñavalkya" (p. 113) [all emphases mine]. Bronkhorst, however, had not taken notice of Eggeling 1882, Renou 1948 and Thieme 1952, and has not discussed the evidence of the unambiguous Mīmāṃsā usage of '*brāhmaṇa*' in the given context, which clearly contradicts his assumption. Furthermore, the late redaction (200-100 BC?) of the BĀU, carried out only *after* Kātyāyana,[70] makes the assumption of a reference by Kātyāyana to the (Yājñavalkya-)*kāṇḍa*s still more unlikely.

Therefore, what we actually meet with here under the designation of *brāhmaṇa*s are single formulations attributed to Yājñavalkya, quoted in direct speech.

The so-called Vṛttikāragrantha section as transmitted through the *Mīmāṃsābhāṣya* displays some exegetical efforts with the aim of reinforcing or defending a Buddhist or the Mīmāṃsaka's position, as the case may be, starting from one Upaniṣadic formulation launched against the Mīmāṃsaka by a Buddhist. Irrespective of the exact time that may be assigned to the anonymous Vṛttikāra and which might range between the 3rd and the 5th century as the latest possible *terminus ante quem*, the present exegeses of the BĀU are at any rate considerably, namely almost half a millennium, older than Śaṅkara (the second half of the 7th century), who is commonly regarded the earliest preserved Vedānta commentator of the BĀU (Kāṇva).[71] By this fact alone, these early hermeneutics, dealing with an Upaniṣad and authored by a Mīmāṃsaka, deserve our close attention. The BĀU(M) is the only Upaniṣad found quoted in the *Śābarabhaṣya*, albeit embedded in the Vṛttikāragrantha. This fact, however, may be explained from the point of view of Parpola,

---

[70] Witzel 2003: § 9, p. 135.

[71] On Śaṅkara's knowledge (or rather: ignorance) of the BĀU in both its recensions as well as for other essentials regarding his Bhāṣya on the BĀU, cf. Rau' s revealing "Remarks" (Rau 1959-61); see also notes 84 f.

whose meritorious investigations into the prehistory of the Mīmāṃsā[72] yielded – among others – also the result that Vājasaneyins such as Kātyāyana would have been involved in the early development of the *Pūrvamīmāṃsāsūtra*. In addition, the Sāmavedic affiliation of Jaimini reflects a close connection between the (Mādhyandina-) Vājasaneyins and the Kauthuma-Sāmaveda branch at the formative time of the *Mīmāṃsāsūtra*, as attested to elsewhere.[73]

1. Recensional bifurcation in the commentaries

Quite contrary to Śaṅkara, who commented upon the BĀU in its Kāṇva recension, the quotes in the *Śābarabhāṣya* are almost exclusively, i.e. with the exception of one indeterminate reading, taken from the Mādhyandina recension alone.[74] This exclusive BĀU affiliation of the early (Pūrva-)Mīmāṃsā to the Mādhyandina branch could indeed reach back to the initial period of its formation.[75] The Mādhyandinas were very prominent already well before the Vāja-

[72] Parpola 1981; 1994.

[73] Parpola 1994: 304, 305, n. 68.

[74] In general this was already observed by Strauss 1932: 491 [= *Kl. Schr.*, p. 401], but entirely overlooked by Biardeau in her 1968 study, which she based on a comparison with the Kāṇva recension only (cf. on p. 114, n. 1 and p. 120, n. 1). In the absence of a critical edition (cf. also Reinvang 2000: 163, n. 23) nothing definite can, however, be said with regard to the readings the ancient Mīmāṃsakas may have recited. I have pointed out elsewhere (WS (II), p. 301) that there is substantial reason to assume that by the times of the Vṛttikāra and Śabara the wording and the structure of the BĀU might indeed in some passages have differed from our received recensions of today. Yet, I do not want to enter here into a discussion of the textual prehistory of the Yājñavalkyakāṇḍas in the ŚPB. The solution of such a problem would above all require a critical edition of early commentaries and other works of *both* the Mīmāṃsā and Vedānta traditions explaining or transmitting BĀU quotations. Cf. Rau 1959-61: 299 (121): "kritisch ediert wird [das Bṛhadāraṇyakopaniṣadbhāṣya] den ältesten uns vor der Hand erreichbaren K-Text der BĀU enthalten." ... "Die Varianten des mūlagrantha wurden ... in die MSS des bhāṣya verschleppt. Das einzige Mittel, dieser Verwirrung ein Ende zu setzen, ist die Aufstellung eines Stemmas aller erreichbaren bhāṣya-MSS und eine darauf gegründete kritische Edition."

[75] Parpola 1994: 305, n. 68. Note, however, that in later times Kumārila preferred to draw mainly upon the *Chāndogyopaniṣad* (see K. Yoshimizu's paper in the present volume, chapter 4).

saneyin Kātyāyana (ca. 248-180 BC), and certainly also during Megasthenes' presence at the Maurya court (ca. 300 BC), who left us a reference to them.[76] Thus, there is a direct line from Yājñavalkya Vājasaneya, the probable redactor and most prominent figure[77] of the corpus of White Yajurveda texts including the BĀU, to some key-figures of the early Mīmāṃsā, as were Jaimini and Kātyāyana. So it will not really come as a surprise that the Vājasaneyin Kātyāyana expressly referred to formulations (*brāhmaṇas*) of Yājñavalkya (see above), that a coherent set of such formulations was cited from the BĀU in its Mādhyandina recension by the Vṛttikāra and that the BĀU(M) is the only Upaniṣad incorporated into the *Śābarabhāṣya* at all. Thus up to a certain point in history the Pūrva-Mīmāṃsā seems to have stood in an unbroken line of Mādhyandina recitation, leading right back into the formative period of the BĀU. The same can hardly be said of the Kāṇva recension as commented upon by Śaṅkara.

2. Exegetical stratagems in the *Śābarabhāṣya*

From the quotations in the *Śābarabhāṣya*, it becomes clear that Yājñavalkya's Janaka- and Maitreyī-dialogues[78] were regarded as highly authoritative already in comparatively early times. In addition, Yājñavalkya's conceptions, word-formations and sayings have become extraordinarily influential for subsequent doctrinal developments. This is in particular true with reference to his statements on self-knowledge (*ātmajñāna*) and to the doctrine of nonduality (*advaita*). The formation and initial coinage of the latter term (*advaita*) go doubtlessly back to Yājñavalkya himself, as Witzel has achieved to demonstrate in his investigation into Yājña-

[76] *Maduandinoi*, cf. Witzel 2003: §9, p. 137.

[77] For a study of Yājñavalkya, his personal language and his involvement in the canonical development of the White Yajurveda corpus see now Witzel 2003.

[78] Strikingly, Bhāskara replaces the feminine *maitreyī* by the masculine *maitreya*. A misprint can safely be ruled out in this case since the masculine stem occurs more than once and is also inflected in the instrumental case (*maitreyeṇa*), cf. ŚMBh 80.2, 5, 17 (*ad* BSū 1.4.18: *vākyānvayāt*).

valkya's language and personality.[79] Given the unconcealed allusions in Gauḍapāda's *Āgamaśāstra* (ĀŚ 2.2-5) to Yājñavalkya's dialogue with Janaka (BĀU 4.3), the frequent occurrence of *advaita*/*advaya*[80] in this earliest extant Advaita-Vedāntaśāstra may be connected with this fact.

In the Mīmāṃsā texts, on the other hand, it is Yājñavalkya's *ātman* doctrine as imparted to Maitreyī, which is given a prominent role, but not the *advaita* doctrine. This might be due to the Buddhists' preference to quote from the dialogue in their own favour. Should the Buddhists really have used to refer to this passage in the way as testified to by the Vṛttikāra, which from a historical viewpoint is not entirely unlikely, their peculiar interpretation of this quote quite naturally necessitated a refutation. This refutation was carried out by way of sentence contextualisation, always from the angle of the narrowest possible context. As such, the procedure is indigenous to Mīmāṃsā hermeneutics, as a theoretically reflected method[81] as well as an exegetically applied strategy.[82] Each of the single quotes can exclusively, or at least also, be located in the fourth *kāṇḍa* of the BĀU, forming as such part of the so-called Yājñavalkyakāṇḍa, in *adhyāyas* 2-4 (= Janaka) and 5 (= Maitreyī). The majority of the citations, however, were demonstrably taken from the Maitreyī dialogue in the fourth *kāṇḍa* (4.5). Not really unexpected for a Mīmāṃsaka, the quotes under consideration were interpreted by way of *contextualizing* the statements by pointing out their meaningful relationship. Thus, the respective immediate context is assigned a prominent criterion for a correct understanding of the intention of the whole. If compared, e.g., to Śaṅkara's way of interpretation, it is noticeable that he absolutely would have tried to supply *as many quotes as possible* from as many different

[79] See above, fn. 77.

[80] *advaita*: ĀŚ 1.10, 16, 17; 2.18, 36; 3.18. *advaya*: ĀŚ 2.33, 35; 3.30; 4.4, 45, 62, 80, 85. *advayatā*: ĀŚ 2.33.

[81] Cf. the sixfold hierarchy (*pramāṇa*) as established to determine Vedic sentence meanings when they relate to ritual matters (ŚBh *ad* MSū 3.3.14).

[82] Cf. Bronkhorst 1997. See also below, fn. 95.

śruti passages as possible with a view to prove their internal coherence according to his own claims. There are roughly 65 quotes I have cursorily counted in his comments on the Maitreyī dialogues (2.4 and 4.5). Among these, only one citation (*neti neti*), occurring three times, actually stems from Yājñavalkya. The rest was taken from elsewhere, from different *śruti* and *smṛti* text-places obviously considered apt to prove the point Śaṅkara was trying to make himself. The authoritativeness of his interpretation is thus derived from a *maximum of matching quotes, which were associatively accumulated.* The method in the *Śābarabhāṣya*, however, is decidedly different, at least as can be judged from the comparatively short text-piece as retained there. The interpretations comply with the immediate context of the respective quote, and whenever a supporting statement is adduced to reinforce a position, it not only is directly taken from Yājñavalkya, but also seems to have been justifiably contextualized. So, incidentally, did Kumārila and Pārthasārathi.[83] It is possible that some Mīmāṃsakas, as they can historically be somehow attached to the Vājasaneyi branch, regarded the statements of Yājñavalkya Vājasaneya as making up a coherent system of thought in its own right. It was probably also handed down as such by the exegetical tradition of the Mādhyandinas. Contrary to Śaṅkara, who, as convincingly demonstrated by W. Rau,[84] is not likely to have received a traditional Vedic training and could hardly ever have had direct access to an unbroken exegesis of the BĀU,[85] Yājñavalkya's formulations were meaningfully *inter-*

[83] See ŚV, ātmav. 146 and NR thereon. See also ŚD, the Mokṣavāda section (pp. 125 ff) of the Vṛttikāragrantha (p. 89, 2 – p. 132, 15), abounding in interpretations of Upaniṣadic quotes.

[84] Rau 1959-61: 295 (117): "Für mich unterliegt es keinem Zweifel, daß Śaṅkara traditionellen Unterricht im vedischen Sinne nie genossen hat, daß er die Rezensionen der BĀU nach MSS verglich, die womöglich noch nicht einmal akzentuiert waren, kurz, daß er *vielerlei* Versionen *las*, wo das Altertum *eine* Version *auswendig* kannte." Cf. also footnotes 71, 85.

[85] This is mirrored by Śaṅkara's following remark on BĀU 4.5.15 (the Maitreyī dialogue): *śrutismṛtivākyāni śataśa upalabhyanta itaretaraviruddhāni* | Cf. Rau 1959-61: 297 (119).

preted in context by the Mīmāṃsakas without further quotation aid to be supplied from elsewhere. Śaṅkara on his part knew Mādhyandina variants (*śrutyantara*) only from Bhartṛprapañca's (now lost) commentary on the BĀU. The interesting point, however, is, that Bhartṛprapañca not only commented upon the Mādhyandina recension,[86] but also shared with many Mīmāṃsakas their characteristic *karmajñānasamuccaya* orientation.[87]

3. Detailed exposition of Yājñavalkya-brāhmaṇas in the Vṛttikāragrantha

In the following, I shall try to briefly analyse the Vṛttikāra's treatment of some of Yājñavalkya's instructional formulations.

A Buddhist opponent[88] cites a *brāhmaṇa* (BĀU 4.5.13/2.4.12) in his own favour. By way of conclusion he makes use of this quote for supporting his arguments put forward against the Mīmāṃsaka's doctrine of a permanent substrate (*ātman*) of cognition. For, being a Sautrāntika, the opponent advocates impermanent 'mind-constituents' (*vijñāna-skandha*) only. All this is preceded by a concluding statement of the Mīmāṃsaka, who had argued thus: "Memory with reference to [what is] an impermanent mind-constituent only is therefore implausible" (*tasmāt kṣaṇike vijñāna-skandha-mātre smrtir anupapanneti*, ŚBh(F) 54.15 f). The Buddhist opponent took up this expression of *vijñāna-skandha-mātra* by [*vijñāna*]-*skandha-ghana*, thus terminologically preparing, as it were, for his *vijñāna-ghana* quote from the Upaniṣad by anticipating an understanding of °*mātra*/°*ghana* in the sense of "mere/only/nothing but". Since the argument had already been pushed forward to 'memory' (*smṛti*) and to the problem with reference to what memory could arise in the absence of a permanent substrate, the Buddhist counteracted the

---

86 Rau 297 (119).

87 See above, section I, *sub* 3.2.

88 Most probably a Sautrāntika as might be judged from the (*vi*)*jñāna-santāna* doctrine. Cf. Schmithausen 1967. On the frequent exegetical preoccupation of Jainas and Cārvākas with BĀU(K) 2.4.12, cf. Uno 1999.

Mīmāṃsaka with the help of a definition of memory that would not necessarily presuppose any permanent substrate. According to him, it is indeed possible that a constituent of 'mind alone' (*vijñāna-skandha-mātra/-ghana*) be directed at a previous series (*santati*) of 'mind alone' and that from such a perspective it would actually be mind alone, which remembers mind.[89] Accordingly, no permanent substrate needs to be postulated. Therefore, he carries on to argue:

> *anyasmin skandhaghane 'nyena skandhaghanena yaj jñānam, tat tatsantati-jenānyenopalabhyate, nātatsantatijena. tasmāc chūnyāḥ skandhaghanā iti. athāsminn arthe brāhmaṇaṃ bhavati – vijñānaghana evaitebhyo bhūtebhyaḥ samutthāya tāny evānuvinaśyati. na pretya saṃjñāstīti* (ŚBh(F) 54.19-23)
>
> [If] one [previous] mere constituent [of mind becomes] known by another mere constituent [of mind, then] this [previous one] is perceived by the other, [subsequent] one, [only if it was] caused by the series of this [previous mind-constituent, but] not [if] it was not caused by this [very] series. Therefore, the mere constituents [are] empty [of any permanent substrate].[90] Now, on this subject matter (/ in [exactly] this sense) there is an *instructional formulation* [of Yājñavalkya]:[91]
>
> [It is] actually mind alone (*-ghana*) [which] emerges from these elements; [and,] after [having thus emerged from them], it [again] disperses along with them [and] only them. There remains no consciousness [of an individual substrate] after dying (/ no [permanent] *post mortem* awareness persists).[92]

In the course of refuting the Buddhist's peculiar, although from a historical perspective perhaps not entirely implausible,[93] utilization

---

[89] *pūrvavijñānasadṛśaṃ vijñānaṃ pūrvavijñānaviṣayaṃ vā smṛtir ity ucyate* (ŚBh(F) 54.17 f).

[90] This passage has something in common with the Śrāvakabhūmi. The Vṛtti-kāra's use of *iti* could indeed point to a reference of such a kind. The following is the quote of a cognate Śrāvakabhūmi passage from the text as given by Schmithausen (1987: 297, n. 221): *tad evaṃ sati skandhamātram etan, nāsty eṣu skandheṣu nityo dhruvaḥ śāśvataḥ svā<mi>bhūtaḥ kaścid ātmā* ... | *iti hi śūnyā ete saṃskārāḥ ātmavirahitāḥ* ... |

[91] The present translation has, in the attempt of historical faithfulness, to adopt the intention of the Buddhist opponent. For the probable original Upaniṣadic meaning cf. WS (III), pp. 214 ff.

[92] For the possibility of an alternative translation cf. WS (II) 319, nn. 20, 27.

[93] Cf. on this WS (I); WS (II).

of Yājñavalkya's statement, which forms the starting-point for the Upaniṣadic hermeneutics under consideration, the Mīmāṃsaka quotes a series of additional statements, all stemming from Yājña-valkya, and in the majority of cases presumably all taken from BĀU 4.5.[94] With a view to disprove the Buddhist's conclusion that nothing but a mind-series exists, the Mīmāṃsaka makes his point by showing that a permanent substrate of cognition, as would be the *ātman*, must necessarily be presupposed. The Mīmāṃsaka quite obviously argues here from the *context*, a frequently applied exe-getical principle,[95] and by way of this he tries to demonstrate that Yājñavalkya's intention was totally different from what the Buddh-ist had attempted to interpret:

> *athāpy asminn arthe brāhmaṇaṃ bhavati – sa vā are 'yam ātmeti pra-kṛtyāmananty – aśīryo na hi śīryata iti.*[96] *tathā – avināśī vā are 'yam ātmā, anucchittidharmeti.*[97] *vinaśvaraṃ ca vijñānam. tasmād vinaśvarād anyaḥ sa ity avagacchāmaḥ* (ŚBh(F) 56.12-15).

> Furthermore on this subject matter (/ in [exactly] this sense) there is an *instructional formulation* [of Yājñavalkya which] they hand down as
> "– [The self] is indestructible, for it does not perish –"
> by [making another formulation of his] the referential of [this] quote:
> "– Look, this certainly is the self [of yours] here."
> In the same way [, by relating it to the same referential statement, they also hand down]:
> "– Look, actually imperishable, this [your] self here bears [indeed] the prop-erty of indestructibility."
> Mind, to be sure, [is] impermanent. Therefore we understand [it] in this way [that] the [self must be] different from what is impermanent.

---

[94] We have to assume this in the light of the other quotes. From the narrower context of 2.4 a similar procedure would not have been possible, because virtual-ly all of the counter-statements relevant for the Mīmāṃsaka are entirely lacking there.

[95] See above, fn. 82.

[96] BĀU 4.5.15 (*not* in 4.4). There are more occurrences of this statement in the BĀU, cf. Frauwallner's apparatus (1968: 56). However, all the citations here are based on context and were therefore in all likeliness also taken from the Maitreyī dialogue of 4.5.

[97] BĀU 4.5.14 (not in 4.4).

To the Buddhist, who challenged the Mīmāṃsaka to point out an agent (/subject) of cognition (*vijñātṛ*) which would be independent of mind, the Mīmāṃsaka replies that one's self can always be experienced only by oneself (*svayaṃsaṃvedya*) and thus cannot be presented to any other person.[98]

In support of this point the Mīmāṃsaka quotes again another set of instructions formulated by Yājñavalkya:

> *athāsminn arthe brāhmaṇaṃ bhavati – śāntāyāṃ vāci kiṃjyotir evāyam puruṣaḥ. ātmajyotiḥ samrāḍ iti hovāceti.*[99] *pareṇa nopalabhyata ity atrāpi brāhmaṇaṃ bhavati – agṛhyo na hi gṛhyata*[100] *iti. pareṇa na gṛhyata ity etadabhiprāyam etat. kutaḥ? svayaṃjyotiṣṭvavacanāt. atrāpi brāhmaṇaṃ bhavati – atrāyaṃ puruṣaḥ svayaṃjyotir bhavatīti.*[101] *kena punar upāyenāyam anyasmai kathyata iti? atrāpy upāye brāhmaṇaṃ bhavati – sa eṣa neti nety ātmeti hovāceti*[102] (ŚBh(F) 58.7-14).

> Now there is an *instructional formulation* on this subject matter (/ in [exactly] this sense):
>
> "When the voice is stilled,[103] what light [of knowledge] exactly has this person here? He has his self as the light [of knowledge], Your Majesty. Thus spoke [Yājñavalkya]."
>
> On [the meaning of this statement, namely] that [one's self] cannot be perceived by another, there is yet another *instructional formulation*:
>
> "It is not perceptible, for it cannot be perceived."

---

[98] The plural usage shows that the existence of a number of "selves" was clearly presupposed. *sarve svena svenātmanātmānam upalabhamānāḥ santy eva* | (ŚBh(F) 58.6). On the Vṛttikāra's dependency on particular doctrines characteristic of early Vaiśeṣika (as is also the assumption of a plurality of eternal souls) cf. Jacobi 1914; Strauss 1932: 490-492 [= *Kl. Schr.*, pp. 400-402]; Biardeau 1968: 111, 115 ff; Frauwallner 1968: 95-98 (Bhavadāsa), 111 f (Vṛttikāra).

[99] BĀU(M) 4.3.6.

[100] BĀU(M) 4.2.6 (K 4); (M) 3.9.28 (K 26); (M) 4.4.27 (K 22); (K) 4.5.15 (*not* in M).

[101] BĀU(M) 4.3.10/16 (K 9/14). Cf. for this passage Slaje 1993.

[102] Only 4.2.4 (K) / 4.2.6 (M) ends with *iti hovāca yājñavalkyaḥ*. For further instances of *neti neti* formulations cf. BĀU 3.3.6 (M/K), (M) 3.9.28 (K 26), (M) 4.2.6 (K 4), (M) 4.4.27 (K 22), (K) 4.5.15 (not in M).

[103] Cf. Olivelle 1998: 111.

The intention of this [formulation] is that [one's self] cannot be perceived by another. Why? Because of [Yājñavalkya's] declaration [that the self] is by itself the light [of knowledge].

On this [subject matter] also there is an *instructional formulation*:

"Here [in dream] this person is himself the light [of knowledge]."

By what means then [can] this [self] be described for another? There is an *instructional formulation* also on this means:

"It is this self here [which is referred to] by means of (*iti*) [all that with reference to what it is] *not* (*na*)."[104] Thus spoke [Yājñavalkya]."

The Vṛttikāra continues his explanation along exactly the same line of negative references to the self, i.e. by way of exclusion, of which I shall give one example:

asāv ayam evaṃrūpa iti na śakyate nidarśayitum. yac ca paraḥ paśyati, tatpratiṣedhas tasyopadeśopāyaḥ. śarīraṃ paraḥ paśyati. tenātmopadiśyate. śarīraṃ nātmā. asti śarīrād anyaḥ sa cātmeti śarīrapratiṣedhenātmopadiś-yate (ŚBh(F) 58.14-18).

It is not possible to present [the self] as: "This is N.N. (*asau*), of such [and such] an appearance." The means of pointing it out [to another] consists in the negation of what indeed (*ca*) the other sees. [It is] the body [which] the other sees. [It is] through the [body that] the self is indicated: "The body is *not* the self. There exists [something] different from the body, and this is the self." [It is] in this way [that] the self is indicated through the negation of the body.

After having supplied some additional reasons to prove the existence of a permanent substratum as would be the self[105] the Mīmāṃsaka concludes that an eternal soul must be accepted which is different from its properties. On the basis of this he rounds off the matter by returning to the initial *vijñānaghana* quote with a view to

---

[104] The present translation adopts the intention of the Mīmāṃsaka which reveals itself by the following set of examples: *a-gṛhya*, *a-śīrya*, etc. Hence my rendering of the double negation (*na*, *na*) by: "all that with reference to what it is *not*".

[105] E.g., completing one's work on the following day [ŚBh(F) 58.21-24]; by comparing one's own experiences of oneself to those of others [ŚBh(F) 58.25–60.4].

invalidate the Buddhist's interpretation by another set of contextually related quotes from Yājñavalkya's statements:

> *atha yad uktaṃ – vijñānaghana evaitebhyo bhūtebhyaḥ samutthāya tāny evānuvinaśyati, na pretya saṃjñāstīti,*[106] *atrocyate – atraiva mā bhagavān mohāntam āpīpadad iti*[107] *paricodanottarakāle 'pahnutya mohāntābhiprāyam asya vacanasya varṇitavān – na vā are 'haṃ mohaṃ bravīmi, avināśī vā are 'yam ātmānucchittidharmā, mātrāsaṃsargas tv asya bhavatīti.*[108] *tasmān na vijñānamātram* (ŚBh(F) 60.17-22).
>
> Now, to [the quotation] as put forward [by you]:
> "[It is] actually mind alone [which] emerges from these elements; [and,] after [having thus emerged from them], it [again] disperses along with them [and] only them. There remains no consciousness [of an individual substrate] after dying (/ no [permanent] *post mortem* awareness persists)",
> we reply:
> Immediately after[109] [Maitreyī's] reproach:
> "With regard to exactly this point (*atraiva*)[110] 'Venerable Sir has driven me into utter confusion'",
> [Yājñavalkya], by denying [any] intention of [causing] utter confusion, [carried on to] explain this instruction:[111]
> "Look, I certainly do not speak in order to confuse[112] [you]. Look, actually imperishable, this self [of yours] here bears [indeed] the property of indestructibility. However, it joins with (*saṃsarga*) 'material' components (*mātrā*)."[113]
> By reason of this [it can] not [be claimed that] only mind [would exist].

---

[106] BĀU 4.5.13 (M/K) / 2.4.12 (M/K)

[107] BĀU 4.5.14 (M)

[108] BĀU 4.5.15 (M)

[109] Note that here again the argument derives its validity from the immediate Upaniṣadic context.

[110] I.e. by having said that "no consciousness [of an individual substrate] remains after dying".

[111] Despite the given word order the possibility of construing the two genitives *asya vacanasya* with °*abhiprāyam* cannot be ruled out: "... denying [that] the instruction had the intention of ..."

[112] For *moh-am* as a possible *ṇamul* gerund cf. WS (III), p. 215, n. 23.

[113] For the probable original meaning of *saṃsarga* in the Upanisadic context ('to rejoin') cf. WS (II), pp. 303 f, 320, n. 33; WS (III), p. 207, n. 7 and pp. 215 f, n. 24. Cf. also the definitions of *mokṣa* and *bandha* in Pārthasārathi's ŚD 125.32 f: *so 'yaṃ prapañcasaṃbandho bandhas, tadvimokṣaś ca mokṣaḥ.*

Thus by contextually pointing out the interrelationship of Yājña-valkya's instructional formulations the Vṛttikāra demonstrates the implausibility (*vaiṣamya)* of the Buddhist argument and doctrine.

Let it be noted, however, that the section comprising the dispute under consideration here commenced with the refutation of an opponent attacking the validity of Vedic utterances. The opponent's objection reads as follows:

> *dṛṣṭaviruddham api, bhavati kiṃcid vaidikaṃ vacanam. pātracayanaṃ vidhāyāha – "sa eṣa yajñāyudhī yajamāno 'ñjasā svargaṃ lokaṃ yāti" iti*[114] *pratyakṣaṃ śarīraṃ vyapadiśati. na ca tat svargaṃ lokaṃ yāti. pratyakṣaṃ hi tad dahyate. na caiṣa yātīti vidhiśabdaḥ* (ŚBh(F) 34.6-9).
>
> Although contradicting perceived [facts], there is indeed[115] a particular Vedic utterance [which must be regarded as authoritative]. After having prescribed the piling up of the receptacles it says: "This [deceased] institutor of the sacrifice here instantly proceeds to the heavenly world, furnished with [his] sacrificial utensils", [a statement, which] clearly (*pratyakṣaṃ*)[116] indicates the body. However, the [body] does not ascend to the heavenly world. For in front of [our] eyes (*pratyakṣaṃ*) it is consumed by fire. Furthermore, the expression [in the indicative mood] 'he (/it) ascends' is no injunction.[117]

The refutation starts with a reference to the above-mentioned objection:

> *yat tu pratyakṣaviruddhaṃ vacanam upanyastaṃ "sa eṣa yajñāyudhī yajamāno 'ñjasā svargaṃ lokaṃ yāti" iti pratyakṣaṃ śarīraṃ vyapadiśatīti, tad ucyate ...* (ŚBh(F) 50.1-4).
>
> We reply to the statement mentioned [by you as one] contradicting direct perception insofar as it clearly indicates the body, [namely]:

---

[114] According to Frauwallner (1968: 34, n. 2) the sentence is quoted in ĀpŚS 31.2.21, with its ultimate source unknown. Cf. Strauss 1932: 507 [= *Kl. Schr.*, p. 417], n. 1, and, for the identification of the first part of the quote (= ŚPB 12.5.2.8), see Biardeau 1968: 110.

[115] Note the emphatic position of *bhavati*.

[116] Alternatively: "... indicates the perceptible (*pratyakṣaṃ*) body".

[117] An injunction requires the use of the optative mood. It is only because it is in the indicative that the present statement could be taken to refer to events that will really take place.

– "This [deceased] institutor of the sacrifice here instantly ascends to the heavenly world, furnished with [his] sacrificial utensils" ... –.

The immediately following dispute, occasionally alluding to the subject under consideration,[118] eventually terminates with the following reference to the same, which concludes the argument:

> *yad uktam – na caiṣa yātīti vidhiśabda iti, mā bhūd vidhiśabdaḥ. svargakāmo yajeteti vacanāntareṇāvagatam anuvadiṣyate. tasmād avirodhaḥ* (ŚBh(F) 60.23-25).
>
> The objection made [by you] as
>
> – "Furthermore, the expression [in the indicative mood] 'he (/it) ascends' is no injunction'" – [admittedly], it may be no injunction. [However, the ascent to heaven] will be conveyed [by this expression] in conformity with the understanding [gained] by another statement, [which is an injunction in the optative mood] that "[someone] desirous of heaven *should* sacrifice". Therefore [there is] no inconsistency [on our part].

Thus the instructional formulations of Yājñavalkya, forming in fact part of the Jñānakāṇḍa, were so to speak sandwiched[119] by a dispute on the contradictoriness of Vedic utterances and injunctions, which form part of the Karmakāṇḍa.

Clearly, the Upaniṣadic instructions on the self (*ātman*) were used for supporting some of the vital points of Pūrva-Mīmāṃsā doctrines. Such integration may corroborate Parpola's assumption of an originally unified Mīmāṃsā tradition. However, I would rather maintain that this supposed "unity" was confined just to a common interest in the interpretation of the respective *kāṇḍa*s, and in this wider sense in the exegesis of the Veda as a whole. The knowledge of the self (*ātmajñāna*), being essential also to the sacrificer occupied with the ritual part of the Veda, may initially have formed a common ground of interest. As convincingly pointed

---

[118] "This, [namely the experience of the notion of 'I' as different from properties] being the case, [it is] the very [self-experience, which] is referred to by 'furnished with [his] sacrificial utensils'." (*evaṃ cet, sa eva yajñāyudhīti vyapadiśyate*. ŚBh(F) 56.19 f).

[119] Cf. Also Strauss 1932: 493 [= *Kl. Schr.*, p. 403]; Frauwallner 1968: 110 f.

out by J. Bronkhorst in his present contribution, ideas of rebirth and liberation (*mokṣa*) from *saṃsāra*, as they were not accepted and thus also not aimed at by the sacrificing faction, could hardly have fulfilled such a uniting function. The same, incidentally, would quite justifiably apply to the monistic ontology (*advaita*) as well, pursued by the ritually passive group only. However, the respective ontological and soteriological notions of *advaita* and *mokṣa* possibly constituted a subcutaneous point of fracture right from the times of their introduction into the Upaniṣadic corpus. They would eventually have caused the tradition, after it had broken up, to fully develop into bipartite, more or less independent schools of isolated Pūrva- and Uttara-Mīmāṃsās. Parpola, too, underlines that their philosophies became mutually exclusive only after Kumārila and Śaṅkara.[120] Moreover, it was not earlier than from the 6th century onwards that some Buddhist (Bhavya) and Jain (Siddhasena Divākara) doxographers started treating the 'Vedānta' as a separate tradition in its own right.[121]

4. Yājñavalkya in context: rough structure of the argument

1. Buddhist (Sautrāntika):

No need for a Mīmāṃsaka to postulate a permanent substrate (*ātman*) of cognition for explaining memory. The assumption of the existence of mind alone (*vijñānaghana*) is sufficient. Even a Yājña-valkya-*brāhmaṇa* corroborates this:

> Starting quote [BĀU(M) 2.4.12/4.5.13 (=K)]:
> *vijñānaghana evaitebhyo bhūtebhyaḥ samutthāya tāny evānuvinaśyati, na pretya saṃjñāsti* (ŚBh 54.22 f).

---

[120] Parpola 1981: 153 ff; cf. also Frauwallner 1968: 110; Mesquita 1994: 451, n. 1 f.

[121] See Qvarnström 1989; 2003. It is perhaps worthy of note that Guṇaratna characterises the Pūrva-Mīmāṃsakas as *brahmasūtrinaḥ* (TRD 283.8 *ad* ṢDS Adhikaraṇa 6: Jaiminīyas).

1.1. Mīmāṃsaka:

Mind constituents are impermanent. For recollection, a permanent substrate must be presupposed. It is the latter what the *brāhmaṇa* intends to express:

1.1.1. Establishing a referential statement for the *brāhmaṇa*s to follow

[~ K 4.5.13]: *sa vā are 'yam ātmā* (ŚBh 56.12 f)

Contextualising the referential statement:

1.1.1.1.

[M 4.2.6 (= K 4)] *aśīryo, na hi śīryate* (ŚBh 56.13)

1.1.1.2.

[M 4.5.15 (= K 14)] *avināśī vā are 'yam ātmānucchittidharmā* (ŚBh 56.13 f)

1.1.2. Buddhist objection:

A permanent substrate (/agent) of cognition being different from its cognition must be pointed out.

1.1.2.1. Mīmāṃsā refutation: A substrate of cognition (*ātman*) can be experienced only by itself (*svasaṃvedya*).

Quote [M 4.3.6]: *śāntāyāṃ vāci kiṃjyotir evāyaṃ puruṣaḥ. ātmajyotiḥ samrāḍ iti hovāca* (ŚBh 58.8 f)

1.1.2.1.1. Therefore one's own substrate cannot be exposed directly to other subjects of cognition.

Quote [M 4.2.6 (= K 4)]: *agṛhyo, na hi gṛhyate* (ŚBh 58.9 f)

1.1.2.1.1.1. The correctness of the above follows from another Yājñavalkya-*brāhmaṇa*:

Quote [M 4.3.10/16 (= K 9/14)]: *atrāyaṃ puruṣaḥ svayaṃjyotir bhavati* (ŚBh 58.11 f)

1.1.2.1.2. The means of pointing out the substrate of cognition is an indirect one, viz. by way of negating what is not the substrate:

Quote [M 4.2.6 (= K 4)]: *sa eṣa neti nety ātmā iti hovāca* (ŚBh 58.14)

1.2. Mīmāṃsaka:
Conclusion: Clarification of the true meaning of the *vijñānaghana* formulation from the context of Yājñavalkya's statements as immediately connected to it.
1.2.1. Repetition of the *brāhmaṇa*-quote

[M 2.4.12/4.5.13 (K)]: *vijñānaghana evaitebhyo bhūtebhyaḥ samutthāya tāny evānuvinaśyati, na pretya saṃjñāsti* (ŚBh 60.17 f)

1.2.1.1. The Buddhist opponent quoted the formulation out of context and interpreted its meaning against the background of his own presuppositions as quite self-evident:
1.2.1.1.1. The meaning of the formulation is far from being self-evident:

Quote [M 4.5.14]: *atraiva mā bhagavān mohāntam āpīpadat* (ŚBh 60.18 f)

1.2.1.1.2. Still the formulation was not intended to cause confusion:

Quote [M 4.5.15]: *na vā are 'haṃ mohaṃ bravīmi* (ŚBh 60.20 f)

1.2.1.1.3. On the basis of this the Sautrāntika can no longer hold on to interpreting the instruction in the light of the doctrine that no permanent substrate of cognition, but only mind constituents would exist.
1.2.1.1.3.1. There is a permanent substrate of cognition bearing the property of indestructibility:

Quote [M 4.5.15 (= K 14)]: *avināśī vā are 'yam ātmānucchittidharmā* (ŚBh 60.21)

1.2.1.1.3.2. It joins with material components in the state of bondage:

Quote [M 4.5.15]: *mātrāsaṃsargas tv asya bhavati* (ŚBh 60.21 f)

III

Summary

Mīmāṃsā prehistory

- Yājñavalkya Vājasaneya was involved in the formation of the Śukla Yajurveda corpus of which the BĀU forms part. The Vājasaneyin Kātyāyana was a key-figure in the early history of Mīmāṃsā.
- As a sacrificing householder (*karmin*) with a deep concern also for self-knowledge (*jñānin*) Yājñavalkya may be seen as a representative of keen interest in ritual *and* knowledge of Vedic lore, long before two one-sided traditions with differently shaped emphases gradually began to emerge in later times only. Yājñavalkya may even have been the first *pra-vrājaka* from the householder state in Indian tradition and may as such have served as a model for aged Mīmāṃsakas.

The period of established systemic traditions of the two Mīmāṃsās

(1) *Canonical affiliation*

- The learned exponents of the Pūrva-Mīmāṃsā remained first and foremost attached to the Kriyākāṇḍa, accepting the Jñānakāṇḍa as auxiliary to enhancing a given, natural certainty about one's self.
- Advaita-Vedāntins were exclusively attached to the study of the Jñānakāṇḍa, by according the Kriyākāṇḍa a subordinate, preparatory value at the most.

(2) *Recensional bifurcation*

- The early development of the Pūrva-Mīmāṃsā was in its initial phase closely related to the Mādhyandina branch of the Vājasaneyins. This may indeed account for the Upaniṣadic references made by them to Yājñavalkya's words on self-knowledge (*ātmajñāna*) as quoted from the Mādhyandina recension of the BĀU. Mīmāṃsā interpretations therefore deserve attention, as they supposedly could be more faithful to Yājñavalkya's original thought in historic terms than, e.g., Śaṅkara's.

- Śaṅkara and the subsequent Advaita-Vedānta tradition were basing themselves on the Kāṇva recension of the BĀU. Yājñavalkya's influence on Śaṅkara's thought is recognisable first – through Gauḍapāda – on account of the ontological concept of *advaita*, adopted by him as a word-formation of Yājñavalkya. No *direct* lineage connecting Śaṅkara with the formative period of the BĀU has so far become discernible. His adaptation of the BĀU to a radical, idealistic *advaita* monism was achieved by a particular mode of interpretation (below, 5). Although Śaṅkara must indeed have had predecessors in the field of illusionistic monism,[122] it was possibly he who was instrumental in disintegrating with a lasting effect an originally unified 'tradition of exegetics' occupied with the Karma- *and* the Jñānakāṇḍa.

(3) *Social aspects*

- Pūrva-Mīmāṃsakas referred to themselves as *lifelong* sacrificing householders (*gṛhastha*s and *karmin*s). They carried the triple staff (*tridaṇḍin*) and were clearly identifiable (in literature) by specific additions to their names such as *bhaṭṭa* etc.
- Uttara-Mīmāṃsakas or Advaita-Vedāntins in the tradition of Śaṅkara were self-knowledge seeking, ideally *lifelong* renouncers (*saṃnyāsin*s and *jñānin*s), who carried the single staff (*ekadaṇḍin*) and were clearly identifiable (in literature) as married men by specific additions to their names such as *parivrājakācārya*, etc.

(4) *Ideologies*

- The positive approach to a *karmajñānasamuccaya*, which would be quite natural for lifelong sacrificing householders, makes the Pūrva-Mīmāṃsā continuing Yājñavalkya's engagement in sacri-

[122] Quoted by Bhartṛprapañca, see Rüping 1977: 2, 69 ff.

ficing activities *and* in the search for self-knowledge. On account of that, also the idea of *jīvanmukti* – '*liberation from* (°*mukti*) attachment to the fruits of activities, though nevertheless actively *participating in* (*jīvan*°) the world of ritual and social duties' – ties in remarkably with the *karmajñānasamuccaya* ideology.

Bhedābheda-Vedāntins such as Bhartṛprapañca and Bhāskara similarly favoured a *karmajñānasamuccaya* plus (Bhāskara) the ideal of a *jīvanmukta* state. Another common feature consists in Bhartṛprapañca's recitation of the BĀU according to the Mādhyandina recension.

On the other hand, a negative approach to the *karmajñānasamuccaya* would be quite natural for advocates of ritual and social inactivity (*saṃnyāsin*) as were the extreme Advaita-Vedāntins, who considered their way of life alone as privileged for liberation. The *jīvanmukti* idea became an integrative part of their doctrinal system comparatively late, as an unavoidable reaction to the ideology of socially active *jīvanmukta*s. The abovementioned Bhedābheda-Vedāntins, who besides the Mādhyandina recitation also shared the *karmajñānasamuccaya* and *jīvanmukti* ideals with the Pūrva-Mīmāṃsakas became superseded by Śaṅkara and the subsequent Advaita-Vedānta tradition and could not gain wide acceptance.

(5) *Hermeneutics*

- Pūrva-Mīmāṃsakas applied the exegetical principle of 'context' (*prakaraṇa*) for interpreting Yājñavalkya's formulations.
- The correctness claimed by Advaita-Vedāntins for their interpretation of BĀU passages was based on a maximum of *matching quotes associatively accumulated* from as many different *śruti* and *smṛti* text-places as possible.

REFERENCES

Texts and abbreviations

ĀpŚS *Āpastambaśrautasūtra*

ĀŚ [*Āgamaśāstra*] *The Āgamaśāstra of Gauḍapāda*. Ed., transl. and annotated by Vidhushekhara Bhattacharya. Reprint: Delhi 1989.

BĀU *Bṛhadāraṇyaka-Upaniṣad*. In: V. P. Limaye& R. D. Vadekar (eds.), *Eighteen Principal Upaniṣads*, I. Poona 1958. (Also in Olivelle 1998.)

BĀU(M) [*Bṛhadāraṇyaka-Upaniṣad*, Mādhyandina Recension] *Bṛhadāraṇjakopanishad in der Mādhjaṃdina-Recension*. Hrsg. u. übers. von Otto Boehtlingk. St. Petersburg 1889.

BĀUBh (Śaṅkara:) *Bṛhadāraṇyakopaniṣadbhāṣya*. In: *Complete Works of Sri Sankaracharya in the Original Sanskrit*, X. Samata revised edition. Madras 1983.

BĀUBhV [(Sureśvara:) *Bṛhadāraṇyakopaniṣadbhāṣyavārttika*] *Shri Sureshvarāchārya's Brihadāraṇyakopanishad-Bhashyavārtikam*. With the commentary Shāstraprakāshika of Ācharya Shri Ānandagiri, II. Ed. by S. Subrahmanya Shastri. (Advaita Grantha Ratna Manjusha Ratna, 30.) Varanasi 1990.

BhGBh [(Śaṅkara:) *Bhagavadgītābhāṣya*] *Bhagavadgītā with Śāṅkarabhāṣya*. (Works of Śaṅkarācārya in Original Sanskrit, 2.) Reprint [of the edition Poona 1929]: Delhi 1981.

BhGBh(Bh) [(Bhāskara:) *Bhagavadgītābhāṣya*] *Bhagavadgītā Bhāṣya by Bhāskarācārya*. (Sarasvatī Bhavana Granthamālā, 94.) Varanasi 1965.

Br [(Prabhākara:) *Bṛhatī*] *Bṛhatī. A Commentary on Sabarabhashya*, I-III. By Prabhakara Misra. With the commentary The Ṛjuvimala of Salikanatha Misra. Ed. By A. Chinnaswami Sastri. (Chowkhamba Sanskrit Series, 391, 406, 414.) Benares 1929-33.

BS [(Maṇḍana:) *Brahmasiddhi*] *Brahmasiddhi by Acharya Maṇḍanamiśra*. With commentary by Saṇkhapāni. Ed. by S. Kuppuswami Sastri. Second edition. (Sri Garib Das Oriental Series, 16.) Delhi 1984.

BSū *Brahmasūtra*

BSūBh [(Śaṅkara:) *Brahmasūtrabhāṣya*] *Brahmasūtra-Śāṅkarabhāsyam. With the commentary Bhāṣyaratnaprabhā of Govindānanda, Bhāmatī of Vācaspatimiśra, Nyāya-Nirṇaya of Ānandagiri*. Ed. by J. L. Shastri. Delhi 1980.

BVP [*Brahmavaivartapurāṇa*] *Brahmavaivartapurāṇa of Kṛṣṇa Dvaipāyana Vyāsa*, I.2. Ed. by J. L. Shastri. Index and Introduction by Satkari Mukhopadhyaya. Delhi 1984-85.

LPr [(Kṣemendra:) *Lokaprakāśa*] *Lokaprakasha of Kshemendra*. Ed. by Jagaddhar Yadoo Shastri. (The Kashmir Series of Texts and Studies, 75.) Srinagar 1947.

LYV [*Laghuyogavāsiṣṭha*] *Śrīmattarkavāgīśvarasāhityācāryābhinandapaṇḍitasamuddhṛtaḥ laghuyogavāsiṣṭhaḥ. vāsiṣṭhacandrikāvyākhyāsahitaḥ*. 2. āvṛttiḥ. Paṇaśīkaropāhvavidvadvara Lakṣmaṇaśarmatanujanuṣā Vāsudevaśarmaṇā saṃśodhitaḥ. Mumbayyāṃ śākaḥ 1859, san 1937.

Mbh [*Mahābhāṣya*] *The Vyākaraṇa-Mahābhāṣya of Patañjali*, II: Adhyāya III, IV and V. Ed. by F. Kielhorn. Third edition by K. V. Abhyankar. Poona 1965.

MSū *Mīmāṃsāsūtra*

NR (Pārthasārathimiśra:) *Nyāyaratnākara*. In ŚV.

NRD [(Ānandānubhava:) *Nyāyaratnadīpāvalī*] *Nyāyaratnadīpāvaliḥ. With the commentary Vedāntaviveka by Ānandagiri*. Critical ed. with introduction by V. Jagadisvara Sastrigal and Kalyanasundara Sastrigal. (Madras Government Oriental Series, 166.) Madras 1961.

ṚjV (Śālikanātha:) *Ṛjuvimalā*. In: Bṛ.

ŚBh [(Śabarasvāmin:) *Mīmāṃsāsūtrabhāṣya*] *Mīmāṃsāsūtrabhāṣya*, I-VI. Ed. by K. V. Abhyankar, G. Jośī et al. (ĀSS, 79.) Poona 1976-84.

ŚBh(F) *Śābarabhāṣya*. Partial edition in Frauwallner 1968.

ŚD [(Pārthasārathimiśra:) *Śāstradīpikā*] *The Shāstradīpikā*. Ed. by Srī Dharmadattasūrī. Bombay 1915.

ṢDS [(Haribhadra:) *Ṣaḍdarśanasamuccaya*] *Shaddarśana-Samuchchaya by Haribhadra. With Guṇaratna's commentary Tarkarahasya-Dipikā*. Ed. by Luigi Suali. Calcutta 1905. (Also in Qvarnström 1999.)

ŚMBh [(Bhāskara:) *Śārīrakamīmāṃsābhāṣya*] *Brahmasutra with a Commentary by Bhāskarāchārya*. Ed. by Vindhyesvari Prasada Dvivedin. Second edition. (Chowkhamba Sanskrit Series, 20.) Varanasi 1991.

ŚPB *Śatapathabrāhmaṇa*

SRBh [*Subhāṣitaratnabhāṇḍāgara*] *Subhāṣita-Ratna-Bhāṇḍāgara or Gems of Sanskrit Poetry*. Selected and arranged by Kāshinātha Pāṇdurang Parab. Sixth edition. Revised by Wāsudev Laxmaṇ Śāstrī Pāṇśīkar. Bombay 1929.

ŚV [(Kumārila:) *Ślokavārttika*] *Ślokavārttika of Śrī Kumārila Bhaṭṭa. With the commentary Nyāyaratnākara of Śrī Pārthasārathi Miśra*. Ed. and rev. by Swāmī Dvārikādāsa Śāstrī. (Prāchyabhārati Series, 10.) Varanasi 1978.

TRD (Guṇaratna:) *Tarkarahasyadīpikā*. In ṢDS.

VC (Ātmasukha:) *Vāsiṣṭhacandrikā*. In LYV, Prakaraṇa 1-3.

YS [*Yājñavalkyasmṛti*]. *Aparārkāparābhidhāparādityaviracitaṭīkāsametā yājñavalkyasmṛtiḥ*. ... Hari Nārāyaṇa Āpṭe ity anena ... prakāśitam. (ĀSS, 46.) Poona 1904.

Studies

BIARDEAU, Madeleine 1968. L'Ātman dans le commentaire de Śabarasvāmin. In: *Mélanges d'Indianisme. A la mémoire de Louis Renou.* (Publications de l'Institut de Civilisation Indienne, Série in-8:o, 28): 109-125. Paris: Éditions E. De Boccard.

BRONKHORST, Johannes 1993. *The Two Traditions of Meditation in Ancient India*. Second edition. Delhi: Motilal Banarsidass.

—— 1997. Philosophy and Vedic exegesis in the Mīmāṃsā. In: Eli Franco & Karin Preisendanz (eds.), *Beyond Orientalism. The Work of Wilhelm Halbfass and its Impact on Indian and Cross-Cultural Studies.* (Poznan Studies in the Philosophy of the Sciences and the Humanities, 59): 359-371. Amsterdam: Rodopi.

CLOONEY, Francis X. 1990. *Thinking Ritually. Rediscovering the Pūrva Mīmāṃsā of Jaimini*. (Publications of the De Nobili Research Library, 17.) Vienna: Institute for Indology, Vienna University.

EGGELING, Julius (transl.) 1882. *The Śatapatha-Brāhmaṇa. According to the text of the Mādhyandina School*, I. (Sacred Books of the East, 12.) Oxford: Clarendon Press.

FIŠER, Ivo 1984. Yājñavalkya in the Śruti tradition of the Veda. *Acta Orientalia* 10: 55-87.

FRAUWALLNER, Erich 1968. *Materialien zur ältesten Erkenntnislehre der Karmamīmāṃsā*. (SB ÖAW, 259.2. = VKSKS, 6.) Wien: Österreichische Akademie der Wissenschaften.

—— 1972. Zum Vṛttikāragranthaḥ. WZKS 16 (1972): 165-167.

HANEFELD, Erhardt 1976. *Philosophische Haupttexte der älteren Upaniṣaden.* (Freiburger Beiträge zur Indologie, 9.) Wiesbaden.

HINÜBER, Oskar von 1992. *Sprachentwicklung und Kulturgeschichte. Ein Beitrag zur materiellen Kultur des buddhistischen Klosterlebens* (AWL Mainz, Abhandlungen der Geistes- und Sozialwissenschaftlichen Klasse, 1992, 6]. Stuttgart: Franz Steiner Verlag.

HOFFMANN, Carmen Undine 2005. Zur Möglichkeit einer „Erlösung zu Lebzeiten" (*jīvanmukti*) vor dem Hintergrund der absoluten Zweitlosigkeit des Brahman. Eine Übersetzung und Textanalyse des vierten Kapitels der Nyāyaratnadīpāvalī. Unpublished M.A. Thesis, Halle.

JACOBI, Hermann 1914. Über die ältere Auffassung der Upaniṣad-Lehren. In: *Festschrift für Ernst Windisch zum siebzigsten Geburtstag*: 153-157. Leipzig: Harrassowitz. [= *Kl. Schr.*, pp. 750-754].

KATAOKA, Kei 2003. Kumārila's critique of omniscience. *Indo Shisōshi Kenkyū* 15: 35-69.

MANI, Vettam 1975. *Purāṇic Encyclopaedia*. Delhi: Motilal Banarsidass.

MESQUITA, Roque 1994. Die Idee der Erlösung bei Kumārilabhaṭṭa. *WZKS* 38: 451-484.

—— 2000. *Madhva: Viṣṇutattvanirṇaya. Annotierte Übersetzung mit Studie*. (Publications of the De Nobili Research Library, 28.) Vienna: Institute for South Asian, Tibetan and Buddhist Studies, Vienna University.

OLIVELLE, Patrick 1986. *Renunciation in Hinduism. A Medieval Debate*, I. (Publications of the De Nobili Research Library, 13.) Vienna: Institute for South Asian, Tibetan and Buddhist Studies, Vienna University.

—— 1993. *The Āśrama System. The History and Hermeneutics of a Religious Institution.* New York: Oxford University Press.

—— (transl.) 1998. *The Early Upaniṣads. Annotated Text and Translation.* (South Asia Research.) New York: Oxford University Press.

PARPOLA, Asko 1981. On the formation of the Mīmāṃsā and the problems concerning Jaimini. With particular reference to the teacher quotations and the Vedic schools. *WZKS* 25: 145-177.

—— 1994. On the formation of the Mīmāṃsā and the problems concerning Jaimini. With particular reference to the teacher quotations and the Vedic schools. (Part II) *WZKS* 38: 293-308.

QVARNSTRÖM, Olle 1989. *Hindu Philosophy in Buddhist Perspective. The Vedāntaviniścaya Chapter of Bhavya's Madhyamakahṛdayakārikā.* (Lund Studies in African and Asian Religions, 4.) Lund: Plus Ultra.

—— 1999. Haribhadra and the beginnings of doxography in India. In: N. K. Wagle & Olle Qvarnström (eds.), *Approaches to Jaina Studies: Philosophy, Logic, Rituals and Symbols.* (South Asian Studies Papers, 11): 169-210. Toronto: Centre for South Asian Studies, University of Toronto.

—— 2003. Early Vedānta philosophy preserved by the Jain tradition: The Vedavādadvātriṃśikā of Siddhasena Divākara. In: Olle Qvarnström (ed.), *Jainism and Early Buddhism: Essays in Honour of Padmanabh S. Jaini*: 575-593. Fremont, Calif.: Asian Humanities Press.

RAU, Wilhelm 1959-61. Bemerkungen zu Śaṅkaras Bṛhadāraṇyakopaniṣadbhāṣya. *Paideuma* 7: 293-299.

REINVANG, Rasmus 2000. A critical survey of the dialogue between Yājñavalkya and Maitreyī in Bṛhadāraṇyaka Upaniṣad 2.4 and 4.5. *Acta Orientalia* 61: 145-202.

RENOU, Louis 1948. Les relations du Śatapathabrāhmana avec la Bṛhadāraṇyakopaniṣad et la personnalité de Yājñavalkya. *Indian Culture* 14.3: 75-89. [= N. Balbir & Georges-Jean Pinault (eds.), *Choix d'Études Indiennes*, II: 885-899. Paris 1977.]

RÜPING, Klaus 1977. *Studien zur Frühgeschichte der Vedānta-Philosophie*, I: *Philologische Untersuchungen zu den Brahmasūtra-Kommentaren des Śaṅkara und des Bhāskara*. (Alt- und Neu-Indische Studien, 17.) Wiesbaden: Franz Steiner Verlag.

SAWAI, Yoshitsugu 1992. *The Faith of Ascetics and Lay Smārtas. A Study of the Śaṅkaran Tradition of Śṛṅgeri*. (Publications of the De Nobili Research Library, 19.) Vienna: Institute for Indology, Vienna University.

SCHMITHAUSEN, Lambert 1967. Sautrāntika-Voraussetzungen in Viṃśatikā und Triṃśikā. *WZKS* 11: 109-136.

—— 1987. *Ālayavijñāna. P. 1.2.* (Studia Philologica Buddhica, 4ab.) Tokyo.

SCHMÜCKER, Marcus 2001. *„Weder als seiend noch als nichtseiend bestimmbar". Vimuktātmans Lehre von der „Realität" der Welt.* (Publications of the De Nobili Research Library, 29.) Vienna: Institute for South Asian, Tibetan and Buddhist Studies, Vienna University.

SLAJE, Walter 1993. BĀU 4.3.14 (M 16) und die Entwicklung des subjektiven Illusionismus im älteren Vedānta. *Studien zur Indologie und Iranistik* 18: 223-250.

—— 2000a. Liberation from intentionality and involvement: On the concept of jīvanmukti in the Mokṣopāya. *JIP* 28.2: 171-194.

—— 2000b. Towards a history of the jīvanmukti concept: The Mokṣadharma in the Mahābhārata. In: Ryutaro Tsuchida & Albrecht Wezler (eds.), *Harānandalaharī. Volume in Honour of Professor Minoru Hara on his Seventieth Birthday*: 325-348. Reinbek: Dr Inge Wezler Verlag für Orientalistische Fachpublikationen.

—— 2001. Rājavidyā. *Studien zur Indologie und Iranistik* 22 (1999) [publ. 2001]: 131-166.

, forthcoming. Quellen des Jñānakarmasamuccayavāda.

(See also WS, below)

SPROCKHOFF, Joachim Friedrich 1979. Die Alten im alten Indien. Ein Versuch nach brahmanischen Quellen. *Saeculum* 30.4: 374-433.,

—— 1981. Āraṇyaka und Vānaprastha in der vedischen Literatur. *WZKS* 25: 19-90.

STEINKELLNER, Ernst 1997. Kumārila, Īśvarasena, and Dharmakīrti in dialogue. A new interpretation of Pramāṇavārttika I 33. In: Petra Kieffer-Pülz & Jens-Uwe Hartmann (eds.), *Bauddhavidyāsudhākaraḥ. Studies in Honour of Heinz Bechert on the Occasion of His 65th Birthday*. (Indica et Tibetica, 30): 625-646. Swisttal-Odendorf: Indica et Tibetica Verlag.

STEPHAN, Peter 2002. *Erlösung im Spannungsfeld von aktivem Leben und Entsagung. Eine Studie zu Śaṅkaras Exegese der Bhagavadgītā.* (Geisteskultur Indiens. Texte und Studien, 3.) Aachen: Shaker Verlag.

STRAUSS, Otto 1932. Die älteste Philosophie der Karma-Mīmāṃsā. *Sitzungsberichte der Preußischen Akademie der Wissenschaften* 1932: 469-532. [= *Kl. Schr.*, pp. 379-442]

THIEME, Paul 1952. Bráhman. *ZDMG* 102: 91-129. [= *Kl. Schr.*, pp. 100-137]

THRASHER, Allen Wright 1993. *The Advaita Vedānta of Brahma-Siddhi*. Delhi: Motilal Banarsidass.

UNO, Tomoyuki 1999. A debate between materialists and Jainas on the interpretation of Bṛhadāraṇyakopaniṣad 2.4.12. In: N. K. Wagle & Olle Qvarnström (eds.), *Approaches to Jaina Studies: Philosophy, Logic, Rituals and Symbols* (South Asian Studies Papers, 11.): 238-249. Toronto: Centre for South Asian Studies, University of Toronto.

VERPOORTEN, Jean-Marie 1987. *Mīmāṃsā Literature*. (A History of Indian Literature, 6.5.) Wiesbaden: Otto Harrassowitz.

VETTER, Tilmann 1969. *Maṇḍanamiśra's Brahmasiddhiḥ. Brahmakāṇḍaḥ. Übers., Einl. u. Anm.* (SB ÖAW, 262.2.) Wien: Österreichische Akademie der Wissenschaften.

—— 1979. *Studien zur Lehre und Entwicklung Śaṅkaras*. (Publications of the De Nobili Research Library, 6.) Vienna: Institute for Indology, Vienna University.

VIDYABHUSANA, S. C. 1915. Vatsyayana, author of the Nyayabhasya. *Indian Antiquary* 44: 82-88.

WITZEL Michael 1994. The Brahmins of Kashmir. In: Yasuke Ikari (ed.), *A Study of the Nīlamata. Aspects of Hinduism in Ancient Kashmir*: 237-294. Kyoto: Institute for Research in Humanities, Kyoto University.

—— 2003. Yājñavalkya as ritualist and philosopher, and his personal language. In: S. Adhami, (ed.), *Paitimana. Essays in Iranian, Indo-European, and Indian Studies in Honor of Hanns-Peter Schmidt*: 103-143. Casta Mesa, Calif.: Mazda Publishers.

WS (I) = Walter SLAJE, Water and salt (I): Yājñavalkya's Saindhava Dṛṣṭānta (BĀU II 4,12). *Indo-Iranian Journal* 44.1 (2001): 25-57.

WS (II) = Walter SLAJE, Water and salt (II): 'Material' causality and hylozoic thought in the Yājñavalkya-Maitreyī dialogue? *Indo-Iranian Journal* 44.4 (2001): 299-327.

WS (III) = Walter SLAJE, Water and salt (III): An analysis and new translation of the Yājñavalkya-Maitreyī dialogue. *Indo-Iranian Journal* 45.3 (2002): 205-220.

YOSHIMIZU, Kiyotaka 1997. *Der ‚Organismus' des urheberlosen Veda*. (Publications of the De Nobili Research Library, 25.) Vienna: Institute for South Asian, Tibetan and Buddhist Studies, Vienna University.

ZANGENBERG Fritz 1962. Śabaraḥ und seine philosophischen Quellen. *WZKS* 6: 60-77.

Kumārila the Vedāntin?

JOHN TABER

In an important article that appeared in the *Wiener Zeitschrift* in 1994 Roque Mesquita undertook a systematic study of Kumārila's doctrine of liberation as it has been preserved in three texts: the *Ślokavārttika*, the *Tantravārttika*, and extant fragments relating to this theme from the *Bṛhaṭṭīkā*.[1] Mesquita made the somewhat surprising discovery that Kumārila appears to shift his position regarding the practices that lead to liberation from what could be called, perhaps, a *karmamārga* in his *Ślokavārttika* to a version of the *jñānakarmasamuccaya* doctrine in his *Tantravārttika* and *Bṛhaṭṭīkā* that in fact emphasizes the importance of knowledge over *karma*.

Specifically, in the Sambandhākṣepaparihāra (SĀP) chapter of his ŚV (see Appendix, Text I) Kumārila emphasizes that liberation can only be achieved as a result of the extinction of *karma*, which is to be brought about by the exhaustion of the fruits of past *karma* and the avoidance of any further *karma*, through not engaging in any optional (*kāmya*) or forbidden (*niṣiddha*) acts, while continuing to carry out regular (*nitya*) and occasional (*naimittika*) obligatory acts. Kumārila says there that "knowledge of Sāṃkhya, etc." cannot be the cause (*nimitta*) of *mokṣa* (SĀP 102); nothing that is caused can be eternal. Only as a result of the elimination of the cause of rebirth, i.e., *karma*, can *mokṣa* come about (SĀP 106). (I believe, by the way, that the parallel here to the Four Noble Truths

[1] Mesquita 1994.

of Buddhism is not without significance.) And he regards the injunctions of self-knowledge in the Veda as subserving the sacrifice, insofar as it provides a reason for undertaking ritual acts (SĀP 103); for only on the basis of an understanding that the self survives the body would one undertake actions whose consequences are to be enjoyed in another world.

In the TV, on the other hand (see Text II), in the context of a discussion of whether the use of words in accordance with the rules of grammar, which can be seen as enjoined by the Veda (insofar as the grammatical *sūtra*s are considered part of the Veda), is subordinate to other ritual purposes or has a benefit of its own, Kumārila states unambiguously that self-knowledge, as enjoined in various Upaniṣad passages, is *puruṣārtha*, not *kratvartha*. That is to say, the actions of seeking, knowing, thinking about, realizing, and meditating on the self are to be carried out for the sake of their own results, in the form of both the attainment of higher powers known to be possessed by yogins and the attainment of the highest self and liberation from the cycle of rebirth, referred to in this text as "non-return" (*apunarāvṛtti*). Kumārila, however, goes on to say that "the injunction of knowledge does not exclude a connection with action"; for *nitya* and *naimittika karmas*, specific to *āśrama* and *varṇa*, are also to be performed "for the sake of destroying previous sin and avoiding future sin due to the non-commission of prescribed acts." Mesquita suggests that in this passage Kumārila has demoted the ritual path laid out in the ŚV to a "subordinate" (1994: 463-464) or "preparatory" role (p. 469). "Although he expressly maintains that the *karmamārga* and *jñānamārga* are equally important, he teaches that extinguishing the force of *karma* follows from exhausting its consequences and carrying out ritual works. Knowledge of the *ātman*, on the other hand, leads directly to liberation" (p. 479). Mesquita also finds this confirmed in a few verses relating to the means of attaining liberation that have been preserved from the BṬ (see Text III). He follows their presentation by Śrīdhara in his *Nyāyakandalī*, who embeds them in a more extensive discussion that Mesquita also believes reflects the teaching of the BṬ. In these verses Kumārila begins (if Śrīdhara faithfully reproduces their order) with statements to the effect that it is *karma* that binds one in the cycle of rebirth; only by the exhaustion of *karma* by experiencing its consequences and carrying out obligatory works does liberation gradually come about. However, he mentions that this occurs for someone who knows the nature of the self (*ātmasvarūpajña*), and he concludes the passage by saying (I prefer the reading of this verse given by Someśvarabhaṭṭa in his *Nyāyasudhā*; see Mesquita 1994: 465),

> One who is destroying sin by regular and occasional *karma*, purifying his knowledge (*jñānaṃ ca vimalīkurvan*), and bringing it to fruition by means of practice (*abhyāsena pācayan*) – such a person whose knowledge is ripened as a result of dispassion (*vairāgyāt*) experiences liberation (*kaivalya*) (fragment 6).

Thus, again, it seems that Kumārila has identified self-knowledge as the proximate means of liberation, as is taught in Vedānta.

Not only does Mesquita see a shifting of positions in Kumārila's statements about this matter; he also postulates on that basis a later date for the BṬ than the ŚV, since otherwise (if the BṬ had been earlier) Kumārila would have, implausibly, gone from the *jñānakarmasamuccayamārga* of the BṬ to the *karmamārga* of the ŚV, then back again to the *jñānakarmasamuccayamārga* in his TV, which we may safely suppose is later than the ŚV.

My purpose in this paper is to raise some questions about the picture Mesquita has presented.[2] I shall not in the allotted space be able to take on all the issues – I shall leave out of consideration altogether the matter of the sequence of Kumārila's works, on which I have written elsewhere. I shall also not attempt to grapple with the opinions of Kumārila's commentators, in particular, Pārthasārathi and Sucarita, on Kumārila's position regarding libera-

[2] I certainly do not claim to refute Mesquita here; his interpretation remains a viable possibility. Mainly, I am grateful to Mesquita for drawing attention to the problem of Kumārila's apparent shift of position on this matter.

tion; for another purpose of mine in this paper is just to look at Kumārila's texts relating to this question without any filters. There are two points on which I shall focus, but even these will be dealt with incompletely. First, I believe that the texts to which Mesquita has drawn attention are more consistent with one another than he has depicted. Second, even if Kumārila over the course of his career moved closer to a position that might be described as a *jñānamārga* – i.e., a *jñānakarmasamuccayavāda* that sees *karma* as the remote and *jñāna* as the proximate means – still, his position would be far removed from that articulated by Śaṅkara, e.g., in his *Brahmasūtrabhāṣya* – which should come as no surprise, since Śaṅkara's position is usually, if misleadingly, presented as diametrically opposed to the *jñānakarmasamuccaya* (e.g., by his disciple Sureśvara) – but even from the position of Maṇḍanamiśra in his *Brahmasiddhi*, which is often referred to as a *jñānakarmasamuccayavāda*. Indeed, there is a range of positions that can be called *jñānakarmasamuccayavāda*s. Thus, it remains questionable whether Kumārila really shifted closer to Vedānta.

Let us begin, however, by considering Jaimini's views on self-knowledge as cited in the *Brahmasūtra*.[3] According to BS 3.4.2-7 (I am following Śaṅkara's reading; I shall have occasion later to refer to Rāmānuja's) Jaimini rejects Bādarāyaṇa's opinion that self-knowledge is enjoined in the Veda as *puruṣārtha*, "for the purpose of man." We need to carry further the investigation into the meaning of this expression that was begun by Frank Clooney,[4] but for the purpose of this essay I shall consider *puruṣārtha* an action that yields a desired result for the human being who undertakes it, such as heaven, as opposed to an action that has no result for the sacrificer but merely contributes to an action that does (and so is *kratvartha*). Thus, the position of Jaimini is that the statements of the Veda that praise knowledge of the self as the highest end of man are mere *arthavāda*s, which encourage one to attain self-

[3] Cf. Mesquita 1994: 451-452.
[4] See Clooney 1990: 139-149, 161 ff.

knowledge as an auxiliary to carrying out the sacrifice, not for its own sake; as such, they may not even be intended literally.[5] Self-knowledge subserves the sacrifice, Jaimini suggests, because the self is a subsidiary as the agent of the ritual act. Knowledge that the self is different from the body would seem to have no other use than to assure the person undertaking the sacrifice that he will indeed be able to enjoy its effects in another world. This position is consistent with another well-known statement of Jaimini's often cited in this connection, namely, MS 1.2.1: "Action is the purport of scripture. Thus, whatever does not refer to action is purposeless."[6]

Elsewhere in the *Brahmasūtra* we find other references to views of Jaimini about liberation: the path of the sun, mentioned in ChU 8.6, BĀU 6.2.15, etc., leads to the highest Brahman (BS 4.3.12; this position is rejected by Śaṅkara, who points out that there cannot, strictly speaking, be any movement toward the highest Brahman, which is omnipresent); the liberated soul manifests its true nature, as free from sin, possessed of true intentions (*satyasaṅkalpa*), omnipotent, etc. (see ChU 8.7.1) (BS 4.4.5); and the released soul has a body (BS 4.4.11). Thus, it seems clear enough that Jaimini did accept the possibility of liberation, though it is uncertain whether he conceived of it as the full identification of the individual soul with the highest Brahman, as the Śāṅkara Advaitins did (especially in light of his belief that the liberated self has a body). However, his rejection of the injunction of self-knowledge as *puruṣārtha* would seem to imply that he did not believe that liberation comes about from knowledge of the true nature of the self alone. Unfortunately, the *Brahmasūtra* does not record what his own understanding of the means of attaining liberation was. We are given only another negative fact in 4.1.17 (once again, accord-

---

[5] See MS 1.2.10, on *arthavāda*.

[6] *āmnāyasya kriyārthatvād ānarthakyam atadarthānām.* ... These words occur within a *pūrvapakṣa*. However, Jaimini accepts this principle, only rejecting it as a basis for excluding statements of fact in the Veda as meaningful sentences. He believes that such statements relate to the sacrifice as *arthavādas*.

ing to Śaṅkara's interpretation of this *sūtra*), namely, that both Jaimini and Bādarāyaṇa believed that *kāmya karma* does not contribute to the origination of knowledge (*vidyāṃ praty anupakārakatva*, BSBh *ad loc.*[7]). Although this suggests that Jaimini did think that knowledge is somehow important, it is still possible that he held an essentially ritualistic view of the attainment of liberation: liberation results from the performance of certain religious acts in which self-knowledge is somehow instrumental. In fact, Śaṅkara documents such a view in the *pūrvapakṣa* of his commentary on BS 1.1.4. I quote from the Thibaut translation:

> Vedānta texts give information about Brahman only insofar as it is connected with injunctions of actions. We meet with injunctions of the following kind, "Verily the self is to be seen", etc. ... These injunctions arouse in us the desire to know what that Brahman is. It, therefore, is the task of the Vedānta texts to set forth Brahman's nature, and they perform that task by teaching us that Brahman is eternal, all-knowing, etc. ... From the direct meditation of this Brahman there results as its fruit final release which, although not to be discerned in the ordinary way, is discerned by the *śāstra*.[8]

I take this to be the view that liberation results, not from self-knowledge, but from the act of meditation (*upāsanā*) on Brahman, for which knowledge of the nature of the self or Brahman is an indispensable aid. Such a theory is consistent with all of the ideas about liberation attributed to Jaimini in the *Brahmasūtra*, and especially with MS 1.2.1 – "Action is the purport of scripture. Thus, whatever does not refer to action is purposeless" – and so one might hypothesize that this was in fact Jaimini's view.

This, certainly, is not the sort of theory we find being presented by Kumārila in his *Ślokavārttika*! There, Kumārila is clear that liberation, being eternal, cannot have a specific cause – caused things endure for only a limited period of time. Thus, liberation, conceived as the cessation of embodied existence, can come about only with the removal of its cause, *karma*. This is the idea at the

---

[7] BSBh, p. 961, 9-10.

[8] Thibaut 1962, I: 25; BSBh, p. 112, 4 – p. 113, 2.

heart of his discussion, and it seems quite cogent. It entails the rejection of any philosophy that conceives of liberation as caused by knowledge, in particular, Sāṃkhya and Vedānta. (It is important to keep in mind here that Kumārila considers knowledge or cognition to be an action carried out by the self as agent – a real event; see, e.g., *Ātmavāda* 76ab. Śaṅkara will later insist that self-knowledge is not an action and does not in any way cause liberation.) However, the principle that liberation cannot be caused would also exclude the kind of view I hypothetically ascribed to Jaimini, which conceives of liberation as brought about by acts of meditation aided by knowledge. Thus, for Kumārila in the ŚV, liberation is reached chiefly by exhausting one's past *karma* by experiencing its effects while both refraining from further, unnecessary or forbidden *karma* and continuing to perform obligatory *karma*. The performance of obligatory *karma* is necessary to avoid further sin that would result from its omission.[9]

Yet he does not completely rule out a role for knowledge. He indeed asserts at the beginning of the ŚV passage I have cited that self-knowledge is enjoined not for the sake of *mokṣa* but in order to motivate qualified persons to undertake sacrifices, as Jaimini apparently did. But later in the text he says that "a body does not arise again ... for those who have realized the truth of the self" (v. 108), and in vv. 110-111 he spells out precisely the function of self-knowledge in his scheme. Regular and occasional obligatory *karma* (such as the *agnihotra*) serve to prevent sin only when they are performed without desire for their results (e.g., heaven), and self-knowledge eliminates such desire (again, this sounds remarkably Buddhist).

[9] Krishan (1994) suggests that the Mīmāṃsakas introduced the idea that *nitya* and *naimittika karma* are to be performed for their own sake, just because they are enjoined. See, e.g., MS 6.3.1-7. Other ritualistic schools believed that such obligatory acts as the *pañca mahāyajñas* – i.e., *adhyayana*, *pitṛyajña*, *agnihotra*, *bali*, and *atithipūjana* – have an ulterior purpose. They serve to neutralize the taint (of *hiṃsā*) incurred by making use of the five domestic "slaughterhouses" (*sūnā*), the hearth, the grindstone, the broom, the mortar and pestle, and the water jar. See *Manusmṛti* 3.68-74.

Thus, according to Kumārila in his ŚV, liberation is attained chiefly just by the enjoyment of the fruits of past *karma* combined with the *detached* performance of obligatory *karma* for the sake of avoiding further sin. The necessary detachment, it seems, is brought about by knowledge of the transmigrating self (not, it is to be emphasized, of the higher Self, Brahman, which is not subject to transmigration), in particular, the knowledge that it is distinct from the body and cognitive faculties. Thus, self-knowledge contributes to the attainment of liberation by playing a kind of auxiliary role.[10] (But we cannot rule out the possibility that Kumārila conceived of a reciprocal relationship between *karma* and self-knowledge: self-knowledge is necessary for *karma* to have its sin-destroying effect, but the performance of obligatory *karma* also somehow supports the emergence of knowledge.) We saw that knowledge also played an auxiliary role in the hypothetical scheme of Jaimini. There, however, it is not auxiliary to *nitya* and *naimittika karma*, but to *upāsanā*.

With this understanding of Kumārila's discussion in the Sambandhākṣepaparihāra before us we can begin to see that his statements in the TV may not deviate so radically from the ŚV as first appears. In the text in question – once again, a discussion of whether the use of correct grammatical forms yields an *apūrva* – Kumārila essentially says that injunctions of self-knowledge in the Veda serve two purposes simultaneously. They are *kratvartha* insofar as they enjoin the knowledge of the transcendent nature of the self, which motivates one to undertake actions the results of which can only be enjoyed in another world; and they are *puruṣārtha* insofar as knowledge of the self leads to benefits in this world as well as the highest good (*abhyudayaniḥśreyasa*), in the form of supernatural powers born of yoga on the one hand (*yogajanyāṇimādyaṣṭaguṇaiśvaryaphalāni*) and liberation consisting in the attainment of the highest self (*apunarāvṛttyātmakaparamātmaprāptyavasthāphala*) on the other. In this sense, injunctions of self-knowledge are

---

[10] See Mesquita 1994: 458-459.

comparable to the two sentences pertaining to the *agniṣomīya* rite, "He ties [the victim] to a stake made of *khadira*" (*khādire badhnāti*), and "One who desires strength should make a post of *khadira*" (*khādiraṃ vīryakāmasya yūpaṃ kuryāt*). These sentences express essentially the same injunction: to use a stake made of *khadira* wood. But because they occur in different contexts – one occurs in close connection with the *agniṣomīya* sacrifice, the other not – it is considered that one has to do with an injunction that is both *kratvartha* and *puruṣārtha* (MS 4.3.5).[11] Although this certainly represents a retreat by Kumārila from Jaimini's position that injunctions of self-knowledge are strictly *kratvartha*, which he himself implies in SĀP 103-104, it is not equivalent to the Advaita Vedānta position of, say, Śaṅkara that knowledge *per se* yields liberation. For it would appear that self-knowledge is being conceived here as an action; liberation and the other benefits of self-knowledge are referred to as "fruits" (*phalāni*) of acting in accordance with the injunctions of self-knowledge. In general, it would seem that if something is prescribed it is something to be done. Śaṅkara is able to avoid this consequence in his *Brahmasūtrabhāṣya* and other works (especially the *Bṛhadāraṇyakopaniṣadbhāṣya*) only by insisting that such statements as "The self is to be seen, heard, thought about," etc. are not really injunctions! They motivate one to strive to know the self, but not thereby to do anything. Kumārila supplies no such caveat here.

Thus, even in his TV Kumārila could still very well be operating within a ritualistic framework. Indeed, he explicitly states that "a connection with *karma* is not excluded by the injunction of knowledge." This is probably directed against the sort of position that will later be articulated by Śaṅkara, that knowledge alone is the means of liberation. Liberation is not something to be brought about by action in any way (nor is knowledge itself an action); for

---

[11] Cf. Kumārila's discussion of the injunction to use proper grammatical forms, TV 1.3.27 : p. 221, 21 ff., which gives a more complete explanation of MS 4.3.5 than the *Ṭupṭīkā*.

it is neither perishable, nor associated with pleasure or pain, while the results of *karma* are the opposite of that. It is in this connection that Kumārila comes back to the importance of *nitya* and *naimittika karma*, which he stressed in the ŚV: even while striving to attain liberation (and other ends) through knowledge, he says, *nitya* and *naimittika karma*, which both destroy sin and prevent its further accumulation, are still to be performed. The function of *destroying* sin is explicitly mentioned in this text for the first time; but there is no reason why Kumārila could not have already had it in mind when he emphasized the necessity of performing *nitya* and *naimittika karma* in the ŚV.[12] (This emphasis on obligatory *karma*, by the way, would appear to preclude *sannyāsa* either as a requirement or even an option for the person striving for liberation – another important difference from Śaṅkara.) Injunctions of self-knowledge and of these actions, Kumārila continues, do not contradict each other, nor are they alternatives, nor do they stand in a relation of subordinate and superior to each other (any or all of these positions can be seen as being defended by Śaṅkara). Thus, Kumārila seems to be saying that it is not by means of knowledge by itself, but knowledge together with obligatory *karma*, that one achieves liberation. Precisely how these two practices (if knowledge can be considered a practice) support each other is not something he explains here.

Thus, the TV may not represent a wholesale change of position from the ŚV on this topic. Although Kumārila seems to be modifying a traditional Mīmāṃsā teaching that self-knowledge is only *kratvartha*, never *puruṣārtha*, it is by no means clear that he has

[12] The idea that the carrying out of obligatory *karma* is "for the purpose of destroying previously committed sin" (*pūrvakṛtaduritakṣayārtham*) is consistent with the traditional belief that it neutralizes the effects of inadvertently committed acts of violence. See fn. 9. Kumārila's emphasis on *nitya karma* may also have been motivated by a desire to respond to certain Mīmāṃsakas who had denied that *nitya* or *niṣiddha karma* have any beneficial or detrimental results. These are the Mīmāṃsakas to whom Kumārila refers at ŚV, Pratijñā 10 as having made Mīmāṃsā into a "materialist" teaching (*lokāyatīkṛtā*), according to Pārthasārathi (*Nyāyaratnākara*, *ad loc.*), who specifically mentions Bhartṛmitra.

gone all the way over to an Advaita-type position that knowledge is a means of liberation *qua* knowledge (and not *qua* action), or that it is the sole means of liberation. Indeed, as I stated, he may still be viewing knowledge itself as an action; that, after all, would appear to be one implication of saying it is *puruṣārtha*, a term which is typically applied to ritual acts. In this connection we should note that according to Rāmānuja in his *Śrībhāṣya*, the "knowledge" of the self (*ātmavidyā*) enjoined in various Upaniṣad texts (and declared to be *puruṣārtha* in BS 3.4.1) is *upāsanā*, meditation on the self, which is clearly a kind of mental act. And in the *Śāstradīpikā* of Pārthasārathimiśra, who in my opinion is the most reliable guide to Kumārila's thought, we find confirmation of the idea that when *ātmajñāna* is enjoined for its own sake, it is in the form of *upāsanā* (p. 283, 6 ff), which might be considered a kind of internal ritual act.[13]

A more striking discrepancy between the ŚV and the TV on the question of attaining liberation, in my view, is the fact that Kumārila, according to the interpretation I have just offered, has now abandoned the principle, so clearly enunciated in the ŚV, that liberation cannot be caused. By saying that liberation, among other things, is the "fruit" of carrying out the injunction of self-knowledge, of course, he is saying just that. The position he appears to embrace in the TV, which remains fundamentally oriented toward the Jaiminiyan principle of MS 1.2.1 that only what is connected with action in the Veda has meaning, seems to represent the rejection of a sound philosophical insight, then – and without any explanation as to why it has been rejected. Thus, in my mind, the passage of the TV, construed in this way, represents not an advance over the ŚV, but a retreat.

However, there is another way in which to read the TV passage as compatible with the verses of the Sambandhākṣepaparihāra that lacks even this discrepancy and is perhaps more straightforward than the reading I have just suggested. Various Upaniṣad passages

[13] ŚD, p. 283, 6 ff.

seem to require Kumārila to acknowledge that self-knowledge contributes, not just to the sacrifice, but also to the attaining of liberation and other human ends. However, as I noted, he does not specify *how* it functions in this capacity. He certainly does not assert that self-knowledge by itself leads directly to the destruction of all *karma* and liberation (as, once again, Śaṅkara does); in fact, he implies the opposite – the performance of obligatory acts for the exhaustion of *karma* remains essential. Thus, because of this lack of specificity, the passage is consistent – at least, not inconsistent – with the view that self-knowledge serves to destroy desire, so that the continued performance of obligatory *karma*, combined with the "enjoyment" of the effects of past *karma*, does not bind one further in *saṃsāra*, which is the teaching of the Sambandhākṣepaparihāra. Self-knowledge – on this view, considered *qua* knowledge, not *qua* action – is *puruṣārtha*, then, insofar as it functions *together* with *karma* and *bhoga* to bring about liberation. The statement that knowledge and *karma* "cannot cancel each other out, nor be alternatives, nor stand in a relation of subordinate and superior" can also be accommodated on this reading. Although I suggested in my discussion of the Sambandhākṣepaparihāra that knowledge is viewed there as a kind of auxiliary, it may not be necessary to see it as *subordinate* at all – certainly, Kumārila himself does not use that language anywhere. Rather, Kumārila could consider that self-knowledge, *bhoga*, and *karma* contribute equally to the realization of liberation. That, after all, would seem to be the idea behind a "conjunction" or "combination" (*samuccaya*) of these factors.

Finally we come to the fragments from the BṬ. Here we find Kumārila very much back within the ambit of considerations that occupy him in his ŚV. He is trying to explain precisely why omitting a *nitya* or *naimittika karma* can cause further sin, which binds one to rebirth, even though not doing something is, strictly, an *abhāva*, which ought not to have any effect. However, he explains (fragment 3), if one is not doing the *nitya* or *naimittika karma* at the time it is prescribed, then one is doing something else one is *not* supposed to be doing at that time, and that is a sin, the fruit of which one will have to experience.[14] Obviously, this discussion is based on the belief, evident in the ŚV, that liberation comes about only as a result of the elimination of rebirth's cause, *karma*. The rest of the fragments, then, appear to reiterate the idea, also found in the ŚV, that the carrying out of obligatory *karma*, together with the exhaustion of past *karma* through experiencing its effects, supported by self-knowledge (which neutralizes desire), yields liberation. Here, too, one should note, the destruction of sin as a result of the carrying out of obligatory *karma* is explicitly mentioned, as in the TV (see fragment 6). However, as I said above, I do not see any reason why Kumārila could not have already had this function in mind when he stressed the importance of *nitya* and *naimittika karma* in the ŚV. Although there is also mention in this text of "bringing knowledge to fruition by means of practice," this needn't refer to anything other than the attainment of full clarity of knowledge of the self, such that detachment, the extinguishing of desire for the fruits of action, really sets in. Or, perhaps it could even refer to a reciprocal causal relationship, i.e., the fact that the performance of obligatory *karma* actually helps give rise to self-knowledge, which in turn makes the performance of obligatory *karma* efficacious in destroying sin. (The teaching that *nitya* and *naimittika karma* help bring about knowledge by "purifying the mind" is accepted by Śaṅkara in BSBh 4.1.16.) However, this also, strictly speaking, would not be incompatible with what Kumārila says in the Sambandhākṣepaparihāra. Thus, I do not see any irresolvable incompatibility between these fragments and the text of the ŚV. In any case, I do not think one is justified in suggesting, either on the basis of this passage or even the TV passage, that Kumārila conceives of *karma* as playing a merely preparatory role, while self-knowledge leads directly to liberation – a position that would be hard to distinguish from Śaṅkara's.[15]

---

[14] This provides a cogent response to the "materialist" Mīmāṃsaka mentioned in fn. 12.

Nevertheless, there remains the apparent discrepancy between the ŚV and the TV in regard to the point whether self-knowledge is *puruṣārtha* or *kratvartha*: the TV clearly states that it is both, whereas the ŚV implies that it is just *kratvartha*. Even though this may not amount to a real discrepancy in the end, how might one account for the fact that Kumārila in these two texts appears to be thinking about the role of self-knowledge within quite different frameworks? Indeed, in the ŚV and TV (and the *Ṭupṭīkā*) Kumārila is thinking according to different sets of rules. In commenting on the latter portions of the *Mīmāṃsāsūtra* in the TV – i.e., not the *Tarkapāda* but the main part of the *śāstra*, which analyzes the sacrifice in great detail – he has to conform to a more traditional understanding of dharma. His view of liberation there is constrained by what is actually prescribed and not prescribed in the

[15] Mesquita's reading of the fragments of the *Bṛhaṭṭīkā* is heavily influenced by the discussion of Śrīdhara in which they are embedded. See Mesquita 1994: 470-473. Although Śrīdhara seems to follow the first four verses closely, arguing that liberation can be achieved only by the exhaustion of one's *karma* through experience, he deviates wildly from Kumārila's text thereafter (beginning p. 687, 7), expounding the idea that, once self-knowledge has become vivid (*spaṣṭī bhavati*) and one attains the state of *jīvanmukta*, one is completely absorbed in the Self and loses external consciousness (*bahiḥsaṃvedana*). In that state the non-performance of obligatory *karma* does *not* result in sin. After a while, the body drops away and one is completely released. It is in this connection that he cites fragment 5. Then, as if returning to his senses, Śrīdhara reiterates that liberation results for the dispassionate knower of the self as distinct from the body, from the exhaustion of *karma* through experience and the avoidance of further sin by the performance of obligatory acts. In this connection he cites fragment 6. The reason for Śrīdhara's excursus into a Vedāntic-sounding account of liberation through self-knowledge is a mystery; in any case, it is certainly not justified by the half-verse fragment from Kumārila he cites. In fact, fragment 5 *prima facie* denies the loss of identity associated with *jīvanmukti* (given that Kumārila never abandons the principle that *nitya* and *naimittika karma* must always be carried out.) Śrīdhara's treatment of these fragments stands in sharp contrast to that of Prabhācandra, who keeps to the *karmabhogavāda* throughout. See PKM, p. 307, 20 – p. 310, 13. However, even if everything that Śrīdhara's treatment of these fragments suggests to Mesquita about Kumārila were true – i.e., even if Kumārila embraced the idea of a *jīvanmukta* and thought that *nitya* and *naimittika karma* were no longer obligatory for such a person – still, as we shall see, there would remain significant differences between Kumārila and Vedāntins such as Śaṅkara and Maṇḍanamiśra on the question of how liberation is attained.

Veda and Dharmaśāstras. In the ŚV, on the other hand, he is thinking as a philosopher; he is guided mainly by principles of reason. The Upaniṣads may indeed say that liberation results merely from self-knowledge; the Veda may therefore enjoin self-knowledge not just as *kratvartha* but also as *puruṣārtha*. But as a philosopher, Kumārila is convinced that knowledge cannot *cause* liberation; indeed, nothing can cause it. Therefore, we ought, if we can, to construe those injunctions as merely *kratvartha*. Śaṅkara will feel compelled to reconstrue them for different reasons. He will be motivated to say that they are not really injunctions at all!

In general, I believe one must be careful when drawing conclusions from an apparent inconsistency between what Kumārila says in his ŚV and what he says in his TV. By itself, such an inconsistency is an insufficient basis for establishing a shift or evolution in Kumārila's thought.

In the course of my discussion I have had occasion to allude to differences between Kumārila and Śaṅkara, but it will be helpful to summarize those differences now.[16] Knowledge, Śaṅkara stresses – the *loci classici* are BSBh 1.1.4 and BĀUBh 1.4.7 – has absolutely nothing to do with action. Knowledge and action pertain to completely different spheres: action to what has to be accomplished, knowledge to what is the case. I quote again from the Thibaut translation, with minor emendations:

> But, it will be said here, knowledge itself is an activity of the mind (*mānasī kriyā*). By no means, we reply, since the two are different in nature. An action is that which is enjoined as being independent of the nature of existing things and dependent on the activity of a person's mind (*puruṣacittavyāpārādhīna*); compare for example the following passages: "To whichever deity the offering is made, on that let him meditate when about to say *vaṣaṭ*" (Ait. Br. 3.8.1); and "Let him meditate in his mind on the *sandhyā*." Meditation and reflection are indeed mental, but as they depend on the person they may either be performed, not performed, or performed differently. Knowledge, on the other hand, arises from the means of knowledge, and those have for their objects things such as they are (*yathābhūtavastuviṣaya*). Knowledge can

[16] Cf. Ram Prasad 2000a and 2000b.

> therefore not be made or not made or made otherwise, but depends entirely on the thing it knows (*vastutantra*), and not either on Vedic statements or the mind of man. Although mental, it thus differs widely from actions like meditation.[17]

Śaṅkara has said before this that knowledge of the identity of the self with Brahman is not of the nature of a "fanciful combination" of ideas (*sampadrūpa*); nor of the nature of an *adhyāsa*.[18] It is not associated with action in any way, especially not as a purification (*saṃskāra*) performed in connection with a sacrifice (such as looking at the victim) or as the object of an act of meditation (*upāstikriyākarma*).[19] Although self-knowledge appears to be enjoined in many passages, it cannot really be the object of an injunction:

> ... Although imperative and similar forms referring to the knowledge of Brahman are found in the Vedic texts, yet they are ineffective because they refer to something which cannot be enjoined, just as the edge of a razor becomes blunt when applied to a stone. For they have for their object something which can neither be endeavored after nor avoided. What, then, is the purport of those sentences which, at any rate, have the appearance of injunctions, such as "The self is to be seen, to be heard"? They have the purport of diverting men from the objects of natural activity (*svābhāvikapravṛttiviṣayavimukhīkaraṇārthāni*). For when a man acts intent on external things, and only anxious to attain the objects of his desire and to eschew the objects of his aversion, and does not thereby reach the highest aim of man although desirous of attaining it, such texts divert him from the objects of natural activity and turn the stream of his thoughts on the inward self....[20]

And so on.

It is clear from all this that the designation of self-knowledge as *puruṣārtha* could only be figurative for Śaṅkara, even though he accepts Bādarāyaṇa's opinion to that effect. As he says, BSBh 3.4.8,

---

[17] Thibaut 1962; I: 34-35 (with minor emendations); BSBh, p. 128, 8 – p. 129, 5.

[18] BSBh, p. 123, 3-4.

[19] BSBh, p. 123, 6; p. 124, 5.

[20] Thibaut 1962, I: 35-36 (with minor emendations); BSBh, p. 129, 11 – p. 130, 4.

> If the Vedānta texts taught that the transmigrating embodied self which is an agent and enjoyer is something different from the mere body, the statements as to the fruit of knowledge of the self would ... be mere *arthavāda*s [insofar as such knowledge would subserve the sacrifice and not be an end in itself]. But what the Vedānta texts really teach as the object of knowledge is something different from the embodied self, viz., the non-transmigrating Lord who is free from all attributes of transmigràtory existence such as agency and the like.... And the knowledge of that self does not only not promote action but rather cuts all actions short....[21]

Self-knowledge is completely removed from the ritual context for Śaṅkara, but for Kumārila it appears still very much embedded in it, even in his discussion in the TV. Kumārila in the end remains true to the attitude toward the Veda that seems to distinguish Mīmāṃsā above all else, that the Veda has only to do with action, and that any statement that cannot be shown to refer to action in some way is purposeless or even meaningless.

Śaṅkara, however, may have adopted one thing from Kumārila, and that is the idea that liberation, being eternal, cannot have a positive cause; rather, it can only be brought by the removal of the cause of rebirth, which for Kumārila is *karma*. That is precisely how Śaṅkara conceives of the operation of self-knowledge. It simply removes ignorance, which is the cause of the false idea of an individual personality, which in his philosophy is the condition for rebirth.

Perhaps, however, it makes more sense to compare Kumārila's views on liberation with those of a Vedāntin who explicitly defends a *jñānakarmasamuccayavāda*, for example, Maṇḍanamiśra. Here, too, we notice considerable differences. According to Maṇḍana, liberation is attained by knowledge of the true nature of the self as Brahman, which instantly destroys all *karma*, the cause of bondage. Even *prārabdha karma* needn't be exhausted by experiencing its effects; if there is a delay in final release, if the body continues for a certain length of time, that is due only to the *saṃskāras* of *prā-*

---

[21] Thibaut 1962, II: 290; BSBh, p. 873, 16 – p. 874, 1.

rabdha karma, not *prārabdha karma* itself.[22] However, full clarity of self-knowledge is achieved only when the *saṃskāra* of *avidyā* is completely suppressed. That occurs by strengthening the opposed *saṃskāra* of true knowledge through repetition (*abhyāsa*) of the liberating insight and the performance of "sacrifices, etc." (*yajñādayaḥ*).[23] While the latter may not be absolutely essential, they can accelerate the rise of knowledge.[24]

This of course is quite different from the *jñānakarmasamuccaya* of Kumārila, even as presented in his TV and BṬ. It emphasizes the instrumentality of self-knowledge in achieving liberation in a way Kumārila does not. It is one thing to say that self-knowledge is enjoined in the Upaniṣads as *puruṣārtha*, quite another to say that it is the principal if not sole means of attaining liberation (or, more precisely, of destroying the cause of bondage, *avidyā*), as Maṇḍana does. Maṇḍana also does not suggest that *karma* must be exhausted by "enjoyment," *bhoga*, as is clearly maintained by Kumārila in his BṬ (fragment 4). Indeed, he states the opposite: only knowledge can eliminate *karma* (again, by destroying its condition, *avidyā*). Finally, Maṇḍana does not talk of the necessity of the continued performance of obligatory *karma* to avoid sin, as Kumārila emphasizes. Rather, for the *ātmajñānin*, according to Maṇḍana, the performance of *nitya* and *naimittika karma* is optional.[25]

Maṇḍana actually does give a favorable assessment of two views of the relation of *jñāna* and *karma* that are reminiscent of Kumārila's.[26] One is that "*karma*s not requiring other effects" (*kāryāntaranirākāṅkṣa*), i.e., not subsidiary to other rites, are an

---

[22] BS, p. 130, 17 – p. 131, 6.

[23] BS, p. 35, 1-8.

[24] BS, p. 36, 18 – p. 37, 3.

[25] One other difference might be mentioned. Maṇḍana is well known as having considered that one may immediately attain final release upon knowing the truth, or else, at the very latest, at the end of one's life, after the subsidence of the activity of *prārabdha karma*. Kumārila, on the other hand, speaks of attaining liberation "after many millions of years"!

[26] BS, p. 36, 12-17.

auxiliary to knowledge (*vidyāṅga*) "because of connection and separation" (*saṃyogapṛthakva*). This reference to MS 4.3.5 brings Kumārila's TV passage to mind. The other is the view that *karma* serves as a "preparation" (*saṃskāra*) for self-knowledge. However, Maṇḍana's acknowledgement of these views is perfectly consistent with his position that "sacrifices, etc." support self-knowledge by helping to counteract the ingrained tendencies of *avidyā*, while self-knowledge itself – and decidedly not the enjoyment of the effects of *karma* – is the chief means of liberation. They would hardly serve as a basis for claiming that Kumārila and Maṇḍana hold essentially the same position. Nor would the sixth fragment from Kumārila's BṬ, which has a certain Maṇḍanesque ring to it:

> One who is destroying sin by regular and occasional *karma*, purifying his knowledge, and bringing it to fruition by means of practice – such a person whose knowledge is ripened as a result of dispassion experiences liberation.

As I argued above, I believe that this verse-and-a-half are quite compatible with the teaching of the Sambandhākṣepaparihāra that self-knowledge must be cultivated in order to perform obligatory *karma* without desire.

Thus, I conclude that the thesis that Kumārila shifted toward Vedānta philosophy in successive expositions of his soteriology remains to be proven.

APPENDIX

Text I. *Ślokavārttika*, Sambandhākṣepaparihāra, vv. 102-111[27]

Sanskrit text:

jñānaṃ mokṣanimittaṃ ca gamyate nendriyādinā I
na ca sāṃkhyādivijñānān mokṣo vedena codyate II 102 II
ātmā jñātavya ity etan mokṣārthaṃ na ca coditam I
karmapravṛttihetutvam ātmajñānasya lakṣyate II 103 II
vijñāte cāsya pārārthye yāpi nāma phalaśrutiḥ I
sārthavādo bhaved eva na svargādeḥ phalāntaram II 104 II
sukhopabhogarūpaś ca yadi mokṣaḥ prakalpyate I
svarga eva bhaved eṣa paryāyeṇa kṣayī ca saḥ II 105 II
na hi kāraṇavat kiṃcid akṣayitvena gamyate I
tasmāt karmakṣayād eva hetvabhāvena mucyate II 106 II
na hy abhāvātmakaṃ muktvā mokṣanityatvakāraṇam I
na ca kriyāyāḥ kasyāścid abhāvaḥ phalam iṣyate II 107 II
tatra jñātātmatattvānāṃ bhogāt pūrvakriyākṣaye I
uttarapracayāsattvād deho notpadyate punaḥ II 108 II
karmajanyopabhogārthaṃ śarīraṃ na pravartate I
tadabhāve na kaścid dhi hetus tatrāvatiṣṭhate II 109 II
mokṣārthī na pravarteta tatra kāmyaniṣiddhayoḥ I
nityanaimittike kuryāt pratyavāyajihāsayā II 110 II
prārthyamānaṃ phalam jñātaṃ na cānicchor bhaviṣyate I
ātmajñe caitad astīti tajjñānam upayujyate II 111 II

Translation:

That knowledge is the cause of liberation is not understood by means of the senses; nor is it prescribed by the Veda that liberation comes from knowledge of Sāṃkhya, etc. (102)

When it is said that the self is to be known, this is not prescribed for the purpose of liberation. It is indicated [rather] that knowledge of the self is the cause of carrying out *karma*. (103)

---

[27] ŚV, p. 474-476. Cf. Mesquita 1994: 455-458.

Given that it is for the sake of something else, the declaration of its fruit is an *arthavāda*. There is no other fruit [of *karma*] than heaven, etc. (104)

And if liberation is conceived as the experience of happiness, this would be heaven by another name, and that is perishable. (105)

For nothing that has a cause is understood to be imperishable. Therefore, only through the absence of the cause, due to the destruction of *karma*, is one released. (106)

For there is no cause of the eternality of liberation other than that which has the nature of non-being; and non-being is not the fruit of any action. (107)

For those who know the truth of the self, when previous *karma* is destroyed as a result of experience, since there is no further accumulation [of *karma*], the body does not arise again. (108)

A body, which is for the sake of experiencing that which is produced by *karma*, does not come forth (*pravartate*). When [*karma*] is absent there remains no cause of [the body]. (109)

Someone desirous of liberation should not take up optional and prohibited [actions]. Let him only do regular and occasion [obligatory rites] with the desire of removing sin. (110)

But the desired result [of these rites] which is known [from scripture] does not arise for someone who does not desire it, and this is the case for the knower of the self. Thus, that knowledge is of use. (111)

Text II. *Tantravārttika* ad MS 1.3.27[28]

Text:

sarvatraiva hi vijñānaṃ saṃskāratvena gamyate I
parāṅgaṃ cātmavijñānād anyatrety avadhāraṇāt II

ātmajñānaṃ hi saṃyogapṛthaktvāt kratvarthapuruṣārthatvena jñāyate tena vinā paralokaphaleṣu karmasu pravṛttinivṛttyasambhavāt. tathā ya ātmāpahatapāpmā vijaro vimṛtyur viśoko vijighatso

[28] TV, p. 227, 11 – p. 228, 18. Cf. Mesquita 1994: 460-462.

'pipāsaḥ satyakāmaḥ satyasaṅkalpaḥ so 'nveṣṭavyaḥ sa vijijñāsitavyaḥ tathā mantavyo boddhavyaḥ tathātmānam upāsīta iti. kāmavādalokavādavacanaviśeṣair jijñāsāmananasahitātmajñānakevalāvabodhaparyantaspaṣṭātmatattvajñānavidhānāpekṣitavākyāntaropāttadvidhābhyudayaniḥśreyasarūpaphalasambandhaḥ sa sarvāṃś ca lokān āpnoti sarvāṃś ca kāmān āpnotīti. tarati śokam ātmavit tathā sa yadi pitṛlokakāmo bhavati saṅkalpād evāsya pitaraḥ samuttiṣṭhanti tena pitṛlokena sampanno mahīyata ityādinā yogajanyāṇimādyaṣṭaguṇaiśvaryaphalāni varṇitāni. tathā sa khalv evaṃ vartayan yāvadāyuṣam brahmalokam abhisampadyate na sa punar āvartata ity apunarāvṛttyātmakaparamātmaprāptyavasthāphalavacanam. aprakaraṇagatatvenānaikāntikakratusambandhāsambandhāc ca nāñjanakhādirasruvavākyādiphalaśrutivad arthavādatvam.

na ca jñānavidhānena karmasambandhavāraṇam |
pratyāśramavarṇaniyatāni nityanaimittikakarmāṇy api pūrvakṛtaduritakṣayārtham akaraṇanimittānāgatapratyavāyaparihārārthaṃ ca kartavyāni. na ca teṣām bhinnaprayojanatvād bhinnamārgatvāc ca bādhavikalpaparasparāṅgāṅgībhāvāḥ saṃbhavanti.

Translation:

In every instance knowledge is understood as a purification and as an auxiliary to something else, except for self-knowledge.

For self-knowledge is known as both *kratvartha* and *puruṣārtha*, because of connection and separation (*saṃyogapṛthaktvāt*; see MS 4.3.5[29]), since without it the performance and non-performance of actions that have their results in another world would not be possible. In the same manner, [there are the injunctions:] "That self which is free from sin, ageless, immortal, free from sorrow, without hunger, without thirst, whose desires and intentions are true – one should investigate it, one should seek to know it" (ChU 8.7.1); also [there are the injunctions] "It is to be thought about, to be known,"

---

[29] Śabara, however, apparently reads the expression *saṃyogapṛthaktva* as 'separateness of context'.

and also, "One should meditate on the self." By means of the particular statements of the *kāma-* and *lokavādas* [there is established] a connection with the two-fold fruit of prosperity and the highest good, obtained from other sentences dependent [in turn] on injunctions of the vivid knowledge of the reality of the self, which culminates in the pure awareness of self-knowledge (?*ātmajñāna-kevalāvabodha*) and is accompanied by thinking and the desire to know, [that is to say, this connection is obtained by the statements:] "He attains all worlds, he attains all desires" (ChU 8.7.1). By such statements as "The knower of the self crosses over sorrow" (ChU 7.1.3), as well as, "If he desires the world of the ancestors, then simply due to his desire the ancestors rise up; having secured the world of the ancestors, he rejoices" (ChU 8.2.1), the fruits arising from yoga, consisting of the eight powers such as minuteness of size (see YSBh 3.45) are mentioned. Also, there is the statement of the fruit consisting in the attainment of the highest self and non-return: "Conducting himself in this way his entire life, he attains the world of Brahman; he does not return again" (ChU 8.15). And, since there is a lack of an exclusive connection with sacrifice, due to its not occurring in the same context, this is not an *arthavāda*, like statements about the ointment, the post made of khadira wood, the ladle, and other *phalaśrutis*.

> But a connection with action is not excluded by the injunction of knowledge.

Regular and occasional obligatory acts, specified for each *āśrama* and *varṇa*, are also to be carried out for the sake of destroying previously committed sin as well as for the purpose of avoiding future sin occasioned by the non-performance [of those acts]. But, since these [injunctions of self-knowledge, on the one hand, and *nitya* and *naimittika karma* on the other] pertain to different purposes and different paths, they cannot cancel each other out, nor be alternatives, nor stand in a relation of subordinate and superior to each other.

Text III. Fragments from the *Bṛhaṭṭīkā*
(as cited in *Nyāyakandalī*, except fragment 6, which is cited as per the *Nyāyasudhā* of Someśvarabhaṭṭa)[30]

Text:

(1) *yāni kāmyāni karmāṇi pratiṣiddhāni yāny api* ।
tāni badhnanty akurvantaṃ nityanaimittikāny api ॥

(2) *karmaṇām prāgabhāvo yo vihitākaraṇādiṣu* ।
na cānarthakaratvena vastutvān nāpanīyate ॥

(3) *svakāle yad akurvaṃs tat karoty anyad acetanaḥ* ।
pratyavāyo 'sya tenaiva nābhāvena sa janyate ॥

(4) *kurvann ātmasvarūpajño bhogāt karmaparikṣayam* ।
yugakoṭisahasreṇa kaścid eko vimucyate ॥

(5) *brāhmaṇatvānahaṃmānī kathaṃ karmāṇi saṃsṛjet* ॥

(6) *nityanaimittikair eva kurvāṇo duritakṣayam*।
jñānaṃ ca vimalīkurvann abhyāsena ca pācayan।
vairāgyāt pakvavijñānaḥ kaivalyaṃ bhajate naraḥ ॥

Translation:

(1) Optional and prohibited actions bind a person [who performs them], as do obligatory actions a person who does not perform them.

(2) And the previous non-existence of actions, when enjoined actions are left undone, does not fail to be excluded from being a real thing by the fact that it brings about something evil (*anarthakaratvena*).

(3) A person who fails to do something in its proper time unwittingly does something else. Thus, his sin is not produced by non-being [but by doing the wrong thing at a particular time].

(4) One who, knowing the nature of the self, brings about the destruction of *karma* through experiencing [its effects] – some such person is liberated after many millions of years.

---

[30] NKand 684-689. Cf. Mesquita 1994: 465-467.

(5) ... How could someone who does not think he is a Brahmin bring about action?
(6) One who is destroying sin by regular and occasional *karma*, purifying his knowledge, and bringing it to fruition by means of practice – such a person whose knowledge is ripened as a result of dispassion experiences liberation.

REFERENCES

Texts and abbreviations

BS [(Maṇḍanamiśra:) *Brahmasiddhi*] *Brahmasiddhi by Acharya Maṇḍanamiśra with Commentary by Saṅkhapāni*. Ed. by S. Kuppuswami Sastri. (Sri Garib Das Oriental Series, 16.) Delhi: Sri Satguru Publications, 1984.

BSBh [(Śaṅkara:) *Brahmasūtrabhāṣya*] *Brahmasūtra Śāṅkara Bhāshya with the Commentaries Bhāmatī, Kalpataru and Parimala*. Ed. by Anantakrishna Śāstri & Vasudev Laxman Shāstri Paṇsikar. Varanasi: Krishnadas Academy, 1982.

NKand *Nyāyakandalī*. In: *Praśastapādabhāṣya (Padārthadharmasaṅgraha) with Commentary Nyāyakandalī by Śrīdhara Bhatta, along with Hindi Translation*. Ed. by Durgādhara Jhā. (Gaṅgānātha Jhā Granthamālā, 1.) Varanasi: Sampurnand Sanskrit Vishvavidyalaya, 1977.

PKM [(Prabhācandra:) *Prameyakamalamārtanḍa*] *Prameyakamala-Mārtanḍa by Shri Prabha Chandra*. Ed. by Pt. Mahendra Kumar Shastri. (Sri Garib Dass Oriental Series, 94.) Delhi: Sri Satguru Publications, 1990.

ŚD *Śāstradīpikā*. Ed. by Subrahmaṇyam Śāstrī & Kiśordās Svāmī. Varanasi: Śrī Sādhuvelā Saṃskṛtamahāvidyālaya, 1977.

ŚV [(Kumārila:) *Ślokavārttika*] *Ślokavārttika of Srī Kumārila Bhaṭṭa with the Commentary Nyāyaratnākara of Śrī Pārthasārathi Miśra*. Ed. by Svāmī Dvārikadāsa Śāstrī. (Prāchyabhārati Series, 10.) Varanasi: Tara Publications, 1978.

TV *Tantravārttika*. In: *Mīmāṃsādarśana with the Tantravārttika of Kumārilabhaṭṭa and the Śābarabhāṣya, 1.2-2.1*. Ed. by Gaṇeśaśāstrī Jośī. (ĀSS, 17.) Varanasi: Ānandāśrama Press, 1981.

Studies and translations

MESQUITA, Roque 1994. Die Idee der Erlösung bei Kumārilabhaṭṭa. *WZKS* 38: 451-484.

CLOONEY, Francis X. 1990. *Thinking Ritually. Rediscovering the Pūrva Mīmāṃsā of Jaimini*. (Publications of the De Nobili Research Library, 17.) Vienna: Institute for Indology, Vienna University.

KRISHAN, Y. 1994. Nitya and Naimittika Karmas in the Pūrva Mīmāṃsā. *ABORI* 75: 177-184.

RAM PRASAD, C. 2000a. Knowledge and action I: Means to the human end in Bhāṭṭa Mīmāṃsā and Advaita Vedānta. *JIP* 28: 1-24.

—— 2000b. Knowledge and action II: Attaining liberation in Bhāṭṭa Mīmāṃsā and Advaita Vedānta. *JIP* 28: 25-41.

THIBAUT, George (transl.) 1962. *The Vedānta Sūtras of Bādarāyaṇa with the Commentary of Śaṅkara*, I-II. New York: Dover Publications.

Mīmāṃsā- and Vedānta-sentences in Padmapāda's *Pañcapādikā* (Chapter 2)

J. M. VERPOORTEN

§ 1 Padmapāda lived in the 9th century (*floruit* ca. 820), was a disciple of Śaṅkara, and wrote a treatise divided into five chapters (*Pañca-pādikā*) where he comments on the *bhāṣya* of his master on the first four aphorisms of the *Brahmasūtra*.

The edition of the *Pañcapādikā* used here, by S. Śrīrāma Śāstrī and S. R. Krishnamurthi Śāstrī (1958), contains several commentaries of which the *Vivaraṇa* of Prakāśātman is a well-known one. In chapter 2, there is a debate between a M(īmāṃsaka) and a V(edāntin), about whether a later *(uttara)* Mīmāṃsā should be added to the former *(pūrva)* Mīmāṃsā in order to scrutinize the Upaniṣadic sentences and make out their meaning. This discussion is not easy to follow because the arguments – some of them very short – succeed each other without any indication that the speaker has changed. The nature of the problems and the style of the exchanges are such that, at first glance, some views seem interchangeable. Although the issues in the debate are few and constantly repeated, it is difficult to point out at which stage we are in the dialectical development and what is precisely the approach of each opponent.

An English translation of the *Pañcapādikā*, accompanied by rich and illuminating notes, has been produced by D. Venkataramiah.[1] There the M debater is called *anūrambhavādin*, 'the one who does not admit [a new] inquiry', and his opponent, the V, is called *ārambhavādin*, 'the one who admits [a new] inquiry'.

A. DELIBERATIONS CONCERNING THE UPANIṢADIC SENTENCES

§ 2 Chapter 2 abruptly opens with an objection of the M: "Sorry (*nanu*) but the inquiry into *brahman* is complete"[2] with what Jaimini has said in his collection of *sūtra*s beginning with the words "Then, therefore, comes the inquiry into dharma",[3] and ending with the appendix entitled Saṃkarṣakāṇḍa.[4] Thus no additional uncertainty (*abhyadhikāśāṅkā*) remains about the essence of *dharma*.

But some (*ke cit*, p. 180/6) authorities are prepared to undertake (*ā-√rabh*)[5] a separate (*pṛthag*, p.181/7) investigation. Śabara indeed defines *dharma* exclusively as *codanā* 'mandate'. Now, in the Upaniṣads, there are important statements that are not mandatory, e.g. ChU 6.2.1: 'In the beginning, my dear, there was being alone.'[6]

§ 3 There are also mandatory sentences like

- BĀU 2.4.5: *ātmā vā are draṣṭavyaḥ*
- ChU 8.1.1: *tasmin yad antas tad anveṣṭavyam, tad vāva vijijñāsitavyam.*[7]

---

[1] Venkataramiah 1948. I thank Dr. A. Pelissero, Turin, to have provided me with photocopies of the pages of the Madras edition here used.

[2] P. 180/2: *siddhā-eva nanu brahmajijñāsā.*

[3] *atha-ato dharmajijñāsā.* Cf. below § 14. Concerning this *sūtra* and its commentary cf. Verpoorten 1986.

[4] On this addendum to the MS, cf. Verpoorten 1987: 6-7. Saṃkarṣa[kāṇḍa] still occurs in chapter 2, pp. 184/5, 187/8.

[5] In our text, the forms of this verb and the noun *ārambha* refer to the new treatise, the one dealing with the Vedānta.

[6] *sad eva somya-idam agra āsīt*, quoted on p. 181/1. On p. 188/5 and 193/2, we find a second non-mandatory phrase, viz. BĀU 4.5.7: *idaṃ sarvaṃ yad ayam ātmā* 'What all this (= the universe) is, that is *ātman*', cf. below § 7.

In them however the injunctive suffix (*kṛtya* or *tavya-pratyaya*)[8] bears on the object (*karman*) and not on the action (*kriyā*). It is *karmābhidhāyin*[9], which is, in the eyes of the M, an undesirable situation.

Another moot point is that *ātman-brahman* is, by essence, beyond the range of acts, even the one of knowing. It cannot be brought about nor modified, nor attained,[10] nor sacralized, because it is eternal (p. 182/1-2).

In the sentence BĀU 1.4.8: *ātmānam upāsīta* 'One should revere the Self', to consider *ātmānam* as a genuine accusative and therefore to qualify it as 'the most desirable [thing]' (*īpsitatama*), sounds freakish in the ear of the M.

In order to address and settle these difficulties, a new inquiry and a new method are necessary under the name of *śārīrakārambha* (p. 187/11), that is Vedānta.

§ 4 The answer of the M (p. 182) and the reaction of the V.

The M argues that the Upaniṣadic statements must be integrated into the *dharma*-science or Pūrva-Mīmāṃsā. After all, what is the difference between *ātmā draṣṭavyaḥ* coming from an Upaniṣad, and *svādhyāyo 'dhyetavyaḥ*[11] which is sheer Mīmāṃsā? And, as far as *ātmānam upāsīta* is concerned, we should appeal to the Mīmāṃsā rule called *saktunyāya*[12] that allows us to consider the accusative as

---

[7] 'Mark well, it is the Self that should be seen' (Zaehner 1966: 46). 'What is within that is what [you] should seek: that is what [you] should really want to understand' (Zaehner 1966: 122).

[8] *Kṛtya* is the technical name of the injunctive suffix used by Pāṇini, e.g. 3.3.171. *Tavya* is a common injunctive ending. In this context *pratyaya* means 'suffix' and not 'knowledge'.

[9] The word occurs on p. 183/6 and contrasts with *bhāvābhidhāyin*, p. 181/4-5.

[10] These three options are familiar in Indian grammar. Cf. Bhartṛhari, *Vākyapadīya* 3.7, *kārikā* 45 (or Rau 2002: 301).

[11] 'One should engage into the study [of the Veda].' The text known as *adhyayana-vidhi* shows up in *Śatapathabrāhmaṇa* 11.5.6.3. In chapter 2, we meet it on pp. 185/7, 191/5 (*svādhyāyakāla*), 195/7, 210/2 (*svādhyāyādhyayana-vidhi*), 204/5, 206/5 (*adhyayana*) and 208-209 (*vedādhyayana*).

a hidden instrumental. Thereby *ātmānam* – actually *ātmanā* – loses the first place in the sentence and hands it over to the verb. As an instrumental, *ātman(ā)* becomes a simple means of gaining heaven and not the main purpose, prior to the act.

But, according to the V, even this solution is unsatisfactory and the above-mentioned phrases must be accounted for by a new method, because they are not ritual prescriptions (*vidhi*s)[13]. Thus we should undertake a new treatise, the *Brahmasūtra*.

§ 5 After a remark on the ritual bath at the completion of study (*snāna*),[14] which should be delayed if a Upaniṣadic teaching is delivered, Padmapāda turns to the agent who is the beneficiary of the mandatory act, namely the *adhikārin*.

In common parlance, we hear orders such as
– *kaṭas tvayā kartavyaḥ* 'The mat must be made by you'
– *grāmas tvayā gantavyaḥ* 'The village has to be reached by you',
where a commander or *niyoktar* is supposed to be present. And if a sentence contains an act to be done and a material, it is to be completed by the supposition of such a person in order to be purposeful (*prayojana*)[15].

The V replies that this view is wrong. We clearly perceive that the injunction "The Self should be seen" aims at destroying nescience conducive to *saṃsāra*.[16] Such a purpose is valid by itself without the mention of any instigator to whom the benefit accrues.

---

[12] MS 2.1.11-12 (analysing TS 3.3.8.4): *saktūn pradāvye juhuyāt* 'He should offer grits in the forest fire.'

[13] It is the opinion of the V. If he held the Upaniṣadic sentences as genuine *vidhi*s similar to the ritual ones, he would play the game of the M.

[14] Pp. 183/5, 203/1, 209/1.

[15] P. 183/7-9: *na niyoktṛtvaṃ nirākartuṃ śakyate … dravyaparatve prayojanābhāvād ānarthakyaṃ niyogasya*. This passage echoes the grammatical ideas of Kumārila; cf. Joshi 1993: 34-36.

[16] Pp. 183-184: *avidyocchedasya-upalabhyamānatvāt. avidyā ca saṃsārahetubhūtā*.

§ 6 Other (*apare*) authorities have a different approach: if somebody thinks that the elucidation of the Veda ends with the Saṃkarṣakāṇḍa (see § 2) – i.e., is confined to Pūrva-Mīmāṃsā – and that no new treatise of Vedānta[17] is to be undertaken, we must draw his attention to the fact that the knowledge of *ātman*, that is of reality (*tattvāvabodha*, p.185/1), is a *kārya*, 'ought to be done'. And this duty or *niyoga* is to be performed by a qualified person (*adhikārin*).

The last three Sanskrit words are met again after an intricate confrontation between M and V concerning the nature of *ātmaviṣaya* (pp. 186-187). Each of the opponents expounds his view of the content of the word. For the M, *ātman* is the individual ego (*ahaṃpratyaya*)[18]; for the V it is the cosmic entity the cognition of which brings the *saṃsāra* to an end.[19]

The new development about *kārya*, *niyoga* and *adhikārin* within the Vedānta is called 'another doctrine' (*matāntaram*) (p. 187/7) or *śārīrakārambha* (p. 187/11). And it is immediately refuted (*pratyukta*, p. 187/12) by the M on the two contrary grounds: either *brahman-ātman* is *siddha*, that is 'already there' and known by everybody, or it is *asiddha* 'not there', 'inexistent', and thereby unknowable. In both cases, the fresh inquiry contemplated by the V is useless.[20]

§ 7 The V sets forth his stance: the Veda is no doubt an object of duty, but not exclusively in the ritual sphere (p. 188/1; cf. below fn. 57). Another object of duty (*kāryaviṣaya*) is knowing the essence

---

[17] Chapter 2 ignores the words *pūrva-* and *uttara-mīmāṃsā*. Incidentally (pp. 183/4, 187/9), it employs the term *vedānta*. On these questions of terminology, see Bronkhorst in this volume.

[18] Cf. p. 200/4: *ataḥ ahaṃpratyayāvaseya eva-ātmā. na tasya śabdāvaseyam atīndriyaṃ rūpāntaram asti.*

[19] Cf. fn. 15 and p. 186/6-8 where the M refutes the Vedantic conception of *ātman* as impossible by saying: *yat punar ātmajñānād avidyocchedaḥ, tad-ucchedāt saṃsāranivṛttiḥ phalam ity upanyastaṃ tad asat.*

[20] P. 187/11-12: *brahmāvagamasya siddhatve 'siddhatve ca kāryatvāsaṃbhavena pratyuktam.*

of reality (*vastutattva*) as revealed by BĀU 4.5.7: *idaṃ sarvaṃ yad ayam ātmā* 'What all this (= the universe / what ever exists / the supreme all) is, that is *ātman*'.[21]

At this point, a difficulty arises: if there is identity between *ātman* and the universe, etc., the former is at least partly *acetana* 'insentient', and that jeopardizes the existence of a knower, and, consequently, of his object of knowledge: the Vedic Revelation (*śabda*).

The answer of the V is as follows: *ātman* does not have the form of the [supreme] All (*sarvarūpatā*), but this latter has the essence of *ātman* (*ātmasvabhāvatā*).[22] The M then points out that in such a view, *ātman* does not require the presence of a *vidhi*, because it is obvious, known by itself without extra help.[23]

§ **8** The parallel of TS 2.6.8.5.

The V wishes to turn the BĀU passage into a *vidhi*[24] in the same way as the M claims that the sentence *tasmāt pūṣā prapiṣṭa-bhāgaḥ*[25] is injunctive although we hardly ever see a form like *yaṣṭavya* 'must be honoured (with ...)' inside this statement.[26] Thus the V proposes to introduce the mandatory form *jñātavya* 'must be known' in BĀU 4.5.7.[27] If, indeed, we did not do so, the Upani-

---

[21] In the opinion of the M, these words are not a *prayogavacana*, a 'rule of performance', pp. 191/6-7, 197/5, 198/4.

[22] Cf. p.199/7-8: *sarvasya ātmasvabhāvatā sidhyati*. That presumably involves that the [supreme] All has no independent existence.

[23] P. 189/3-4: *pratīte 'rthe śabdaṃ kalpayatā kiṃ kṛtaṃ syāt ? Śabda(m)* is probably a synonym of *vidhi*, which the next phrase suggests by using *vidhiṃ kalpayitvā*.

[24] P.189/1: *evaṃ tarhi kalpyatāṃ vidhiḥ*.

[25] 'Therefore Pūṣan [is endowed] with a portion of kneaded flour.' The next phrase in the TS is *adantako hi* 'for he is toothless'.

[26] By adding the verbal form, the M assumes the right of transforming the assertion of the TS into a injunction. Nowhere else, e.g. in Śbh 3.3.46 that examines the same text, we discover the word *yaṣṭavya*. It is assumed by Venkataramiah (1948: 151, n. 20) to account for the expression *aśrūyamānavidhi* 'an unexpressed *vidhi*', p. 189/6.

ṣadic sentence would be truncated[28] without support (*nirālambana*, p. 189/11). On the other hand, *jñātavya* gives to the statement the strength of an experience (*anubhava*) or an evidence (*akṣakaraṇa/kāra/bhāva*).[29]

§ 9 Is it right to complete BĀU 4.5.7 with the injunctive form *jñātavya*?

The V emphasizes that *ātman* under the aspect of the universe is not recognized as a conscious enjoyer except in a mandatory (*niyoga*) frame.[30] In other words, to link *ātman* and *idaṃ sarvam* is hardly possible without a mandatory verb.

As far as the M is concerned, he says that the *niyoga*, instead of being required by *ātman*, requires (*ā-√kṣip*) it, because, deprived of a personal agent (*puruṣa*, i.e. *ātman*), it would be neither perceptible (*anupalabdha*) nor effective.

Moreover, for making a *niyoga-vidhi* perceptible, a *dhātu* or 'verbal root' is necessary. Which one?[31] *Kartavya* is excluded as unfit because, even resting on this form, BĀU 4.5.7 fails to eradicate the unconscious nature of [at least a part of] the universe (*idam sarvam*).[32]

Thus the command "Be the universe / whatever exists made (= turned) into *ātman*" cannot be performed by lack of a suitable procedure (*itikartavyatā*).[33] *Jñātavya* is also objectionable and the

---

[27] P. 190; the form *kartavya* is also proposed as the mandatory verb to be supplemented.

[28] P. 194/6: *avāntaravākya*. In such a phrase, there is no connection with *prāmāṇatva*.

[29] This idea is defended by the V on p. 195/3, 6 and p.196/1; cf. fn. 43.

[30] P.190/1: *nanv atra-apy ātmapadaṃ cetanasya bhoktur vācakam.*

[31] Venkataramiah (1948: 153, n. 25) points out that the answer to this question is "no one", since neither *kartavya* nor *jñātavya* are suitable.

[32] P.190/7-8: *yadi tāvat kartavyam iti, tatra-anātmasvabhāvatā na nivṛttā prapañcasya*; cf. § 7.

[33] An illustration is given: it is not because you model the offerings of dough (*piṣṭapiṇḍa*) into lion shapes that their nature of dough disappears. Cf. Śbh 8.3.24 cited and commented in Verpoorten 2001: 84.

translation 'Be whatever exists / the universe known as *ātman*' must be rejected because a [concrete?] object as *idaṃ sarvam* cannot be transformed by cognition into a different entity (*ātman*).[34]

§ 10 The V desperately tries to bolster the proposed *jñātavya* against the thorough criticism of the M. According to the M, however, a statement affirming (*vidhāyaka*) such and such a content cannot make it mandatory at the same time.[35]

The V argues that something can subserve two goals simultaneously[36] and, therefore, that a *śabda* – viz., an Upaniṣadic 'great utterance' (*mahāvākya*) – asserts its own meaning and the obligation of knowing (*pratyaya*) it as well (p. 182/6-7).[37]

For the M, this thesis is *anirūpita* 'doubtful'. BĀU 4.5.7 actually conveys a message that cannot be demonstrated from elsewhere (*anyato 'siddhatva*, p. 193/4). So it has no right of obtaining the status of 'object of injunction' (*vidher viṣaya*, p.193/4). Conversely, if it should become a mandate, it would be unable to have its content known[38]. So the conclusion is that both aspects cannot coexist in the same sentence for fear of disjunction.[39].

§ 11 The V then raises a question familiar to anyone acquainted with the Mīmāṃsā: if a *vidhi* is limited to one command, where and what are the details (*guṇakarma*, p. 193/7) of the performance? To

---

[34] P.191/1-2: *na hi vastu vastvantarātmanā jñātuṃ śakyate.*

[35] This point is seemingly the main topic of the obscure pages 191-193 and particularly on p. 192/1-3.

[36] I skip over the comparison between the *mantra*s and the Upaniṣadic sentences developed from p. 191/6 onwards. The example of a double goal object is given in fn. 45.

[37] Here *pratyaya*, as the compound *saṃpratyaya*, means 'knowledge' and not 'suffix' like above in fn. 8.

[38] P.193/4-5: *atha vidher viṣayo na prameyam avagamayitum alam.*

[39] P.193/5-6: *na ca yugapad ubhayaṃ saṃbhavati vairūpyaprasaṅgāt.* It is obvious that *vairūpya* (mentioned again on p. 194/5) is the Vedantic synonym of *vākyabheda* 'split in the sentence', usual with Śabara; cf. Verpoorten 1987, § 22.

make them available, it is easier to postulate that the sentence might provide us with more than one enjoined thing.

This time, the M is in trouble, as proven by his lengthy and embarrassed answer. He tries to get out of this fix by laying down a difference between the ritual sphere and the one of his opponent.[40] In the first case, the object (*karman*) of the act, e.g., the rice to be sprinkled and purified, is something *siddha* 'already present'; in the second, *brahman-ātman* is something *asiddha* (p. 193/8–194) 'not present', 'unable to be the target of an act', and thus outside the scope of the *kārya* or duty.[41]

The V proceeds to say again that BĀU 4.5.7, as a meaningful explanation, contains in itself the injunctive power of having its message known.[42] So, this latter should be prescribed in order to be intelligible and valid, somewhat like, according Anselmus of Canterbury, God must exist in order to be perfect.

For the M, on the contrary, the message in question remains illusory because it is beyond the scope of perception.[43] And even if it were not illusory, it could be grasped through the *svādhyāya-vidhī* (p. 185/7), at the exclusion of any other prescription. Furthermore, nowhere in the (ritual) Veda is a means of experiencing *ātman*[44] provided, and, if it was, it would make it useless to complete BĀU 4.5.7 with the imperative participle *jñātavya*.

---

[40] The Vedantic sphere is denoted by the words *yatra-tatra* 'where/when ... there'. The couple *iha punaḥ* indicates that the M comes back to his own doctrine and stresses the difference with his opponent. Cf. pp. 194/10, 196/8, 199/3-4 (cf. below fn. 49) etc.

[41] In an other respect, *brahman-ātman* is *siddha* 'accomplished' and not *sādhya* 'to be carried out' with the help of a rite since it is eternal. See fn. 42.

[42] P. 184/7: *arthavādapadānām iva ... kaṃ cid artham avabodhya vidhisabandham anubhavet.* The M calls BĀU 4.5.7 an 'association of words' (*padasamanvaya*, pp. 193/2-3, 194/10), which is informative and not injunctive, because it describes something *siddha*, i.e. *ātman*.

[43] As explained by Venkataramiah (1948: 160, n. 41). In the text (p. 195/3-4), perception is called *sākṣāt-karaṇa/bhāva* or *anubhava*. Cf. § 8.

[44] According to the M, this means might be called *abhyāsa* 'training, practice', synonym of *upāsana* (p.186/3). BĀU 1.4.8 uses the verb *upāsīta*; cf. above § 3.

§ 12 As far as the other argument is concerned, viz., the possibility for an entity of fulfilling two missions, the M opines that it should be denied as well.[45] Therefore, a *vidhi* that apparently conveys two commands,[46] e.g., several deeds and their succession, actually prescribes the former one only. That does not mean that the 'succession' (*krama*) itself does not exist but it pertains to the sphere of the 'remembrance' (*smṛti*) and is to be ascertained by *arthāpatti*.[47] And once again the M concludes that it is a mistake to say that the Veda is able to reveal the essence of reality since its unique object is *kārya* or 'duty'.[48]

§ 13 Differences between BĀU 4.5.7 as a piece of verbal knowledge and perception.

a. In case (*tatra*) of perception – so the M says – the eye is an independent means of knowledge in reference to each object. But when the *tātparya* or 'intention' of an Upaniṣadic sentence is object of cognition (*prameyatā*), it is not understood word by word.[49]

b. The V wishes the verbal cognition (*abhidhānika pratyaya*) to be an object of command (*vidhiviṣaya*), but the M notices that enjoined knowledge (*pratipattividhi)* does not necessarily lead to a link with the object (*vāstavaṃ saṃsargam*, p.199/6-7, 10). This

---

[45] The example already adduced (p. 192/4) was the one of the irrigating canal which is helpful for the crops as well as for quenching one's thirst. Cf. Śbh 3.1, *sūtra* 12; transl. Jha 1933, I: 351. This example is here dismissed as unfit (p. 187/3: *apeśala*).

[46] Likely reference to AB 2.4: *samidho yajati / tanūnapātaṃ y° / iḍo y° / barhir y° / svāhākāraṃ y°*. 'He offers (to) the fire-sticks, (to) Tanūnapāt, (to) the oblation, (to) the sacrificial grass, (to/with) the cry of "hail".'

[47] Suggestion of Venkataramiah 1948: 164, confirmed by the occurrence of the word *arthāt*, p.199/7.

[48] P. 198/8-9: *tasmād asad etat: kāryaviṣayo 'pi vedo vastutattvam avagāmayati*.

[49] P. 199/3-5: *tatra yad yad avabodhayati cakṣuḥ tatra svatantram eva pramāṇam. Iha punaḥ yatra tātparyaṃ tasya* [*mahāvākyasya*] *prameyatā, na yad yat pratīyate tasya tasya*. A literal translation provides an unsatisfactory meaning, because the parallelism is defective.

paradoxical reasoning seems to be meant to disconnect cognition and injunction, whereas the V seeks to connect them tightly.

The M reminds us that *ātman* is just the individual ego, knowledgeable without a revelation (*śabda*). Granted that *ātman* is such, no obstacle prevents you from meditating on its Upaniṣadic qualifications, namely *brahman*, *antaryāmin* and so on.[50]. If all that occurs in the frame of the Mīmāṃsā, what room is left for a further investigation called Vedānta?[51]

B. DELIBERATIONS CONCERNING THE FIRST TWO SŪTRAS OF JAIMINI

§ 14 Why did Jaimini use the word *dharma* in MS 1.1.1?

The V tries to show that his view is already the one of Jaimini, and accordingly he quotes the initial *sūtra* of the MS.[52] He emphasizes the wide range of meanings included in the word *dharma* mentioned here, ranging from a Vedic ceremony (like the *agnihotra*) to the adoration in a Buddhist temple (*caityavandana*).[53] Jaimini, of course, chooses the former meaning as the topic of his *śāstra* (p. 203/2), the *Mīmāṃsā*, but the ritual *dharma* – the V says – does not include the whole object of the Veda (*sarvavedārtha*). There is another topic dealing with what has 'an accomplished form' (*siddharūpa*, p. 203/3) and escapes the injunctive power of the *adhyayanavidhi* (p. 204/4-5).

And when Jaimini uses *dharma*, instead of *vedārtha*, in MS 1.1.1, he strives to bring to the reader's mind the presence of this unsaid possibility: investigating into the essence of reality.[54]

---

[50] E.g. BĀU 2.5.9, 3.7.3; ChU 6.8.7 (*tat tvam asi*), cited on p. 200.

[51] P.201/3: *kim aparam avaśiṣṭaṃ yataḥ brahmajijñāsārambhaṃ prayuñjīta?*

[52] The text of MS 1.1.1 is given in fn. 3 and fn. 15. It is mentioned in the text on pp. 201/5, 202/8, 204/7.

[53] P. 202. The same problem is resumed on p. 211, in a less clear context, cf. below § 16.

[54] P. 205/3-4: *kaś cid asya (= vedasya) bhāgaḥ kāryatāśūnye vastutattve vartate.*

Dharma is as important for what it suggests as for what it states. On the other hand, it contains a much stronger incentive force than the weak *vedārtha* (p. 204).[55]

§ 15 Why did Jaimini use the word *codanā* in MS 1.1.2?

The M seeks to reaffirm the priority of the *kārya* with the help of the word *codanā* present in MS 1.1.2, without explicitly quoting it at this stage.[56] According to him, *dharma* is nothing but *codanā* 'impulsion / mandate to act ritually' (p. 206/1-5).

The V retorts in a rather tortuous way and comes out with the idea that Jaimini chose *codanā* to denote what this word does not say as much as to denote what it says. Through *codanā*, it is pointed out that the injunctive part of the Veda is not tantamount to the whole of it.[57] We may have to understand that the other part deserves an investigation even if the Sūtrakāra himself is not concerned with it.[58] Despite the texts adduced by the M as proofs of the mandatory nature of the Veda,[59] the V does not declare himself defeated and appeals to the *bhāṣya* on MS 1.1.1 where Śabara proclaims:

> We will transgress this mandate (the one of holding the Veda as purely injunctive). If we do not transgress it, we will be rendering the Veda meaningless when it is fraught with meaning ..." (p. 209/1-2).[60]

---

[55] P. 204/6-8: *jijñāsām arhati-iti vadituṃ dharmagrahaṇaṃ yuktam. "atha-ato dharmajijñāsā", na "vedārthajijñāsā-iti" yato na vedārthatayā jñāne pravṛttiḥ.*

[56] On p. 205/1 he speaks of 'the second *sūtra*' (*dvitīyaṃ sūtram*) but quotes the text *codanālakṣaṇo 'rtho dharmaḥ* for the first time on p. 212/4.

[57] Pp. 207/6–208/1: *(yena) vedārthamātrasya dharmatvaṃ mā bhūd iti codanā-iti avocat* '(The Sūtrakāra, p. 207/4) said *codanā* [after thinking]: "be [the ritual] dharma not the unique [object] of the Veda".' Cf. also p. 188/1: *satyaṃ kāryaviṣayo vedaḥ, na tu tāvanmātre* 'It is true that the Veda has duty as its object, but not merely that.'

[58] P. 208/1-2: *tad evaṃ sūtrakāra eva svaśāstraviṣayātiriktaṃ vedabhāgam avicāritam asūsucat.*

[59] P. 208/3-4, citing Śbh *ad* MS 1.1.1 (= Frauwallner 1968: 12/12-13); MS 1.1.25 (= Clooney 1990: 90); MS 1.2.1 (see below fn. 61) (= Clooney 1990: 103); see also Taber in this volume.

Such a declaration shows that Śabara extends the 'sense of the Veda' (*vedārtha*) beyond the scope of *kārya* (p. 209/8-9).

C. CLOSING DELIBERATIONS AND CONCLUSION

§ 16 The last 28 Sanskrit lines of chapter 2 are very difficult.[61] First of all, the view of *ke cid*[62] is presented. They seem to think that a new *śāstra* should not be undertaken to lay down the priority of *dharma* as ritual action over *dharma* as veneration in a Buddhist temple (see § 14), but to settle discrepancies within the orthodoxy concerning the import of this word.

Eventually (p. 215), the chapter ends with the expected restatement that *dharma* has been deliberately mentioned in MS 1.1.2, instead of *vedārtha*, to keep an opportunity available for starting a further inquiry, namely Vedānta.

The content of chapter 2 can be summarized in the form of several contrasts:

- The contrast between (1) Pūrva-Mīmāṃsā according to which everything has been said by Jaimini, etc. about *Veda-dharma* so that no new research is needed, and (2) Uttara-Mīmāṃsā which is prepared to further look into the Upaniṣads for the essence of reality (*vastu-tattva* = *ātman-brahman*).
- The contrast between (1) the ritual injunctions and (2) the Upaniṣadic statements and the difference between (1) the Upaniṣadic statements and (2) *mantra*s and *arthavāda*s. *Mantra*s and *arthavāda*s are subordinate to *vidhi*s and draw their sense from

---

[60] *atikramiṣyāma imam āmnāyam, anatikrāmanto vedam arthavantaṃ santam anarthakaṃ kalpayema* (text in Frauwallner 1968: 12/11-13). The rest of the sentence rather helps the cause of the M.

[61] They are preceded by a discussion on MS 1.2.1: *āmnāyasya kriyārthatvād ānarthakyam atadarthānām* (p. 209/9) 'Action is the purport of scripture. Thus, whatever does not refer to action is purposeless' (transl. by Taber in this volume), a *sūtra* which could be a major obstacle on the path towards an non-ritual *mīmāṃsā*.

[62] According to Venkataramiah (1948: 175), resuming an indication of the *Vivaraṇa* (p. 211/10), these "some" are the Prābhākaras.

them. *Mahāvākya*s are significant by themselves and thus independent.

- The contrast between (1) *ātman* regarded as the individual ego in the Mīmāṃsā but (2) as a universal and supreme entity by the Vedānta.

If one tries to join both aspects of each contrast in one whole, he gets into trouble, especially if he strives to build a sentence which would be both denotative and injunctive. That would result into *vākyabheda* or 'split in the sentence' (see § 10).

Finally, Padmapāda explains the first two *sūtra*s of Jaimini in a way of his own. He argues that the Sūtrakāra uses *dharma* in MS 1.1.1 and *codanā* in MS 1.1.2 in order to show the limits of his own task: the study of the mandatory part of the Veda. Implicitly he invites others to explore areas he could not or would not investigate himself. So he tacitly acknowledges the legitimacy of the Uttara-Mīmāṃsā.

REFERENCES

Texts, translations and abbreviations

AB *Aitareyabrāhmaṇa*. See Aufrecht 1975; Keith 1920.

ABHYANKAR, K. V. & G. A. JOSHI 1929-34. *Jaimini's Mīmāṃsā Sūtra*, I-VII. [Edited together with *Śābara-bhāṣya*, *Prabhā*-commentary, Kumārila's *Tantravārttika* and *Ṭupṭīkā*.] (ĀSS, 97.) Poona: Ānandāśrama. (Reprint: 1972.)

AUFRECHT, Theodor (ed.) 1879. *Das Aitareya Brāhmaṇa*. Bonn: Adolph Marcus. (Reprint: Hildesheim: Georg Olms Verlag, 1975.)

BĀU *Bṛhadāraṇyaka-Upaniṣad*. See Zaehner 1966; Senart 1934.

ChU *Chāndogya-Upaniṣad*. See Zaehner 1966; Senart 1930.

FRAUWALLNER, Erich 1968. *Materialien zur ältesten Erkenntnislehre der Karmamīmāṃsā*. (SB ÖAW, 259.2. = VKSKS, 6.) Vienna: Österreichische Akademie der Wissenschaften. [Sanskrit text and German translation of MS 1.1.1-5 and Śbh on this passage]

JHA, Ganganatha (transl.) 1933. *Śābara-Bhāṣya Translated into English*, I-III. (GOS, 66, 70, 73.) Baroda: Oriental Institute. (Reprint: 1973.)

KEITH, A. B. (transl.) 1914. *The Veda of the Black Yajus School Entitled Taittirīya Sanhitā*, I-II. (HOS, 18-19.) Harvard University Press.

KEITH, A. B. (transl.) 1920, *Rigveda Brahmaṇas. The Aitareya and Kauṣītaki Brāhmaṇas of the Rigveda.* (HOS, 25.) Cambridge Mass.: Harvard University Press.

M = Mīmāṃsaka

MS *Mīmāṃsā-sūtra* of Jaimini. See Abhyankar & Joshi 1929-34; Jha 1933; Frauwallner 1968.

Pañcapādikā of Padmāpada. See Śrīrāma Śāstrī & Krishnamurthi Śāstrī 1958; Venkataramiah 1948.

RAU, Wilhelm 2002. *Bhartṛharis Vākyapadīya. Versuch einer vollständigen deutschen Übersetzung nach der kritischen Edition der Mūla Kārikās.* Hrsg von O. von Hinüber. Stuttgart: Franz Steiner Verlag.

Śbh *Śābara-bhāṣya.* See Abhyankar & Joshi 1929-34; Jha 1933.

SENART, Emile (ed. & transl.) 1930. *Chāndogya-Upaniṣad traduite et annotée.* Paris: Société d'Édition "Les Belles Lettres" [Contains also the Sanskrit text in transcription,]

—— (ed. & transl.) 1934. *Bṛhad-Āraṇyaka-Upaniṣad traduite et annotée.* Paris: Société d'Édition "Les Belles Lettres". [Contains also the Sanskrit text in transcription.]

Śrīrāma Śāstrī, S. & S. R. Krishnamurthi Śāstrī 1958. *Pañcapādikā of Śrīpadmācārya with Prabodhapariśodhinī of Ātmasvarūpa and Tātparyārthadyotinī of Vijñānātman and Pañcapādikāvivaraṇa of Śrī Prakaśātman with Tātparyadīpikā of Citsukhācārya and Bhāvakāśikā of Nṛsiṃhāśrama.* (Madras Government Oriental Manuscript Series, 155.) Madras: Government Oriental Manuscripts Library.

TS *Taittirīyasaṃhitā.* See Keith 1914.

V = Vedāntin

Vākyapadīya of Bhartṛhari. See Rau 2002.

VENKATARAMIAH D. (transl.) 1948. *The Pañcapādikā of Padmapāda* (GOS, 107.) Baroda: Oriental Institute.

ZAEHNER, R. C. (transl.) 1966. *Hindu Scriptures.* (Everyman's Library.) London: J. M. Dent & Sons. [Translations from the Ṛgveda, Atharvaveda, Upaniṣads and the Bhagavadgītā]

Studies

CLOONEY, Francis X. 1990. *Thinking Ritually. Rediscovering the Pūrva Mīmāṃsā of Jaimini.* (Publications of the De Nobili Research Library, 17 Vienna: Institute for Indology, Vienna University.

JOSHI, S. D. 1993, Kauṇḍa Bhaṭṭa on the Meaning of Sanskrit Verbs (1). *Saṃbhāṣā* 14: 1-40. Nagoya: Nagoya Studies in Indian Culture and Buddhism.

VERPOORTEN, J. M. 1986. Le premier sūtra de la Mīmāṃsā et ses commenaires, *Bulletin d'Études indiennes* 4: 353-366.

—— 1987. *Mīmāṃsā Literature*. (A History of Indian Literature, 6.5.) Wiesbaden: Otto Harrassowitz.

—— 2001. Le bestiaire des philosophes indiens. In: C. Cannuyer et al. (eds.), *L'animal dans les civilisations orientales / Animals in the Oriental Civilizations. Henri Limet in honorem* (Acta Orientalia Belgica, 14.): 67-100. Bruxelles: Société Belge d'Études Orientales.

Kumārila's Reevaluation of the Sacrifice and the Veda from a Vedānta Perspective

KIYOTAKA YOSHIMIZU

INTRODUCTION

Among the many scholars of Indian philosophy, Kumārila Bhaṭṭa is deserving of special attention for his original thoughts in various disciplines. Besides elaborating logic, epistemology, theories of language and verbal cognition, theories of ethics and social system, he also contributes to the development of the ritual Mīmāṃsā into a philosophical system by his own theory of liberation. Recently, K. Harikai investigated Kumārila's theory of liberation in the *Tantravārttika* (TV) and discovered some fragments about liberation from his lost work, the *Bṛhaṭṭīkā* (BṬ). Adding more fragments to the extant BṬ, R. Mesquita explained how Kumārila developed his theory of liberation in his three works, the *Ślokavārttika* (ŚV), the TV and the BṬ[1]. Thanks to their careful studies, it has been clarified that, in the Sambandhākṣepaparihāra of the ŚV, Kumārila considers liberation as the state of consciousness in which the self is completely dissociated not only from pain but also from pleasure,[2]

[1] Cf. Harikai 1989; 1990: 133-145 and Mesquita 1994.

[2] ŚV, Sambandhākṣepaparihāra, k. 105: "If liberation were held to consist in the enjoyment of pleasure, then it would be synonymous with heaven, which is perishable." (*sukhopabhogarūpaś ca yadi mokṣaḥ prakalpyate | svarga eva bhaved eṣa paryāyeṇa kṣayī ca saḥ* ||); Sambandhākṣepaparihāra, k. 107ab: "Except for the non-existence [of all feelings], liberation surely has no other grounds

as asserted in the Nyāya school.[3] At the end of the Vyākaraṇādhikaraṇa of the TV, however, Kumārila advocates a position of the Vedānta. Quoting some passages mainly from the *Chāndogyopaniṣad* (ChU),[4] he asserts that the knowledge of the self (*ātmajñāna*) is valuable not only to rituals (*kratvartha*) but also to human beings (*puruṣārtha*), because this knowledge, if culminated in meditation, brings about supernatural power and even leads to liberation.[5] Here Kumārila characterizes liberation as the attainment of a supreme self (*paramātmaprāpti*) and as the non-return to this world (*apunarāvṛttyātmaka*).[6] In the BṬ, Kumārila seems to have strengthened his inclination to the Vedānta even further, since there are portions from the BṬ where he professes a particular theory of Vedāntic

---

for its eternity." (*na hy abhāvātmakaṃ muktvā mokṣanityatvakāraṇam* |). Cf. Mesquita 1994: 456.

[3] Cf. NBh, p. 83, 1-2: "Just as one should not accept a food mixed with honey and poison, one should not accept the pleasure connected with pain." (*tad yathā madhuviṣasaṃpṛktānnam anādeyam ity evaṃ sukhaṃ duḥkhānuṣaktam anādeyam iti*); NBh, p. 1028, 4-5: "Just as, indeed, the connection with passion as well as the connection with pleasure and pain are cut off from one who is sleeping well without dreaming, so [they are cut off] also in the state of liberation." (*yathā suṣuptasya khalu svapnādarśane rāgānubandhaḥ sukhaduḥkhānubandhaś ca vicchidyate tathāpavarge 'pīti*).

[4] The following passages from the ChU are quoted in the Vyākaraṇādhikaraṇa (TV, p. 288, 8-15 : TV', II, p. 227, 13-21): "*ya ātmā apahatapāpmā vijaro vimṛtyur viśoko vijighatso 'pipāsaḥ satyakāmaḥ satyasaṃkalpaḥ, so 'nveṣṭavyaḥ so vijijñāsitavyaḥ*" (ChU 8.7.1); "*sa sarvāṃś ca lokān āpnoti sarvāṃś ca kāmān* [TV: *āpnoti*]" (ChU 8.7.1); "*tarati śokam ātmavit*" (ChU 7.1.3); "*sa yadi pitṛlokakāmo bhavati saṃkalpād evāsya pitaraḥ samuttiṣṭhanti tena pitṛlokena saṃpanno mahīyate*" (ChU 8.2.1); "*sa khalv evam vartayan yāvadāyuṣam brahmalokam abhisaṃpadyate na ca* [TV: *sa*] *punar āvartate*" (ChU 8.15.1). Cf. Harikai 1990: 140-141. The translations from the ChU in the present article are those by Olivelle (1996).

[5] TV, p. 288, 7 : TV', II, p. 227, 13: "The knowledge of the Ātman is recognized to be valuable to rituals as well as to human beings on account of its diverse connections [with rituals and human beings]" (*ātmajñānaṃ hi saṃyogapṛthaktvāt kratvarthapuruṣārthatvena jñāyate*). Cf. Harikai 1990: 140. For the *saṃyogapṛthaktvanyāya* and its application to the Mīmāṃsā theory of liberation, see Kurata 1980.

[6] *apunarāvṛttyātmakaparamātmaprāptyavasthāphalavacanam* (TV, p. 288, 16 : TV', II, p. 227, 22-23). Cf. Harikai 1990: 143-144.

practice, namely, *jñānakarmasamuccaya*, which means that both the gnostic knowledge of the self (*jñāna*) and Vedic sacrifices (*karman*) should be equally pursued together (*samuccaya*) because both are necessary for liberation.[7] In another fragment from the BṬ, Kumārila remarks that the self is inseparable from happiness (*ānanda*).[8]

In the present paper, I shall investigate Kumārila's theory of liberation illustrated in his less famous and fragmented work, the *Ṭupṭīkā* (ṬṬ), namely, the last volume of his trilogy on the *Śābarabhāṣya*. Afterwards I will attempt to elucidate what he means by the supreme self (*paramātman*), which is to be ultimately attained through self-contemplation and Vedic sacrifices.

1. ELIMINATION OF FAULTS (*PĀPAKṢAYA*) AS A PURPOSE OF *BHĀVANĀ* IN THE SACRIFICE

In the first section of JS 6.3, it is discussed how to perform periodical (*nitya*) sacrifices following the injunctions such as *yāvajjīvaṃ darśapūrṇamāsābhyāṃ yajeta* or *yāvajjīvam agnihotraṃ juhoti*, which are qualified by the phrase "as long as one is alive" (*yāvajjīvam*), instead of "one who desires heaven" (*svargakāmaḥ*).[9]

---

[7] A BṬ fragment in NSu, p. 329, 5-6: "[The opponent would contend] 'But the supreme bliss arises from the knowledge, not from the ritual, which is nothing else but the cause of bondage.' [Reply: the supreme bliss] does not [arise] from either one [of the two], but [it arises] from the combination of the knowledge and the ritual." (*nanu *niḥśreyasaṃ jñānād* [NSu: *niḥśreyasajñānād*] *bandhahetor na karmaṇaḥ* | *naikasmād api tat kiṃ tu jñānakarmasamuccayāt* ||) Cf. Harikai 1989: 954; NSu, p. 329, 29-30: *bandhahetukarmakṣayāt.*

[8] A BṬ fragment in ŚVK, II, p. 130, 11-12 and ŚD, p. 361, 3-4: "Intellect, happiness, eternity, ubiquity and other properties of the Ātman are recognized to be inherent [in the Ātman] by nature; the Ātman is never separated from them." (*nijaṃ yat tv ātmacaitanyam ānandaś *ceṣyate ca yaḥ* | *yac ca nityavibhutvādi **tair ātmā naiva mucyate* ||) Cf. Mesquita 1994: 475.

* ŚD: *ānandaś ceṣyate*; ŚVK: *ānando 'dhyakṣyate*

** ŚD: *tair ātmā*; ŚVK: *tenātmā*

[9] The two *yāvajjīva* injunctions are quoted in ŚBh, p. 1406, 12-13 : ŚBh', V, p. 242, 4-5. Cf. also ṬṬ, p. 1406, 20 : ṬṬ', V, p. 242, 9 (on JS 6.3.1): *yāvajjīvike prayoge cintyate.*

This kind of injunction, which we can call "*yāvajjīva* injunction", was recognized in the first section of JS 2.4 to be a direction (*codanā*), i.e., a fundamental injunction that issues an order to perform a sacrifice without depending on other injunctions.[10] Based on the independence of the *yāvajjīva* injunction, it is ascertained in the first section of JS 6.3 that the primary offerings of the periodical sacrifices must be performed in due time even if secondary offerings are omitted owing to unavoidable circumstances.[11] One of the *siddhānta sūtra*s (JS 6.3.3) declares that the reason for the compulsory performance of the primary offerings is that one would commit a fault (*doṣa*) if one neglects to perform them.[12]

In this connection, Kumārila shifts the topic of discussion to the significance of periodical sacrifices as a necessary means to liberation. The first half of his commentary on the *siddhānta sūtra* 6.3.2 is exclusively devoted to the view of "some scholars" (*kecit*).[13] With regard to the main topic of this section, these scholars justify the performance of periodical sacrifices without secondary offerings for the reason that the periodical sacrifices, if performed as

[10] For the content of the first section of JS 2.4 and the demonstration of the independence of the *yāvajjīva* injunction from the *svargakāma* injunction, see Yoshimizu 2004b, sections I-II.

[11] Cf. Yoshimizu 2004b, section IV.

[12] JS 6.3.3: "And in case it (= the primary offering) is not performed, [the sacrificer] commits a fault. On account of this, [the primary offering has] distinction from that (= auxiliaries) because it depends on [the performance of] the primary offering [whether the sacrificer commits a fault]" (*tadakarmaṇi ca doṣas tasmāt tato viśeṣaḥ syāt pradhānenābhisaṃbandhāt*).

[13] The description of the view of "some scholars" begins with ṬṬ, p. 1408, 6 : ṬṬ', V, p. 243, 25 and ends in ṬṬ, p. 1409, 19 : ṬṬ', V, p. 245, 18. In the middle of the ṬṬ on JS 6.3.2, Kumārila announces the end of the quotation of "some scholars" saying *iti kecid evaṃ varṇayanti* (ṬṬ, p. 1409, 19 : ṬṬ', V, p. 245, 18). In the lines preceding this announcement, we cannot find a phrase that would announce the beginning of the view of "*kecit*". Pārthasārathi begins his commentary on ṬṬ 6.3.2 saying *ekadeśimatena tāvat siddhāntam āha* (TR, p. 495, 21). Thus it is certain that "some scholars" (*kecit*) appear from the beginning of the ṬṬ on JS 6.3.2. Because "some scholars" comment on a word of JS 6.3.2: *ekadeśe*, and criticize some interpretations of this word (ṬṬ, p. 1408, 26 – p. 1409, 5 : ṬṬ', V, p. 244, 22 – p. 245, 4), Kumārila seems to quote the view of some existent Mīmāṃsakas of those days.

lifelong duties in accordance with the *yāvajjīva* injunction that prescribes the occasion (*nimitta*) of performance, do not bring any result (*phala*) that would need secondary offerings as well.[14] With regard to the necessity of desiring a result in the performance of periodical sacrifices, these scholars discuss the way of integrating periodical sacrifices into the practice towards liberation (*mokṣa*). They maintain that one who wishes for liberation, instead of heaven (*svarga*), still has to perform the periodical sacrifices such as the new and full moon sacrifices (*darśapūrṇamāsa*), because the *yāvajjīva* injunctions put anyone who is alive under the obligation to perform these sacrifices without promising the attainment of heaven.[15] In this case, the significance of a periodical sacrifice becomes defensive in nature because one would, by the performance

---

[14] ṬṬ, p. 1408, 6-9 : ṬṬ', V, p. 243, 25 – p. 244, 2: "[In periodical sacrifices] there is no [specified] manner of performance (*itikartavyatā*) [inclusive of secondary offerings] because there is no *apūrva*. Why is there no *apūrva*? Because there is no result. Why is there no result? Because the occasion [to perform a sacrifice] and the [desire of a] result are incompatible in one and the same (sacrifice). Why are they incompatible in one and the same (sacrifice)? Because they cannot be taken up [by human beings for a sacrifice], a sacrifice is enjoined according to them.* Once either [an occasion or a result] is settled, [the enjoinment of a sacrifice] becomes ready; [a sacrifice] is therefore enjoined according to only one of them. If [one and the same sacrifice] would be enjoined according to both, then a syntactical split would occur [in the interpretation of one and the same injunction]. [In the case of the enjoinment of the *yāvajjīva* injunction, the sacrifice] is enjoined according to [the sacrificer's] occasion [to be alive], because it is mentioned in the text." (*nāstītikartavyatā, apūrvābhāvāt. katham apūrvābhāvaḥ. phalābhāvāt. kathaṃ phalābhāvaḥ. nimittaphalayor ekatrāsaṃbhavāt. katham ekatrāsaṃbhavaḥ. nimittaphalayor anupādeyatvāt te prati karmopādīyate* [Ānandāśrama ed.: °*opādīyete*; TR, p. 496, 7: °*opādīyete [yate]*]. *tatrānyataropādāne kṛtārthatvād ekaṃ praty upādīyate. ubhayopādāne vākyabhedaḥ. nimittasya śrutatvāt tat praty upādīyate.*)

* Kumārila includes occasion (*nimitta*) and the desire of a result (*phala*) in the five kinds of those that cannot be taken up (*anupādeya*). One of them must be settled in advance when one performs a sacrifice. Cf. Yoshimizu 2003.

[15] ṬṬ, p. 1408, 17-18 : ṬṬ, V, p. 244, 11-12: "For one who seeks liberation without desiring heaven for the reason that heaven inevitably binds [one who is attached to it], it is obligatory to perform only the essential part of the [periodical] sacrifice, because [even one who seeks liberation] is given the occasion [to be alive]." (*yaḥ svargaṃ na kāmayate bandhātmakatvān mokṣārthī, tasya karmasvarūpa eva kartavyatā, nimittasaṃbhavāt.*)

of the sacrifice, aim at nothing other than the non-occurrence of an offence (*pratyavāyānutpatti*). Just as one puts on shoes so as not to be injured when one happens to tread on thorns, one can, by performing a periodical sacrifice as a duty, be relieved of an offence (*pratyavāyaparihāra*) one would commit if one carelessly neglects the duty.[16] Kumārila's theory of liberation in the Sambandhākṣepaparihāra of the ŚV seems to be influenced by these "some scholars" (*kecit*), because he approves of the defensive character of periodical sacrifices by saying that one who wishes for liberation should perform them for the purpose of avoiding an offence (*pratyavāyajihāsā*).[17]

In the second half of the ṬṬ on JS 6.3.2[18], however, Kumārila protests against these "some scholars". Here he declares that nobody would commence periodical sacrifices without desiring any result even if they are compulsory duties.[19] He points out that, if

---

[16] ṬṬ, p. 1409, 6-9 : ṬṬ, V, p. 245, 4-7: "How then is it possible for a person to undertake such a [sacrifice that does not bring any result]? [One undertakes such a sacrifice] for the purpose of the non-occurrence of an offence. It is, in fact, prescribed in a *smṛti* text* that one commits an offence in case one neglects to perform anything that is enjoined. Besides, people wish to avoid something harmful as well as they wish to attain something beneficial. Just as, in the ordinary world, one puts on shoes so as not to be injured when one happens to tread on thorns, [we can recognize] in the interpretation of this (*yāvajjīva* injunction) also [that one performs periodical sacrifices] so as to be relieved of an offence." (*katham tarhīdṛśe puruṣapravṛttiḥ. pratyavāyānutpattyarthā. vihitākaraṇād dhi pratyavāyaḥ smaryate. puruṣeṇa ca hitaprāptir yatheṣyate 'hitanivṛttir api tatheṣyate. yathā loke upānaddhāraṇādikā kriyā kaṇṭakaparihārārthā, evam ihāpi pratyavāyaparihārārthā.*)

* As a source *smṛti*, Pārthasārathi [TR, p. 500, 2] quotes "*akurvan vihitaṃ karma prāyaścittīyate naraḥ*" (Manu 11.44a&d).

[17] ŚV, Sambandhākṣepaparihāra, k. 110: "Among those (varieties of actions), one who desires liberation should not undertake the actions that are either enjoined for desirable things or prohibited [but] should perform the actions enjoined periodically or on a special occasion in order to avoid an offence." (*mokṣārthī na pravarteta tatra kāmyaniṣiddhayoḥ* | *nityanaimittike kuryāt pratyavāyajihāsayā* ||). Although Pārthasārathi glosses *pratyavāya* as "*pūrvakṛtādharma*" (NR, p. 476, 15), Kumārila uses *pratyavāya* in the sense of an offence against a rule without temporal specification. Cf. ŚV, Codanāsūtra, k. 250 & k. 256; Manu(K&M) 4.245.

[18] ṬṬ, p. 1409, 20 – 1411, 25 : ṬṬ', V, p. 245, 19 – p. 248, 25.

one were supposed to perform a sacrifice only for the purpose of avoiding an offence (*pratyavāya*), one would then try to keep the offence in the state of non-existence (*abhāva*).[20] But, in fact, no one would become engaged in an action only from defensive motives.[21] Kumārila's new position is that one who wishes for liberation (*mokṣārthin*) performs periodical sacrifices in order to eliminate his own fault (*pāpakṣaya*).[22] He explains the reason why the elimination of one's fault can take the place of the non-occurrence of an offence (*pratyavāyānutpatti*), by applying the theory of *bhāvanā*.[23]

---

[19] TṬ, p. 1410, 6-7 : TṬ', V, p. 246, 4-5: "Indeed, nobody is found who would have no desire at all on the performance of an obligatory action" (*na hīdṛśaḥ puruṣo 'sti yo 'vaśyakartavye phalaṃ na kāmayate*).

[20] "Some scholars" themselves admit that the avoidance of an offence is a kind of non-existence. Cf. TṬ, p. 1409, 10-11 : TṬ', V, p. 245, 8-9: "[Some one would contend:] Then, the non-offence would be the result [of the sacrifice]. We [some scholars] reply: In the first place, a result is something existent, and the non-offence is the non-existence [of an offence]. Why on earth, the latter could be the result of an action?" (*nanv evam apratyavāyaḥ phalaṃ syāt. ucyate. phalaṃ tāvad bhāvaḥ. apratyavāyaś cābhāvaḥ. katham asau kriyāphalaṃ syāt*).

[21] In the TV, Kumārila often calls a human being "one who applies his intellect in advance of action" (*buddhipūrvakārin*) and describes that a *buddhipūrvakārin* concerns himself about his own benefit on the occasion of any action. Cf. TV, p. 113, 3 : TV', II, p. 10, 22 (*kecit*): "In fact, people who apply their intellect in advance of action would not take on that thing if it were not useful for themselves." (*na hy ātmānupakāriṇaṃ santaṃ enaṃ buddhipūrvakāriṇaḥ puruṣāḥ prayatnena dhārayeyuḥ*); TV, p. 134, 22 : TV', II, p. 37, 17: "First in the ordinary world, people who apply their intellect in advance of action do not undertake even the slightest part of a work that would bring no benefit." (*loke tāvad buddhipūrvakāriṇaḥ puruṣā mātrām api na niṣprayojanāṃ prayuñjate*); TV, p. 383, 22-23 : TV', II, p. 350, 18-19: "One who applies his intellect in advance of action does not carry out an unworthy work even if being asked for hundred times." (*na ca buddhipūrvakārī puruṣaḥ puruṣārtharahitaṃ vyāpāraṃ vacanaśatenāpy ukto 'nutiṣṭhati*); TV, p. 662, 11-12 : TV, IV, p. 19, 12-13: "In fact, no one who applies his intellect in advance of action desires heaven just to take place, but [one desires it] to come to be enjoyed by himself." (*na hi kaścid buddhipūrvakāry evaṃ kāmayate svarga ātmānaṃ labhatām iti. kiṃ tarhi, mamopabhogyaḥ syād iti.*)

[22] TṬ, p. 1410, 7-8 : TṬ', V, p. 246, 5-6: "['Some scholars'] would contend that one who seeks liberation [does not have any desire]. That is not right. Even such a person must inevitably desire the elimination of [his own] fault, because liberation would not take place as long as that (fault) exists." (*mokṣārthīti cet. tan na. tenāpy avaśyaṃ pāpakṣaya eṣitavyaḥ. tasmin sati mokṣābhāvāt.*)

Bhāvanā, which consists of the verbal root *bhū* in the causal form *bhāv* and the suffix LYUṬ (*anā*), can be literally rendered as "bringing into being". In the TV on the first section of JS 2.1 (Bhāvārthādhikaraṇa), Kumārila holds *bhāvanā* to be expressed by the suffixes of the verbs in all injunctions.[24] The reason why human activity is expressed in a causative form is that the Mīmāṃsakas consider that human activity, unlike physical movements, consists in intentional actions performed with the aim of realizing a purpose. When one is engaged in an action, one always tries to bring a purpose into realization. For any kinds of actions of human agent A, we can find the realization of purpose B to be expressed in an abstract form "A makes B" (*karoti*)[25], which is further analyzed into a causal expression of the activity, i.e., "A brings B into being" (*bhāv-aya-ti*). The agent of being (*bhavitṛ*), i.e., the agent (*kartṛ*) of an activity, turns into the object (*karman*) of a human action that promotes the activity.[26] Accordingly, when one finds an action ex-

---

[23] ṬṬ, p. 1409, 20-21 : ṬṬ', V, p. 245, 19-20: "That (= the view of 'some scholars') would not be tenable. How? On the basis [of a verbal expression] of *bhāvanā*, there occurs the threefold requirement, namely, 'What for [is it to be done?],' 'By what means [is it to be done?]' and 'How [is it to be done?].' The manner of performance [is put into practice] on the basis of that (the last requirement), and in this case [of the interpretation of the *yāvajjīva* injunction] there is that (requirement)." (*tan nopapadyate. katham. bhāvanātas tisra ākāṅkṣā utpadyante. kiṃ kena katham iti. tannimittā cetikartavyatā. sā ceha vidyate.*)

[24] In the ŚV, Kumārila does not specify which part of a verb indicates *bhāvanā* (cf. Vākyārthādhikaraṇa, kk. 248-250; Kuroda 1980), whereas he suggests in the TV that *bhāvanā* is indicated by the verbal endings of all verbs that include intransitive verbs (cf. Yoshimizu 2004a, n. 2).

[25] Cf. Frauwallner 1938: 221-222. Kuroda (1979) remarks that Patañjali demonstrates the congruence (*sāmānādhikaraṇya*) of a general verb *karoti* with *pac* and other verbs that express a particular action (*kriyāvacana*) (MBh, I, p. 254, 20-21) and Kumārila applies this congruence to the proof of the existence of *bhāvanā*.

[26] TV, p. 377, 14 : TV', II, p. 342, 15: "The agent of the action of being turns into the object of making." (*bhavatikriyāyāḥ kartā karoteḥ karma saṃpadyate*); TV, p. 377, 24-25 : TV', II, p. 343, 3-4: "The agent of making is the causal agent for the agent of being. In contrast with the (causal agent), the agent of being turns into the causal object." (*karotyarthasya yaḥ kartā bhavituḥ sa prayojakaḥ | bhavitā tam apekṣyātha prayojyatvaṃ prapadyate*); TV, p. 378, 16-17 : TV', II,

pressed by a verb in an injunction, one notices that there is a *bhāvanā*, which requires a purpose to be realized (*sādhya*) by action.

After having thus demonstrated the existence and the expression of *bhāvanā* in the Bhāvārthādhikaraṇa, Kumārila asserts that the required purpose is the heaven indicated by the phrase "one who desires heaven" (*svargakāmaḥ*) when one follows the *svargakāma* injunction of a periodical sacrifice.[27] The *svargakāma* injunction enjoins one to bring heaven into being by means of a sacrifice. The present section, i.e., the first section of the JS 6.3, however, deals with the *yāvajjīva* injunction that orders the obligatory performance of a periodical sacrifice without referring to an object of desire (*kāma*). If one who seeks liberation instead of heaven still has to exert one's *bhāvanā* through the performance of a periodical sacrifice, Kumārila says, the requirement of a purpose for the periodical sacrifice can be fulfilled by the elimination of one's existent fault,[28] not by the non-occurrence of a non-existent offence.[29]

---

p. 344, 4-5: "Therefore, people well versed in *bhāvanā* proclaim *bhāvanā* to be the action that causes a thing to become an agent of being." (*tena bhūtiṣu kartṛtvaṃ pratipannasya vastunaḥ* I *prayojakakriyām āhur bhāvanāṃ bhāvanāvidaḥ* II).

[27] Cf. TV, p. 383, 18 – p. 384, 19 : TV', II, p. 350, 14 – p. 351 19. After having determined a purpose (*sādhya*), the *bhāvanā* in an injunction requires the means (*sādhana*, *karaṇa*) to be applied for the realization of the purpose (cf. TV, p. 384, 20-23 : TV', II, p. 351, 20-23) and then requires to specify the manner of performance (*itikartavyatā*) in which the means is arranged (cf. TV, p. 385, 23-26 : TV', II, p. 351, 24 – p. 352, 2). The three requirements by a *bhāvanā* were investigated since the time of Śabara. Cf. ŚBh, p. 2113 (corr.: 3013), 24 – 2114 (corr.: 3014), 2 : ŚBh', VII, p. 20, 23 – p. 21, 1: "A verb has 'being' as its primary meaning and denotes 'bringing something into being', since [the verb] has the requirements of a series of factors to be applied for [bringing something into] being, [i.e., the requirements formulated as follows] 'With what, for what and how should one perform a sacrifice?'" (*bhāvapradhānam ākhyātam. bhāvanāṃ kasyāpi brūte. bhāvaprayuktasya sādhanagrāmasyāpekṣitatvāt. yajeta, kena, kimartham, katham iti.*)

[28] ṬṬ, p. 1410, 9-10 : ṬṬ', V, p. 246, 7-8: "Therefore, after it has been revealed that the periodical sacrifices are the means to attain that (liberation: *mokṣa*), they require the manner of performance. For one who has lost desire for any result [inclusive of heaven], only this (elimination of one's fault: *pāpakṣaya*)

Kumārila had contrastively admitted in the Sambandhākṣepaparihāra of the ŚV that there is no means to eliminate one's fault unless one actually experiences its result (*bhoga*).[30] In the TV, however, he seems to make a shift to the position that one can eliminate one's own faults by means of periodical sacrifices. In the Apūrvādhikaraṇa on JS 2.1.5, where he demonstrates the existence of *apūrva* as a potency (*śakti*) of the self, he examines the possibility that the *apūrva* potentially inherent in the self becomes manifest by means of a periodical sacrifice. At the end of this examination, he changes the significance of the periodical sacrifice from the reinforcement of the inherent potency to the removal of the impediments that obstruct its manifestation, since he says as follows:

> Or, it may be recognized that the self of a man is, always by nature, capable of attaining all things; but that (self) has certain impediments, which are removed by means of sacrifices.[31]

In the present section of the ṬṬ, Kumārila, by applying the theory of *bhāvanā*, more explicitly demonstrates that the impediments attached to the self are removed by means of periodical sacrifices. When he says that the requirement of a purpose for periodical

is [considered as] the result of the sacrifice." (*tasmān nityāni karmāṇi tasya upāyatvena codyamānānītikartavyatām apekṣante. vītāyāṃ ca phalecchāyāṃ karmaṇa idam eva phalam.*)

[29] Kumārila's conviction that the *bhāvdnā* of any kinds of actions requires a positive purpose to be realized as a result is reflected in the following question addressed to "some scholars." ṬṬ, p. 1408, 10-11 : ṬṬ', V, p. 244, 3-4: "The requirement [of a purpose] by a word that expresses *bhāvanā* in the form 'For what?' is, once generated, neither satisfied by an occasion nor by the sacrifice. By what, then? [It can be satisfied] only by a result." (*nanu bhāvanāvacanasya kim ity ākāṅkṣotpannā na nimittena pūryate na yāgena. kena tarhi. phalenaiva.*)

[30] ŚV, Sambandhākṣepaparihāra, k. 108: "In that case, if one who has cognized the true nature of the self extinguishes one's previous deeds (= *karman*) by experiencing their retribution, then one's body would never be produced again because [one's deeds] would not be piled up afterwards." (*tatra jñātātmatattvānāṃ bhogāt pūrvakriyākṣaye | uttarapracayāsattvāt deho notpadyate punaḥ ||*)

[31] TV, p. 400, 10-11 : TV', II, p. 372, 10-11: *sarvāvāptisamartho vā prakṛtyātmā sadeṣyate | kaścit tu pratibandho 'sya karmabhiḥ so 'panīyate* || (Cf. Clooney 1990: 244; Yoshimizu 2000: 158.)

sacrifices can be fulfilled by the elimination of one's existent fault, he seems to have taken the *Nirukta* of Yāska into consideration.[32] Since the time of the *Nirukta*, it was well recognized that there are six modifications of "being" (*bhāva*) that is the essential meaning of verbs.[33] On the ground that not only occurrence (*jāyate*) and increase (*vardhate*) but also decay (*apakṣīyate*) and extinction/elimination (*vinaśyati*) are included in these modifications, Kumārila seems to designate the fault one actually bears as an agent of being (*bhāva*), and he considers its elimination as the purpose (*sādhya*) to be realized through *bhāvanā* in the performance of a periodical sacrifice as a necessary means to liberation. Even if one keeps an offence in the state of non-existence (*abhāva*) through performing a duty, the continuing non-existence of an offence cannot be the purpose of the performance, because *abhāva* is excluded from the sphere of being (*bhāva*) where a purpose to be realized through the *bhāvanā* of the performance takes place. One who is always intent only on keeping himself from harm would not be worthy of being called the agent of an action.

From the view of the traditional Mīmāṃsā, the ritual to be performed for the purpose of eliminating a fault is not the periodical sacrifice but expiation (*prāyaścitta*).[34] But the idea that periodical sacrifices can purify the performer is very old and can be traced

---

[32] *Nirukta*, p. 29, 6-11: *ṣaḍbhāvavikārā bhavantīti vārṣyāyaṇiḥ. jāyate 'sti vipariṇamate vardhate 'pakṣīyate vinaśyatīti. ... vardhata iti svāṅgābhyuccayam, sāṃyaugikānāṃ vārthānām. ... apakṣīyata ity etenaiva vyākhyātaḥ pratilomam. vinaśyatīty aparabhāvasyādiṃ ācaṣṭe. na pūrvabhāvam ācaṣṭe na pratiṣedhati*: "According to Vārṣyāyaṇi, there are six modifications of being: genesis, existence, alteration, growth, decay and destruction. ... Growth denotes the increase of one's own limbs or of objects which are associated (with one's self), ... The term decay denotes its antithesis. Destruction denotes the commencement of the later state, but neither affirms nor denies the former." (transl. by Sarup [1967, The Nirukta: 6-7])

[33] Cf. MBh, I, p. 258, 13-14; VP 1.3, 3.1.36-39, 3.8.26-34; BD(M) 2.121 = BD(T) 2.91. For the passages quoted from the *Nirukta* in the ŚBh, see Garge 1952: 233-235. Cf. also *Nirukta*, p. 27, 8 and the ŚBh in n. 27: *bhāvapradhānam ākhyātam.*

[34] Cf. JS 2.4.3, 12.3.16.

back to the age of the Brāhmaṇas.[35] This idea was carried over into the Vedānta school. The *Brahmasūtra* (BS 4.1.13-19) distinguishes two types of *karman*,[36] i.e., the *karman* in which the retribution has already been set in motion (*prārabdhakārya*) and the *karman* in which the retribution has not been set in motion yet (*aprārabdhakārya*). The *prārabdhakārya* cannot be annulled by human effort and can be extinguished only through the experience of its result.[37] Nevertheless, the *aprārabdhakārya* is abolished upon enlightenment with the help of the performance of the Agnihotra and other periodical sacrifices.[38] Hence, the idea of self-purification by means of periodical sacrifices may have been prevalent at the time of Kumārila under the influence of the Vedānta school. It is, however, Kumārila's original idea in the ṬṬ that he considers elimination of faults (*pāpakṣaya*) as the purpose (*sādhya*) of the *bhāvanā* in the periodical sacrifices for liberation.

---

[35] In ŚB 11.1.1-2.7, which deals with the secret significance of the new and full moon sacrifices, it is stated that one who reveres one's self (*ātmayājin*) by purifying one's self through sacrifices is superior to one who reveres deities (*devayājin*) through sacrifices (ŚB 11.2.6.13; Bodewitz (1973: 304) remarks that the *ātman* in this context refers to the whole body rather than to the soul). In his commentary on Śaṅkara's BSBh, Vācaspatimiśra quotes ŚB 11.2.6.13 as the source for the view that periodical sacrifices purify a person by extinguishing faults (Bhm, p. 84, 10-14; Suryanarayana Sastri & Raja 1992: 84, n. 71; Alston 1989a: 66).

[36] *Scilicet*: *agha* in BS 4.1.13. For Śaṅkara's view on these two types of *karmans*, see Alston 1989b: 211-235.

[37] BS 4.1.19: "But, after having extinguished the other [good and bad *karmans*] by means of their experience, one enters into [*brahman*]." (*bhogena tv itare kṣapayitvā saṃpadyate*).

[38] BS 4.1.15: "But only the previous [good and bad *karmans*] in which the retribution has not been set in motion yet [can be extinguished by means of the knowledge of the self], because [the liberation is said to occur] after that (annihilation of one's body)" (*anārabdhakārye eva tu pūrve tadavadheḥ*); 4.1.16: "But the sacrifices such as Agnihotra and the like [should be performed] for the same purpose, because it is thus directly enjoined in the sacred texts" (*agnihotrādi tu tatkāryāyaiva taddarśanāt*). BS 4.1.15-16 restrict the general statement of BS 4.1.13-14 that the attainment of Brahman brings good and bad *karmans* to extinction.

2. CHRONOLOGICAL SEQUENCE OF KUMĀRILA'S WORKS

Since E. Frauwallner collected some fragments of the BṬ and concluded that Kumārila had written the BṬ in his later years, little textual evidences for or against Frauwallner's hypothesis have been adduced.[39] We can only note that R. Mesquita pointed out Kumārila's reference to the ŚV, Ātmavāda, k. 74 ff, in the TV on the Apūrvādhikaraṇa (JS 2.1.5) as a piece of evidence that the ŚV chronologically precedes the TV.[40] But critically speaking, it is not impossible that here Kumārila is referring to a certain lost section of the BṬ, not the ŚV. In the following, I will indicate some textual evidence for the sequence of Kumārila's works proposed by Frauwallner. My point is that the ṬṬ is to be placed between the TV and the BṬ in view of the theory of liberation. Before going into this topic, I would like to make an excursus to prove that the ŚV precedes the TV.

It is well known that Śabara, after having written his own commentary (*bhāṣya*) on JS 1.1.5, quotes another's commentary (*vṛtti*) on JS 1.1.3-5. This *Vṛtti* divides JS 1.1.4 into two parts in order to make the first part a definition of perception (*pratyakṣa*) and the last part an opposing *sūtra* that introduces JS 1.1.5. The author of the *Vṛtti* then criticizes the Yogācāra idealism, adding five more *pramāṇa*s to *pratyakṣa*, scrutinizing the Mīmāṃsā theories of words and meaning, and defending the authority of the Vedic ritual scriptures as well as demonstrating the existence of one's soul (*ātman*).[41] In the ŚV, Kumārila devotes one chapter to each of these

---

[39] J. Taber, on the contrary, raised the possibility that Kumārila wrote the ŚV in his later years as a summarizing work of the BṬ. Cf. Taber 1986-92.

[40] Cf. TV, p. 397, 30 : TV', II, p. 369, 9: *ātmavāde sthitaṃ hy etat kartṛtvaṃ sarvakarmasu*; Mesquita 1994: n. 11. Cf. also TV, p. 404, 22 : TV', II, p. 378, 9-10: *ātmavādoktasvasvāmibhāvavyavasthānāt*.

[41] The passage *bādarāyaṇagrahaṇam uktam* (ŚBh(F), p. 48, 15) is to be considered as inserted by Śabara himself in the midst of the quotation from the *Vṛtti,* because it refers to his own previous remark on Bādarāyaṇa (ŚBh(F), p. 24, 14-15). Following the editor of the ŚV of the Bibliotheca Indica edition, Jacobi

topics. But curiously enough, he identifies the definition of perception alone as a quotation from the *Vṛtti*[42] and the remaining discussions as Śabara's own writing, since he ascribes the criticism of the Yogācāra idealism (Nirālambanavāda) to "*bhāṣyakṛt*" and "*bhāṣyakāra*", which are none other than titles of Śabara.[43] Kumārila refers to Śabara and his *Bhāṣya* also in several chapters of the ŚV on the remaining parts of the *Vṛtti*.[44] Judging from this, he must have held the view, however distorted, that it is not the Vṛttikāra but Śabara who established the definition of each "means of valid knowledge" (*pramāṇa*) in the Mīmāṃsā school.[45]

I conjecture that Kumārila's misunderstanding might be based on a passage presented by Śabara at the beginning of his commentary on the JS 2.1.1: "In the first Adhyāya, the definition of *pramāṇa* was accomplished" (*prathame 'dhyāye pramāṇalakṣaṇaṃ vṛttam*).[46] Although Śabara thereafter summarizes exegetic topics discussed in the four Pādas of the first Adhyāya, this passage gives the impression that the examinations of the six kinds of *pramāṇa*s were included in the traditional topics of the first Adhyāya of the JS itself. When Kumārila, however, undertook to compose the TV, he came to maintain a critical attitude towards Śabara's

---

(1911: 15) considers Śabara's quotation from the *Vṛtti* to end just before this passage of his own and Strauss (1932: 21) follows Jacobi. Zangenberg (1962: 63), however, insists that Śabara inserts his own word here and then resumes the quotation from the *Vṛtti*, which continues until the end of the investigation on the existence of the self (*ātman*). Frauwallner (1968: 110-112, n. 42: "Der Vṛttikāraḥ") supports Zangenberg for the reason that in the investigation of *ātman* that consists of polemics with Buddhists there are references to the Śūnyavāda section of the *Vṛtti*.

[42] ŚV, Pratyakṣasūtra, k. 13.

[43] Jacobi (1911: 15) adduces the following instances: ŚV, Nirālambanavāda, k. 16d (*bhāṣyakṛtā*), 29a (*bhāṣyakāreṇa*).

[44] Cf. Anumānapariccheda, k. 52d (*bhāṣyakāras*); Abhāvapariccheda, k. 57b (*bhāṣye*); Sambandhākṣepaparihāra, k. 8a (*bhāṣye*); Sambandhākṣepaparihāra, k. 42b (*bhāṣye*); Ātmavāda, k. 148b (*bhāṣyakṛt*).

[45] We could say, at the best, that Kumārila considers Śabara as a proponent of the theories of the Vṛttikāra without going into the authorship.

[46] ŚBh, p. 370, 4 : ŚBh', II, p. 333, 4.

Bhāṣya. With regard to the beginning passage of Śabara's commentary on JS 2.1.1, Kumārila restricts the meaning of *pramāṇa* to the direction (*codanā*), i.e., the fundamental injunction of a sacrifice,[47] or the object to be comprehended by means of the direction, i.e., *dharma*, on the basis of JS 1.1.2: *codanālakṣaṇo 'rtho dharmaḥ.*[48]

Before laying down this restriction, Kumārila says that the first Adhyāya never gives the definition of *pramāṇas* in the sense of "the means of valid knowledge". Inference (*anumāna*) is not mentioned in the *sūtras* at all. Perception is mentioned in JS 1.1.3, but it is just contrasted with *codanā* because it cannot be the means of knowing *dharma.* Scripture (*śabda*) is demonstrated to have an authority (*pramāṇa*) about *dharma.* Its definition (*lakṣaṇa*) is, however, subsequently going to be investigated in the second Adhyāya.[49] Then, Kumārila explicitly states that it is the Vṛttikāra who, although deviating from the main topic of the first Adhyāya, established the definitions of the six kinds of *pramāṇas.*[50] It is

---

[47] TV, p. 370, 16-20 : TV', II, p. 333, 17-22.

[48] TV, p. 370, 20-22 : TV', II, p. 333, 22 – p. 334, 4. In the ŚV on JS 1.1.2, Kumārila makes an epistemological excursus about the self-validity of knowledge (*svataḥprāmāṇya*) with regard to all kinds of knowledge (Codanāsūtra, k. 33a: *sarvavijñānaviṣayam*).

[49] TV, p. 370, 7-11 : TV', II, p. 333, 7-12.

[50] TV, p. 370, 11-15 : TV', II, p. 333, 12-16: "It is true that the Vṛttikāra presented the definitions of all (*pramāṇas*), but [these definitions] cannot be integrated into the topics of the [first] Adhyāya, because they are not integrated into those topics that [appear (cf. NSu, p. 536, 30-32: *ārūḍha*)] in the *sūtras* of the Adhyāya. How can it be possible for those *sūtras* to cease to work with a reference to the (definitions of *pramāṇas*) that are different from any topics [of those *sūtras*]. Besides, in view of the fact that the Vṛttikāra asserted that the six *pramāṇas* based on perception cannot be topics of investigation, they are, at any rate, out of definition. Because [the Vṛttikāra], in fact, admitted that they are not worth investigating at all on account of being well known in the ordinary world (cf. ŚBh(F), p. 24, 18-19), it is impossible to integrate them into the topics of the first Adhyāya." (*yad api ca vṛttikāreṇa sarveṣāṃ lakṣaṇaṃ pradarśitaṃ na tad adhyāyārthatvenopasaṃhartuṃ yuktam. sūtrādhyāyārthānupasaṃhārāt. katham ca samastalakṣaṇārthavyatirikta evārthe sūtrāṇi kṣīyeran. api ca vṛttikāreṇa yo 'py uktaḥ ṣaṭkaḥ pratyakṣapūrvako 'parīkṣyatayā so 'pi naiva lakṣaṇagocaraḥ.*

uncertain whether Kumārila ascertained the extent of the quoted *Vṛtti* by himself or was taught it by someone else.[51] In all cases, however, he cleared up the ambiguity about the extent of the quotation of the *Vṛtti* when he began to compose the TV. Once he arrived at this conclusion in the TV on JS 2.1, it is inconceivable that he would afterwards take Śabara to be the author of the remaining sections of the *Vṛtti*. Consequently, we can safely say that the ŚV chronologically precedes the TV.[52]

Let us now proceed to the order of the TV and the ṬṬ. At the end of the Vyākaraṇādhikaraṇa, as mentioned in the introduction of this article, Kumārila examines the relation between sacrifice and the knowledge of the self as an appendix to the inquiry of the significance of the science of grammar. Here, he suggests the following suspicion: If the most essential part of the Upaniṣads is held to be an injunction to cognize one's true self for the purpose of liberation, then this injunction would invalidate compulsory sacrifices, which are enjoined by injunctions in the Brāhmaṇas, for attaining liberation. Kumārila, however, straightforwardly dispels this suspicion.[53] According to him, one who seeks liberation has no

---

lokaprasiddhārthāni hi 'tāny aparīkṣyatvenoktāni na prathamādhyāyaviṣayatvenopasaṃhāram (TV': *°viṣayatvepasaṃhāram*) *arhanti*.)

[51] At least in the two commentaries, Aj, p. 4, 14-15 and NSu, p. 536, 9-11, there are no comments that would suggest that Kumārila takes over the view from someone else that the definition of *pramāṇa*s was given by the Vṛttikāra, not by Śabara. In the Mīmāṃsā school of those days there seems to have been an uncritical but influential trend, in which even Kumārila was once inclined to consider the investigations of the means of valid cognition to be included in the traditional sections compiled by Śabara into his *Bhāṣya*. Mīmāṃsakas may have been motivated to this uncritical trend by the spirit of competition with other brahmanical schools *sūtra*s of which contain the sections for the means of valid cognition. Even about one century after Kumārila, Śaṅkara has the misunderstanding about the extent of the *Vṛtti* since he insists that Ācārya Śabarasvāmin demonstrated the existence of the self in his "*pramāṇalakṣaṇa*" borrowing the topic from BS 3.3.53-54. Cf. BSBh, p. 424, 1-2; Jacobi 1911: 18.

[52] In Yoshimizu 2000, I tried to trace the process in which Kumārila, from the ŚV to the TV, developed his own theory of *apūrva* in confrontation with traditional views held in the Mīmāṃsā school at his times.

difficulty in following the injunctions of both kinds together, because they respectively enjoin an action with different purposes and different courses of performance, although they ultimately aim at one and the same goal, i.e., liberation.[54] Kumārila admits that the cognizing of one's own self is a special kind of action enjoined by Upaniṣads in view of liberation.[55] But sacrifices also have some significance for liberation. Concerning this point, he says: As far as the practice aiming at liberation is concerned, the performance of compulsory sacrifices serves not only to prevent a future offence (*akaraṇanimittānāgatapratyavāyaparihāra*), but also to eliminate the faults already committed (*pūrvakṛtaduritakṣaya*).[56] The dual-purpose enumerated here suggests Kumārila's first step of his alienation from "some scholars", whom he once followed in the

---

[53] TV, p. 288, 18 : TV', II, p. 228, 15: "Besides, the connection of the sacrifice [with liberation] would not be disturbed [by the knowledge of the self] even though [the Upaniṣads] enjoin to cognize [one's self]." (*na ca jñānavidhānena karmasaṃbandhavāraṇam* I).

[54] TV, p. 288, 20-21 : TV', II, p. 228, 17-18: "Besides, because they [i.e., the injunction to cognize one's self and injunctions of periodical and occasional sacrifices] have [their own] different purposes and different ways [of practice, i.e., *jñānamārga* and *karmamārga*], there is neither contradiction, nor alternative, nor hierarchical relation between them." (*na ca teṣāṃ bhinnaprayojanatvād bhinnamārgatvāc ca bādhavikalpaparasparāṅgāṅgibhāvāḥ saṃbhavanti.*)

[55] TV, p. 288, 11-12 : TV', II, p. 227, 17-18: "The two kinds of result, i.e., the prosperity and the supreme bliss, laid down in the sentences that require an injunction to cognize the essence of the self distinctively" (*-spaṣṭātmatattvajñānavidhānāpekṣitavākyāntaropāttadvividhābhyudayaniḥśreyasarūpaphala-*)

[56] TV, p. 288, 19-20 : TV', II, p. 228, 16-17: "One should perform the duties confined to each stage of life and each class of society, namely, the periodical duties as well as the occasional duties [even if one seeks liberation], in order to eliminate one's fault already committed as well as to prevent a future offence one would commit if one does not perform them." (*pratyāśramavarṇaniyatāni nityanaimittikakarmāṇy api pūrvakṛtaduritakṣayārtham akaraṇanimittānāgatapratyavāyaparihārārthaṃ ca kartavyāni*). In this context, the *nityanaimittikakarmāṇi* are not restricted to *śrauta* sacrifices but comprise all kinds of duties in each *āśrama*. Because a student (*brahmacārin*) has not installed his own *śrauta* fires yet, the student is not entitled to *śrauta* sacrifices but has duties of other kinds. Besides, Kumārila may not take the fourth *āśrama*, i.e., renouncer (*saṃnyāsin*), into consideration because one must renounce one's *śrauta* fires (Manu 6.34; 43) and thereby intentionally neglect the *yāvajjīva* injunction when one proceeds to the stage of *saṃnyāsin*.

ŚV. In the ṬṬ, at last, he proclaims his secession from "some scholars" by strengthening his conviction that one concerns oneself only with something "being" (*bhāva*) through all sorts of actions inclusive of the practice for the purpose of liberation.

Lastly, we have come to examine the order of the BṬ and other works of Kumārila. R. Mesquita (1994: 466-467) has indicated that six verses[57] of the BṬ are quoted in the *Nyāyakandalī* of Śrīdhara.[58] In the sixth verse, Kumārila advocates the elimination of one's fault by means of the performance of periodical and occasional sacrifices,[59] just as he did in the ṬṬ. Hence, the BṬ turns out to have been composed after the TV. The chronological order between the ṬṬ and the BṬ is to be presumed on the ground of the third verse:

> When an imprudent person, without performing that (enjoined action),[60] is engaged in something else, an offence is brought to the person only by that (engagement in something else), not by the non-existence [of the performance of the enjoined action].[61]

---

[57] The quotation of the fifth verse contains the first half only, whereas a half verse is attached to the sixth verse.

[58] It is appropriate to consider all these verses to be quoted from one and the same text although they are separately introduced with *yathoktam* without reference to the author or the name of the text, because they consistently advocate the liberation through *jñānakarmasamuccaya*, with which Śrīdhara himself declares to agree (NK, p. 683, 11-12). And the source text in question must be the BṬ because the sixth and the last half verses (cf. fn. 59) coincide with the verses quoted by Someśvara with the introduction *bṛhaṭṭīkāyām uktam* with a slight variant (NSu, p. 330, 2-4).

[59] A BṬ fragment in NK, p. 689, 10-12: "One should eliminate one's own defect by means of periodical and occasional sacrifices, purify one's knowledge and bring it to ripening through the exercise [of *yoga*]. Once having made one's knowledge ripen owing to the perfect freedom from passions, one would partake of isolation [i.e., liberation]." (*nityanaimittikair eva kurvāṇo duritakṣayam* | *jñānaṃ ca vimalīkurvann abhyāsena tu pācayet* || *vairāgyāt** *pakvavijñānaḥ kaivalyaṃ labhate naraḥ* | [Mesquita 1994: 467]).

* NSu: *vairāgyāt*; NK: *abhyāsāt*.

[60] *tat* refers to the *vihita* in the foregoing verse.

Here, Kumārila asserts that what causes the offence of the Vedic duty is not the non-existence (*nābhāvena*) of the performance of sacrifices, but the actual engagement in some other irrelevant things (*yad ... karoty anyad ... tenaiva*). In the ŚV and the TV, Kumārila approved of the traditional idea proclaimed in JS 6.3.3[62] that one commits a fault if one does not perform a periodical sacrifice. Also in the ṬṬ, Kumārila does not dare to deny this idea when he comments on this very *sūtra* 6.3.3. But in the BṬ, at last, Kumārila decided to part from this traditional idea in order to give priority to his own ontological idea. The reason for his decision is expressed in the immediately foregoing verse (the second verse):

> And, the reason why the previous non-existence (*prāgabhāva*) of actions, which consists in the non-performance of enjoined (actions), is not excluded from the reality (*vastu*) is not that it causes a bad effect.[63]

According to Kumārila's view advocated in the ŚV, the non-existence (*abhāva*) of something in a spot is real (*vastu*) insofar as we can classify it into one of the four kinds of non-existence.[64] Thus, the non-performance of periodical sacrifices surely comes to be included into the reality (*vastu*) only for the reason that it is put into the class of previous non-existence (*prāgabhāva*). As regards the inclusion of non-existence into reality, Kumārila has been consistent since his younger years in holding that it does not matter at all whether non-existence has an effect.

---

[61] A BṬ fragment in NK, p. 684, 13-14: *svakāle yad akurvaṃs tat karoty anyad acetanaḥ | pratyavāyo 'sya tenaiva, nābhāvena sa janyate ||* cf. Mesquita 1994: 466.

[62] Cf. n. 12.

[63] BṬ fragment in NK, p. 684, 11-12: *karmaṇāṃ prāgabhāvo yo vihitākaraṇādiṣu | na cānarthakaratvena vastutvān nāpanīyate ||* cf. Mesquita 1994: 466.

[64] Cf. ŚV, Abhāvapariccheda, k. 8ab: "Besides, these [four] kinds [of non-existence, i.e., the previous non-existence (*prāgabhāva*), the subsequent non-existence (*pradhvaṃsābhāva*), the mutual non-existence (*anyonyābhāva*) and the absolute non-existence (*atyantābhāva*) (cf. Abhāvapariccheda, kk. 2cd-4)] would not hold good with regard to non-reality. Hence the (non-existence) belongs to the reality." (*na cāvastuna ete syur bhedās tenāsya vastutā*).

3. THE SUPREME SELF (*PARAMĀTMAN*) RESIDING IN THE BODY CALLED "VEDA"

With regard to the question of what the "supreme self" (*paramātman*) is, Kumārila provides an answer, which may very well overthrow our image of Kumārila as a Mīmāṃsaka. In the ṬṬ, as elucidated in the foregoing sections, Kumārila advocates a theory that periodical sacrifices purify one's self from faults. One who adheres to this theory is required to oppose the religious position that liberation is attained without following the Vedic tradition of sacrifices. As regards the influence of a particular religious group on this theory, we can conjecture some relation to the Vedānta school from BS 4.1.13-19, according to which the *karman* in which the retribution has not been set in motion (*aprārabdhakārya*), can be abolished by means of the knowledge of the self with the help of periodical sacrifices. In the section of the TV on which we are going to focus immediately below, moreover, Kumārila proclaims that a *paramātman* reveals sacrifices through its body called "Veda", and he further insists that his proclamation is attested to by some phrases in a particular Upaniṣad (*vedānta*).

In the TV on JS 3.1.13, Kumārila discusses why it is possible to ascertain whether a verbal expression in an injunction, such as the grammatical number of a noun, is intended (*vivakṣita*) or not, while at the same time maintaining that the Veda is not composed by human beings (*apauruṣeya*).[65] Kumārila examines three possibili-

[65] At the beginning of this section, Śabara quotes some injunctions that contain a noun in the singular (*graham*, *agnes*, and *puroḍāśam*) and asks whether one who follows these injunctions should deal with one single implement or with all implements available in each sacrifice: *asti jyotiṣṭomaḥ "ya evaṃ vidvān somena yajate" iti. tatra śrūyate "daśāpavitreṇa grahaṃ saṃmārṣṭi" iti. tathā, agnihotre śrūyate, "agnes tṛṇāny apacinoti" iti. tathā darśapūrṇamāsayoḥ śrūyate, "puroḍāśaṃ paryagnikaroti" iti. tatra saṃdehaḥ. kim ekasya grahasya, ekasyāgneḥ, ekasya puroḍāśasya ca saṃmārjanādi kartavyam uta sarveṣāṃ grahāṇāṃ sarveṣām agnīnāṃ sarveṣāṃ puroḍāśānām iti* (ŚBh, p. 699, 2-7 : ŚBh', IV, p. 65, 7-12). Whereas Śabara occasionally uses the expression *avivakṣita* in the discussion of this section, Kumārila explicitly integrates the word "be intended" (*vivakṣyate*) into the question formulated at the beginning as follows: "In all these cases, an action is enjoined with reference to something

ties about what is to be considered as the "intention" (*vivakṣā*) in a sentence of the *apauruṣeya* Veda, without discussing the relative superiority and inferiority of these three possibilities. First, one can use the term "intention" figuratively (*upacāra*) by comparing the impersonal injunctions of the Veda to the instructions by a speaker in ordinary communications.[66] Second, Kumārila points out the possibility that when we investigate the intention of a Vedic sentence we are, in fact, trying to ascertain the intention of the commentators (*vyākhyātṛ*) who traditionally handed down the Vedic scriptures.[67]

After having presented these two possibilities, Kumārila declares in the concluding part of this discussion, that a supreme self (*paramātman*) resides as a "knower of the field" (*kṣetrajña*)[68] in each Vedic corpus just as intelligent souls reside in material bodies. Hence, it becomes legitimate to say that a verbal expression in a Vedic sentence is intended (*vivakṣita*) or not in the primary meaning of *vivakṣā*. In order to demonstrate this remarkable idea, Kumārila composes sixteen verses with an insertion of a portion of prose right in the middle. Kumārila begins with the declaration that a "knower of the field" resides in each Vedic corpus.

> (1) Or, what is thought of [in this section] might be whether [a grammatical expression is] intended or not intended by the "knowers of the field" who reside in the *Ṛgveda* and all other [Vedic scriptures].[69]

---

particular. Then there arises a question as to whether the grammatical number of a word that refers to the particular thing is intended or not" (TV, p. 699, 11-12 : TV', IV, p. 65, 22-23: *sarvatra ca kiṃcid uddiśya kriyā vidhīyate. tatroddiśyamānasya kiṃ saṃkhyā vivakṣyata uta neti saṃśayaḥ*). For the main arguments in this section, see Yoshimizu 2006 and Yoshimizu, forthcoming.

66 TV, p. 700, 16 – p. 701, 17 : TV', IV, p. 67, 9 – p. 68, 17.

67 TV, p. 701, 18 – p. 702, 3 : TV', IV, p. 68, 18 – p. 69, 7.

68. For *kṣetrajña*, see ŚvU 6.16, MaitrU 2.5, BhG 13 and Zaehner 1969: 333-334. Zaehner refers to *a-kṣetrajña* (one who does not know the field) in ChU 8.3.1 and illustrates the usage of *kṣetrajña* in the sense of "man who knows his own subject" in the *Mahābhārata*.

69 TV, p. 702, 4-5 : TV', IV, p. 69, 8-9: (1) *ṛgvedādisamūheṣu kṣetrajñā ye pratiṣṭhitāḥ* I *teṣāṃ vāyam abhiprāyaḥ syād vivakṣāvivakṣayoḥ* II To comment on

Instead of elucidating what the "knower of the field" in the Veda is, Kumārila immediately draws our attention to the fact that bodies of living beings are endowed with souls and their intention is cognized by others who examine the sentences pronounced by them.

> (2) In material bodies, for example, there reside intelligent souls, who intend certain things and do not intend others. (3) Although their intention is cherished in the inside, it is nevertheless cognized by the people who examine their sentences, as if it sparkled into the outside only through the potencies of words.[70]

Kumārila continues to talk about material bodies of living beings in this world. After having indicated that there are various forms of bodies for souls on account of a particular material composition caused by their own previous action (*karman*), he goes into a fanciful illustration of particular forms and constituents of bodies in the four spheres of the world, namely, on the earth, in the sphere of water, in the sphere of sky, and in the sphere of heaven. Although the souls in this context are expressed as *paramātmanām* in the plural in the Ānandāśrama edition, we should probably supply an *avagraha* for the omitted *a-* after *dṛśyante* in accordance with Someśvara's gloss *aparamātmanāṃ jīvānām* (NSu, p. 1009, 17-18). It is unlikely that there are many *paramātman*s and they come

---

this verse, Someśvara quotes the following Upaniṣadic passage: "*yo vai vedeṣu tiṣṭhan vedān antaro yamayati yo vedān vetti yaṃ vedā na viduḥ yasya vedā śarīraṃ eṣa ta ātmāntaryāmy amṛta*" *ity upaniṣatprāmāṇyād* (NSu, p. 1008, 12-14). This passage seems to be modeled on BĀU 3.7.3-23, where Yājñavalkya teaches to Uddālaka Āruṇi the inner controller (*antaryāmin*) of various constituents of the macrocosm and the microcosm, in which constituents, however, the Vedas are not included.

[70] TV, p. 702, 6-9 : TV', IV, p. 69, 10-13: (2) *mahābhautikadehasthā yathātmānaḥ sacetanāḥ* I *kaṃcid artham vivakṣanti na vivakṣanti cāparam* II (3) *teṣām antargatāpīcchā tadvākyārthavicāribhiḥ* I *jñāyate* **śabdaśaktyaiva* ***sphurantīva bahiḥ sthitā* II

* India Office Library San. Ms. 2158: *śabdaśaktyaiva*; Ānandāśrama ed.: *śabdaśakyaiva*.

** Ānandāśrama ed.: *sphurantīva*; India Office Library San. Ms. 2158: *visphurantī*.

to be bound into material bodies on account of their own previous *karmans*.

> (4) We find that the diverse kinds of bodies are determined by the power of actions performed by the souls that are not the supreme one (**aparamātmanām*), because these (bodies) diversely emanate from the primordial matter (*prakṛti*). (5) On the earth, we find four kinds of bodies, namely, chorion-born and the like, limbs of which are mostly made up of the element of earth assisted by water and the rest. (6) It is reported that in the sphere of Varuṇa there exist the bodies with transparent limbs, which are made mainly of water combined with other elements. (7) And in the sphere of the sky, there float many living beings with the light and subtle bodies, which are made of air assisted by earth and the rest. (8) In the sphere of heaven, there are brightly shining bodies made mainly of light, which grow larger by the light poured from the sun.[71]

Without scrutinizing the existence of fanciful bodies in other spheres than on the earth,[72] Kumārila resorts to the authority of

---

[71] TV, p. 702, 11-19 : TV', IV, p. 69, 14-23: (4) *dehabhedaprakārāś ca karmaśaktivaśānugāḥ* | *prakṛtyārambhavaicitryād dṛśyante* **'paramātmanām* || (5) *pārthivāvayavaprāyāḥ śeṣatoyādyanugrahāt* | *jarāyujādayo dehā dṛṣṭā bhuvi caturvidhāḥ* || (6) *bhūtāntarānubaddhena toyenaiva vinirmitāḥ* | *śrūyante vāruṇe loke dehāḥ svacchāṅgalakṣaṇāḥ* || (7) *antarikṣe ca bahavaḥ prāṇino vātanirmitaiḥ* | *bhramanti laghubhiḥ sūkṣmair dehair bhūmyādyanugrahāt* || (8) *svarloke taijasaprāyā dehāḥ śuddhaprabhānvitāḥ* | *āpyāyante vikīrṇena bhānavīyena tejasā* ||

* An *avagraha* is explicitly written in India Office Library San. Ms. 2158: *'paramātmanām*.

[72] In the *Vaiśeṣikasūtra* we find a root of Kumārila's fanciful description of four spheres and various types of bodies. According to the commentator Candrānanda, VS 4.2.1 and 4.2.2 respectively refute the assumptions that the bodies on the earth are made of five or three (earth, water and fire) kinds of elements, thereby demonstrating that they are essentially made only of earth. Then VS 4.2.3 admits that the elements other than earth are connected (*saṃyoga*) with each other in the bodies on the earth although they are not inherent in the bodies. The remaining *sūtras* 4.2.4-9 enumerate the reasons for the existence of bodies not born from womb (*ayonija*) in the spheres of water and other elements. Candrānanda introduces this topic with the following remark: *jalādibhir ayonijam eva śarīram ārabhyate varuṇalokādau* (VSV, p. 35, 15-16). In the *Praśastapādabhāṣya* there are more detailed descriptions akin to Kumārila's. The bodies on the earth are classified into *yonija* and *ayonija*, the former is again classified into chorion-born (*jarāyuja*) and egg-born (*aṇḍaja*) (PBh [31]). In the spheres of water, light (*tejas*) and wind, the subtle bodies made of each element are able to

śruti and *smṛti* that attest that the people who accumulated good deeds in this world acquire shining bodies in the world of heaven.

> It is likewise declared in the following supplement to the chapters on the oblations to the lunar mansions (*nakṣatreṣṭi*) "The pious people, indeed, go to the heavenly world, where the lunar mansions are their lights," and the *Manusmṛti* also describes those who go to heaven as follows "Having a body of light, [he goes to the supreme state (*paraṃ sthānam*)] through a straight way."[73]

Then Kumārila comes back to the main issue of discussion, i.e., the intention of the *apauruṣeya* Veda.[74] First, he suggests that there is a *śruti* that attests to the existence of a supreme self (*paramātman*) embodied in space (*vyoman*). Since four spheres of the world have

---

enjoy objects owing to the assistance by earth elements (PBh [38]: *tatra śarīram ayonijam eva varuṇaloke pārthivāvayavopaṣṭambhāc copabhogasamartham*; [45]: *śarīram ayonijam evādityaloke pārthivāvayavopaṣṭambhāc copabhoga-samartham*; [52]: *tatrāyonijam eva śarīraṃ marutāṃ loke pārthivāvayavopa-ṣṭambhāc copabhogasamartham*). I thank Prof. H. Isaacson for drawing my attention to Vaiśeṣika texts.

73 TV, p. 702, 20-22 : TV', IV, p. 69, 24 – p. 70, 2: *tathā ca nakṣatreṣṭi-vākyaśeṣe 'bhihitaṃ "ye hi janāḥ puṇyakṛtaḥ svargaṃ lokaṃ yanti teṣāṃ etāni jyotīṃṣi yan nakṣatrāṇi."* tathā ca manunāpi svargaṃ lokaṃ gacchann abhi-hitaḥ, "tejomūrtiḥ patharjunā"** iti.*

* Cf. TS 5.4.1.3 (Agnicayana): *nakṣatreṣṭakā upa dadhāty, etāni vai divo jyotīṃṣi, tāny evāva runddhe, sukṛtāṃ vā etāni jyotīṃṣi yan nakṣatrāṇi, tāny evāpnoti.* There is no approximate phrase in the chapter on the *nakṣatreṣṭi* of TB 1.5. Cf. Dumont 1954.

** Manu(M) 3.83: *evaṃ yaḥ sarvabhūtāni brāhmaṇo nityam arcati* I *sa gacchati paraṃ sthānaṃ tejomūrtiḥ patharjunā* II Although Kullūka reads *tejomūrti* congruent with *sthānam*, he notes a variant reading *tejomūrtiḥ* by commenting on Manu(K) 3.93 as follows: ... *paraṃ sthānaṃ brahmātmakaṃ tejomūrti prakāśam. ... tejomūrtir iti savisargapāṭhe prakṛṣṭabrahmabodhasvabhāvo bhūtveti vyākhyā.*

74 Someśvara assumes the following suspicion of the opponent: "It is possible for individual souls to occupy a body in order to experience the result brought by their own action. You imagine the supreme self to occupy the Veda. It is, however, impossible for it to occupy a body, because [the supreme self] is neither the agent of action nor the agent of experience. Furthermore, the Veda cannot be the body of the (supreme self), because the Veda is permanent and therefore cannot be brought about by means of an action of the self" (NSu, p. 1009, 29-32: *nanu jīvātmanāṃ svakarmopāttaphalopabhogadehādhiṣṭhātṛtvasaṃbhave 'pi vedādhiṣṭhātṛtvenābhimatasya paramātmanaḥ kartṛbhoktṛtvābhāvād dehādhi-ṣṭhātṛtvaṃ na saṃbhavati vedānāṃ ca nityatvenātmakarmānupāttatvān na tad-dehatve sambhavati*).

been enumerated so far one after another, Kumārila, in this context, imagines space to permeate the whole universe comprising the four spheres vertically. We shall examine the meaning of this *śruti* later.

> (9) In the same manner, it is attested in a *śruti* that there is a supreme self embodied in space, [a supreme self] that is constantly revered by means of water and also indicated[75] [through the phrase] "Space (*kha*) is Brahman."[76]

Kumārila then abruptly changes the topic to the *guṇas* of material elements (*mahābhūta*). Since he offers "color" (*rūpa*) and "touch" (*sparśa*) as examples, what is being talked about here is not the three kinds of constituents (*triguṇa*) of the primordial matter (*prakṛti*), but the five kinds of qualities to be perceived through five kinds of sense organs.

> (10) Whatever qualities of material elements, say color, touch and others, may respectively be fixed upon particular souls, they build up the bodies as the basis for experience.[77]

In the first three quarters of verse (10), Kumārila suggests that not only the material elements of bodies, but also the perceptible qualities of them variously differ according to the spheres where the bodies are located. With regard to the last quarter, we should pay attention to the agent of experience (*sambhoga*), namely, the agent of perception on the basis (*hetu*) of the perceptible qualities.[78] The

---

[75] One should construe this *codita* not as a single past participle but as *ca* and *udita*, following NSu, p. 1010, 9-10: *kham brahmeti śrutyā vyomaśarīratayodita ity uktam.*

[76] TV, p. 702, 23-24 : TV', IV, p. 70, 3-4: (9) *tathā vyomaśarīro 'pi paramātmā śrutau śrutaḥ* I *ijyate vāriṇā nityaṃ yaḥ khaṃ brahmeti coditaḥ* II

[77] TV, p. 702, 25 – p. 703, 5 : TV', IV, p. 70, 5-6: (10) *rūpasparśādayo ye 'pi mahābhūtaguṇāḥ sthitāḥ* I *pratyekam ātmanāṃ te 'pi dehāḥ saṃbhogahetavaḥ* II Someśvara glosses *saṃbhogahetu* with "*saṃbhogādhiṣṭhānatā*" (NSu, p. 1010, 18).

[78] In the Saṃbandhākṣepaparihāra (kk. 100, 108-109) and the Ātmavāda (kk. 4, 8, 13, 34-38 etc.), Kumārila uses the derivative nouns from *bhuj*, i.e., *[upa-] bhoga*, *bhoktṛ* and *bhogya*, based on the sense of retribution of one's previous *karmans*. The *saṃbhoga* in verse (10), however, does not mean karmic retribution because one's body is the result (*phala*) of one's *karman*, not the cause

agent in question is not the soul that occupies the body possessed of color, touch and other qualities, because these qualities are not sense organs but the objects of perception. The agent is someone else who perceives the body through his own sense organ. Color, touch, and other qualities make the body perceptible for other living beings. Accordingly, the soul that resides in a body with perceptible qualities turns into an object to be experienced. One who has blue eyes, for example, never sees the world blue. Instead, others identify such a person as a one of European descent.

Here Kumārila comes back to the Veda. He alluded to "color and touch" in the previous verse in anticipation of reference to the quality that is acoustically perceived by living beings and particular to space (*vyoman*, *ākāśa*), namely, sound (*śabda*).[79] *Śabda* also means a word endowed with a meaning, and the Veda consists of words *par excellence*. Borrowing the term *śabdabrahman* from grammarians,[80] Kumārila demonstrates that the Veda forms the body of the supreme self (*paramātman*).

> (11) As regards the Vedic scripture that is called "*brahman* of words (sounds)" [by grammarians], its entirety is occupied by one single supreme self.[81]

In the preceding verse (10), Kumārila admitted that not only an entire set of five kinds of perceptible qualities, but also a single kind of them (*pratyekam*) can constitute the body of a soul.[82] Here

---

(*hetu*). Perceptible qualities in a body also cannot be the cause of retribution because they come to appear in a body that has already been brought into existence. Even if *saṃbhogahetavaḥ* were a Bahuvrīhi compound, *saṃbhoga* cannot mean retribution. Retribution cannot be the cause of one's body because retribution itself is the result of one's previous *karmans*.

[79] Cf. BhG 7.8cd: *praṇavaḥ sarvavedeṣu śabdaḥ khe pauruṣaṃ nṛṣu* ||; MBhr 12.177.35ab: *tatraikaguṇam ākāśaṃ śabda ity eva tat smṛtam* |; VS 2.1.26: *liṅgam ākāśasya*.

[80] Prof. J. Bronkhorst informed me that the word *śabdabrahman* is never used in the *Vākyapadīya*. Cf. Rau 1988: 146.

[81] TV, p. 703, 6-7 : TV', IV, p. 70, 7-8: (11) *śabdabrahmeti yac cedaṃ śāstraṃ vedākhyam ucyate* | *tad apy adhiṣṭhitaṃ sarvam ekena paramātmanā* ||

in (11), he holds the Veda that consists of sounds alone to be able to constitute the body of the supreme self.

Kumārila is of the opinion that it is impossible for an individual person to completely master the innumerable scriptures of the Veda.[83] Nevertheless, each scripture of the Veda transmitted in a brahmin branch, one by one, forms a complete body of the same *paramātman*. Although there is only one and the same *paramātman* in reality (verse 9), it appears as many "knowers of the field" (verse 1: *kṣetrajña*) that reside, one by one, in various Vedic scriptures.

> (12) In the same manner, the individual bodies that are respectively named, such as *Ṛgveda* etc., are always endowed with consciousness (*caitanya*)[84] insofar as they are [the bodies] to be received (*bhogya*) by some souls [called "knowers of the field" (*kṣetrajña*)].[85]

---

[82] NSu, p. 1010, 19-20: "[Kumārila] said 'respectively' in order to dispel a suspicion that color and other qualities form a body only when being put together [with other kinds of perceptible qualities] as in the case of earth and other elements." (*pṛthivyādimahābhūtavat samuditānām eva rūpādīnāṃ dehatva-śaṅkānirāsārthaṃ pratyekam ity uktam*).

[83] In the TV on JS 2.4.9, Kumārila recommends to concentrate on studying the text of one's own Vedic branch (*śākhā*): "Just as one and the same universal inheres in each individual [of the same sort], so the universal property of the Veda belongs to each branch. Hence, it holds good that one studies the text of one branch since the single number of the word 'Veda' (*svādhyāya*) is intended in the injunction 'One should study the Veda' for the reason (cf. JS 3.1.13-15) that the Veda is enjoined for the purpose of knowing the duties" (TV, p. 635, 24-26 : TV', III, p. 223, 12-14: *yathaivākṛtiḥ prativyakti samavaiti tathaiva svādhyāyatvam ekaikasyām śākhāyām. ataś ca "svādhyāyo'dhyetavya" iti karmāvabodhanaṃ praty upādīyamānatvād vivakṣitaikasaṃkhyaikā śākhādhy-etavyā*). Kumārila ironically warns against an attempt to master the texts of other branches: "If someone, on account of being too clever, were to study the texts of other branches that belong to the same Veda, he had better perform a sacrifice by means of an oblation made of rice and barley mixed up when he becomes very rich." (TV, p. 636, 14-15 : TV', III, p. 223, 21-22: *ataś ca yo nāmātimedhāvitvād ekavedagatāni śākhāntarāṇy apy adhīte sa samṛddhaḥ san vrīhiyavair api miśrair yajet*).

[84] Kumārila indicates *caitanya*, *dravya* and *sattā* as the properties inseparable from an individual self (ŚV, Ātmavāda, k. 26cd) and asserts the identity of the consciousness of an individual in spite of its different appearances in accordance with the objects (ŚV, Śabdanityatādhikaraṇa, k. 404).

After having thus elucidated the Veda as the body of a supreme self, Kumārila finally comes back to the original question about the intention (*vivakṣā*) in the *apauruṣeya* Veda. Generally speaking, if we want to understand someone else in front of us as a human being, we have to not only perceive his or her physical body but also comprehend his or her intention through his or her speech (verse 3). If the *Ṛgveda* and other Vedic scriptures, which themselves are nothing but aggregates of sounds, respectively form the bodies in which the supreme self resides as "knower of the field", it is not enough for the understanding of the Veda only to hear the sounds that constitute the Veda, however accurate the perception may be acoustically. It is also necessary to comprehend the intentions the supreme self announces through each sentence of the Veda. Just as a hearer understands the intention of a speaker through verbal usages in the ordinary world, we can understand the intention of the supreme self about how to perform the sacrifice through "the potency of the injunction" (*vidhiśakti*).

> (13) When these [souls in Vedic scriptures] who cherish a certain aim within themselves reveal the meaning of sentences, we can understand, through the potencies of the words, whether [a verbal expression of a sentence] is intended or not intended by them. (14) In fact, whatever [the supreme self] accepts by means of the potency of the injunction is "intended", while we should explain that that which [the supreme self] abandons is "not intended". (15) Hence, we should argue, on the basis of the potency of the injunction, whether [a verbal expression of a Vedic text is] intended or not intended by the [supreme self] that is the self of "*brahman* of words" and penetrates the whole of the Vedas.[86]

[85] TV, p. 703, 8-9 : TV', IV, p. 70, 9-10: (12) *tathargvedādayo dehāḥ proktā ye 'pi pṛthak pṛthak* I *bhogyatvenātmanāṃ te 'pi caitanyānugatāḥ sadā* II In this verse, *bhogya* may mean the body to be received in this world. Cf. n. 78; NSu, p. 1011, 9-10: *tathargvedādayo 'pi ... jñānañ ca vinā bhogāyogāc caitanyākhya-jñānānvitā ity arthaḥ.*

[86] TV, p. 703, 10-15 : TV', IV, p. 70, 11-16: (13) *teṣāṃ cāntargatecchānāṃ vākyārthapratipādane* I *vivakṣā vāvivakṣā vā jñāyate śabdaśaktitaḥ* II (14) *vidhi-śaktyā gṛhītaṃ yat tat sarvaṃ hi vivakṣitam* I *tathaiva tu parityaktaṃ vyākhyeyam avivakṣitam* II (15) *śabdabrahmātmano 'py evaṃ sarvavedānusāriṇaḥ* I *vivakṣā vāvivakṣā vā vaktavyā vidhiśaktitaḥ* II

Thus considered, even without recourse to a figurative usage (*upacāra*), one can examine whether a verbal expression of a sentence in the eternal Veda is "intended" or "not intended" in the primary meaning (*mukhyavṛtti*) of "intention". Kumārila concludes the discussion with the following verse, borrowing an expression of Brahman, *anādinidhanam*, from Bhartṛhari.

> (16) Thus then, even in the primary meaning [of "intention"], we can explain the intention and the non-intention with reference to the meanings of [the sentences of individual] Vedas, although the Veda is beginningless and endless.[87]

In the Vyākaraṇādhikaraṇa of the TV, Kumārila held that the *paramātman* is the goal to be attained with the help of sacrifices by one who has cognized the true nature of one's own self. Presenting the aforecited verses (1) to (16), he also proclaims the *paramātman* to be the agent who reveals sacrifices through the perceptible bodies called "Veda". Just as one can perceive the bodies of others by seeing their colors and touching their shapes, one can perceive the Veda as the body of the *paramātman* by hearing its constituent parts, namely, the sounds *par excellence* manifested in space through recitation. It is also requested that one comprehend the intention of the *paramātman* from each sentence of the Veda by adopting exegetic technique, just as one attempts to comprehend the intention of a speaker in the ordinary world by various means. Thus considered, Kumārila professes *jñānakarmasamuccaya* in the BṬ, as mentioned in the introduction of this article,[88] in order to express his conviction that one who daily recites Vedic texts and performs periodical and occasional sacrifices in conformity with Vedic injunctions for his whole life constantly accumulates experience (*saṃbhoga*) of the supreme self revealed in space.[89]

---

[87] TV, p. 16-17 : TV', IV, p. 70, 17-18: (16) *anādinidhane 'py evaṃ vede vedārthagocare* | *vyākhyānaṃ mukhyavṛttyāpi syād vivakṣāvivakṣayoḥ* || Cf. VP 1.1: *anādinidhanaṃ brahma śabdatattvaṃ yad akṣaram* | *vivartate 'rthabhāvena prakriyā jagato yataḥ* ||

[88] Cf. fn. 7.

4. CONFORMITY OF THE IDEA OF THE SUPREME SELF WITH THE *ŚLOKAVĀRTTIKA*

One might suspect the idea of *paramātman* and the structure of the world elucidated in the aforecited verses of the TV not to be consistent with Mīmāṃsā theories in the *Ślokavārttika* (ŚV), because in the ŚV Kumārila demonstrates that the Veda and this world have never been created. Besides, he criticizes some opponents who shaped the theories presupposed in the idea of *paramātman*: He refutes the proof of the impermanence of sound (*śabdānityatā*) offered by Vaiśeṣikas who hold that sound is the quality of space, and he opposes the *sphoṭa* theory of Bhartṛhari, who says that the Vedas are manifestations of the *brahman*. Upon careful examination, however, there is no inconsistency although it might be unexpected that the author of the ŚV declares such a metaphysical view in the TV.

In the fanciful illustration of various bodies in diverse spheres of the world, as presented in verses (1) to (9), Kumārila keeps away from the cosmogonic explanation of the origin of each sphere. He just describes the characteristics of the body possessed by a soul in a particular sphere. Apart from the transmigration of individual souls into various bodies owing to their *karman*s, as mentioned in verse (4), Kumārila says nothing about the formation of each sphere or about the origin of the system of rebirth in each sphere. Hence, according to him, living beings must have beginninglessly been and will endlessly be transmigrating in these spheres. The supreme self also has beginninglessly been and will endlessly be embodied in the permanent sounds that constitute the Veda. Accordingly, Kumārila holds also in this section that the Veda and this world have no beginning, thereby he does not go against his

---

[89] In the aforecited sixteen verses we could read Kumārila's rivalry against the *saṃnyāsa* movement advocated, for example, in the *Muṇḍakopaniṣad*. MuU 1.1.4-5 underestimates the knowledge gained through various Vedic studies, and MuU 3.2.3 declares that the Ātman cannot be attained by means of Vedic studies.

refutation of the various theories about the creation of this world in the ŚV, Sambandhākṣepaparihāra, kk. 42cd-113.

As regards the descriptions of sound in the ŚV, we can say that Kumārila admits that sound is the quality of space (*ākāśa*, *vyoman*) as held in the Vaiśeṣika school in spite of the controversy as to the permanence of sound. In the Śabdanityatādhikaraṇa of the ŚV, Kumārila refutes the opponent's proof that sound is impermanent because it appears immediately after the effort of pronunciation (*prayatnānantarā dṛṣṭiḥ*), on the ground that this reason is inconclusive (*anaikāntika*).[90] He alludes to space (*ākāśa*) as a counter-example to which this reason is applicable. Although space is permanent and all-pervading, it is not perceived in a place occupied by earth or water and appears immediately after they are removed by means of human effort.[91]

Presupposing that space is the substratum of sound, Kumārila demonstrates the local manifestation of permanent sounds: Sounds can be manifested only close to the place where space is connected (*saṃsarga*) with sounding objects.[92] Although sounds become manifested in the all-pervading space, a deaf person cannot hear them owing to the defects of his auditory organs caused by his own *dharma* and *adharma*.[93] The manifestation of voice is caused by inner winds in the speaker's vocal organs and transmitted through outer winds to the hearer's auditory organs.[94] On one hand, Kumārila admits that it is traditionally acknowledged in the ordinary world that a part of space forms auditory organs as the Vaiśeṣikas insist.[95] On the other hand, he holds auditory organs to be a part of

---

[90] ŚV, Śabdanityatādhikaraṇa, k. 19.

[91] ŚV, Śabdanityatādhikaraṇa, kk. 30cd-32ab.

[92] ŚV, Śabdanityatādhikaraṇa, kk. 74cd-76ab.

[93] ŚV, Śabdanityatādhikaraṇa, kk. 76cd-78ab.

[94] ŚV, Śabdanityatādhikaraṇa, kk. 121cd-130ab.

[95] ŚV, Śabdanityatādhikaraṇa, kk. 146cd-149ab. According to Pārthasārathi, Kumārila approves of the Vaiśeṣika's idea of auditory organs as a view prevalent in the ordinary world in order to refute Bhartṛmitra's opinion that an auditory

directions (*diśaḥ*) appealing to a Vedic testimony in order to demonstrate that his position is more orthodox than the Vaiśeṣika's position.[96] However, his position is, in the end, nothing other than the Vaiśeṣika's since he approves of the Vaiśeṣika explanations of the process of aural comprehension for the reason that both space and directions are all-pervading.[97] Thus in the ŚV, Kumārila turns the Vaiśeṣika view that space is the substratum of sound to his own advantage, and concludes that sound is just as permanent as space.[98]

It is true that Kumārila criticizes Bhartṛhari's illusionistic monism in the ŚV. He refutes Bhartṛhari's monistic views on language: The figurative (*upacāra*) cognition of a word as its meaning,[99] the manifestation of a single *sphoṭa* as a meaningful word,[100] and the manifestation of a single intuition (*pratibhā*) as a sentence divided

---

organ is produced by sounds (cf. NR, p, 540, 9-11 on ŚV, Śabdanityatādhikaraṇa, k. 130cd).

[96] ŚV, Śabdanityatādhikaraṇa, kk. 150-152cd. In k. 150c, Kumārila quotes "*diśaḥ śrotram*" from TB 3.6.6.2: "Make its eye go to the sun; let its breath go to the wind; its hearing to the quarters, its life to the atmosphere, its body to the earth" (transl. by Dumont [1962: 254]) (*sūryaṃ cakṣur gamayatāt, vātaṃ prāṇam anvavasṛjatāt, diśaḥ śrotram, antarikṣam asum, pṛthivīṃ śarīram*), which is a part of the *adhrigu* litany recited by the Hotṛ at the slaying of the victim.

[97] ŚV, Śabdanityatādhikaraṇa, kk. 152cd-154ab: "The quarters are all-pervading and [in reality] one, and extend as far as space. [The quarter] limited by an ear-hole becomes an auditory organ just as [the Vaiśeṣikas holds] a part of space [to be an auditory organ]. Whichever theories the Vaiśeṣikas may propound in order to demonstrate [their position that auditory organs consist of] a part of space, all of them can be applied to [our position that auditory organs are] a part of the quarters. But [our position] is superior [to theirs] on the ground of the Vedic tradition." (*dik ca sarvagataikā ca yāvadvyoma vyavasthitā* || *karṇacchidraparicchinnā śrotram ākāśadeśavat* | *yāvāṃś ca kaṇabhugnyāyo nabhobhāgaprakalpane* || *digbhāge tu samasto 'sau āgamāt tu viśiṣyate* |). Unlike the Vaiśeṣikas (cf. VS 1.1.4, 2.2.12-15; PBh [4], [23]-[24], [73]-[74]), Kumārila assumes no substantial difference between space and directions except for nominal difference.

[98] ŚV, Śabdanityatādhikaraṇa, k. 350ab: "On account of the aforementioned all-pervasiveness, that (sound) is established as just permanent as space" (*prāguktena vibhutvena vyomavac cāsya nityatā* |).

[99] ŚV, Pratyakṣasūtra, kk. 171-172 ff.

[100] ŚV, Sphoṭavāda.

into an illusional aggregate of words.[101] In the aforecited verses (11) and (12), our attention may be drawn to the apparent affinity to Bhartṛhari's idea that one and the same Veda, which is a duplicate (*anukāra*) of Brahman, has been handed down in many recensions (VP 1.5). We should, however, note that Kumārila explicitly distinguishes the supreme self (*paramātman*) from the Veda, which is nothing but the body it occupies in space. He can therefore, even in these verses, by no means be called a monist.

In the ŚV, Sambandhākṣepaparihāra, kk. 82cd-86, Kumārila criticizes the theory of cosmogony held in monistic subjectivism that there exists only the self (*puruṣa*, *ātman*) in reality. Kumārila directs his criticism towards two types of monistic metaphysics, namely, the theory of real modification (*vikṛti*) and the theory of illusionistic manifestation. Against the former theory, he points out that the Self considered as a pure soul (*śuddhapuruṣa*) cannot be modified into the impure phenomenal world.[102] After having formulated the latter theory with allusions to dream and ignorance (*avidyā*),[103] he denies the cosmogonic appearance of illusion from both sides: If someone else brought ignorance into the Ātman, then monism would be abandoned. If, conversely, ignorance were a property of the Ātman by nature, nothing could change the nature of the Ātman, because, in the position of the opponent, there is no real entity except for the Ātman.[104]

---

[101] ŚV, Vākyādhikaraṇa, kk. 325cd-327cd, kk. 336cd-340ab.

[102] ŚV, Sambandhākṣepaparihāra, kk. 82cd-83: "It is impossible, on one hand, for a soul that is totally pure to undergo impure modification. And because merit and [demerit] are regulated by the [pure] self, it is not reasonable that one suffers affliction due to them. Or, if [the modification were nevertheless] set in motion on account of them, then something else [that controls merit and demerit] would be accepted." (*puruṣasya ca śuddhasya nāśuddhā vikṛtir bhavet* || *svādhīnatvāc ca dharmādes tena kleśo na yujyate* | *tadvaśena pravṛttau vā vyatirekaḥ prasajyate* ||).

[103] ŚV, Sambandhākṣepaparihāra, k. 84: "Because, on the other hand, [the self is said to be] pure by nature and there exists no other object [than the self], what could, for the (self), bring about the activity of ignorance just like a dream?" (*svayaṃ ca śuddharūpatvād asattvāc cānyavastunaḥ* | *svapnādivad avidyāyāḥ pravṛttis tasya kiṃkṛtā* |).

Although Kumārila thus definitively criticizes monistic theories of cosmogony, it would not be appropriate to conclude that the ŚV allows no scope for any kinds of Vedānta views. As mentioned in the introduction of the present article, Kumārila asserts in the Sambandhākṣepaparihāra of the ŚV that one does not enjoy pleasure (*sukhopabhoga*) in the state of liberation. This view may sound incompatible with the typical Vedāntic description of Brahman as "being, consciousness and happiness" (*sat-cid-ānanda*). But whether happiness (*ānanda*) is regarded as important varies according to individual scholars in the early medieval Vedānta. Maṇḍanamiśra, for example, intensively demonstrates that Brahman has the nature of *ānanda* in the first chapter of his *Brahmasiddhi*. Śaṅkara, however, does not emphasize the feeling of happiness in the state of liberation, except for the cases when he comments on the *Brahmasūtra* or Upaniṣads that refer to *ānanda*.[105]

In the ŚV, there are some passages where Kumārila lightly suggests the Vedāntic teachings of self-awareness. In the Vyākaraṇādhikaraṇa of the TV, as mentioned in the introduction of the present paper, Kumārila explains the efficacy of the knowledge of the self in two ways: On one hand, the knowledge of the self is helpful for performing sacrifices (*kratvartha*) because one feels like undertaking the periodical sacrifices to attain heaven in one's next life, only if one understands that one's own soul does not perish but

[104] ŚV, Sambandhākṣepaparihāra, kk. 85-86: "If [the activity of ignorance] were held to occur due to something else, then you would fall into dualism (*dvaita*). And if ignorance were held to be [a property of the self] by nature, then nobody could cut off such ignorance. A natural (ignorance) could, by any chance, be extinguished if something divergent [from the Ātman] were applied to it. But for those who admit only the Ātman [as a real thing], there is no cause distinct [from the Ātman].*" (*anyenopaplave 'bhīṣṭe dvaitavādaḥ prasajyate | svābhāvikīm avidyāṃ tu nocchettuṃ kaścid arhati || vilakṣaṇopapāte hi naśyet svābhāvikī kvacit | na tv ekātmābhyupāyānāṃ hetur asti vilakṣaṇaḥ ||*).

* Referring to Nirālambanavāda k. 198ab, Pārthasārathimiśra mentions the Vaiśeṣika explanation that the black color of an earthy pot is changed to red on account of its contact with fire. Cf. NR, p. 470, 28-29; p. 471, 1-2.

[105] Cf. Hacker 1950: 276-277; 1968: 129-135; Ingalls 1952: 2.

continues after death.[106] On the other hand, the knowledge of the self is also helpful directly to human beings (*puruṣārtha*), because it brings about prosperity (*abhyudaya*) and supreme bliss (*niḥśreyasa*). Kumārila holds the prosperity in this context to be the eight kinds of supernatural power gained through meditation,[107] whereas he considers the supreme bliss as the non-return to this world and the attainment of the supreme self.[108] In the Sambandhākṣepaparihāra, k. 103, however, Kumārila explicitly states that the injunctions in the Upaniṣads such as "The Self is to be known" (*ātmā jñātavyaḥ*) are not laid down with a view to the attainment of liberation through cognizing one's own self, because its purpose is to promote the performance of sacrifices (*karmapravṛttihetu*), in other words, it is *kratvartha*.[109]

---

[106] TV, p. 288, 7-8 : TV', II, p. 227, 13-14: *tena* (= *ātmajñāna*) *vinā paralokaphaleṣu karmasu pravṛttinivṛttyasaṃbhavāt.*

[107] TV, p. 288, 14 : TV', II, p. 227, 21: *yogajanyāṇimādyaṣṭaguṇaiśvaryaphalāni.*

[108] TV, p. 288, 16 : TV', II, p. 227, 22-23: *apunarāvṛttyātmakaparamātmaprāptyavasthāphalavacanam.* Combining *abhyudaya* with the eight supernatural powers enumerated in the *Yogasūtra* 3.45 (cf. Harikai 1990: 217, n. 129), Kumārila may have introduced the pair of notions "*abhyudaya* and *niḥśreyasa*" from the *Manusmṛti* and modified it in accordance to the intellectualism of the Vedānta without abandoning the significance of sacrifices. Manu(K&M) 12.88-89 declares that *abhyudaya* is attained through the engagement (*pravṛtti*) of the *kāmya* actions that increase pleasure (*sukhābhyudayika*) whereas *niḥśreyasa* through the cessation (*nivṛtti*), which is, however, nothing else than the action (*karma*) based on knowledge without secular desires (*niṣkāmaṃ jñānapūrvam*).

[109] ŚV, Sambandhākṣepaparihāra k. 103: *ātmā jñātavya ity etan mokṣārthaṃ na ca coditam* | *karmapravṛttihetutvam ātmajñānasya lakṣyate* || In the next verse, k. 104, Kumārila asserts that the Upaniṣadic phrases that refer to the result of cognizing of one's self should be regarded as explanatory sentences (*arthavāda*) for the injunction of a sacrifice: "Once it is accepted that the (knowledge of the self) is serviceable to other things (i.e., rituals), the description of its result turns to be an explanatory sentence, and [the knowledge of the self has] no result except for heaven etc." (*vijñāte cāsya pārārthye yāpi nāma phalaśrutiḥ* | *sārthavādo bhaved eva na svargādeḥ phalāntaram* ||). In the Vyākaraṇādhikaraṇa of the TV, however, he declares that such phrases refer to the result particular to the *ātmajñāna*.

We should not, however, overlook the context in which this verse is located. Kumārila refutes the Sāṃkhya theory of cosmogony in kk. 87-112, in which he propounds his own theory of liberation for the purpose of criticizing the gnostic intellectualism that is prone to incite the lifestyle of renunciation. He has no intention to restrict the role of *ātmajñāna* only to *kratvartha*. After having recommended concentration on obligatory sacrifices and not to indulge in pursuing secular desires if one wishes for liberation,[110] he immediately says that one can diminish secular desires through *ātmajñāna* and thereby refrain from optional (*kāmya*) sacrifices.[111] Hence, we can say that Kumārila admits even in the Sambandhākṣepaparihāra that the knowledge of the self is helpful for the attainment of liberation, although not directly as stated in the Vyākaraṇādhikaraṇa. At the end of the Ātmavāda of the ŚV too, Kumārila suggests his concern with the Vedānta. He recommends studying the Upaniṣads (*vedānta*) in order to confirm the knowledge of the existence of the *ātman*.[112]

5. AFFINITY TO THE *CHĀNDOGYOPANIṢAD*

In verse (9) among the aforecited sixteen verses, Kumārila says that a *śruti* attests to (*śrutau śrutaḥ*) the existence of a *paramātman* embodied in space (*vyomaśarīra*). The content of the *śruti* suggested here consists of the three phrases (1) *vyomaśarīro 'pi para-*

[110] Cf. ŚV, Sambandhākṣepaparihāra, k. 110 in fn. 17.

[111] ŚV, Sambandhākṣepaparihāra, k. 111: "We understand that [one can acquire] the result [of a sacrifice] only if one desires it, and it would not be brought about to one who has no desire of it. Since this (indifference to the result) exists in one who has cognized his own self, the knowledge of the (self) is [indirectly] helpful [for the attainment of liberation]" (*prārthyamānaṃ phalaṃ jñātaṃ na cānicchor bhaviṣyati | ātmajñe caitad astīti tajjñānam upayujyate ||*).

[112] ŚV, Atmavāda, k. 148: "Thus the author of the Bhāṣya [cf. fn. 44] established the existence of the soul by means of reasoning, in order to refute the theory of the non-existence of the soul. One can reinforce the idea thus acquired by devoting oneself to the Upaniṣads" (*ity āha nāstikyanirākariṣnur ātmāstitāṃ bhāṣyakṛd atra yuktyā | dṛḍhatvam etadviṣayaś ca bodhaḥ prayāti vedāntaniṣevaṇena ||*).

mātmā, (2) *ijyate vāriṇā nityam*, and (3) *yaḥ khaṃ brahmeti coditaḥ*. Since there are too many passages where the absolute being is related to space (*ākāśa*, *vyoman*) in the Upaniṣads, I shall first investigate the possible source of phrases 2 and 3.

Someśvara, a commentator on the TV, explains that phrase 2 is concerned with the *sāvitrī* verse, i.e., a *gāyatrī* verse for Savitṛ (*Ṛgveda* 3.62.10), as follows:

> Against the suspicion that [the supreme self (*paramātman*)] does not occupy a body because it has no purpose [in possessing a body], [Kumārila] said "[the supreme self that is constantly] revered by means of water" in order to establish [that the supreme self is] the receiver [of a body]; and [the "water" in this phrase means] the water that is [constantly] splashed up with [the recitation of] the *gāyatrī* verse [that begins with] *tat savitur vareṇyam*, which by means of the word *tat* refers to the supreme self called *brahman* whose abode is the Savitṛ.[113]

Quoting the beginning of the *sāvitrī* verse, Someśvara asserts that the *paramātman* occupies the Savitṛ, i.e., the sun, (*savitradhiṣṭhāna*) instead of space (*vyoman*). He then grounds this on *Aitareyāraṇyaka* 2.2.4, which identifies the sun with the Ātman on the basis of a congruent expression of *sūrya* and *ātman* in *Ṛgveda* 1.115.1: *sūrya ātmā jagatas tasthuṣaś ca.*[114] In order to make his explanation conform to Kumārila's idea of the *paramātman* embodied in space, he then says that the *paramātman*, in fact, occupies space (*vyoman*) for the reason that the sun occupied by the *paramātman* is located in space. He alludes to the fact that the in-

---

[113] NSu, p. 1010, 1-4: *prayojanābhāvād dehānadhiṣṭhātṛtām āśaṅkya bhoktṛtvasiddhyai "ta[t] savitur vareṇyam" iti savitradhiṣṭhānatacchabdavācyabrahmākhyaparamātmābhidhāyinyā gāyatryotkṣipyamāṇena "vāriṇejyata" ity uktam.*

[114] NSu, p. 1010, 4-6: "On the ground of a phrase of an *upaniṣad* 'What I am, he is; what he is, I am' (transl. by Keith [1909: 215]), and also on the ground of the phrase of a *mantra* 'And the sun is the *ātman* of anything that goes or stands,' there occurs the idea that the *brahman* occupies the sun." (*"tad yo 'haṃ so 'sau, yo 'sau so 'ham" ity upaniṣacchruteḥ "sūrya ātmā jagatas tasthuṣaś ca" iti mantravarṇāc ca brahmaṇaḥ savitradhiṣṭātṛtvāvagatiḥ*). Cf. AiĀ 2.2.4: *tad yo 'haṃ so 'sau yo 'sau so 'ham. tad uktam ṛṣiṇā. sūrya ātmā jagatas tasthuṣaś ceti. etad u haivopekṣetopekṣeta.*

dividual *ātman*, in fact, occupies the entirety of one's body including the heart, although one meditates (*upāsana*) on one's *ātman* as that which occupies one's heart.[115] This explanation by Someśvara is, however, not convincing at all because Kumārila hints at neither the *sāvitrī* verse nor the sun in the sky.

When Someśvara explains phrase 2 by recourse to the *sāvitrī* verse, he seems to refer to the ceremony called *saṃdhyopāsana* to be performed everyday in the morning and in the evening, because the sprinkling of oneself with water (*mārjana*), the muttering of the *sāvitrī* (*japa*) and the offering of water (*tarpaṇa*) are included in the series of ceremonies that form the daily *saṃdhyopāsana*.[116] It has been, however, clarified by Sh. Einoo that the daily *saṃdhyopāsana* accompanied with *mārjana*, *japa* and *tarpaṇa* was formed in the later period of the *Gṛhya* literature.[117] Thus we can safely say that Kumārila does not take the *saṃdhyopāsana* into consideration

---

[115] NSu, p. 1010, 6-8: "Just as one meditates on one's *ātman* as that which occupies one's heart, although it occupies the whole of one's body in truth, there is no inconsistency in meditating on [the *paramātman*] as that which occupies the sun located in space, although [the *paramātman*] occupies the whole space in truth." (*kṛtsnadehādhiṣṭhānasyāpi cātmano hṛdayādhiṣṭhānopāsanavat kṛtsnavyomādhiṣṭhānasyāpi vyomāntargatasavitṛmaṇḍalā*[corr.: °*maṇḍala-*]*dhiṣṭhānopāsanāvirodhaḥ*.)

[116] Kane 1997: 312-321, 668; Gonda 1980: 460.

[117] Sh. Einoo classifies the ritual texts that deal with *saṃdhyopāsana* into two groups: *gṛhyasūtra*s in one group, *pariśiṣṭa*s and *śeṣasūtra*s added to the *gṛhyasūtra*s in another group. Comparing these two groups, he has discovered a historical change of the performer of the ceremony (Einoo 1992; 1993: 299-313). According to the former group, the ceremony is to be performed by students (*brahmacārin*), and the rituals performed with water are not laid down except for *Jaiminīyagṛhyasūtra* 1.13.15-16, where *mārjana* is prescribed. Einoo (1993: 305 enumerates the following instances: *Kāṭhaka-GS* 1.25-28; *Mānava-GS* 1.2.1-5; *Vārāha-GS* 5.30; *Āśvalāyana-GS* 3.7.3-6; *Śāṅkhāyana-GS* 2.9.1-3; *Kauṣītaki-GS* 2.6.3-4. According to the latter group, contrastively, the *saṃdhyopāsana* including *mārjana*, *japa* and *tarpaṇa* is to be performed by householders (*gṛhastha*) in a more complicated process. The *saṃdhyopāsana* prescribed in the former group is not included in the Agnihotra, i.e., the *śrauta* sacrifice to be performed every day in the morning and in the evening. The Agnihotra as a ceremony for revering the sun is supposed to have been changed in a more abridged form into the morning and evening *homa* in the *gṛhyasūtra*s (Einoo 1993: 274-299; Kane 1997: 681-688).

in phrase 2, because it is not a ritual revealed in a *śruti* text. It is neither likely that the splashing up of water in the *saṃdhyopāsana* is expressed with the verb *yaj* (*ijyate*), which indicates the act of putting an oblation into the sacrificial fire in a *śrauta* ritual (JS 4.2.27).

I propose to interpret phrase 2 as a brief summary of the first three stages of "the doctrine of five fires" (*pañcāgnividyā*) because it is possible to consider the first three stages of the *pañcāgnividyā* as a symbolical speculation of the rainfall that occurs in the vast space from heaven to the earth. The doctrine of five fires was completed in *Chāndogyopaniṣad* (ChU) 5.4.1-9.1 and *Bṛhadāraṇyakopaniṣad* (BĀU) 6.2.9-13 (in the Mādhyandina recension: 6.1.12-16), which are preceded by *Jaiminīyabrāhmaṇa* (JB) 1.45-46 and 49-50 and *Śatapathabrāhmaṇa* (ŚB) 11.6.2.6-10.[118] H. W. Bodewitz focuses on the first oblation in the JB, i.e., the immortal water (*amṛtam āpaḥ*), and he remarks that it is more original than faith (*śraddhā*) in the BĀU and the ChU and that the water doctrine was originally neither cyclic nor connected with the transmigration theory, because the *āpaḥ* in the JB are the heavenly waters.[119] Bodewitz finds the main reason for the Upaniṣadic transformation of the *pañcāgnividyā* into a transmigration theory in the textual evidences in Vedic literature that *śraddhā* is frequently associated with water and especially with truth (*satya*), which itself is identified with water.[120]

The idea of the circulation of water in nature seems to have been prevalent among the scholars of the Vedānta, when they put importance to the *pañcāgnividyā* as a theory of transmigration in the first section of the *Brahmasūtra* (BS) 3.1. BS 3.1.1 declares that the soul of a living being is enveloped by subtle materials when it leaves the body at death.[121] Summarizing the *pañcāgnividyā*

---

[118] Bodewitz 1973: 110-123; Schmithausen 1994.

[119] Bodewitz 1973: 113.

[120] Bodewitz 1973: 117, n. 3; Schmithausen 1994: 45.

with respect to the five fires (*dyu-parjanya-pṛthivī-puruṣa-yoṣit*) and five oblations (*śraddhā-soma-vṛṣṭy-anna-retas*), Śaṅkara holds water to be the subtle material mentioned in this *sūtra* and refers to the two passages of the ChU in which Pravāhaṇa Jaivali poses a question about "the water that takes on a human voice"[122] and draws a conclusion[123] before and after the teachings of the *pañcāgnividyā* respectively.[124] It is quite certain that the *Brahma-sūtra* itself deals with the Upaniṣadic *pañcāgnividyā*, because BS 3.1.5 anticipates an objection that water (*āpaḥ*), expressed by the feminine pronoun *tāḥ*, is not directly mentioned at the first stage.[125] This objection exactly refers to the description of the first oblation in the ChU and the BĀU version, namely, faith (*śraddhā*) instead of water. In the light of the wide recognition of the Upaniṣadic *pañcāgnividyā* as confirmed in BS 3.1 and the commentary there-

[121] BS 3.1.1: *tadantarapratipattau raṃhati saṃpariṣvaktaḥ praśnani-rūpaṇābhyām*. "In obtaining a different (body) (the soul) goes enveloped (by subtle parts of the elements), (as appears from) question and explanation." (transl. by Thibaut [1904: 101]).

[122] ChU 5.3.3: "Do you know how at the fifth offering the water takes on a human voice?" (Olivelle 1996: 140) (*vettha yathā pañcamyām āhutāv āpaḥ puruṣavacaso bhavantīti*).

[123] ChU 5.9.1: "at the fifth offering the waters take on a human voice" (Olivelle 1996: 141) (*iti tu pañcamyām āhutāv āpaḥ puruṣavacaso bhavantīti*). The BĀU version of *pañcāgnividyā* lacks this conclusion in 6.2.14-15 although it contains the question on the water that takes on a human voice (6.2.2).

[124] BSBh, p. 325, 6-10.

[125] BS 3.1.5: *prathame 'śravaṇād iti cen na tā eva hy upapatteḥ*. "If an objection be raised on the ground of (water) not being mentioned in the first fire, we refute it by remarking that just it (viz. water) (is meant), on the ground of fitness." (transl. by Thibaut [1904: 106]). In his commentary on this *sūtra*, Śaṅkara brings forward several arguments (*upapatti*) to justify the interpretation of the word *śraddhā* in the sense of water (BSBh, p. 327, 22 – p. 328, 12). These explanations are not peculiar to Śaṅkara, because Bhāskara also, likewise but more concisely, comments on BS 3.1.1 and 3.1.5 referring to the *pañcāgnividyā* and the usage of the word *śraddhā* in the sense of water (BSBh(Bh), pp. 152-153). As pointed out by W. Halbfass (1991: 326), Śaṅkara propounds a peculiar theory of *apūrva* in his commentary on BS 3.1.6: Once offered into the Āhavanīya fire, the water ingredients of an oblation are transformed into *apūrva*, adhere to the performers of faithful sacrifices (*śraddhāpūrvakakarma*), envelop their souls (*jīva*), and lead them to the yonder world (BSBh, p. 328, 25 – p. 329, 5).

on, it is likely that Kumārila laid down phrase 2 *ijyate vāriṇā nityam* for the purpose of describing the *paramātman* embodied in space, by alluding to the process of rainfall described as a cosmic periodical (*nitya*) sacrifice in the first three stages either of the ChU or of the BĀU version of the *pañcāgnividyā*. The *paramātman* embodied in space is said to be constantly (*nityam*) revered (*ijyate*) as a deity (*devatā*) by means of the three successive modifications of water (*vāri*), viz., faith (ChU & BĀU: *śraddhā*), *soma* and rain (ChU: *varṣa*; BĀU: *vṛṣṭi*) offered respectively into the three symbolical fires settled in space vertically, viz., heaven (ChU & BĀU: *asau lokas*), rain-cloud in the sky (ChU & BĀU: *parjanya*) and the earth (ChU: *pṛthivī*; BĀU: *ayaṃ lokas*).

As regards phrase 3 (*yaḥ khaṃ brahmeti coditaḥ*), it is much easier to find its source in the Upaniṣads. Kumārila quotes *khaṃ brahmeti* from the teachings of three sacrificial fires to Upakosala in ChU 4.10.4-5:

> The fires then said to each other ... And they told him: "*Brahman* is breath. *Brahman* is joy (*ka*). *Brahman* is space (*kha*)." He replied: "I can understand that brahman is breath. But I don't understand how it can be joy or space." "Joy is the same as space," they replied, "and space is the same as joy." And they explained to him both breath and space (*ākāśa*).[126]

We find the phrase *khaṃ brahma* also in BĀU 5.1.1: *oṃ khaṃ brahma. khaṃ purāṇam. vāyuraṃ kham. iti ha smāha kauravyāyaṇīputraḥ*. It is nevertheless probable that Kumārila quotes this phrase not from the BĀU but from the ChU, because he, in the aforecited verse (7), describes the sky (*antarikṣa*) as the sphere where the bodies made mainly of wind (*vāta* = *vāyu*) float, thereby distinguishing the sphere of wind from the whole space (*vyoman*). But BĀU 5.1.1 does not distinguish *vāyuraṃ* and *kham*. Additionally, the ChU is much more impressive as a textual source than the

[126] Olivelle (1996: 133) on ChU 4.10.4-5: *atha hāgnayaḥ samūdire. ... tasmai hocuḥ. prāṇo brahma kaṃ brahma khaṃ brahmeti. sa hovāca. vijānāmy ahaṃ yat prāṇo brahma. kaṃ ca tu khaṃ ca na vijānāmīti. te hocuḥ. yad vāva kaṃ tad eva kham. yad eva khaṃ tad eva kam iti. prāṇaṃ ca hāsmai tad ākāśaṃ cocuḥ.*

BĀU in this context, because *khaṃ brahma* is revealed from sacrificial fires in ChU 4.10.4-5, whereas it is just a peripheral saying by a human being in BĀU 5.1.1. In that case, phrase 2 also probably refers to the ChU.

If phrase 2 and 3 are based on the ChU, it may be right to assume that phrase 1 (*vyomaśarīro 'pi paramātmā*) also reflects a certain passage in the ChU. Among the ChU passages where the absolute being is related to space[127], Kumārila may refer to a scene of Aśvapati Kaikeya's teachings on the "Ātman common to all men" (*vaiśvānarātman*) in the ChU 5.11-24. In the dialogue of King Aśvapati with six brahmins, each brahmin asserts what is to be considered as the absolute being, and then Aśvapati replies to each brahmin that what they have asserted is just a part of the *vaiśvānarātman*. In the ChU 5.15 and 5.18, Aśvapati replies to Jana Śārkarākṣya that the space (*ākāśa*) Jana holds to be the *vaiśvānarātman* is, in fact, just the body (*saṃdeha*) of it.[128] Unlike Bhartṛhari who identifies Brahman with the essence of words (*śabdatattva*), Kumārila distinguishes the *paramātman* from the Veda manifested as sounds *par excellence* in space (verses 9-11) just as

[127] For the *ākāśa* identified with the absolute being in the ChU, see 1.9.1: *asya lokasya kā gatir iti. ākāśa iti hovāca. ... ākāśaḥ parāyaṇam*; 3.12.7-9: *yad vai tad brahmetīdaṃ vāva tad yo 'yaṃ bahirdhā puruṣād ākāśaḥ. ... ayaṃ vāva sa yo 'yam antaḥ puruṣaḥ ākāśaḥ ... ayaṃ vāva sa yo 'yam antarhṛdaya ākāśaḥ*; 3.14.1-2: *sarvaṃ khalv idaṃ brahma ... ākāśātmā*; 3.18.1: *athādhidaivatam ākāśo brahmeti*; 7.12.1-3: *ākāśo vāva tejaso bhūyān ... sa ya ākāśam brahmety upāste... smaro vāvākāśād bhūyaḥ*; 8.1.1 *daharo 'sminn antarākāśaḥ*; 8.14.1: *ākāśo vai nāma nāmarūpayor nirvahitā, te yad antarā, tad brahma, tad amṛtam, sa ātmā.*

[128] ChU 5.15.1-2: "'Space, Your Majesty,' he replied. 'What you venerate as the self', Aśvapati told him, 'is this ample self here, the one common to all men. ... This, however,' he said, 'is only the trunk of the self. And if you had'nt come to me,' he continued, 'your trunk would have crumbled to pieces!" (Olivelle 1996: 145) (*ākāśam eva bhagavo rājan iti hovāca. eṣa vai bahula ātmā vaiśvānaraḥ ... saṃdehas tv eṣa ātmana iti hovāca. saṃdehas te vyaśīryad yan māṃ nāgamiṣya iti*); ChU 5.18.2: "Now, of this self here, the one common to all men, ... the ample is the trunk." (Olivelle 1996: 146) (*tasya ha vā etasyātmano vaiśvānarasya ... saṃdeho bahulaḥ*). For the *saṃdeha* in another meaning than "doubt", Böhtlingk and Roth (1872-75: 638) remark: "Zusammenkittung: *anna-* ŚB 10.5.3.8, verächtliche Bez. des menschlichen Leibes 14.7.2.17, ChU 5.15.2."

he distinguishes other souls from the bodies (*deha*) they occupy in various spheres (verses 4-8). Thus it may be appropriate to assume Aśvapati's reply to Jana to be the chief source of phrase 1.[129] Then we can say that it is from his own Vedāntic perspective that Kumārila propounds the existence of a *paramātman* that resides in the Veda, since he most probably resorts to some phrases in the ChU as the authority that attests to his view.

Granted that the three phrases in verse (9) refer to the ChU, one may ask why Kumārila designates the absolute being embodied in the Veda with "*paramātman*", a word that does not appear in the ChU.[130] We find a clue for approaching this question in an interpretation of the world advocated by Bhartṛprapañca, a Vedāntin who was very famous as a *jñānakarmasamuccaya-vādin* although all of his works are lost. His date may not be far from Kumārila's because Bhartṛprapañca is frequently criticized by Śaṅkara and Sureśvara. Bhatṛprapañca is said to have maintained that the world consists of three layers (*rāśitraya*), i.e., the highest layer of the supreme self (*paramātmarāśi*), the middle layer of individual souls (*jīvarāśi*) and the lowest layer of corporeal and incorporeal

---

[129] For the *ākāśa* as a body of the absolute being in other Upaniṣads, see BĀU 3.7.12: *ya ākāśe tiṣṭhann ākāśād antaro yam ākāśo na veda yasyākāśaḥ śarīram ya ākāśam antaro yamayaty eṣa ta ātmāntaryāmy amṛtaḥ*; BĀU 4.1.2: *vāg evāyatanam ākāśaḥ pratiṣṭhā prajñety enad upāsīta*; TU 1.6: *etat tato bhavati. ākāśaśarīraṃ brahma. satyātma prāṇārāmaṃ mana-ānandam. śāntisamṛddham amṛtam*; MuU 2.2.7cd: *divye brahmapure hy eṣa vyomny ātmā pratiṣṭhitaḥ* ||. Cf. Jacob 1891: 154-157.

[130] The word *paramātman* appears in later Upaniṣads. Cf. Jacob 1891: 525. In the MaitrU, there are two instances, i.e., MaitrU 6.9: *prāṇo 'gniḥ paramātmā vai pañcavāyuḥ samāśritaḥ*; 6.17: *anūhya eṣa paramātmāpdrimito 'jo 'tarkyo 'cintyaḥ. eṣa ākāśātmā*. Both instances are, however, included in the "editorial interpretations" ascertained by van Buitenen (1962: 109, 111). In the BhG, there are some verses that refer to the *paramātman*. Cf. BhG 13.22cd: *paramātmeti cāpy ukto dehe 'smin puruṣaḥ paraḥ*; 31: *anāditvān nirguṇatvāt paramātmāyam avyayaḥ | śarīrastho 'pi kaunteya na karoti na lipyate* ||; Zaehner 1969: 222 (on BhG 6.7): "It is true that *param'ātmā* would normally mean the 'highest Self,' that is God *qua* timeless, eternal Brahman, as it certainly does in 13.22 ... and in 15.17 ... The only other place it occurs in the Gītā is 13.31, where it might mean either self-in-self or God-in Himself."

materials (*mūrtāmūrtarāśi*).[131] According to the fragments which Ānandagiri, a commentator on Sureśvara's *Vārttika* on Śaṅkara's *Bṛhadāraṇyakopaniṣadbhāṣya*, quotes from Bhartṛprapañca's commentary (*bhāṣya*) on the BĀU,[132] the *paramātman* is in the undifferentiated and unmanifested state (*avasthā*).[133] Since individual selves emanate from the supreme consciousness,[134] the nature of being beyond sorrow and perplexity as well as the nature of self-illuminating we find in our inner consciousness (*vijñānamaya*) belong to the *paramātman* too.[135] And the unification with the *paramātman* is considered the result (*kārya*) of the discernment (*darśana*) of *paramātman*.[136] It is difficult to judge whether Kumārila knows Bhatṛprapañca or vice versa on account of the scarcity of materials, and Kumārila definitively refuses any kinds of cosmogony including that of the Vedānta. It is nevertheless possible that Kumārila and Bhartṛprapañca share similar views on the absolute being insofar as they never abandon the significance of sacrifices and consider liberation as the ultimate result (*phala*, *kārya*) of religious practice. The term *paramātman* seems to be preferred within the wide range of the *jñānakarmasamuccaya-vādin*s of those days,[137] whether they had affinity to the ChU as did, perhaps, Kumārila, or to the BĀU as did Bhartṛprapañca.

---

[131] Cf. BĀUBh, p. 328, 4-7; BĀUBhV, p. 1011 : kk. 112-113; Kanakura 1932: 42.

[132] The following quotations in the ŚP are included in Hiriyanna 1925.

[133] A fragment in ŚP, p. 769, 14: *yā tv aviśeṣāvasthā 'nabhivyaktā paramātmāvasthaiva seti bhāṣyeṇāvasthāntaram āha.*

[134] A fragment in BĀUBhṬ, p. 560, 8: *vijñānaṃ paraṃ brahma tatprakṛtiko jīvo vijñānamaya iti bhartṛprapañcair uktam anuvadati.* Cf. Nakamura 1955: 181, n. 45.

[135] A fragment in ŚP, p. 1242, 2-3: *śokamohādyatītatā prakāśamātrarūpatā ca vijñānātmany ucyamānā paramātmani siddhā bhaviṣyatīti tadukter ity arthaḥ.*

[136] A fragment in ŚP, p. 664, 21-22: *paramātmadarśanāvasthāyāḥ paramātmabhāva eva kāryam iti bhāṣyeṇāha.* For Bhatṛprapañca's view on the practice towards liberation through the intermediate state of Hiraṇyagarbha, see Hino 1984.

[137] Śaṅkara frequently uses the term *paramātman* despite criticizing *jñānakarmasamuccayavāda*. For Śaṅkara's ambivalent notion of *paramātman*, see the

As mentioned in the introduction of the present article, Kumārila quotes some passages from the ChU to attest to his view on the significance of the knowledge of the self in the Vyākaraṇādhikaraṇa. When he demonstrates the attainment of the supreme self (*paramātmaprāpti*) as the ultimate goal of human beings, he has recourse to the very last sentence of ChU 8.15: "someone who lives in this way all his life attains the world of *brahman*, and he does not return again."[138] From the viewpoint of the *jñānakarmasamuccaya-vāda*, this quotation especially indicates Kumārila's close affinity to the ChU.[139] What is meant by "lives in this way all his life" is enjoined as follows in ChU 8.15 just before the quotation:

> From the teacher's house – where he learned the Veda in the prescribed manner during his free time after his daily tasks for the teacher – he returns, and then, in his own house (*kuṭumba*), he does his daily Vedic recitation in a clean place, rears virtuous children, draws in all his sense organs into himself, and refrains from killing any creature except for a worthy person.[140]

---

following remarks by Hacker (1950: 278): "und auch Paramātman ist 'etwas anderes als der Jīva' ... das gerade Gegenteil: Īśvara, Paramātman oder Brahman ist identisch mit der Einzelseele."

[138] Olivelle 1996: 176 on ChU 8.15: *sa khalv evam vartayan yāvadāyuṣam brahmalokam abhisaṃpadyate na ca punar āvartate*. This passage is quoted in TV, p. 288, 15 : TV', II, p. 227, 21-22 before "*ity apunarāvṛttyātmaka-paramātmaprāptyavasthāphalavacanam*."

[139] In the Vyākaraṇādhikaraṇa there are two sentences quoted from other Upaniṣads than the ChU: *tathā "mantavyo bodhavyaḥ" tathā "ātmānam upāsīta"* (TV, p. 288, 9-10 : TV', II, p. 227, 16). As noted by Harikai (1990: 217), Kumārila seems to refer to BĀU 2.4.5 "*ātmā vā are draṣṭavyaḥ śrotavyo mantavyo nididhyāsitavyo maitreyī*" with "*mantavyo bodhavyaḥ*" and to BĀU 1.4.8 "*ātmānam eva priyam upāsīta*" with "*ātmānam upāsīta*". These two quotations suggest Kumārila's preference of the ChU to the BĀU because they are no more than instances of Upaniṣadic injunction (*vidhi*) to cognize the self with ambiguous wording, instances appended to the preceding full quotation of an injunction from ChU 8.7.1: *ya ātmāpahatapāpmā vijaro vimṛtyur ... so 'nveṣṭavyaḥ sa vijijñāsitavyaḥ*.

[140] Olivelle 1996: 176 on ChU 8.15: *ācāryakulād vedam adhītya yathāvidhānaṃ guroḥ karmātiśayeṇābhisamāvṛtya kuṭumbe śucau deśe svādhyāyam adhīyāno dhārmikān vidadhad ātmani sarvendriyāṇi saṃpratiṣṭhāpyāhiṃsan sarvabhūtāny anyatra tīrthebhyaḥ*.

Here the text enumerates various duties of a householder (**kuṭumbin*) to be performed for his whole life (*yāvadāyuṣam*), namely, Vedic recitation, bringing-up of children, self-control, and non-injury of living beings except for occasions for hospitality including sacrifices. Kumārila, as a *jñānakarmasamuccaya-vādin*, may have cast a glance at the preceding enumeration of these lifelong duties, when quoting the last sentence of ChU 8.15. The exegetic term *samuccaya*[141] in the *jñānakarmasamuccaya* suggests that the knowledge of the self and periodical sacrifices are equally indispensable for liberation. As far as the means to liberation is concerned, Kumārila holds all duties of each life-stage (*āśrama*) including those of a householder to have equality with the knowledge of the self, because he excludes not only contradiction (*bādha*) and alternative (*vikalpa*) but also hierarchy (*aṅgāṅgibhāva*) from the relation between the two ways of practice.[142] Hence, Kumārila maintains that the duties of a householder including periodical sacrifices are, as ChU 8.15 enjoins, to be performed for one's whole life (*yāvajjīvam*), and they are never preliminaries that one could renounce at a certain advanced stage of the religious practice towards liberation.[143]

In addition, the first section of the ChU, which reveals the *udgīthavidyā*, is concluded with the following remark that literally corresponds to the tenet of *jñānakarmasamuccaya*:

> Only what is performed with knowledge, with faith, and with an awareness of the hidden connections (*upaniṣad*) becomes truly potent (ChU 1.1.10).[144]

---

[141] For exegetic arguments whether one of the two rituals (*vikalpa*) or both of them (*samuccaya*) are to be performed, see the third and the fourth Pādas of the twelfth Adhyāya of the JS.

[142] TV, p. 288, 19-21 : TV', II, p. 228, 16-18. Cf. fn. 54 and fn. 56

[143] Although the BS emphasizes the significance of periodical sacrifices and other duties in the four life-stages (*āśrama*) for the reason that they are enjoined by *śruti* (BS 3.4.26, 32, 34, 48-49), the BS does not proclaim the *jñānakarma-samuccaya* in the strict sense of the word, because the BS regards these duties as an assistance (*sahakārin*) to the knowledge (BS 3.4.33) and thereby leaves room for renunciation (BS 3.4.25).

Here it is declared that a ritual associated with knowledge brings its result more efficiently. It is certain that, since early times, the recommendation of ritual performance associated with knowledge in ChU 1.1.10 and the enumeration of lifelong duties of a householder in ChU 8.15 were highly valued as guiding principles of their religious life by the Mīmāṃsakas who were oriented also to the Vedānta, because both sentences are quoted by Śaṅkara in his BSBh as textual sources that support the position of Jaimini.[145] Hence, although the word *paramātman* does not appear in the ChU, this Upaniṣad must have been most important for Kumārila as an authority that supports his *jñānakarmasamuccaya-vāda*. Whether Kumārila's affinity to the ChU only shows his personal preference or suggests any regional and institutional milieu remains to be investigated.[146]

---

[144] Olivelle 1996: 98 on ChU 1.1.10: *yad eva vidyayā karoti śraddhayopaniṣadā tad eva vīryavattaraṃ bhavatīti.*

[145] Cf. BSBh on BS 3.4.4 and 3.4.6. See also NSu, p. 23, 24-26 (on JS 1.2.7) that quotes ChU 1.1.10 as noted by Harikai (1990: 138-139). According to Śaṅkara, BS 3.4.48 says that the reason why the ChU ends with the enumeration of the duties of a householder is that his *āśrama* includes the duties of all other *āśramas*. One cannot, however, hold the ChU to be thoroughly advocating *jñānakarmasamuccaya*, because the ChU contains a few teachings that are not consistent with it too, for example, the teachings by Raikva who is living under a cart (ChU 4.1.8) and the teachings of the "path leading to the gods" (*devayāna*) to be trodden by those who perform austerity in the wilderness (ChU 5.10.1).

[146] Among 44 quotations found in Śaṅkara's Bhāṣya on the 17 *sūtra*s that express the opinions of Jaimini (including BS 3.4.3-7 and 4.3.13; cf. Parpola 1981: 156), 24 (i.e., 55%) are quoted from the ChU, whereas only 4 (i.e., 9%) from the BĀU. Among 37 quotations on the 12 *sūtra*s that express the opinions of Bādarāyaṇa (including BS 3.4.9-11), on the contrary, only 12 (i.e., 32%) are quoted from the ChU against 14 (i.e., 38%) from the BĀU. Although Śaṅkara may have added some quotations to the original explanations handed-down to him on these *sūtra*s, the obvious difference in the frequency of quotation suggests that Jaimini must have belonged to the group of scholars who were engaged mainly in the interpretation of the ChU, whereas Bādarāyaṇa paid equal attention to the ChU and to the BĀU. In the TV, Kumārila seems to synthesize the positions of Jaimini and Bādarāyaṇa with regard to liberation, because the positions of Jaimini and Bādarāyaṇa were opposed to each other with respect to whether the knowledge of the self is *kratvartha* (BS 3.4.2-7 by Jaimini) or *puruṣārtha* (BS 3.4.1, 8-17 by Bādarāyaṇa), whereas Kumārila maintains that it

REFERENCES

Texts and abbreviations

AiĀ [*Aitareyāraṇyaka*] *The Aitareya Āraṇyaka*. Ed. & transl. by A. B. Keith. Oxford 1909. (Reprint: Delhi 1995.)

Aj *Ajitā*. In: Kunio Harikai, Ajitā and Vijayā on the verbal meaning (Bhāvārtha Adhikaraṇa, Mīmāṃsā Sūtra 2.2.1-4). *Acta Eruditiorum* 9 (Saga Medical School): 1-50. 1990.

BĀU *Bṛhadāraṇyakopaniṣad*. See ChU.

BĀUBh *Bṛhadāraṇyakopaniṣadbhāṣya*. In: *Bṛhadāraṇyakopaniṣat Ānandagirikṛtaṭīkāsaṃvalitaśāṅkarabhāṣyasametā*. Ed. by Kaśīnātha Śāstrī Āgāśe. (ĀSS, 15.) Reprint: Poona 1982.

BĀUBhṬ *Bṛhadāraṇyakopaniṣadbhāṣyaṭīkā*. See BĀUBh.

BĀUBhV *Bṛhadāraṇyakopaniṣadbhāṣyavārttika*. In: *Śrīmadsureśvarācāryaviracitaṃ bṛhadāraṇyakopaniṣadbhāṣyavārttikam ānandagirikṛtaśāstraprakāśikākhyaṭīkāsaṃvalitam*, I-II. Ed. by Kaśīnātha Śāstrī Āgaśe. (ĀSS, 16.) Poona 1893-94.

BD(M) [*Bṛhaddevatā*] *The Bṛhad-Devatā*, I. Ed. by A. A. Macdonell. (HOS, 5.) Cambridge, Mass. 1904.

BD(T) [*Bṛhaddevatā*] *The Bṛhaddevatā*. Ed. by Muneo Tokunaga. Kyoto 1997.

BhG *Bhagavadgītā*. In Zaehner 1969.

Bhm *Bhāmatī*. *Bhāmatī of Vācaspatimiśra*. Ed. & transl. by S. S. Suryanarayana Sastri & C. Kunhan Raja. Adyar 1933. (Reprint: Adyar 1992.)

BS *Brahmasūtra*. See BSBh; Thibaut 1904.

BSBh *Brahmasūtraśāṅkarabhāṣya*. In: *Works of Śaṅkarācārya in Original Sanskrit*, III. Delhi 1985.

---

is both *kratvartha* and *puruṣārtha* by applying the *saṃyogapṛthaktvanyāya*. Kumārila, however, quotes Upaniṣadic phrases almost exclusively from the ChU. The reason might be found in the fact that the ChU has almost no explicit recommendation of renunciation unlike the BĀU, which depicts the scene of farewell to his wife by the leading character of the Upaniṣad, i.e., Yājñavalkya (4.5.15). In addition, also Prabhākara is concerned with the ChU, since ChU 8.3.1 *ta ime satyāḥ kāmā anṛtāpidhānāḥ* and 3.14.1 *sarvaṃ khalv idaṃ brahma tajjalān iti śānta upāsīta* are quoted in the Pūrvapakṣa on the Svargakāmādhikaraṇa (JS 6.1.1-3) of the *Bṛhatī*. Cf. Yoshimizu 1997: 397-399.

I wish to express my sincere gratitude to Prof. J. Bronkhorst, who offered me an opportunity to present an earlier version of this article at the panel on the relation between Mīmāṃsā and Vedānta during the 12th World Sanskrit Conference (Helsinki, July 2003). Thanks are due to Prof. Bronkhorst also for improving my English in this article.

BSBh(Bh) [(Bhāskara:) *Brahmasūtraśāṅkarabhāṣya*] *Śrībhāskarācāryaviracitam brahmasūtrabhāṣyam*. Ed. by Vindhyeśvarī Prasāda Dvivedin. (Chowkhamba Sanskrit Series, 20.) Varanasi 1915. (Reprint: 1991)

ChU *Chāndogyopaniṣad*. In: *Eighteen Principal Upaniṣads*, I. Ed. by V. P. Limaye & R. D. Vadekar. Poona 1958.

JB [*Jaiminīyabrāhmaṇa*] *Jaiminīya-Brāhmaṇa of the Sāmaveda*. Ed. by Raghu Vira & Lokesh Chandra. (Sarasvati Vihara Series, 31.) Nagpur 1954. (Reprint: Delhi 1986.)

JS *Mīmāṃsāsūtra*. See TV.

MaitrU *Maitrāyaṇyupaniṣad*. See ChU.

Manu(K) [*Manusmṛti*] *Manusmṛti with the Sanskrit Commentary Manvarthamuktāvalī of Kullūka Bhaṭṭa*. Ed. by Jagadīśalāla Śāstrī. Delhi 1983.

Manu(M) [*Manusmṛti*] *Manusmṛti with the "Manubhāṣya" of Medhātithi*. Ed. by Ganganath Jha. Calcutta 1920-39. (Reprint: Delhi 1999.)

MBh [*Mahābhāṣya*] *The Vyākarạna-Mahābhāṣya of Patañjali*, I. Ed. by F. Kielhorn; rev. by K. V. Abhyankar. Fourth edition. Poona 1985. [First edition: 1880.]

MBhr [*Mahābhārata*] *The Mahābhārata*, XV: *The Śāntiparvan* (Part III: Mokṣadharma, A). Ed. by S. K. Belvalkar. Poona 1954.

MuU *Muṇḍakopaniṣad*. See ChU.

NBh *Nyāyabhāṣya*. In: *Nyāyadarśanam*, I-II. Calcutta 1936-44.

Nirukta In: *The Nighaṇṭu and the Nirukta*. Ed. & transl. by Lakshman Sarup. Oxford and Lahore 1920-27. (Reprint: Delhi 1967.)

NK *Nyāyakandalī*. In: *Praśastapādabhāṣya with the commentary Nyāyakandalī of Śrīdharabhaṭṭa*. Ed. by Durgadhara Jha. (Ganganatha Jha Granthamālā, 1,) Varanasi 1963.

NR *Nyāyaratnākara*. See ŚV.

NSu [*Nyāyasudhā*] *Nyāyasudhā taṃtravārttikaṭīkā bhaṭṭasomeśvaraviracitā*. Ed. by Mukunda Shastri. (Chowkhamba Sanskrit Series, 45-56.) Benares 1901-02.

ŚB [*Śatapathabrāhmaṇa*] *The Śatapatha-Brāhmaṇa in the Mādhyandina-Śākhā*. Ed. by Albrecht Weber. (Chowkhamba Sanskrit Series, 96.) Second edition. Varanasi 1964. [First edition: Berlin 1855.]

ŚBh *Śābarabhāṣya*. See TV.

ŚBh' *Śābarabhāṣya*. See TV'.

ŚBh(F) *Śābarabhāṣya* on JS 1.1.1-5. In Frauwallner 1968.

ŚD [*Śāstradīpikā* (Tarkapāda)] *Śāstradīpikā yuktisnehaprapūraṇyākhyavyākhyayā samalaṅkṛtā*. Ed. by Laxman Shastri Dravid. (Chowkhamba Sanskrit Series, 188-190, 225-226.) Benares 1916.

ŚP *Śāstraprakāśikā*. See BĀUBhV.

ŚV [*Ślokavārttika*] *Ślokavārttika of Śrī Kumārila Bhaṭṭa with the Commentary Nyāyaratnākara of Śrī Pārthasārathi Miśra*. Ed. by Svami Dvarikadasa Sastri. (Prāchyabhārati Series, 10.) Varanasi 1978.

ŚVK II *Kāśikā*. In: *The Mīmāṃsāślokavārttika with the Commentary Kāśikā of Sucaritamiśra*, II. Ed. by K. Sambasiva Sastri. (Trivandrum Sanskrit Series, 99.) Trivandrum 1929.

ŚvU *Śvetāśvataropaniṣad*. See ChU.

PBh *Praśastapādabhāṣya*. In: Bronkhorst & Ramseier 1994.

TB [*Taittirīyabrāhmaṇa*] *The Taittirīya Brāhmaṇa with the Commentary of Bhaṭṭa Bhāskara Miśra*. Ed. by A. Mahadeva Sastri. Mysore 1911. (Reprint: Delhi 1985.)

TR [*Tantraratna*] *Tantraratnam by Pārthasārathimiśra*. Ed. by Paṭṭābhirāma Śāstrī & Rāmanātha Dīkṣita.Sarasvatībhavana Granthamālā, 31.3.) Varanasi 1979.

TS [*Taittirīyasaṃhitā*] *Die Taittirīya-Saṃhitā*. Ed. by Albrecht Weber. (Indische Studien, 11-12.) Leipzig 1871-72. (Reprint: Hildesheim 1973.)

ṬṬ *Ṭupṭīkā*. See TV.

ṬṬ' *Ṭupṭīkā*. See TV'.

TU *Taittirīyopaniṣad*. See ChU.

TV *Tantravārttika*. In: *Mīmāṃsādarśanam*. (ĀSS, 97.) Poona 1929-53.

TV' *Tantravārttika*. In: *Mīmāṃsādarśanam*. Ed. by K. V. Abhyaṃkara & G. Jośī. I-VII. (ĀSS, 97.) Second edition. Poona 1971-81.

VP [*Vākyapadīya*] *Bhartṛharis Vākyapadīya*. Ed. by Wilhelm Rau. Abhandlungen für die Kunde des Morgenlandes, 42.4.) Wiesbaden 1977.

VS *Vaiśeṣikasūtra*. See VSV.

VSV *Vaiśeṣikasūtravṛtti*. In: *Vaiśeṣikasūtra of Kanāda with the Commentary of Candrānanda*. Ed. by Muni Jambuvijayaji. (GOS, 136.) Baroda 1961.

Studies

ALSTON, A. J. 1989a. *Śaṃkara on Discipleship*. (A Śaṃkara Source Book, 5.) London: Shanti Sadan.

ALSTON, A. J. 1989b. *Śaṃkara on Enlightenment*. (A Śaṃkara Source Book, 6.) London: Shanti Sadan.

BODEWITZ, H. W. 1973. *Jaiminīya Brāhmaṇa I, 1-65. Translation and Commentary with a Study Agnihotra and Prāṇāgnihotra*. (Orientalia Rheno-Traiectina, 17.) Leiden: E.J. Brill.

BÖHTLINGK, O. & R. ROTH 1872-75. Sanskrit-Wörterbuch, VII. St. Petersburg.

BRONKHORST, Johannes & Yves RAMSEIER 1994. *Word Index to the Praśastapādabhāṣya*. Delhi: Motilal Banarsidass.

BUITENEN, J. A. B. Van 1962. *The Maitrayaṇīya Upaniṣad.* (Disputationes Rheno-Trajectinae, 6.) The Hague: Mouton.

CLOONEY, Francis X. 1990. *Thinking Ritually. Rediscovering the Pūrva Mīmāṃsā of Jaimini.* (Publications of the De Nobili Research Library, 17.) Vienna: Institute for Indology, Vienna University.

DUMONT, Paul-Emile 1954. The iṣṭis to the nakṣatras (or oblations to the lunar mansions) in the Taittirīya-Brāhmaṇa. *Proceedings of the American Philosophical Society* 98: 204-223.

—— 1962. The animal sacrifice in the Taittirīya-Brāhmaṇa. The part of the Hotar and the part of the Maitrāvaruṇa in the animal sacrifice. *Proceedings of the American Philosophical Society* 106: 246-263.

EINOO, Shingo 1992. Who is the performer of the saṃdhyopāsana? *WZKS* 36, Supplement (Proceedings of the VIIIth World Sanskrit Conference, Vienna 1990): 59-67.

—— 1993. Hindu girei no hen-yō (Transformation of Hindu rituals). In: Yasuke Ikari & Yashuko Nagano (eds.), *Indo Fukugō Bunka no Kōzō* (Structure of the cultural complex in India): 261-318. Kyoto: Hōzōkan.

FRAUWALLNER, Erich 1938. Bhāvanā und vidhiḥ bei Maṇḍanamiśra. *WZKM* 45: 212-252.

—— 1968. *Materialien zur ältesten Erkenntnislehre der Karmamīmāṃsā,* (VKSKSO, 6.) Vienna: Österreichische Akademie der Wissenschaften.

GARGE, D. V. 1952. *Citations in Śabara-bhāṣya. A Study.* Deccan College Dissertation Series, 8.) Poona: Deccan College.

GONDA, Jan 1980. *Vedic Ritual. The Non-Solemn Rites.* (Handbuch der Orientalistik, 2.1.) Leiden: E.J. Brill.

HACKER, Paul 1950. Eigentümlichkeiten der Lehre und Terminologie Śaṅkaras: Avidyā, Nāmarūpa, Māyā, Īśvara. *ZDMG* 100: 246-286.

—— 1968. Śaṅkara der Yogin und Śaṅkara der Advaitin. Einige Beobachtungen. In: *Beiträge zur Geistesgeschichte Indiens. Festschrift für Erich Frauwallner* (WZKS, 12-13): 119-148.

HALBFASS, Wilhelm 1991. *Tradition and Reflection. Explorations in Indian Thought.* Albany: State University of New York Press.

HARIKAI, Kunio 1989. Nyāyasudhā ni in-yō sareru Bṛhaṭṭīkā ni tsuite (Quotations from the Bṛhaṭṭīkā in the Nyāyasudhā). *Journal of Indian and Buddhist Studies* 37.2: 951-957.

—— 1990. *Koten Indo seiten kaishakugaku kenkyū.* (The hermeneutics of Classical India – A study of arthavāda and mantra of the Mīmāṃsā school.) Fukuoka: Kyūshū University Press.

HINO, Shoun 1984. Sureśvara's criticism of Bhartṛprapañca's view of liberation. *Aligarh Journal of Oriental Studies* 1.1: 137-148.

HIRIYANNA, M. 1925. Fragments of Bhartṛprapañca. *Proceedings and Transactions of the Third Oriental Conference, Madras 1924*: 439-450.

INGALLS, D. H. H. 1952. The study of Śaṅkarācārya. *ABORI* 33: 1-14.

JACOB, C. G. A. 1891. *A Concordance to the Principal Upaniṣads and Bhagavadgītā*. Bombay: Government Central Book Depot.

JACOBI, Hermann 1911. The dates of the philosophical Sūtras of the Brahmans. *Journal of the American Oriental Society* 31: 1-29.

KANAKURA, Ensho 1932. *Vedānta tetsugaku no kenkyū*. (The Study of Vedānta Philosophy.) Tokyo: Iwanami Shoten.

KANAZAWA, Akira 2001. *Word-Index to Kumārila's Ślokavārttika*. Tokyo: The Resarch Association of Indian Logic.

KANE, P. V. 1997. *History of Dharmaśāstra. Ancient and Medieval Religious and Civil Law*, II.1. (Government Oriental Series, B 6.) Third edition, Poona: BORI. [First edition: 1941.]

KURATA, Haruo 1980. Saṃyogapṛthaktvanyāya as a basis of the theory of mokṣa. *Journal of Indian and Buddhist Studies* 28.2: 970-975.

KURODA, Hiroshi 1979. Kumārila no bhāvanā setsu ni tsuite (1) (Some problems concerning the bhāvanā theory of Kumārila (1)). *Journal of Indian and Buddhist Studies* 28.1: 456-458.

—— 1980. Kumārila no bhāvanā setsu ni tsuite (2) (Some problems concerning the bhāvanā theory of Kumārila (2)). *Journal of Indian and Buddhist Studies* 29.1: 436-441.

MESQUITA, Roque 1994. Die Idee der Erlösung bei Kumārilabhaṭṭa. *WZKS* 38: 451-484.

NAKAMURA, Hajime 1955. *Vedānta tetsugaku no hatten*. (Development of the Vedānta philosophy.) Tokyo: Iwanami Shoten. (Reprint: 1981.)

OLIVELLE, Patrick 1996. *Upaniṣads*. (Oxford World's Classics.) Oxford: Oxford University Press.

PARPOLA, Asko 1981. On the formation of the Mīmāṃsā and the problems concerning Jaimini. With particular reference to the teacher quotations and the Vedic schools. *WZKS* 25: 145-177.

RAU, Wilhelm 1988. *Bhartṛharis Vākyapadīya: vollständiger Wortindex zu den mūlakārikās*. (Abhandlungen der Geistes- und Sozialwissenschaftlichen Klasse, 11.) Stuttgart: Franz Steiner Verlag.

SCHMITHAUSEN, Lambert 1994. Zur Textgeschichte der Pañcāgnividyā. *WZKS* 38: 43-60.

STRAUSS, Otto 1932. Die älteste Philosophie der Karma-Mīmāṃsā. *Sitzungsberichte der Preußischen Akademie der Wissenschaften* 1932: 469-532.

TABER, John 1986-92. Further observations on Kumārila's Bṛhaṭṭīkā. *Journal of Oriental Research, Madras* 56-62: 179-189.

THIBAUT, George (transl.) 1904. *The Vedānta-sūtras with the Commentary by Śaṅkarācārya*, II. (The Sacred Books of the East, 38.) Oxford: Clarendon Press.

YOSHIMIZU, Kiyotaka 1997. *Der "Organismus" des urheberlosen Veda. Eine Studie der Niyoga-Lehre Prabhākaras mit ausgewählten Übersetzungen der Bṛhatī.* (Publications of the De Nobili Research Library, 25.) Vienna: Institute for South Asian, Tibetan and Buddhist Studies, Vienna University.

—— 2000. Change of view on apūrva from Śabarasvāmin to Kumārila. In S. Mayeda (ed.), *The Way to Liberation, Indological Studies in Japan.* (Japanese Studies on South Asia, 3): 149-165. New Delhi: Manohar.

—— 2003. Kumārila on the dual aspects of the reader's consciousness: Textual comprehension and actual performance. *Studies in the History of Indian Thought* (*Indo Shisōsi Kenkyū*) 15: 5-33.

—— 2004a. Notes on Kumārila's approach to the ritual scripture, In: Shoun Hino & Toshihiro Wada (eds.), *Three Mountains and Seven Rivers. Prof. Musashi Tachikawa Felicitation Volume*: 735-751. Delhi: Motilal Banarsidass.

—— 2004b. The dual significance of a periodical sacrifice: *nitya* or *kāmya* from the Mīmāṃsā viewpoint. *JIP* 32.2-3: 189-210.

—— 2006. The theorem of the singleness of a goblet (*graha-ekatva-nyāya*): A Mīmāmsā analysis of meaning and context. In: Masaaki Hattori (ed.), *Word and Meaning in Indian Philosophy* (Acta Asiatica, Bulletin of the Institute of Eastern Culture, 90): 15-38.

——, forthcoming. The intention of expression (*vivakṣā*), the expounding (*vyākhyā*) of a text, and the authorlessness of the Veda.

ZAEHNER, R. C. 1969. *The Bhagavad-gītā with a Commentary Based on the Original Sources.* Oxford: Clarendon Press.

ZANGENBERG Fritz 1962. Śabaraḥ und seine philosophischen Quellen. *WZKS* 6: 60-77.

INDEX

(Italicized page numbers refer to the footnote section)

abhāva 39, 55, 170, 178-179, 182, 207, 211, 218-219, *236*
abhyudaya 117, 166, 180-181, *217*
adhyāsa 174
Ādiśeṣa 27
Advaita *5*, *22*, *37*, 49-50, 66, 93-94, 99-111, 122, 125-130, 136-137, 147, 150-152, 163, 167, 169
Āgamaprāmāṇya 33
Āgamaśāstra 25-27, 137
agnihotra *68*, *118*, *121*, 165, 195, 203, 212, *220*, *238*
Aitareyāraṇyaka 237
ākāśa 42, 226, 231, 237, 241-243
ānanda 203, 234
Ānandabodha 94, 103-105
Ānandagiri 7, 244
Ānandānubhava 122-125, 128
Ānandavardhana *129-130*
anumāna 215
apauruṣeya 51-52, 220-221, 224, 228
aprārabdhakārya 212, 220
apunarāvṛtti 160, 166, 180, 202, *235*, *245*
apūrva 74, 112, 166, *205*, 210, *216*, *240*
Arjuna 129
arthavāda 15-16, 38-40, 74-75, 162-163, 175, 178-181, *193*, 197, *235*
āśrama 75, 119-126, 160, 180-181, *217*, 246-247
Aśvaghoṣa 31
ātmajñāna *117*, *126*, 136, 146, 151, 169, 178-181, *189*, *235*
ātman 8, 16, *31*, 44, 47, 53, 137, 139, 141-142, 144, 146-149, 160, 186-198, *202-203*, *207*, *212*, 213-214, *230*, 233-238, 242, *245*
Ātmasiddhi *19*, 33, 64
avidyā 51, 55, 95-96, 104-105, 107, 111, 176-177, *188*, 233
Bādarāyaṇa *2*, 16, *21*, *62*, 67, *73*, 75, 162, 164, 174, *213*, *247*
Bhagavadgītā *31*, 107, 129, *226*, *243*
Bhagavadgītābhāṣya 116-118, *128-129*
Bhāmatī *20*
Bhāṇaruci *19*
Bhartṛhari *5*, *12*, *18*, 28-29, 229-230, 232-233, 242
Bhartṛmitra *18*, *168*, *231*
Bhartṛprapañca *18*, 126-127, 139, *151*, 152, 243-244
Bhāruci *18*
Bhāskara *10*, *19*, *21*, 22, *34*, 51-52, 61, 63-64, 66, *116*, 122-127, 129, *131*, *136*, 152, *240*
Bhāskarakaṇṭha *30*
Bhāṣyaratnaprabhā *20*
Bhaṭṭa 122-125, 151
Bhavadāsa 21, *142*
bhāvanā 207-212
Bhāvanāviveka *116*

Bhavya 2, 28, 60-61, 147
Bhedābheda 126, 128, *130*, 152
bhoga *130*, 170, *172*, 176, 178, 210
Bodhāyana 18-22
brahman 3, *31*, *71*, *75*, 93-95, 99, 101-113, *132*, 163-164, 166, 174, 181, 186-187, 189, 193, 195, 197, *212*, 225-226, 228-231, 233-234, 237, 241-243, 245
Brahmadatta *18*, *21*, 22
Brahmānandi(n) *19*
Brahmasiddhi *9*, 53-56, 58, 93, 95, *116*, 127, 162, 234
Brahmasūtra *2*, *4*, 7-11, 13-20, 22, 32, 34-35, 42, 48, 51-52, 63, 65-67, 70-72, 75-76, 94-98, 106, *121-127*, 162-164, 169, *176*, 185, 188, 212, *216*, 220, 234, 239-240, *246-247*
Brahmasūtrabhāṣya 6-10, 15, 27, 35, 38, 45-46, 48, *51*
Bṛhadāraṇyaka-Upaniṣad 44, 58, 112, 126, *131*, 132-144, 147, 150-152, 186-187, 190-195, *222*, 239-245, 247
Bṛhadāraṇyakopaniṣadbhāṣya 17, *44*, *135*, 167, 244
Bṛhaṭṭīkā *118*, 126-127, 159-161, *172*, 176-177, 182-183, 201-203, 218-219, 229
Buddhacarita 31,
Buddhists 2, *5*, 26, 28, 60, 64, 127, 134, 137, 139-142, 144-145, 147-149, 160, 165, 195, 197, *214*
Candrānanda *223*
Cārvāka *5*, *139*
Chāndogya-Upaniṣad *38*, 74, *117*, *135*, 163, 180-181, 186, 202, *221*, 236-247
codanā 9, 17, *75*, 186, 196, 198, 204, 215
Devasvāmin 21-22
Devatākāṇḍa *19*, *21*
dharma 8-9, 16-17, 20, 38, 48-49, 64, 66, 74, 116-117, *122*, 126, 129, 172, 186-187, 195-198, 215, 231
Dharmakīrti *95*, *116*
Dramiḍa *18*
Draviḍācārya *19*
ekadaṇḍin 122-124, 151
Gauḍapāda 25, *28*, 29, 151
Gauḍapādīyakārikā 25, *27*
Gautama 71
Gītābhāṣya 63, 116
Govindānanda *20*
gṛhastha 117, 119-125, 129-130, 151, *238*
Guhadeva *18-19*
Guṇaratna 124, *127*
heaven 1, *4*, 59-60, *64*, 70, 75, 111-112, 117, 145-146, 162, 165, 178-179, 188, *201*, 203-205, 207, 209, 222-224, 234-235, 239, 241
injunction 8-9, 23-25, 35-40, 42-43, 46, 52-53, 73-75, 102, 118, 120, 145-146, 160, 163-164, 166-169, 173-174, 180-181, 188, *190*, 192, 195, 197, 203-209, 215-217, 220-221, *227*, 228-229, 235, *245*
Iṣṭasiddhi 128
Īśvarasiddhi 33
Jaimini *4*, 14-21, *37*, *62*, 67, 72-75, 77, 120-122, 129, *132*, 135-136, 162-167, 186, 195-198, 247
Jaiminīyabrāhmaṇa 239
Jainas *5*, 28, *95*, 127, *139*, 147
Janaka 136-137
Jātinirṇaya 99-100
jīvanmukta 129, 152, *172*
jīvanmukti 126-130, 152, *172*

Jīvanmuktiviveka 128
Jñānakāṇḍa 116-119, 146, 150-151
jñānakarmasamuccaya *126*, *129-130*, 159, 161-162, 175-176, 203, *218*, 229, 243-247
jñānamārga 126, 160-162, *217*
jñānin 119, 129-130, 150-151
kaivalya 161, 182, *218*
kāmya 60-61, 159, 164, 235-236
Kāṇva 134-136, 151
Kapardi(n) *18*
Kapila 71
karman 4, 19, 44, 47, 58, 61, 69, 125-126, 130, 158, 160-162, 164-172, 175-179, 181-183, 187, 193, 203, 208, *210*, 212, 220, 222, *225*, *235*
Karmakāṇḍa 17, 116-120, 146, 151
karmamārga 117-118, 126, 159-161, *217*
karmin 119, 129-130, 150-151
Karṇakagomin *116*
kārya 102, 106-107, 111, 189, 193-197, 244
Kāśakṛtsna *19*, 67
Kauṇḍabhaṭṭa *20*
kratvartha 8, 160, 162, 166-168, 172-173, 179-180, 202, 234-236, *247-248*
Kriyākāṇḍa 150
Kṛtakoṭi 21-22
kṣetrajña 221, 227
Kullūka(bhaṭṭa) *20*, *224*
Kumārila(bhaṭṭa) v, 1, 3-5, 11, 23, *34*, 56, 59-60, 78, 125-128, 133, *135*, 138, 147, 159-177, *188*, 201
liberation v, 1-5, 9, *22*, 25, 27, 33, 42-46, 57-62, 69, 75, 77-78, 101, 105, 108, *117*, 118, 127-128, 130, *144*, 147, 152, 159-179, 183, 201-207, 209, 211-213, 216-220, 234-236, 244, 246-247
lokāyatīkṛtā *168*
Madhusūdana Sarasvatī *21*
Madhyamakahṛdaya *28*
Mādhyandina 132, 135-136, 138-139, 150-152, 239
Mahābhārata 1, *21*, 69-70, 129-130, *221*, *226*
mahāvākya 46, 93-94, 102, 192, *194*, 198
mahāyajña *165*
Maitreyī 136-138, *141*, 144, *245*
Maṇḍana(miśra) *9*, 13, *29*, 37, 53-58, 70, 93-98, *100*, 103, 105, 107, *116*, 121, 123, 125-128, 162, *172*, 175-177, 234
Māṇḍūkya-Upaniṣad 27
Manusmṛti *10*, *20*, 61, *62*, *121*, *206*, *217*, 224, *235*,
māyā 104-105, 111
Meghanādārisūri 94, *99*, 105-113
Mīmāṃsā v-vi, 3-6, 8, 10, 13, 17-18, 23-52, 56-78, *100*, 112, 128, 130-137, 146, 150-151, 168, 175, 185, 187, 192, 195, 197-198, 201-202, 211, 213-214, *216*, 230
Mīmāṃsakas v, 3, 5, 23-25, 32, 34, 37-38, 46, 49-52, 57-61, 71-72, 77-78, 120-122, 124, 130, 133-143, 147-150, *165*, *168*, *171*, 184-197, *204*, 208, *216*, 220, 247
Mīmāṃsāsūtra 3-5, 7-8, 10-18, 20, 22, 35-36, 42, 59, 62, 66-68, 70-71, 73, 76-77, 135, 172, 203-204, 208-211, 213-216
Miśra 123-125
Muṇḍaka-Upaniṣad 68-69, 108-109, *230*, 243
mokṣa see liberation
Mokṣopāya 29-30, 129-130

Mokṣopāyaṭīkā *130*
naimittika 60, 159-160, *165*, 166, 168, 170-172, 176, 178-183, *206*, *217-218*
Naiṣkarmyasiddhi 13, *34*
Nātha(muni) *19*, 32-33, 64
Nayadyumaṇi *94*, *99*, 105-113
niḥreyasa *4*, 166, *203*, *217*, 235
Nirukta 211
niṣiddha 60, 159, *168*, 178-179, *206*
nitya 59-60, 111, 159-160, *165*, 166, 168, 170-172, 176, 178-183, *202*, 203, *206*, *210*, *217-218*, 241
nivṛtti 116-117, 126, *235*
Nyāya 29, 71, 130, 202
Nyāyabhāṣya *34*, *202*
Nyāyakandalī *126*, 127, 160, 182, 218-219
Nyāyamakaranda 94, 103
Nyāyaratnadīpāvali 122, 128
Nyāyaratnākara *118*, *168*, *206*
Nyāyasudhā 161, 182
Padmapāda 16-17, 63, 185, 188, 198
pañcāgnividyā 239-241
Pañcapādikā *16-17*, 63, 185-198
paramahaṃsa 45, 122
Paramārthasāra 27
paramātman 47, 112, 166, 180, 202-203, 220-230, 233, *235*, 236-238, 241-247
paramātmaprāpti 166, 180-181, 202, *235*, 245
Parivrājakācārya 123
Pārthasārathi(miśra) 56, *117-118*, 125-127, *131*, 133, 138, *144*, 161, 168-169, *204*, *206*, *231*, *234*
periodical sacrifices 203-212, 217-220, 229, 234, 241, 246; see also *nitya*
Prabhācandra *172*
Prabhākara 1-2, *21*, 23, 59, 78, *100*, 107-108, 111, *116*, 123-125, 133, *248*
Prābhākara *197*
Prakāśātman 185
Pramāṇaparāyaṇa 99-101, 103
Prapañcahṛdaya 20-22, 64, 66
prārabdhakārya 212, 220
pratyakṣa 93, 98, 100-104, 106-108, 110, 145, 213-214
pratyavāya 58, 60, 178-182, 206-207, 217, *219*
pravrājaka *120*, 124
pravṛtti 52-53, 116-118, 126, 174, 178-179, *196*, *206*, *233*, 235
prāyaścitta *206*, 211
puruṣa 191, *206*, 211, 233
Puruṣanirṇaya 33
puruṣārtha 8, 15-16, 35-36, 41, 53, *75*, 160, 162-163, 166-170, 172-174, 176, 179- 180, 202, *206*, 235, *247-248*
Pūrvamīmāṃsā 3-6, 15, 22, 62, 64-66, 76, 94, 115, *131*, 135-136, 146, 150-151, 185, 187, 189, 197
Pūrva-Mīmāṃsakas 119-122, 125, *147*, 151-152
Rāma 129
Rāmānuja 18-20, 22, 32, *34*, 52, 61, 64, 66, 94, *108*, 111, 162, 169
Ṛgveda 221, 227-228, 237
Ṛgvedabhāṣya *20*, *64*
Śabara 1-2, 4-6, 10-13, 15, 19, 21-23, 39, 59, 73, 77-78, *118*, 120-121, 125, 131-132, *135*, *180*, 186, *192*, 196-197, *209*, 213-216, *220*
Śābarabhāṣya 1, *4*, 8, 11-12, *21*, 23, 42, 59, *64*, 73-74, *132*, 134-139, 203
śabdabrahman *226*

Śālikanātha 93-94, 98-103, 105-110, 125, 133
sāmānya 54, *56*, 93, 95, 98-101, 108-110
sambhoga 225-226, 229
Saṃkarṣakāṇḍa *19*, 21-22, 67, 186, 189
Sāṃkhya 2, *22*, *29*, 71, 159, 165, 178, 238
saṃnyāsa 117, 119, 124, *127*, 168, *230*
saṃnyāsin 117, 119-120, 122-124, 151-152, 168, *217*
saṃsāra *4*, 69, 147, 170, 188-189
Śaṅkara v, 4-13, 15, 17-22, 25, 27, 29, 31, *34*, 35-53, 58, 63, 65, 68, 70, 72-76, 116-122, 126, 128-131, 134-139, 147, 151-152, 162-165, 167-168, 170-175, 185, *212*, *216*, 234, 240, 243-244, 247
sanmātra 93-98, *100*, 106-107, 110
Śārīraka 6-7, 10, 12-14, 19, 24, 63-65, 77
Śārīrakamīmāṃsābhāṣya *34*, 63-64, *124*, *126-127*
Sarva(darśana)siddhāntasaṃgraha *19*
Śāstradīpikā *117-119*, *126-127*, *130-131*, *133*, *138*, *144*, 169, *203*
Śatapathabrāhmaṇa 131-132, *135*, *145*, *187*, *212*, 239
sattva 108, 110
Sautrāntika 139, 147, 149
Sāyaṇa *20*, *64*
Siddhasena Divākara 28, 147
Siddhitraya *64*
Ślokavārttika *56*, 60, 118, *138*, 159-161, 164-166, 168-173, 178-179, 201, 206, *208*, 210, 213-216, 218-219, *227*, 230-236
smṛti *21*, 24, 58, 127, *130*, 138-140, 152, 194, 206, 224
Someśvara(bhaṭṭa) 161, 182, *218*, 222, *224-225*, 237-238
Śrībhāṣya 18-20, 52, 64, 66, 169
Śrīdhara *126*, 127, 160-161, *172*, *218*
Śrīnivāsa *19*, *64*
Śrīparāṃkuśa *19*
Śrīvatsāṅka(miśra) *18*
śruti 27, *37*, 41, *42*, 44, 47, 58, 65, *74-75*, 104, 127, 138, 152, 224-225, 236, 239, *246*
Sucarita(miśra) 123, 125, 161
Sureśvara 13-19, *34*, *43*, 63, *116*, 123, 162, 243-244
Svāmin 125
svarga see heaven
svargakāma *64*, 146, 203-204, 209
svataḥprāmāṇya *215*
Taittirīyopaniṣadbhāṣya 44
Ṭaṅka *18*
Tantravārttika 60, *118*, 125-126, 159-161, 166-169, 171-173, 175-177, 179-181, 201-202, 207-210, 213-230, 234-235, 237, *245-247*
Tattvāloka 100-101, 103
Tattvaratnākara *19*
tridaṇḍin 122-124, 151
Ṭupṭīkā 60, *167*, 172, 203-210, 213-214, 216, 218-220
Uddyotakara 128
Umbeka 56, *116*, 125
Upadeśasāhasrī *21*, 44-47, 50-51, 58, 63
upāsanā 35, 164, 166, 169, *193*, 238
Upavarṣa 6-7, 10, 12-13, 21-22
Uttaramīmāṃsā 3-6, 15, 22, 24, 59, 62, 64-66, 77, 117, *131*, *189*, 197-198

Vācaspati(miśra) 13, *20*, 123, *212*
Vāhaṭa *20*
Vaiśeṣika 2, *95*, *97*, *142*, *224*, 230-232, *234*
Vaiyākaraṇabhūṣaṇa 20
Vākyapadīya 5, 28-29, *187*, *211*, *226*, *229*, 233
vānaprastha 124
varṇa 160, 181
Vārttika 244
Vātsyāyana *34*
Veda v, 12, 14-15, 17-18, 20, 23-38, 42-49, 52-62, 65, *72*, 77, 94-95, 102, 107-108, 146, 160, 162-163, 166, 169, 173, 175, 178, *187*, 189, 193-198, 220-230, 233, 242-243, 245
Vedānta v-vi, 1-3, 13, 17-18, 24-38, 43, 46, 51-52, 56-58, *66*, 75, 78, 92, *97*, 118, 128, 134-135, 147, 161-162, 164-167, 175, 177, *186*, 187, 189, 195, 197-198, 202, 212, 220, 234-236, 239, 244, 247-248
Vedāntadeśika 22
Vedāntakalpalatikā 21
Vedāntins 3, 5, 15, 23-57, 61, 67, 70, 72, 74, 77-78, 120, 122, 126-128, 150-152, *172*, 175, 185-196, 243
Vedārthasaṃgraha 18
vidhi 98, 102, 106, 188, 190-195, 197, *245*
Vidyāraṇya 128
vijñānaghana 139-140, 143-144, 147, 149
vikṛti 233
Vimuktātman 104, *116*, 128
viśeṣa 54, 93-97, 99-101, 107, 110-112
Viśiṣṭādvaita *19*, 32, 93-94, 107, 111-113
Viśiṣṭādvaitins 122
Viśvarūpa 123
vivakṣita 220-222, 227-229
Vivaraṇa 185, *197*
Vṛtti 19, 213-216
Vṛttikāra 11, 19-20, 131-137, 139-140, *142*, 143, 145, 214-216
Vṛttikāragrantha 11-12, 131-134, 138-147
Vyāsa 19-21, *37*
Yādavaprakāśa 32
Yājñavalkya vi, 115, 129, 131-152, *222*, *248*
Yājñavalkyakāṇḍa 133, *135*, 137
Yājñavalkyasmṛti 130
Yāmuna(muni) *18-19*, *21*, 32-33, 64, 66
Yāska 211
Yatīndramatadīpikā 19, *64-65*
Yatipatimatadīpikā 19, *64-65*
Yatīśvara *19*
yāvajjīva 126, 203-209, *217*, 246
Yoga *22*, 26, 130, 166, 181, *218*
Yogabhāṣya 21
Yogācāra 213-214
Yogavāsiṣṭha 29
yogin 26, 49, 160
Yuktidīpikā 27